W9-AMX-706

The Obligation toward the Difficult Whole

MODERN AND CONTEMPORARY POETICS

The Obligation toward the Difficult Whole

Postmodernist Long Poems

BRIAN McHALE

THE UNIVERSITY OF ALABAMA PRESS

Tuscaloosa and London

The author gratefully acknowledges permission to reprint material from the following sources:
From "Confidence Trick," in *Give Em Enough Rope*, by Bruce Andrews (Sun & Moon Press,
1987). Copyright © 1987 by Bruce Andrews. From "A Wave," in *A Wave*, by John Ashbery. Copyright © 1981, 1982, 1983, 1984 by John Ashbery. Reprinted by permission of Georges Borchardt,
Inc., for the author. From "The Skaters," in *Rivers and Mountains*, by John Ashbery. Copyright
© 1962, 1963, 1964, 1966 by John Ashbery. Reprinted by permission of Georges Borchardt, Inc.,
for the author. From "The System" and "The Recital," in *Three Poems*, by John Ashbery. Copyright © 1970, 1971, 1972 by John Ashbery. Reprinted by permission of Georges Borchardt, Inc.,
for the author. From *Gunslinger*, by Edward Dorn. Copyright 1968, 1969, 1971, 1972, 1975, and
1989 by the Estate of Edward Dorn. Used by permission. From *New and Collected Poems, 1952–
1992*, by Geoffrey Hill. Copyright © 1994 by Geoffrey Hill. Reprinted by permission of Houghton Mifflin Company. All rights reserved. From "Pythagorean Silence," "Defenstration of
Prague," and (various excerpts) from *The Europe of Trusts*, by Susan Howe. Copyright © 1990
by Susan Howe. Used by permission of New Directions Publishing Corporation. From *Letter
to an Imaginary Friend*, by Thomas McGrath. Copyright © 1997 Copper Canyon Press. Reprinted by permission of Copper Canyon Press. From *The Changing Light at Sandover*, by
James Merrill. Copyright © 1980, 1982 by James Merrill. Used by permission of Alfred A.
Knopf, a division of Random House, Inc. From *The Tablets*, by Armand Schwerner. Copyright © 1999 by the Estate of Armand Schwerner. Used by permission. From "Harlem Gallery,
Book I: The Curator," in *"Harlem Gallery" and Other Poems*, by Melvin Tolson. Copyright ©
1999. Reprinted by permission of the University of Virginia Press and by permission of
Melvin B. Tolson Jr.

Library of Congress Cataloging-in-Publication Data will be found at the end of this book.

Book of Esther

Contents

Preface

Ordinary unhappiness is a long poem.
David Shapiro, *House (Blown Apart)*, 56

I RESEARCHED AND WROTE this book during the last decade of the twentieth century and of the second millennium. If it possesses any fin de siècle or fin de millennium features or tonalities, I leave them to others to detect. All I can say is that I intended it to be a twentieth-century (and second-millennium) book, but that I woefully underestimated how long it would take for a specialist in narrative and in postmodernist fiction to retool sufficiently to undertake a book on the postmodernist long poem.

One consequence of my taking so long to finish this book is that in the interval between its conception and its completion, its subject threatened to disappear. I don't mean the long poem; quite the contrary. More long poems were begun, continued, or completed during the nineties than ever before (or so it sometimes seemed). Nor am I thinking of the many obituaries for postmodernism that were a staple of cultural journalism (and of the more fashion-conscious wing of academic scholarship) throughout the nineties. Reports of postmodernism's demise have been greatly exaggerated. In any case, even if postmodernism were defunct, that would only mean that my chosen period of expertise had receded into the historical past instead of remaining contemporary, and why should that trouble me any more than the pastness of *their* periods troubles specialists in Romanticism or the Renaissance or the Middle Ages?

No, it's not the putative death of postmodernism that I find threatening, but rather the possibility that it never existed in the first place. This alarming possibility was raised in particularly compelling fashion, just as I was making final revisions on the typescript of this book, by

Marjorie Perloff in her manifesto, *21st-Century Modernism: The "New" Poetics* (2002). Perloff argues that the distinction between modernist and postmodernist poetry was a spurious one all along, and that poets such as Charles Olson who explicitly positioned themselves as "postmodernist" were oriented toward (or away from) a particular, severely reduced and domesticated version of modernism. The genuinely innovative avant-gardism of early modernism—the modernism of the pre-Great War "futurist moment"—fell out of the literary-historical narrative, or was assimilated to it in a normalized form, defanged and declawed. The avant-garde momentum of this first modernism was transmitted through various successor avant-gardes—the objectivists, John Cage and his circle, the performance poetries and ethnopoetics of the seventies, some (but not all) of whom embraced the label "postmodern"—to re-emerge at the turn of the millennium as a "21st-century modernism," the return of the repressed.

There is much truth in what Perloff says, but not the whole truth. In the end, her argument about the spuriousness of postmodernism and the return of the avant-garde is less threatening to a project like mine than it at first appears. For one thing, her way of thinking about the relationship between modernism and postmodernism is hardly alien to the discourse on postmodernism; quite the contrary, versions of a literary-historical narrative akin to Perloff's have long circulated in postmodern studies, and in fact form the basis of my own understanding of postmodernism. The classic formulation is Lyotard's: "Postmodernism . . . is not modernism at its end but in the nascent state, and that state is constant" (79). I understand this as meaning that when, in the second and third decades of the twentieth century, a relatively stable modernist poetics was crystallized out from the churning heterogeneity of early-modernist innovation, what was left out and left over—the "lost" avant-garde—remained available for revisiting and reappropriation by later generations of innovators (see McHale, *Constructing* 55–58). So "postmodernism" signifies the full range of possibilities ("modernism . . . in the nascent state") available before a normalizing modernism had made its choices, and which became available again after normalized modernism had run its course. That was Lyotard's story, anyway, as it is mine and, with some variation, Perloff's.

Modernism's nascent state is constant, says Lyotard—an apparent paradox. By this he implies, I take it, that the relationship of postmodernism to modernism is not unique to the twentieth century, but recurrent; that in the course of cultural history, successive "modernisms" have been crystallized out, leaving behind residues available for recuperation by later generations of "postmodernists." In other words, this is a general mechanism of cultural change. It resembles the mechanism identified by the Russian formalists under the name of the "elevation of the junior branch" or the "canonization of the younger genres": genres expelled from the center of the literary system in one period linger on in the peripheries, where they await revival by a later period (see Shklovsky 189–93; Tynyanov). Literary history traces, not a straight line of succession, but a broken or zigzag path, from center to periphery to center again, from "insider" to "outsider" to "insider." Its narrative is a messy one of successive acts of repression and recovery.

In *21st-Century Modernism* Perloff defends the continuing relevance to turn-of-the-century poetry of the formalist poetics of estrangement and difficulty, so she is surely aware of formalist theory. She must know that her account of the return of the modernist repressed is really only a particular case of the general literary-historical dynamic that the formalists identified. It is the same dynamic as the one that Lyotard captured in his formulation, and the same as the one that animates my own account, in the chapters that follow, of postmodernist poetry's recovery of "lost" and ephemeral genres such as Menippean satire, learnéd wit, and court masque. Formalist-style literary historiography, with its zigzag progress, its leaps and recoils, yields an untidy picture of literary phenomena. Rather than tidy up the mess, I have sought to preserve it, thinking that this was the best way to honor (in a phrase I have lifted from Robert Venturi) the obligation toward the difficult whole.

The obligation toward the difficult whole applies also to the eclecticism of my selection of texts. I have tried not to hew to any particular version of postmodernism in making my selection, or to any particular party line or school or even any representative sampling of schools, but instead to reflect the eclecticism of the postmodern scene itself, its difficult whole. I've sought to combine more familiar poems (including some which might not typically be read in a postmodernist context) with unfamiliar ones. Above all, I've selected the poems that I wanted to become intimate with (or thought I did, since some of them I had read only partially or superficially at the point when I made my selection).

I've deliberately avoided rounding up some of the usual suspects. Conspicuous by their absence from the chapters that follow are those monumental poems that (depending on how one looks at it) exhaust modernism or inaugurate postmodernism or make the transition from one to the other: Pound's late *Cantos*, Williams's *Paterson*, Zukofsky's *"A,"* H.D.'s *Helen in Egypt*, Olson's *Maximus Poems*, or (in another tradition) Perse's *Anabasis* or Jabès's *Book of Questions*. Others have already written authoritatively about these texts, drawing on a breadth and depth of scholarship I could not hope to attain. There are many other poems, however, that could have figured in this project alongside or instead of the poems that *do* figure in it, but that I have passed over just because time and space are limited and one needs to choose. I could easily have chosen a different long poem by Ashbery, for instance. In fact, I had originally paired "The Skaters" with his book-length poem *Flow Chart*, but in the process of revising discovered that I had said nothing new about *Flow Chart* that I had not already said more concisely in connection with "The Skaters"; so *Flow Chart* dropped out of the project almost at the last moment. In the same way, I could have substituted different poems by Susan Howe, but I remained faithful to my first love, her *Europe of Trusts* poems.

Howe's poems and many of Ashbery's, including "The Skaters" (but not *Flow Chart*), could be assimilated to the genre of "pocket epic," a term that Nigel Alderman taught me to use. It is typically used of British poems, including (among my selections) Hill's *Mercian Hymns*, but also MacDiarmid's *A Drunk Man Looks at a Thistle*, Bunting's *Briggflatts*, David Jones's *The Anathémata*, Paul Muldoon's "Yarrow," and two that I've written about elsewhere, Andrew Greig's *Men on Ice* and *Western Swing* (see McHale, "Brit-Pop"). The Canadian long poem, as anthologized by Ondaatje and Thesen, seems generally to be affiliated with the British pocket epic. However, nothing prevents our extending the term to cover poems from the United States like those of Howe, Ashbery, Kathleen Fraser, Rosmarie Waldrop, Leslie Scalapino, or Barrett Watten, or for that matter Michael Harper's "Debridement," a pocket *Iliad*. All of these might have been candidates for inclusion in this book. Other candidates might have been book-length poems such as Gary Snyder's *Mountains and Rivers without End*, Ronald Johnson's *Ark*, Robin Blaser's *The Holy Forest*, Kenneth Koch's *Seasons on Earth*, Muldoon's *Madoc*, Clark Coolidge's *At Egypt*, Lyn Hejinian's *My Life* or *Oxota* or *The Cell*, or Theresa Hak Kyung Cha's *Dictee*; multivolume works, some of them still ongoing, such as Beverly Dahlen's *A Reading*, Rachel Blau DuPlessis's *Drafts*, or Ron Silliman's *The Alphabet;* or discontinuous long poems, their sections interpolated among other poems in the poet's collections, such as Robert Duncan's *Passages* or Nathaniel Mackey's *Songs of the Andoumboulou.*

Apart from the threatened disappearance of my subject, another consequence of taking so long to finish this book is that the textual and scholarly ground has shifted underfoot. During the course of the nineties, new editions of several of these poems appeared: complete editions of McGrath's *Letter to an Imaginary Friend* and Schwerner's *The Tablets*, new editions of Ashbery's "The Skaters," Tolson's *Harlem Gallery*, and (literally as I write these words) Howe's *The Europe of Trusts*. New annotations appeared: Robert Polito's annotations to Merrill's *The Changing Light at Sandover*, Stephen Fredman's and Grant Jenkins's to Dorn's *Gunslinger*, Raymond Nelson's to *Harlem Gallery*. Much relevant new scholarship was published, including the first monograph ever on Howe's poetry (by Rachel Tzvia Back), the second monograph ever on Ashbery's poetry (by John Shoptaw), the second ever on the New York School in general (by David Lehman), and important book-length studies on women's long poems (by Lynn Keller) and on women's Language poetry (by Ann Vickery), among much else. I have had to scramble to stay abreast of these developments, taking some comfort in the thought that all this publishing activity must indicate increasing interest in postmodernist poetry. More sobering developments also occurred. Three of the poets about whom I have written died while I was working on this project: James Merrill in 1995, Edward Dorn in 1999, and Armand Schwerner, also in 1999. I mourn the loss of all three of them, but especially of Armand Schwerner, whom I knew, admired, and loved.

Apart from the quite incalculable debts I owe the poets themselves, in the course of writing this book I have accumulated a mass of personal debts to colleagues, friends, and kin. Some read and commented on chapters or discussed the ideas in them with me; others directed me to key references or gave or lent me books that I might not otherwise have had access to; some just (just!) gave support, encouragement, and sound advice. Let me name some of those people here: Mieke Bal and Ernst van Alphen (for Gorris's *De Stilte Rond Christine M.*); Charles Bernstein; Rachel Blau DuPlessis; Joanne Ferguson; Kathleen Fraser; the late John Funari; Willard Gingerich; Hank Lazer; Alma and Lily Gottlieb-McHale (for the general climate); Bob Griffin; Jim Harms; Lynn Keller; Kevin McHale (for the timely loan of McGrath's *This Coffin Has No Handles*); Carl Malmgren (for Piazza d'Italia updates); Tyrus Miller; Claire and George Milner; Bob Parker; Bob Perelman; Arthur Sabatini; Mark Scroggins; John Shoptaw; David Shumway; Richard Shusterman (for hiphop); David Simpson and Judy Sylvester; Henry Sussman; Barrett Watten; and Tamar Yacobi.

This book was researched, written and rewritten during my tenure as Eberly Family Distinguished Professor of American Literature at West Virginia University. Though by the time it appears I will have taken up a new position at the Ohio State University, nevertheless this is my West Virginia book, and I owe a debt of gratitude to WVU and my colleagues in the Department of English there for time, resources, intellectual stimulation, and an atmosphere of collegiality in which to work. I want especially to thank Duane Nellis, dean of the Eberly College of Arts and Sciences, for a timely semester's sabbatical leave. My thanks also go to my students in the various courses I offered throughout the nineties on topics in postmodernism and poetry, among whom I want to single out Joe Moffett, a fellow student of the postmodernist long poem, and Eddie Christie, my research assistant in spring 2002, when I needed him most. Costs for permissions were partly defrayed by a subvention granted by the Research Committee of the Ohio State University College of Humanities.

Versions of two of these chapters have appeared elsewhere. Part of chapter 4 appeared under the title, "Archaeologies of Knowledge: Hill's Middens, Heaney's Bogs, Schwerner's Tablets," in *New Literary History* 30.1 (Winter 1999): 239–62. A version of chapter 5 appeared as "How (Not) to Read Postmodernist Long Poems: The Case of Ashbery's 'The Skaters,'" in *Poetics Today* 21.3 (Fall 2000): 561–90, the first of three Festschrift issues in honor of Benjamin Harshav. Three of these chapters began life as conference presentations: chapter 4 as a presentation at "Past, Present, Future Tense," Cornell University, April 1995; chapter 6 as a presentation at "Assembling Alternatives," University of New Hampshire, 29 August–2 September 1996; chapter 7 as a presentation at "Poetry and the Public Sphere," Rutgers University, April 1997. I am grateful to the audiences at these events who gave me invaluable feedback, and to the organizers for inviting me in the first place: Jonathan Monroe (Cornell), Romana Huk (UNH), and Kathleen Crown, Harriet Davidson, and Nick Yasinski (Rutgers).

1
Introduction: The Obligation toward the Difficult Whole

DESPITE EFFORTS TO THINK of postmodernism totalistically, as a cultural dominant that inflects practices right across the whole spectrum of culture (see especially Jameson, *Postmodernism*), its usefulness or relevance as a periodizing concept appears anything but uniform from field to field. Concepts of the postmodern have taken firm hold in architecture (as we'll see in some detail below), the dance, and the novel, but less so in the visual arts, cinema, or music. This is not to say that critics, publicists, or even practitioners in these latter fields have no use whatsoever for the term, but only that in these fields its use seems optional or arbitrary, whereas in architecture or dance or the novel it has come to seem difficult or impossible even to speak of contemporary practices without invoking some version of postmodernism—if only to dismiss it as inadequate.

Poetry is another field where the period-concept postmodernism has never seemed inevitable. The term does, of course, have some currency in the discourses of and around poetry; among the Norton anthologies are *Postmodern American Poetry*, edited by Paul Hoover (1994), and Donald Allen's epochal anthology, *The New American Poetry* (1960), which, when it returned in a second edition, bore the new title, *The Postmoderns*. A number of critics and theorists have regularly applied the term to poetry from the mideighties on. Nevertheless, Fredric Jameson, by far the most influential theorist of postmodernism as period concept and "cultural logic," devotes barely three pages of his more than four-hundred-page *Postmodernism, or, The Cultural Logic of Late Capitalism*

2 / Chapter 1

(1991) to poetry, or rather to a single poem, the Language poet Bob Perelman's "China." (I'll return to Jameson on Perelman's "China" in chapter 6). While the term "postmodern" or "postmodernism" appears to have been coined on several independent occasions, dating back at least to the 1870s, few of these early uses can be shown to have any genealogical continuity with contemporary usage. Ironically, one of the earliest that does is Charles Olson's use (207) of "post-modern" in the early fifties in conjunction with "post-humanist" and "post-historic" (see Calinescu 267–68; Bertens 20–22). The irony here is that Olson's context for (re)inventing postmodernism was that of poetry—and poetry, as we have just seen, is one of the cultural forms where no consensus has emerged concerning postmodernism's relevance. More ironic still, in this respect, is Olson's lifelong affiliation with the long poem, of all poetic genres the one evidently least susceptible of being characterized in postmodernist terms.

Special difficulties seem to inhere in thinking about the long poem as postmodernist. The long poem itself, as a distinct historical genre, seems indelibly associated with modernism. It is a modernist invention, a desperate solution to the problem that the high modernists (Eliot, Pound, Williams, Stevens, Hart Crane, MacDiarmid, H.D.) set for themselves of achieving poetry commensurate with the scale of their ambitious designs on literary history and the culture at large, but without violating the doctrine of the image, which held that the individual image was the foundation of poetic value, and without relapsing into overtly narrative modes (see, among others, Riddel; Dickie; Friedman; McHale, "Telling Stories").[1] In a sense, then, to undertake to write a long poem is to engage with a peculiarly high-modernist problematic and to practice a distinctively high-modernist genre; it is, in effect, to *be* a high modernist, no matter whether one is writing under conditions of modernity in 1922 or 1942, or under the "postmodern condition" in 1968 or 1980 or 1991. Unsurprisingly, then, much of the best commentary on the "postmodernist" long poem (whether under that name or some other, such as "modern verse epic" or "modern poetic sequence") has tended to emphasize the continuities between modernist practice and contemporary practices (see, e.g., M. Bernstein; Rosenthal and Gall; Beach). Such continuities demonstrably exist, and emphasizing them has considerable value, bringing important features of these poems to light. But the contrary emphasis on discontinuity and difference, on the *post*modernity of this high-modernist genre in contemporary practice, also has considerable potential value and promises to bring to light other features—precisely those obscured by emphasizing modernist continuities.

How, then, to proceed? How are we to come to descriptive and hermeneutic grips with the postmodernist long poem, to get some purchase on this slippery object, without simply collapsing it into the high-modernist model, acceding to that model's priority and explanatory power? How are we to salvage, and respect, the *difference* of the postmodernist long poem relative to its modernist precursor? One might aspire to describe postmodernist long poems "in themselves," without reference to any precedents whatsoever, high-modernist or otherwise. In actual practice, however, we always approach unknown objects in the light of known models. The question, then, is what models to substitute for the privileged high-modernist model when approaching the postmodernist long poem? I would like to propose two alternative models: first, the model of the postmodernist novel; and second, that of postmodern architecture.

I. THE NOVELISTIC MODEL

Why leave fictive experiments to the prose writers?

Armand Schwerner, "Tablets Journals/
Divagations," *The Tablets* (1999: 128)

One earmark of the modernist long poem, as I've just observed, is its adherence to a ban on narrative in poetry (see Perloff, "From image to action"; McHale, "Telling Stories"). By contrast, of the nine postmodernist long poems discussed in the present book (or eleven, depending on how one is counting), six of them are narrative poems, and the rest entertain some more or less oblique relation to narrative or the novel.

How is it that these poets seem so little constrained by the modernist prohibition on narrative in poetry? One reason, surely, is that so many of them are themselves novelists. Of the nine poets discussed here, four published one or more works of prose fiction.[2] Even more relevant, however, to the postmodernist narrative mode of these long poems is their relationship to certain pre- and para-novelistic genres, modes of fiction that precede the novel historically or coexist with it, but somewhere off to one side of the novelistic mainstream. One such genre is Menippean satire, the realist novel's predecessor and shadowy Other. As I shall argue in chapter 3, both Tolson's *Harlem Gallery* and Dorn's *Gunslinger* can be seen as following in the erratic and discontinuous tradition (or anti-tradition) of Menippean satire, the genre (or antigenre) of Petronius's *Satyricon*, Rabelais's *Gargantua and Pantagruel*, Swift's *Gulliver's Travels*, Flaubert's *Bouvard et Pécuchet*, Flann O'Brien's *At Swim-Two-Birds*, and many so-called novels of the postmodernist period. We might equally plausibly locate all of these fictions, and many others besides, in a tradition of "learnéd wit" (see Moore) extending at least from Erasmus and Rabelais down through Joyce and Flann O'Brien to Borges, Nabokov, Umberto Eco, and the OuLiPians. It is here, alongside these other forms of fictive scholarship and mock learning, that Schwerner's mock-scholarly hoax, *The Tablets*, finds its proper place (see chapter 4). The tradition of learnéd wit also accommodates the linguistic and generic extravagance of, for instance, Dorn's *Gunslinger* or parts 3 and 4 of McGrath's *Letter to an Imaginary Friend.*

These pre- and para-novelistic genres are the precursors of the postmodernist novel. The postmodernist novel returns to these obsolete and marginalized genres seeking models of a type of fiction that is not, as the modernist novel was, dedicated to exploring epistemological questions, but rather to raising ontological ones. The postmodernist long poem, we can assume, returns to these genres for the same reason. Elsewhere (McHale, *Postmodernist Fiction* 6–25) I have traced the shift from the epistemological dominant of modernist fiction, which is oriented toward issues of perception, knowledge, reliability, etc., to the ontological dominant of postmodernism, in which the orientation shifts to issues of fictionality, modes of being, the nature and plurality of worlds, etc. That same shift can be traced in these postmodernist long poems, sometimes over the course of a single poem. Merrill's *Changing Light at Sandover*, in particular, begins in the epistemological mode in its first part, "The Book of Ephraim," but shifts increasingly into the ontological mode in its second and third parts. A similar trajectory is recapitulated on a smaller scale in part 4 of McGrath's *Letter to an Imaginary Friend.*

Moreover, the means of effecting this reorientation are in many cases the same as in postmodernist novels. Shift of dominance is achieved using a specific repertoire of strategies (devices, motifs) that have come to be recognized as characteristic of postmodernism, though many of them can be found in those very same obsolete and marginalized genres, outsiders to the novelistic mainstream, on which both the postmodernist novel and the postmodernist long poem draw. First, the fictional world itself is pluralized through a number of strategies: juxtapositions of this world and the world to come (as in Merrill's *Changing Light at Sandover*) or of historical realities and fiction (as in Schwerner's *The Tablets*, Hill's *Mercian Hymns*, and Howe's "The Liberties"); the creation of ontologically heterogeneous worlds, or "heterotopias" (as in Dorn's *Gunslinger*); or the irruption into our world of beings of a different ontological order from our own (e.g., the spirits and angels of *Changing Light*). Second, the ways in which fictional worlds are made, or in which they *fail* to be made, are laid bare through such strategies as proliferation of narrative levels through embedding or "stacking" (as in Tolson's *Harlem Gallery* and Schwerner's *The Tablets*), erasure and unmaking (as in *The Tablets*, Ashbery's "The Skaters," and Howe's *Europe of Trusts*), and so on. Third, the literalized figures in *Gunslinger* and *Harlem Gallery* and the tension between *use* and *mention* in "The Skaters" and Andrews's "Confidence Trick" are strategies that drive a wedge between text and world, splitting them apart and pitting them one against the other. Fourth, the ultimate ontological grounding of fictional worlds is exposed—their grounding, on the one hand, in the material reality of the book (see especially Schwerner and Howe), and on the other hand in the material activity of an author, whose problematizing is a feature of all these poems. (For further details and examples, see McHale, *Postmodernist Fiction*.)

Even if one is generally skeptical of cross-genre comparisons, it's hard to deny the *heuristic* value of approaching postmodernist long poems in the light of the postmodernist novel. It is something of a mystery why postmodernist long poems have not been read more often in the context of postmodernist prose fiction before now; surely academic specialization is mainly to blame. In any case, the poetics of postmodernist fiction can serve as a bridge to the postmodernist long poem. One reflection of the heuristic value I ascribe to postmodernist novels in this connection is the recurrent allusion to works of postmodernist fiction in the chapters that follow. This is particularly conspicuous in chapter 3, where the entire discussion of Tolson's and Dorn's poems is organized with reference to the fiction of Ishmael Reed, especially his novels *Yellow Back Radio Broke-Down* and *Mumbo Jumbo*. Fiction figures in a similarly pivotal way in chapter 6, where the differences between McGrath's and Andrews's respective methods of appropriative sampling are clarified by juxtaposing the modernist poetics of John Dos Passos's *U.S.A.* with William Burroughs's postmodernist cut-ups. Nabokov's *Pale Fire,* an exemplary fiction of "learnéd wit," functions as a touchstone for the discussion of Schwerner's *Tablets* in chapter 4, as does William Gibson's genre-defining cyberpunk novel *Neuromancer* for the discussion of *Changing Light* in chapter 2; and so on.

Finally, the heuristic function of postmodernist fiction is also reflected in the order in which I take up the poems in the chapters below. If postmodernist narrative poetics is the bridge to these poems, then it makes sense to begin with the poems that yield most readily to analysis in terms adapted from postmodernist fiction, and to proceed from there to poems that elude or resist such analysis more tenaciously. Thus I begin with the most "novelistic" long poems in my corpus: Merrill's *Changing Light* (chapter 2), Tolson's *Harlem Gallery,* and Dorn's *Gunslinger* (chapter 3). (McGrath's *Letter to an Imaginary Friend,* which ought by rights to figure among these "novelistic" poems, is withheld until a later chapter for purposes of contrast.) The middle chapters are devoted to quasinarrative texts, poems in which the narrative element has been deliberately fragmented (Hill's *Hymns* and Schwerner's *Tablets* in chapter 4) or "weakened" (Ashbery's "The Skaters" in chapter 5), but from which something like a narrative poetics can nevertheless be recovered, more or less effortfully. The final chapters are reserved for the most intractably antinarrative texts in this corpus—Andrews's "Confidence Trick" (coupled for contrast with McGrath's *Letter* in chapter 6) and Howe's *Europe of Trusts* trilogy (chapter 7)—though of course the negativity of these antinarratives is inevitably conditioned in part by the expectations of narrativity against which these texts muster their formidable resistance.

II. THE ARCHITECTURAL MODEL

Language is the house of Being. In its home man dwells.
    Martin Heidegger, *Letter on Humanism* (193)

Architectural terms are more than just metaphors for reading,
yet it's difficult to track the parallels without getting impossibly
abstract or painfully elusive.
    Charles Bernstein, "The Book as Architecture," *My Way* (56)

An alternative model for the postmodernist long poem is postmodern architecture. Postmodern architecture has a special status in the public perception of postmodernism—it is, after all, the form in which most people are apt to encounter postmodernist aesthetics, if they encounter it at all, and the one that has occasioned the most public discussion and controversy. But it also has a special status in theories of postmodernism; it is, in a sense, the privileged model, to which all other manifestations of postmodernism are referred.

Postmodern philosophers and theorists have come to regard discourse in the Western tradition as "architectural." The "*will to architecture* is the foundation of Western thought," writes Kojin Karatani (xxxv). Derrida puts it this way: "the deconstruction of ph[iloso]phy should be at the same time the deconstruction of the architectural metaphor, which is at the core of philosophy[,] and of the architectural tradition which is philosophical through and through" (Derrida and Eisenman 105; see also Wigley).[3] Meanwhile, from the other side, postmodern architects and architecture critics have come increasingly to regard architecture as "discursive." Writing is now more freely acknowledged to play an integral role in architectural practice. The writing of architectural manifestos and polemical monographs is one of the legacies that postmodern architects inherited from their high-modernist precursors—Le Corbusier, Gropius, Wright—but it has become so endemic among the postmodernists that for a time it seemed as though architectural writing had displaced building in their practice. Moreover, in becoming writers, postmodern architects also became increasingly "literary," in the sense of incorporating in their texts allusions to many of the same critics and theorists on whom literary scholars rely. Thus, Robert Venturi, in his 1966 manifesto *Complexity and Contradiction in Architecture*, mobilizes the literary modernism of Eliot and the New Critics *against* architectural modernism; Bernard Tschumi alludes knowledgeably to structuralists and poststructuralists such as Genette, Barthes, Eco, and Baudrillard; and Peter Eisenman shows himself to be an attentive reader (or perhaps *mis*reader) of Derrida. Beyond the writing of architectural manifestos, it has also become increasingly clear how much of routine architectural practice can be seen as broadly "discursive." Thus, Mark Wigley (212–13) enumerates no fewer than forty "mechanisms of representation"—"discourses," in the broadest possible sense—that among them constitute a building, ranging from the curricula and pedagogy of schools of architecture, through professional licensing criteria, fee structures, legal contracts, copyright law, and building, zoning and safety codes, to interview and presentation formats, architectural jurying, competition formats, and even model making and photographic techniques and the structure of the architectural monograph.

Not only does the practice of architecture involve writing, but also architecture itself can be conceived along the lines of language. Apologists for postmodern architecture such as Charles Jencks (*Language* 39–79), having absorbed (in however simplified a way) the findings of semiotics, proposed to speak of architecture as a "language" or "code," in which one could discern "words" (door, window, column, cantilever, etc.), "metaphors" (especially metaphors of the human face and body), "syntax" (what the architectural tradition through modernism called "structure"), even entire fields and systems of "semantics" (e.g., the system of the three classical orders—Doric, Ionic, Corinthian; the nineteenth-century system of "revivalist" styles—Greek Revival, Gothic Revival, Italian, Hindu, Old English; etc.). Peter Eisenman, at the outset of his career, devoted himself to exploring the possibilities of architecture as language in a series of private houses, some actually built, others only projected. Like a good Chomskyan, he bracketed off architectural "semantics"—the functional "meanings" that high-modernist architects applied to buildings—in the interests of isolating the units and combinatorial rules of architectural "syntax." At a certain point, however, he seems to have abandoned the model of architecture as language and, no doubt under the influence of Derrida and other poststructuralists, to have shifted to the more radical notion of *the building as text*—a fabric of differences, susceptible of deconstruction (see Gandelsonas; Eisenman, "Misreading"). These two alternatives—related but distinguishable —namely *architecture as language or code,* and *building as text,* serve to indicate, however cursorily, the range of postmodern "discursive" approaches to architecture. One sees with what justice Jameson could conclude that "postmodern architecture is the property of literary critics after all, and textual in more ways than one" (*Postmodernism* 99).

The postmodern rapprochement of architecture and discourse has enhanced the potential of postmodernist architecture to serve as a model for the contemporary long poem. If already in the modernist period architecture could be pressed into service to model the spatialized forms of modernist long poems—as witness the Unreal Cities of *The Waste Land,* the Tempio of *The Cantos*—then surely a "discursivized" postmodern architecture must serve the purpose that much better. Postmodern architecture in fact provides two such models, each with the potential to capture different aspects of the postmodernist long poem's complex form. These two models—one hesitates to call them "types" or "schools," since they cut across the usual typologies with which postmodern architectural criticism abounds—correspond to the two approaches to architectural discourse identified in the preceding paragraph. The first, which proposes to approach architecture as language or code, might be called the "semiotic" or "historicist" model, but would very likely be associated by most lay consumers of architecture with "Post-Modernism" as such. (In what follows, I'll preserve that spelling in order to distinguish this model from postmodernism generally.) The second, corresponding to the building-as-text approach to architecture, might be called the "deconstructivist" model.

The "Post-Modern" model encompasses postmodernist architecture as it exists in the public mind, the Post-Modernism of half-serious historicist allusion: the classical appliqués on Michael Graves's Portland Public Services Building, the shaped crowns of Philip Johnson's skyscrapers, and so on. The defining principle of this model is *legibility*. If architectural meaning is to be accessible to its users, so the theory runs, then architecture must deploy a repertoire of familiar signs, inherited from past architectural systems—mainly, as it turns out, those of classicism, often stylized to the point of caricature. The manifesto of this version of Post-Modernism is *Learning from Las Vegas*, by Robert Venturi, Denise Scott Brown, and Steven Izenour. First published in 1972, *Learning from Las Vegas* posited an architecture based on the principle of the "decorated sheds" of the Las Vegas Strip: merely functional buildings with huge signs plastered to their facades, or freestanding along the roadside. The tension between the legibility of the sign out front and the modernist functionality of the building behind it could be reconciled, according to Venturi and his collaborators, through a saving irony (Venturi, Brown, and Izenour 161). By way of precedent they adduced pop art, with its coupling of populist appeal and avant-garde self-consciousness (130, 162).

It was left to that prolific apologist of Post-Modernism, Charles Jencks, to reformulate Venturi's irony as "double-coding" (*Language* 129–32; *What Is Post-Modernism?* 14–15, 18–19; "Time Fusion" 125). Post-Modern buildings, by this account, communicate on two different levels to two different constituencies. On one level, through their modernist structural techniques (the shed itself) and in-group ironies, they communicate with a minority constituency of architects and connoisseurs; on another level, they reach a broader public of architecture consumers through their historicist allusions (the decoration on the shed). The first true "major monument" of this double-coded architecture, according to Jencks, was not, as other critics had announced, Johnson's Chippendale-top AT&T Building (still too modernist, in Jencks's view), but Charles Moore's Piazza d'Italia in New Orleans (*Language* 133, 146; see Jameson, *Postmodernism* 100–101). An architectural in-joke that doubles as a kind of pocket theme park, simultaneously elitist and populist (though unfortunately not, as it turns out, very popular), the Piazza d'Italia is nothing if not legible: it can be read like a book.[4]

Almost from the outset, Jencks was conscious of the "literariness" of double-coded architecture, not only in the sense of that architecture's own discursiveness, but in the sense of its literary analogues, particularly the postmodernist fiction of Borges, Barth, Eco, and others. On the literary side, it was Linda Hutcheon, in *A Poetics of Postmodernism* (1988) and elsewhere, who adopted Jencks's notion of double-coding and developed it as a model for postmodernist literature. Hutcheon identifies literary postmodernism with a particular genre of novel, that of self-reflexive historical fiction, or "historiographic metafiction"—e.g., *The French Lieutenant's Woman, The Name of the Rose, Ragtime, The White Hotel, Midnight's Children*—and historiographic metafiction, in turn, she characterizes in terms of its double-coding. Like the Piazza d'Italia and other double-coded architectural works, historiographic metafictions are simultaneously legible and avant-garde, historicist reconstructions and self-reflexive parodies; they appeal both to the "common reader" (whoever that might be) and the academic specialist.

Influential though Hutcheon's account has been, hers is not the only direction in which one might develop a literary notion of double-coding on the model of Post-Modern architecture. If Hutcheon's model couples avant-gardism with the historicist aspect of Post-Modern architecture, another approach involves coupling it with Post-Modernism's pop art aspect. This is Larry McCaffery's approach in positing an "avant-pop" tendency in recent fiction, that is, a tendency that "combines pop art's focus on consumer goods and mass media with the avant-garde's spirit of subversion and emphasis on radical formal innovation" (xvii–xviii). While the two versions of double-coded fiction do overlap to some degree—Pynchon, Coover, and DeLillo, for instance, satisfy the criteria of both historiographic metafiction and avant-pop—McCaffery's avant-pop canon accommodates a number of surfictionists and other radical experimentalists (e.g., Acker, Barthelme, Burroughs, Federman, Sukenick) whom Hutcheon would exclude on the grounds of elitist illegibility.

While both Hutcheon and McCaffery range widely over media and genres in their respective accounts of postmodern double-coding, neither sees fit to mention poetic examples, let alone long poems. Nevertheless, a number of postmodernist long poems do seem to satisfy one or other set of criteria for double-coding. Merrill's summoning-up of the spirits of the illustrious dead in *The Changing Light at Sandover* (see chapter 2)—mainly figures from literary history, but also including, for instance, Akhnaton and Nefertiti, Muhammad, and Montezuma— might be seen as a particularly eccentric version of historiographic metafiction. More congruent with the genre as Hutcheon conceived it is Howe's revisionist reflection in "The Liberties" (chapter 7) on the historical relationship between Jonathan Swift and his live-in muse, Esther Johnson (the "Stella" of his poems and correspondence). As for the avant-pop variety of double-coding, here Edward Dorn's *Gunslinger* (chapter 3), with its avant-garde subversion of the genre conventions of Westerns and its affinities with comic-book art and sixties pop, seems a strong candidate for inclusion. Others of these poems, though they don't necessarily adhere to the logic of double-coding, nevertheless adopt the citational aspect of historicist Post-Modernism that one sees so clearly in a project such as Moore's Piazza d'Italia. Ashbery's "The Skaters" (chapter 5), Andrews's "Confidence Trick" (chapter 6), and Howe's *Europe of Trusts* (chapter 7) all treat the discourses circulating around them (everyday colloquial clichés and degraded mass-media discourses in Ashbery and Andrews; texts from the high-literary canon—Spenser's, Shakespeare's, Swift's—in Howe) as *objects for exhibit* rather than *means of expression,* as ornament rather than structure, much as Moore exhibits the classical orders and elements in his Piazza d'Italia. These discourses are *mentioned* rather than *used* (to anticipate terminology that will figure in the relevant chapters below); they signify "mass-media discourse" or "Shakespeare," as the dropped-keystone arches and broken pediments of Post-Modern architecture signify "classicism," or even "architecture" *tout court.*

Not every architect or architecture critic welcomed the Post-Modern aesthetic of historicism and legibility, to say the least. On both the progressive and conservative wings of the profession, architects protested Post-Modernism's reduction of history to Disneyland-style simulacra, its neutralizing of architecture's criticial potential, and its perceived pandering to market and entertainment values. For radicals and conservatives alike, a target of particular hostility has been Robert Venturi for his promotion of the Las Vegas paradigm of semiotic architecture. But in fact Venturi's aesthetics are intriguingly divided, and his theory and practice have at least as much in common with Post-Modernism's radical critics and the architecture of defamiliarization as they do with Post-Modern historicism. Before the manifesto of architectural legibility, *Learning from Las Vegas*, he had produced a different but equally influential manifesto on architectural form, *Complexity and Contradiction in Architecture* (1966; 2nd edn. 1977). Some aspects of his approach to form in *Complexity and Contradiction* are unproblematically compatible with the Las Vegas paradigm, including his account of "vestigial" (i.e., historicist), "rhetorical" (i.e., double-coded) and ironic elements in architecture, his defense of "honky-tonk" (i.e., popular-culture) elements, and his slogan, "Main Street [is] almost all right" (38, 40, 42, 44, 104). Moreover, Venturi betrays a modernist-style anxiety to unify, integrate, and reconcile the disparate and disjunct parts of the mainly baroque and mannerist (including Edwardian neomannerist) buildings he analyzes. But he also reveals an openness toward and acceptance of architectural tensions and disjunctions that can be neither resolved nor easily "read"— "violent adjacencies" and "superadjacencies" (1977:56, 61), complex interiors and residual spaces (70–74), and unresolved contradictions (102), which Venturi compares with those of difficult poetry. One is strongly reminded of the Frank Gehry House, Jameson's touchstone (*Postmodernism* 107–29) of postmodernist disjunction and difficulty, which postdates *Complexity and Contradiction in Architecture* by over a decade. Venturi's resonant slogan for architecture in this complex and contradictory mode, "the obligation toward the difficult whole," seems to anticipate Jameson's enigmatic slogan of postmodernist aesthetics, "difference relates" (Jameson, "Architecture" 59–60; *Postmodernism* 31).

The obligation toward the difficult whole: it may be the phrase's residual modernist connotations that have prevented its adoption as a postmodernist motto. "Obligation" retains more than a trace of modernist architecture's high-minded purism and absolutism; "difficult" evokes the modernist conviction that difficult times call for difficult forms ("poetry in our civilization, as it exists at present, must be *difficult*," wrote Eliot in 1921); while "whole" sounds hopelessly dated, a relic of New Critical organicism (see Perloff, *21st-Century* 10). Taken together, the words can hardly fail to resonate with echoes of modernist constructivism, whereas postmodernist architecture (as distinct from the "Post-Modern" architecture discussed above) tends to favor catchwords evoking or implying *de*construction. So we find *de*-composition in Eisenman (*House X*), *dis*-junction, *dis*integration, and a whole lexicon of other words prefixed by *de-*, *dis-*, or *ex-*in Tschumi, *anti*-architecture and *an*architecture in Derrida's characterization of Eisenman's work (Derrida and Eisenman 8), even *de*-architecture (Wines), as well as, of course, *deconstructivist architecture* itself (Johnson and Wigley). All of these coinages point toward an aspiration to trouble and undo architectural form in ways beyond what Venturi's "difficult whole" implies.

We have already seen above how deconstruction and architecture became implicated in each other's theoretical projects in the postmodern period. The fact that deconstruction and architectural theory have learned to mimic each other's discourse does not, however, make it any easier to understand how deconstruction could be manifested in actual buildings. Derrida himself expressed doubts about this possibility. Bernard Tschumi recounts how, on first approaching Derrida about collaborating on an architectural project (the Parc de Villette scheme in Paris), the latter asked, "But how could an architect be interested in deconstruction? After all, deconstruction is anti-form, anti-hierarchy, anti-structure, the opposite of all that architecture stands for" (Tschumi 250). It remains a good question.

One example of deconstruction in actual practice is the architecture of Peter Eisenman—though, as one might expect, the "actual" is itself one of the concepts that Eisenman's architecture problematizes, since his practice has consisted of buildings, texts about those buildings, texts *in lieu of* buildings, and buildings (actually built or only proposed) understood as texts commenting on *other* buildings. House X, for instance—unbuilt, but elaborately presented and theorized—can be understood as "a critique of the previous houses" in the series (*House X* 44), some of them built (Houses I through III, see *House of Cards;* House VI, see S. Frank), others not.[5] In the House X project Eisenman pulls the building's volumes apart to leave a "void center" (*House X* 88), a concept also underlying his development, in this project and its successor, House El Even Odd, of the "three-dimensional el," a sort of anti-cube that serves as the "base form" of these unbuilt buildings (54; see Macrae-Gibson 30–50). Such houses illustrate, to the degree that a building can, the very notion of "loss of center"; they deny, says Eisenman, the "anthropocentricity of man" (quoted in Macrae-Gibson 38). House X, according to Rosalind Krauss (182), "incorporates the notion of difference at a very deep level," and with it Eisenman's architecture "has assumed the conditions of postmodernism" (184)—by which she means not Post-Modernism in the historicist mode, but deconstructivism.

Another exemplar of deconstructivism is Bernard Tschumi, whose practice of architecture, like Eisenman's, has combined built spaces with the "paper spaces" of architectural drawing and writing (93, 102). He proposes thinking of architecture as sequences of frames—in effect, stagings of events—but at the same time, recognizing the ease with which sequences can be recuperated as narratives, he has sought to disturb and interrupt these architectural sequences in ways that prevent any facile narrativization. In citing precursors for his model of architectural sequence, Tschumi expands the field of architecture well beyond its normal limits to include, for instance, theatrical spectacles and outdoor pageants, from the Renaissance masques of Ben Jonson and Inigo Jones through the *fêtes* of the French Revolutionary period to Russian Constructivist stage designs and even (more sinisterly) stagings of Nazi Party rallies by Albert Speer, Hitler's court architect (117–18, 125–26). One outcome of Tschumi's reflection on "dys-narrative" sequences (204–05) is the elaborate Parc de Villette project (see Johnson and Wigley 92–101), for one part of which he commissioned a collaborative work from Peter Eisenman and Jacques Derrida. This three-way collaboration is documented (inevitably) in a text—an alarmingly peculiar book, *Chora L Works* (1997; see note 3 above). At the outset (as we have seen) skeptical of the possible relevance of deconstruction to architecture, Derrida, by the end of the process documented in the book, could conclude that, together with law (and for similar reasons), architecture figures as one of the "ultimate tests of deconstruction" (Derrida and Eisenman 167).

The same question that troubled Derrida about the notion of a deconstructivist architecture—how can one deconstruct and still have architecture?—troubles long poems modelled on deconstructivist architecture: how can one build large-scale poetic structure and deconstruct it at the same time? The long poems discussed in this book address that question in various ways. The most obvious answer is to build with visual voids—blank spaces, as in Howe's *Europe of Trusts* (see chapter 7)—or even to *build ruins*. According to Eisenman, "the 'post-modern' metaphor of the ruin has superseded the modern metaphor of the machine," and this metaphor is literalized in his House X, which is "strongly colored by metaphoric ideas of ruin, decay, and falling to pieces" (*House X* 34; see Tafuri 178).[6] This same deconstructive metaphor of ruin colors not only Howe's "spaced-out" poetry, but even more explicitly Schwerner's *The Tablets* (chapter 4), which uses spacing and nonalphabetic signs to evoke a literally ruined text. Ashbery illustrates another such strategy, namely that of using one textual segment to contradict, nullify, or semantically evacuate another, pitting segment against segment so that they are mutually consumed. Entire blocs of text, cancelled, reframed, or otherwise "weakened" ontologically, fall under erasure in this way throughout Ashbery's "The Skaters" (see chapter 5). The result is a textual world poised strangely between being and nonbeing, yielding an effect of ontological "hovering." Similar hovering effects are achieved elsewhere by other means—for instance, by suspending elements of textual reality between literal and figurative status, in Tolson's *Harlem Gallery* and Dorn's *Gunslinger* (chapter 3). Merrill in *The Changing Light at Sandover* (chapter 2) generalizes this hovering effect to an entire virtual "other world," which unfolds into provisional reality when Merrill and his partner David Jackson operate the Ouija board, but then contracts back into nonexistence when they set the board aside.

If Eisenman's architecture of de-composition is a good model for some of these long poems, for others Tschumi's disjunctive architecture makes a better fit. Analogues of Tschumi's discontinuous, "dysnarrative" sequences can readily be found in the fragmentary, interrupted, cut-up, and pieced-together poetry of Ashbery, Andrews, and Howe (chapters 5, 6, and 7 respectively). More striking still, however, is the appearance here, as model and *mise en abyme,* of architecture in the extended sense proposed by Tschumi: architecture as pageant, masque, party rally. Certain titles are indicative: the third part of Merrill's *Changing Light* (chapter 2) is entitled "Scripts for the Pageant," while the second part of Howe's "The Defenestration of Prague" bears the title of one of Ben Jonson's court masques, *Speeches at the Barriers.* In both of these cases, masque serves to model a particularly centrifugal and heterogeneous kind of space—a world made up of fragments of many worlds, a heterotopia.

Il n'y a pas de hors-texte, Derrida (158) notoriously asserted: there is nothing outside the text, no "outside-text." Here is one reason (not the only one) why conceiving of a building as a text has such radical consequences for architecture. A building, even a building conceived of as an "utterance" coded in an architectural "language," has more or less sharply delimited boundaries; but a building understood as a text overruns boundaries, opening out into other texts, onto a limitless space of intertextuality. Such are the implications of a textualist, deconstructivist architecture. "The division between inside and outside is radically disturbed. The form no longer simply divides an inside from an outside. . . . [T]he sense of being enclosed, whether by a building or a room, is disrupted. . . . The wall breaks open, and in a very ambiguous way. . . . It no longer provides security by dividing the familiar from the unfamiliar, inside from out. The whole condition of enclosure breaks down" (Johnson and Wigley 18). There is no more apt illustration of the architectural equivalent of *pas de hors-texte* than Jameson's postmodern touchstone, the Gehry House. In the Gehry House as built, the tumbling cube of the kitchen "bursts through the structure, peeling back the layers of the house" (Johnson and Wigley 22), and a new space opens, ambiguously inside and outside, between the outer wall of the old house and the new "skin" that has been wrapped around it. Plans called for further disruption: the house's frame was to erupt through the rear wall into the backyard in an avalanche of scaffolding. (See the models and drawings in Johnson and Wigley 25–26).

Here, then, is one last architectural analogue of the postmodernist long poem. Like the Gehry House, postmodernist long poems burst through their textual enclosures and overrun their boundaries, in the most literal ways. In several cases of poems discussed in this book, we know of outtakes and leftovers, materials perhaps earmarked for inclusion in the poems but for some reason left out and published separately, or materials that in some sense "overflowed" the bounds of the poems. Such outtakes exist in the case of Tolson's *Harlem Gallery,* Dorn's *Gunslinger,* McGrath's *Letter to an Imaginary Friend,* and Merrill's *Changing Light at Sandover.* A related difficulty arises in Howe's *Europe of Trusts,* where it is unclear whether the three constitutent parts ("Pythagorean Silence," "The Defenestration of Prague," and "The Liberties") are designed to be read together as a single, integral long poem, or perhaps as a linked trilogy of poems, or merely as *Selected Poems* (a subtitle that appears in some Howe bibliographies, though nowhere in *The Europe of Trusts* itself). Each alternative implies a different hypothesis of what constitutes the "whole," how its parts are articulated, what lies inside that presumed whole and what outside it. Confronted with such puzzles of inside and outside, inclusion and exclusion, and such evidence of the permeability of textual boundaries, one is forced to acknowledge in all of these poems a compelling obligation toward the difficult whole.

2

Angels in America

James Merrill's *The Changing Light at Sandover*

"WAITING FOR THE ANGEL" ought to be the title of part 1 of Tony Kushner's two-part play *Angels in America* (premiered in 1990). It isn't; the actual title, of course, is *Millennium Approaches*. But waiting for the angel is precisely what occupies Kushner's reluctant hero, Prior, throughout the play's three long acts, from the first feathery intimations of its approach—literally, a feather falls from nowhere—until, heralded by otherworldly lighting effects ("*Very* Steven Spielberg," Prior remarks), it finally comes crashing through the ceiling at the very end of the last scene.

"Waiting for the Angel" is, in fact, one of the subhead titles of the last book of *Mirabell: Books of Number* (1978), which was then published as the second of James Merrill's trilogy of long poems collectively entitled *The Changing Light at Sandover* (1982). The poem's protagonists, Merrill and his partner David Jackson, have been waiting to be put in touch with the angel Michael since book 7.7 (234). Various intimations of the angel's approach appear in intervening books, including a joke about importuning angels for "THE FEATHER OF PROOF" ("Mirabell" 8.9, 258).[1] Michael finally addresses Merrill and Jackson directly through the Ouija board, their device for communicating with the spirit world, in the very last lines of "Mirabell" (9.9, 275–76). Not until the trilogy's third volume, "Scripts for the Pageant" (1980), do their informants in the other world describe the angel to them ("Scripts" Yes, 286; see also 289, 296.)

It is not a question here of one text's direct influence on the other; such influence is unprovable, and in any case not very interesting.[2] Rather, both Kushner's play and Merrill's long poem seem to emerge from the same matrix of postmodernist aesthetics.[3] How else to explain such similarities between *Angels in America* and *The Changing Light* as their multiple worlds (this world and the other world, but also worlds of dream and hallucination, inset worlds of texts-within-the-text, etc.); their mingling of characters of diverse ontological status (historical, fictional, and supernatural in the case of Kushner; in Merrill's, public, private, and mythological or allegorical); their location within and use of a gay subculture of difference; and so on. It might be thought that these similarities between the two texts would be eclipsed by their profound differences of genre; Kushner's, after all, is a theater piece making extensive use of spectacle and music, and generally vernacular in tone, while Merrill's is a long poem in a variety of forms, "fixed" as well as "open," ranging up and down the scale of stylistic registers. Yet these generic differences are perhaps less crucial than they at first appear, especially in view of the pervasive theatricality of Merrill's poem (see section III below).[4]

Harder to dismiss or reconcile are the differences arising from their respective attitudes toward popular culture. If a defining feature of postmodernist aesthetics is the erosion of distinctions between high and popular culture (as many have argued, most persuasively Andreas Huyssen), then Kushner, with his casual melding of high and low, is more fully and unanxiously postmodernist than Merrill. Kushner embraces popular-culture materials without embarrassment ("*Very* Steven Spielberg"); Merrill, by contrast, is transparently anxious about and resistant to the popular-culture materials which contaminate (in his view) the messages transmitted by the Ouija board. How to take seriously revelations cribbed from popular books of pseudoscience and the occult, from von Däniken's *Chariots of the Gods?*, the prophecies of Edgar Cayce (see Mazzocco 216), the subliteratures of near-death experience and alien abduction, etc.? "Dear Wystan," writes Merrill at one point, addressing Wystan Auden, one of his interlocutors in the spirit world, who has just characterized as "VERY VERY BEAUTIFUL" a communiqué from higher-order spirits revealing (among other things) the origin of flying saucers—

Dear Wystan, VERY BEAUTIFUL all this
Warmed-up Milton, Dante, Genesis?
This great tradition that has come to grief

In volumes by Blavatsky and Gurdjieff?
Von and Torro in their Star Trek capes,
Atlantis, UFOs, God's chosen apes—?
Nobody can transfigure junk like that
Without first turning down the rheostat
To Allegory, in whose gloom the whole
Horror of Popthink fastens on the soul,
Harder to scrape off than bubblegum.

. . . .

Some judgment has been passed
On our intelligence—why else be cast
Into this paper Hell out of Doré
Or Disney?

("Mirabell" 2.3, 136)[5]

Merrill confessed, in a 1979 interview with Helen Vendler, to embarrassment about the "silly" (read: trashy, kitschy) materials of his trilogy
(*Recitative* 50–51). In other interviews, he denied any such problems with
accommodating popular culture (see, e.g., *Recitative* 68). Nevertheless, I
think it is going too far to commend Merrill (as Philip Kuberski does)
for the "promiscuous inclusiveness" that allows him to juxtapose material from tabloids and popular occult books with Scripture and visionary
poetry (249, 250). Such juxtapositions certainly occur, but the evidence
of the trilogy itself (as in the passage above) suggests that Merrill was
sufficiently committed to a high-art aesthetic to find them embarrassing
to the end—and this includes the Ouija board itself, an embarrassingly
low-culture prop on which to premise a poem with pretensions to visionary art (see section IV below).[6] More embarrassing still, though for reasons not entirely under Merrill's control, is his iconography of angels.

"There are no angels in America," says a character in Kushner's play,
and when he first said it back in 1990 it was much more nearly true (in
one sense) than it is today. Pop-culture angelology was just entering on
a phase of expansion in 1990; since then, angel imagery has seemingly
penetrated every niche of popular culture—from tabloids to coffee-table
books, from greeting cards and calendars to coffee mugs and T-shirts,
from *Time* magazine (which featured a cover story on angels in its issue of December 27, 1993) to the Victoria's Secret catalog (which used
winged models to introduce a new line of "Angel" undergarments in

summer 1997). Nor have TV and the movies been neglected. After a lapse of several years, angels returned to the small screen when CBS premiered its weekly dramatic series *Touched by an Angel* at the start of the 1994–95 season. Angel movies have continued to be a staple of the Christmas season—for instance, two opened in the weeks before Christmas 1996, *Michael*, starring John Travolta, and *The Preacher's Wife* with Denzel Washington—and they are occasionally to be seen at other times of year as well (e.g., *City of Angels* [1998], the Hollywood remake of Wenders and Handke's 1987 classic, *Der Himmel über Berlin* [*Wings of Desire*]). MTV abounds with angel-themed music videos, of which R.E.M.'s "Losing My Religion" is among the most memorable. Examples could easily be multiplied (see McHale, "Gravity's Angels").

So ubiquitous is angel imagery in popular culture of the late nineties that it is hard to remember a time when angels were *not* popular. Nevertheless, it is the case that popular angel iconography was much less conspicuous when Kushner premiered the two parts of *Angels in America* at the beginning of the nineties, and postively *in*conspicuous (outside of the Christmas season) when Merrill was composing *The Changing Light* in the seventies. Merrill's precedents and models were exclusively high-art angels: the angels of the Renaissance painters and of Dante, Milton, Blake, and Rilke. By an irony of cultural history, Merrill's high-art angelology has been engulfed by pop-culture fashion, his sublime angels reduced post factum to fellowship with John Travolta and sexy underwear models.

And not just Merrill's angels, for a number of other serious postmodernist writers were exploring the iconography of angels at about the same time, among them Donald Barthelme, Gabriel García Márquez, Thomas Pynchon, Milan Kundera, Juan Goytisolo, Salman Rushdie, Steve Katz, and Harold Brodkey.[7] Some of these postmodernist angels were predictably parodic and iconoclastic—Barthelme's, Márquez's, Kundera's, Katz's; but others, including Goytisolo's, Rushdie's, and Brodkey's, not to mention the cinematic angels of Wenders and Handke's *Wings of Desire* and its sequel, *Faraway, So Close* (1993), were clearly meant to be taken seriously, in some sense. The angels of Pynchon's visionary novel, *Gravity's Rainbow* (1973), in particular, have much in common with those of Merrill's *Changing Light* (see Berger, "Merrill and Pynchon," and Merrill's 1981 interview with Fred Bornhauser, *Recitative* 58). It seems clear from all the evidence that the popular-culture angels of the nineties revival owe little if anything to the "serious" postmodernist angels of the seventies and eighties, while the postmodernist angels could hardly have been influenced by the popular angelology that postdates them. So we must conclude that angel imagery emerged independently at these two levels of cultural production. If so, then it becomes even more pressing to explain the striking ubiquity of angels in postmodern culture, high and low alike.

No doubt there are multiple, overlapping, and interfering reasons why cultural producers at all levels should turn to angel imagery as the millennium approached. According to conventional pop-sociological interpretations of this phenomenon, the angelic revival reflected a collective hunger for spirituality in a barrenly materialistic culture. But this is hardly the only explanation for this richly overdetermined phenomenon. Angels, as I have suggested elsewhere (McHale, *Constructing* 125–26, 202–03), belong to a class of motifs that function as "ontological pluralizers." That is, whatever other meanings we may invest it with, whatever other desires it may embody, an angel is also, and preeminently, a representative of the world from which it comes—a world other than our own. By "representative" I mean "synecdoche," the part that stands for the whole, the whole in this case being the other world, or indeed other *worlds* in the plural. A part of another world that has irrupted into this one, the angel stands for the whole of that other world from which it comes and to which it belongs, and beyond that for the general principle of ontological difference. Angels *stand for* the plurality of worlds; whatever else they might mean, angels also mean something like, "There is more than one world."

And by "worlds" here I mean a number of apparently disparate categories of states of being, ranging from alternative psychological realities (daydreaming, fantasies, dreams, hallucinations, psychotic delusions) to the multiple, jostling, clamorous microworlds of the mass media and the arts, to alternative worldviews and models of "reality," to the "other world" with which Merrill and Jackson communicate and from which Kushner's angel comes. I include also alternative subcultures, or what Berger and Luckmann (1966) call "enclaves of meaning," such as the gay subculture that figures so conspicuously in both *Angels in America* and *The Changing Light* (see Shoptaw, "James Merrill" 761). It is surely no accident that gay artists in our time have displayed a particular affinity for angel imagery (see Damon 142–201): these queer angels are synecdoches for a separate world of gayness, a world whose very existence remained largely unsuspected, until relatively recently, by straight "mainstream" culture.

The coming of the angel is explosive, disruptive, traumatic; it sends shock waves through the entire structure of the known world, for by violating the boundaries of that world it forces inhabitants to confront the fact of ontological plurality. With the explosive irruption of the angel into Prior's bedroom, "a membrane has been broken," Kushner writes in his playwright's notes to part 2 of *Angels in America* (8); "there is disarray and debris." Kushner's characters, Prior in particular, suffer what the psychologicist John E. Mack, in a related context, calls "ontological shock," the shock of encountering another world.[8] This encounter with other worlds (in every sense) is one aspect of the postmodern condition; hence the ubiquity of angels in postmodern culture. Hence the angels of *The Changing Light at Sandover*.

I. VISION AND REVISION, OR, THE CHANGING LIGHT

Angels represent the other world not only by *standing* for it, *pars pro toto*, but also by *speaking* for it; that is, they bear messages from the other world. Bearing messages is, of course, the function traditionally ascribed to angels in Scripture and religious art, one they inherited from the messenger-gods of antiquity (see Greene), and which they in turn passed on to their own heirs, the message-bearing aliens of contemporary UFO mythology (see Peebles). As messengers, angels can readily be pressed into service as figures for the circulation of information itself (see Serres). In this role, they have less affinity for the postmodernist poetics of otherness and the plurality of worlds than for the modernist poetics of knowledge, its accessibility and circulation, its reliability or unreliability. This is the function that they play, for instance, in Joseph McElroy's late-modernist novel *Women and Men* (1987). Here "angels" is the name given to a kind of collective consciousness that serves as the connective tissue of the novel, a fluid discursive medium that shuttles the reader's attention from place to place, dipping into characters' minds and then pulling back again to view them from outside, and wrapping everyone and everything in a continuous commentary (see McHale, *Constructing* 188–206). In other words, angels in McElroy's novel *literalize* classic narratological strategies of point of view—internal versus external, omniscient versus limited, shifting focalization. In doing so they thrust into the foreground the modernist problematics of knowledge associated with such strategies, raising such questions as who possesses knowledge? what knowledge do they possess? how reliably do they know what they know? to whom do they transmit their knowledge, and how? and so on.

In Merrill's *The Changing Light*, angels and other spirit-world interlocutors don't just deliver an ontological shock of otherness; they also, and effusively, deliver messages. Certainty or the lack of it, reliability, the gap between appearance and reality, the sources and transmission of knowledge—such epistemological themes are all inevitably foregrounded in a poem much of which has allegedly been spelled out, letter by letter, by the pointer of a Ouija board. These were already the themes of Merrill's earlier poetry, where issues of skepticism, the unreliability of sense data, illusion, and ambiguity abound, and the privileged motifs include the mask, the mirror, and the puzzle (see Moffett 1–19; Humphries). All these epistemological themes and motifs come to a head in *The Changing Light*, which, of all the major visionary poems since Dante, is surely the one that most distrusts and interrogates the substance of its own visions. Indeed, it is "not so much a visionary poem as a revisionary one, I fear," as Merrill once told Fred Bornhauser in an interview (*Recitative* 56).

The light in the other world of Sandover changes constantly throughout the trilogy, and what is glimpsed in and by that light is subject to constant questioning and reevaluation. Epistemological themes of revisionism, skepticism, and recognition or unmasking run throughout *The Changing Light*. New revelations constantly modify or supersede previous ones, and statements received as final truths are regularly shown in retrospect to have been simplifications, convenient fictions, or outright mistakes. No authority is final in *The Changing Light*. Just as the testimony of the partners' first spirit-mentor, Ephraim, is revised and even discredited by their next mentor, Mirabell, so Mirabell's testimony in its turn undergoes revision by still higher authorities (but also by Mirabell himself). Even the archangels' revelations in "Scripts" are subject to qualification. A special, and especially acute, object of epistemological suspicion throughout is the metaphorical character of the spirits' revelations. How much of the elaborate mechanism of otherworldly existence is really just a metaphor for something else, e.g., for laws of physics or aesthetic principles? What are the partners literally being asked to believe? How trustworthy is metaphor as a mode of access to "truth"? The problem is raised time and again, but never resolved. Moreover, *The Changing Light* is "a succession of recognition scenes" (Polito, "After-word" 237), nowhere more so than in the middle and last sections of the third volume, where one after another of the poem's main characters are unmasked as other than we had all along supposed them to be. Maria Mitsotaki, an Athenian acquaintance of Merrill and Jackson and, posthumously, a participant in the Ouija seminars of "Mirabell" and "Scripts," is revealed very late in the third volume to be identical with one of the five immortal souls, none other than Plato himself ("Scripts" No, 466). Ephraim, the earliest and consequently the least knowledgeable and authoritative of all the other-world informants, is revealed to have been all along the archangel Michael in disguise—Michael, the most knowledgeable and most powerful informant of all, the one whose arrival is so eagerly awaited in the closing books of "Mirabell."

Epistemological doubts are never assuaged, no ultimately reliable version of things is ever achieved, and who knows how far the process of unmasking could go? From a very early point, once it starts becoming clear that the epistemological questions will never be conclusively resolved, epistemological issues begin to modulate into issues of a different kind—ontological ones. Questions of what one knows, and how reliably, come gradually to be pre-empted by questions such as, what could there *be* out there? and where *is* "out there," anyway? The chain of transmission, the succession of mentors is alleged also to be a hierarchy of *being*. Earlier and less authoritative informants rank lower in this hierarchy; later and more authoritative ones rank higher.

As early as "Ephraim," the other world is pictured as a nine-level hierarchy of souls. Although, as we have seen, Ephraim's account is subsequently revised, and his hierarchy of souls dismissed as a "great dull bureaucracy" ("Mirabell" 2.8, 145) of minor relevance to the really urgent activities of the spirit world, nevertheless the tiered model of being he proposes seems accurately enough to capture the structure of the other world as it emerges in the accounts of later informants. Above the level occupied by spirits of the human dead such as Ephraim comes a level of nonhuman spirits, who are "superior" to Ephraim's kind at least in terms of seniority (and consequently of knowledge). These are the spirits of the creatures who inhabited the worlds that preceded our own: batlike spirits, fallen angels, one of whom, Mirabell, metamorphoses into a peacock; centaur spirits, among them the gentle being called Unice or Uni, who appears here as a unicorn and accompanies Merrill and Jackson in the final phases of their education. Above these spirits come the archangels of "Scripts," the four brothers Michael, Gabriel, Emmanuel (or Elias), and Raphael (or Elijah); above them, in turn, the God B and his opposite number, Nature or Psyche (also known as Chaos); there are even intimations of a pantheon of other gods, God B's fellows, from whom he is estranged and to whom he memorably signals through the cosmic dark (see "Scripts" Yes, 360, reprised at the very end of "Scripts," 517). As Merrill and Jackson are handed off from one informant to the next, they also "ascend" through this heavenly hierarchy, from the ex-human Ephraim to Mirabell the fallen bat-angel to the archangels and beyond: "Each lesson lifts us to a plane of greater/Power and light? IN-DEED AN ELEVATOR" ("Scripts" Yes, 353–54). This is, in other words, a Gnostic scheme, where levels of knowledge correspond to levels of being (see Humphries 191–92), and where unanswerable epistemological questions precipitate one into ontological speculations.

II. MAKING AND UNMAKING, OR, SANDOVER

Embodying ontological speculations in fictional structure is (as I have argued extensively elsewhere) the trademark of postmodernist poetics and the key to distinguishing it from the modernist poetics of epistemology. But "no one has accused Merrill of being postmodern" (Blasing 156). Perhaps no one has thought to do so because criteria for distinguishing postmodernist poetry have proven so much more elusive than those for postmodernist fiction. Perhaps Merrill's eligibility for the label "postmodernist" would seem stronger if The Changing Light were thought of as a kind of novel (see Polito, "Afterword" 232; Humphries)— a novel-in-verse, to be sure, for which there is distinguished precedent, e.g., Pushkin's Eugene Onegin, Byron's Don Juan.

What makes this move more plausible is the fact that, apart from the trilogy and his ten books of lyric poetry, Merrill also published two novels, as well as a distinctly novelistic memoir. Moreover, one of those novels, The (Diblos) Notebook (1965), has some claim to being regarded as postmodernist. It is, first of all, a roman à clef, mingling fiction and reality (or should that be "fiction" and "reality"?). More than that, it is literally a novel sous rature, under erasure (Yenser 40): many single words and phrases, and a few sentences and whole paragraphs, are scored through, placed sous rature—even its subtitle, A Novel! The narrative is subject to constant revision, with entire episodes, plot twists, characters, etc., being edited out or retrospectively reinterpreted. But this is not Merrill's only novel *sous rature*. Another one has been inscribed between the lines and in the margins, as it were, of "The Book of Ephraim," its traces being especially discernible in sections A, J, N, S, and T (see Polito, "Afterword" 232–36). Merrill claims, in section A, that he had originally decided to cast the story of his and Jackson's "Thousand and One Evenings Spent/ . . . at the Ouija Board/In Touch with Ephraim Our Familiar Spirit" (4) in the form of a prose fiction, but that the manuscript draft of this novel had been lost, literally mislaid (under circumstances described in another poem, "The Will," from *Divine Comedies,* 1976). Remembered fragments of this lost novel survive in "Ephraim," where they are juxtaposed with the "real" events and "real" people (see section D) on which the novel had been based. Like *The (Diblos) Notebook,* then, the first book of the trilogy mingles "fiction" and "reality," juxtaposing a fragmentary roman à clef with the *clef* to unlock that *roman.*

A complex structure; but even more complex is the way it mirrors world making in "Ephraim" in general. The "lost" novel, surviving here fragmentarily, mirrors, in the distorting fun-house mirror of fiction, the people and events of "Ephraim"; but beyond this, the entire process whereby fictional worlds are generated from the raw materials of experience mirrors the process of generating the other world, Ephraim's spirit world, from the letters spelled out on the Ouija board. "Fiction" (the "lost" novel) is to "reality" as This World (the one in which the Ouija seances occur) is to the Other World: in this complex two-tier analogy, the Ouija seances are analogous to the composition of the "lost" novel. In other words, the "lost" novel of "Ephraim"—not only in itself, but in its transformative relationship to the "reality" of "Ephraim"—functions as a *mise en abyme* of the projection of the other world, in all its baroque elaboration.

"Shall I project a world?" Pynchon's heroine Oedipa Maas anxiously asked. "Ephraim," with its complexly inscribed novel *en abyme,* affords us a first glimpse into the mechanism of "projecting worlds" in the trilogy, and such anatomizing of the ways of world making will become a dominant motif as the later books unfold (see Yenser 238; Mazzocco 214). "Projecting *worlds,*" in the plural, since *The Changing Light* projects at least *two* worlds, this one and the other one (even if we don't count the multiple levels of the spirit hierarchy as distinct worlds, though why shouldn't we?). On the one hand, Merrill projects the spaces in which the Ouija messages are received—rooms in a house in Stonington, Connecticut, and other rooms in a house in Athens, as well as the shuttlings between these houses and excursions away from them (including, in "Ephraim," a world tour). On the other hand, treating this experience of straddling continents as the template for an experience of straddling worlds (Yenser 5), Merrill also projects other-world spaces, the spaces described to him via the Ouija board by Ephraim, Mirabell, Auden, Maria, and his other spirit-informants.

These projected spaces of the other world are relatively elusive in "Ephraim" and "Mirabell." It is not clear, for instance, whether the nine-tier hierarchy of "Ephraim" can be visualized in any way (see U, 73), while the "sites" mentioned by Mirabell (such as the Research Lab, see Mirabell 2.5, 140), if they can be regarded as sites at all, tend to be abstract or ambiguous or uncannily mutable ("WHA" is Auden):

> HEAVEN MY FRIENDS IS ODD   IS BOTH
> REALITY & A FIGMENT OF IMAGINATION
> REAL FOR EACH FAITH YET AN UNFAILING SURPRISE FOR THE DEAD:
> A SPACE? A VOID? A FORCE? RATHER AS WHA FIRST SAID
> A NEW MACHINE WHICH MAKES THE DEAD AVAILABLE TO LIFE.
>   ("Mirabell" 9, 260)

> (THERE IS NO CLOUDLAND
> IN THE BERNINI SENSE OF ANGELS DANGLING THEIR FEET ETC.
> HEAVEN, REMEMBER, CD FIT IN THIS CUP OR BE VASTER
> THAN EARTH ITSELF)
>   ("Mirabell" 9.2, 264)

Not until "Scripts" do the spaces of the other world acquire a more or less fully elaborated visual dimension. Indeed, the instruction sessions ("lessons") that make up the trilogy's third book are regularly prefaced by stage directions that establish the setting, and that setting is usually Sandover, an English country house refitted to serve as a school:

> Scene: The schoolroom, once the nursery,
> At Sandover, that noble rosebrick manor

. . . .

Blackboard wall, a dais, little desks
Rorschach'd with dull stains among naively
Gouged initials—MM, WHA,
And others. Star-map, globe and microscope.
A comfy air of things once used and used.
. . . .
Dormer windows overlook the moat,
The maze, the gardens, paddock where a lonely
Quadruped is grazing. Round the whole,
Which seems so vast and is not, a high hedge
Stands for the isolating privilege
Of Learning—as we'll all have felt acutely
By summer's end. Beyond it can be seen,
Faces uplifted to our quarantine,
A gathering of tiny figures: friends
From the Bureaucracy. That tarnished blur
Like smoke at view's end, into which they go
Come dusk, hides (one might think) the ghastly semi-
Detached 'conditions' of their suburb—though
On fine days clearance comes and, ecstasy!
The Greenwood stretches long miles to the Sea
                              ("Scripts" Yes, 319–20)

Within the frame of this literally picturesque space, with its foreground and background, its closely observed details and receding vistas, all kinds of scenic metamorphoses are possible. The schoolroom can become a kind of theater opening onto other, inset scenes, spaces-within-spaces:

Our school has every modern teaching aid.
Green fields ashimmer and great ore-veined peaks
Fill one frame. Then, as Emmanuel speaks,
They are replaced by a 3-D cascade
Overbrimming inexhaustibly
Font upon font of snow above a polar sea.
                              ("Scripts" Yes, 343)

Gothic spires, pagodas, minarets,
Greek columns blazng from each picture-glass—

But it's all tinted like an oleograph
And somehow radiates irreverence.
("Scripts" No, 443)

Faint camel bells. Dry flute. One black-framed scene
All blazing desert, not a blade of grass.
Above the carpet God's magnificent
Somber glory throbs as through a tent.
("Scripts" No, 448)

Sometimes the setting seems weirdly doubled, two superimposed spaces at once—for instance, classroom and amphitheater (or "FORUM"):

The schoolroom, having dressed for the occasion
In something too grown-up, too sheer—the sense,
Through walls, of a concentric audience,
Rank upon blazing petaled rank arisen—
Quickly corrects its blunder, reassumes
Childhood's unruly gleams and chalk-dust glooms.
("Scripts" &, 407)

In the climactic spatial transformation of Sandover, the poem's scene shifts from the refitted nursery to the still-glamorous ballroom of this visionary country house, where Merrill will read his poem aloud to an audience of deceased literary masters ("Coda" 556–60).

At its most "visionary," the other-world space of Sandover seems entirely unconstrained by any earthly model, simulating nothing in *this* world (country house, ballroom, desert landscape, or what-have-you) but freely improvised—as when the Ouija board itself seems to enter the other world and metamorphose into a kind of dance floor ("MM" is Maria Mitsotaki, "DJ" is Jackson, "JM" is Merrill):

Music. A single pure white beam one knows
Floods the mirror room, which undergoes
Instant changes. Dewy garlands deck
The staircase. Statue, pictures, candlestick,
Each is prismatically multiplied.
The Ouija Board drifts upward on a tide

Of crystal light—ethereal parquet
Where guests will presently join WHA
And MM. (DJ and JM appear
Twice, outside and in, both 'there' and 'here'.)
                                    ("Scripts" Yes, 354)

This recalls nothing so much as cyberspace—not cyberspace as we currently know it, i.e., the rather drab and utilitarian World Wide Web, but cyberspace as imagined in cyberpunk science fiction, and in particular the "consensual hallucination" so memorably envisioned by William Gibson in "Burning Chrome," *Neuromancer*, and other texts of the mid-eighties.

The comparison with cyberspace illuminates differences between Merrill's other world and that of earlier visionary poems, in particular Dante's *Comedia*, his primary model (see Jacoff). Dante's other world is a "memory theater" in which literally memorable figures, topoi in the rhetorical sense, are each assigned to a topographic site in visionary space, where they remain eternally. Dante actually tours this world, reviewing its topoi in order. The other world of *The Changing Light*, by contrast, behaves like cyberspace, that is, like computer memory. Accessed through a technological device, a prosthesis—a computer console or, in Merrill's case, a Ouija board—the other world unfolds into existence when that device is operated, and folds back up into nonexistence when the device is turned off. When not being accessed, it has no existence except that of bits of information stored in something like a computer memory. Merrill and Jackson never actually enter this other world, as Dante did his, but—like Gibson's heroes "jacked into" their cyberspace consoles, or like a contemporary Web user—sit at home and read its ephemeral spaces off their equivalent of a computer screen. Nobody in the real world of the trilogy—neither Merrill nor Jackson nor any of their living friends with walk-on roles—has any direct experience of the other world; their experience of it is always mediated by others. Strictly speaking, it is a misnomer to characterize this as a "visionary" poem, since no one here has actually *seen* anything—or rather, the most they have seen are the words picked out for them by the pointer of the Ouija board (see von Hallberg, *American Poetry* 114). Only the otherworldly surrogates, whose putative words they have transcribed—Auden's, Maria's, Ephraim's, Mirabell's, and so on—are in any position to see the places and doings of the spirit world. Merrill and Jackson's "visions" of Sandover are always verbal fictions—always vicarious, never immediate.

Especially revealing is the moment when cyberspace collapses—a moment with no equivalent in Dante. At the end of a session, when one of Gibson's hackers withdraws from cyberspace, it appears to fold up (usually "like an origami crane," Gibson 174) into a dimensionless point. There are also moments when cyberspace is abruptly "interrupted," and it is at such moments that the ephemerality of cyberspace, its ontological instability, is especially foregrounded. Like Gibson's cyberspace, the spaces of Merrill's other world are "self-dissolving landscapes," as Polito says (thinking of Marjorie Perloff's description of Rimbaud; Polito, "Afterword" 243-44.) The other world of Sandover disappears—folds up— at the end of each Ouija session as the mediums return to their everyday lives.

Like cyberspace, Sandover is ontologically unstable, vulnerable to interruptions and temporary eclipses (see Kuberski 243). Rhetorical interruption—the interruption of one voice by another, or of one of the poet's interior voices by a different one—had been a feature of Merrill's poetry since at least the early sixties (see Yenser 62-66, 70). In *The Changing Light*, this stylistic feature acquires an ontological dimension, since the interrupting voice typically emanates from a different world or level than the voice being interrupted, as when a hierarchically superior being censors a lower-order one, or an "unqualified" being is expelled from the scene. Thus, for instance, the first notice of the higher-order bat-angels' existence comes when they unceremoniously interrupt a conversation with deceased friends in "Ephraim," section U (73). But more than that, the world of Sandover is subject to a kind of global or blanket instability, a flaw in its very foundations, so to speak. Sandover itself, the "rosebrick manor house" that is the setting for the lessons and parties of "Scripts," dominating and organizing the space of the other world, amounts to a literalized metaphor. Or perhaps not even a literalized one; perhaps it remains "mere" metaphor to the end. This ambiguity fatally compromises the ontological bases of the trilogy's other world, threatening to shake that world down until it lies flush with the surface of the text—just so many words. If the processes of world making are laid bare in *The Changing Light*, so too are the processes of unmaking worlds (or of letting them unmake themselves).

III. MASQUE

A poetics of disruption, of fluid and destabilizing figurality, of "now you see it, now you don't": where could Merrill possibly have found precedents to authorize such practice? Not in Dante, surely; and not in cyberpunk either, which of course postdates his trilogy. What genre of writing could offer models for such ontological instability? Only the court masque.

"Scripts for the Pageant" is manifestly an appropriate title, and not only for the third volume; it could easily be extended to the trilogy as a whole, since it's all theater. Theatricality pervades *The Changing Light* at all levels. Especially striking is the frequency with which Merrill resorts to theatrical metaphors, not only in the context of the other world but also in connection with this-worldly phenomena. Thus, for example, the painful final phase of David Jackson's troubled relationship with his parents is figured as a play being staged in the theater of his psyche ("Mirabell" 0.2, 100), while the hurricane that passes through Stonington in "Mirabell" 8.1 becomes, metaphorically, an opera (243). However, most of Merrill's theatrical figures bear on the "things unseen" of the spirit world; indeed, their function is often to lend a visual dimension to the invisible.

Thus, for instance, the Research Lab, so difficult to visualize, becomes an indoor theater (an operating theater?) where souls are improved—by contrast, presumably, with the open-air arena of unimproved souls (groundlings?):

This takes place in what he [i.e., Mirabell] calls the *Lab*
Or the *Research Lab:* precinct of intense
Activity his superiors direct.
Outside, the shriek and howl of beasts. Within,
Behind closed doors, as when a troupe retires
From jostling Globe to candlelit Blackfriars,
An EMPTINESS PACKD FULL.
                                        ("Mirabell" 2.5, 140)

This metaphor is Merrill's "own" (whatever that might mean in a "mediumistic" poem like this one). Elsewhere, however, the spirits too use theatrical figures, for instance to convey to Merrill and Jackson their sense of the determinism, literally the "scriptedness," that governs their universe:

OUR PLAY IS WRITTEN AS WE SPEAK
& WE KNOW ITS END EACH TIME AS THE APPLAUSE & LAUGHTER
WEAKEN & ALL START EDGING OUT THE DOORS   YR ENERGIES
MY FRIENDS ARE OUR AUDIENCE, THEATRE & SCRIPT

("Mirabell" 5.2, 191)

Especially resonant, in the context of the spirit world, is the recurrent metaphor of the "wings" of the stage, with its punning side-glance at angelic iconography. One example, from "Mirabell" 7.41, occurs when Mirabell is interrupted at the point of uttering an indiscretion about Mother Nature: the pointer is swept off the Ouija board "Into the wings," as is Mirabell himself by, presumably, a winged being. More elaborate, and more resonant still, is the archangel Michael's cosmological application of the theatrical conceit, "wings" included:

FOR IN REVEALING TO OUR FATHER THE PRIMAL GLOBE ON
    WHICH THE WHOLE PLAY WAS TO BE ACTED OUT,
I WAS THE SWITCH, THE TAPPING STAFF, I IT WAS WHO THEN LIT
    UP THE PLAYERS ON THE STAGE
AND TWICE CHAOS RANG DOWN THE CURTAIN, AS HE WAITS TO
    DO AGAIN,
AND AGAIN OUR GREAT DIRECTOR CALLING: CURTAIN UP! LIGHT!
    LIGHT!
BEGAN THE PLAY AS LIGHT WEPT IN THE WINGS.

("Scripts" Yes, 326–27)

Or, in other words, all the world's a stage, God's the director, and Michael's the stage manager.

The trilogy's theatrical figures are literalized in "Scripts" as theatrical performances. Here the pervasive theatricality of *Changing Light* comes to a head in a series of pageants, *tableau vivants,* and dramatic set pieces staged before the posthumous "eyes" (though they have none, of course) of Auden and Maria, who in turn report to Merrill and Jackson via the board. Three series of stagey "lessons"—in fact more like gala inaugural lectures and celebrity roundtables—are interrupted at intervals by allegorical spectacles: a pageant of the Five Senses in "Yes" (336–40), a kind of burlesque show of nine parodic muses in "&" (400–04), and a grand ceremonial procession in "No" (482–90). By way of epilogue, five relatively low-key ceremonies follow in the "Coda." The terms I have been using to name these various performances—pageant, procession, ceremony, etc.—are all more or less interchangeable, and all related to the same genre term (which is in fact the preferred term for these performances throughout *Changing Light*). The precise term is, of course, *masque* (see Molesworth 175; Polito, "Afterword" 249).

The theatrical masques of the Tudor and Stuart courts—paradigmatically those produced by Ben Jonson and Inigo Jones—were multimedia spectacles, embracing poetry, music, dance, architecture, and stagecraft. Like *Changing Light*, they posited a plurality of worlds, their plots (such as they were; plotting was never the masque's strong suit) often hinging on intrusion from one world into an adjacent one—like Kushner's angel—or the spectacular transformation of one world into another. The most typical transformation, of which Jonson's *Pleasure Reconciled to Virtue* (1618) is an example, involved the displacement of one or more grotesque or burlesque subworlds—the worlds of the "antimasque" or "antemasque"—by a "higher" world; the parodic pageant of the muses in "&" corresponds precisely to this antimasque component of the court masque (Yenser 289). Masques typically mingled characters of different ontological status—historical, fictional, mythological, allegorical—again like *Changing Light*. They especially delighted in the literal masking and unmasking of courtiers, who performed in the masques disguised (but transparently) as mythological heroes or allegorical figures—much as Plato in Merrill's trilogy disguises himself as Maria, or Michael as Ephraim. Finally, like *Changing Light* the masque was philosophical and didactic in purpose, a series of spectacular "lessons," scenes of instruction.

Parallels could easily be multiplied. At only one point does the parallelism appear to break down, for the court masque was oriented—rhetorically but also *optically*, with respect to the perspective and sight lines of the masque stage set—toward the monarch, who sat front and center in the audience. Of course there could be no parallel to such a monarchic orientation in a poem produced in a democratic era; or could there? Auden explains that the grand climactic masque of "No" had been "CENTERED PROPERLY UPON THE MONARCH," by which Merrill understands him to mean the goddess Nature. "TRUE," says Auden,

FROM ONE END OF THE SPYGLASS
And from the other? WHO MY DEARS BUT YOU!
MANKIND: ALL EYES IN HEAVEN FOCUSED ON
THE MORTAL, SACRED (& EXPENDABLE) THRONE
AND OH THE STAGECRAFT! SIMPLE SOLID JOY

("Scripts" No, 491)

It is collective humankind that occupies the monarch's high seat in Merrill's updated masque.

Merrill's revival of the masque appears, on the face of it, implausible, given the genre's in-built ephemerality and occasional character. Court masques were designed to be performed on specific, unique occasions, and few even of Jonson's masques received a repeat performance. The features that distinguish the masque as a genre are also what make it an unlikely candidate for revival in our time: its absolutist ideology, its neoplatonic iconography, its obsolete stagecraft, not to mention its dependence on the monarch's physical presence (though we have just seen how this last difficulty can be finessed). How did the masque genre, this antiquarian curiosity, even become available to Merrill, and why did he choose it as the vehicle for his visionary poetry?

There is no continuous, direct tradition of court masque for Merrill to have drawn upon. Unlike its Continental cognates, the French ballet de cour and the Italian intermezzo—which evolved into, respectively, classical ballet and opera—the masque's historical development was interrupted by the English Civil War and never successfully resumed. Nevertheless, the masques of *The Changing Light* have multiple sources. The first is academic scholarship: Merrill acknowledges in a 1982 interview (*Recitative* 65) the importance to the trilogy of Stephen Orgel's seminal scholarly book on the Jonsonian masque (1965). Another source is canonical plays that incorporate specimens of masque, in particular plays in the Shakespearean canon, especially *The Tempest*, with its inset Masque of Ceres, but also its more diffuse masque-like features. *The Tempest* is a pervasive intertextual presence throughout Merrill's trilogy (see Vendler 169; Yenser 314; Spiegelman). So, too, are Spenser's allegorical pageants from *The Faerie Queene,* another of the sources for the poetics of masque, from which Merrill quotes in "Ephraim," section "Q," and to which he slyly alludes through his use of the Spenserian stanza for the masque of "Scripts," No (Moffett 224).

The Continental cognates of English court masque, and their descendents, are another possible avenue to masque poetics. For instance, Calderón's *autos sacramentales,* in a sense the Spanish equivalent of court masque, have been proposed as a model for Merrill's masques (Saéz 243). Much more obviously relevant, however, is opera, especially the tradition of fantastic opera (see Conrad)—e.g., Mozart's *The Magic Flute,* Wagner's *Ring* cycle, the Strauss/Hofmannstahl collaborations—which has preserved more or less intact various elements of masque poetics, such as the mingling of ontologically diverse characters, masking and unmasking, the antimasque component, and spectacular displacements of one world by another. The relevance of fantastic opera to Merrill's poetics is unmistakable, not only in the trilogy but throughout his entire oeuvre. For instance, his earliest novel, *The Seraglio,* features an elaborate account of the premiere of a fantastic opera based on the Orpheus myth, while "Matinees" (from *The Fire Screen,* 1969), a sequence of eight linked sonnets, recalls his first childhood exposure to an opera—not incidentally, it is Wagner's *Das Rheingold,* the most masque-like of the *Ring* operas. Wagner's presence in *The Changing Light* is conspicuous (see, e.g., "Ephraim" N, 56; Q; "Mirabell" 6.3, 210), as is the presence of opera in general.

Thus, Merrill appears to have reassembled, around the core of a revived scholarly interest in the masque, various components of masque poetics that he found dispersed among a range of sources, including Shakespeare, Spenser, and Wagnerian fantastic opera. One might suppose this was idiosyncratic on Merrill's part, reflecting a preoccupation he shared with, at most, a few academics. Surprisingly, this is not the case, for in fact, versions of masque abound in postmodern culture. Traces of masque can be detected, for example, in various postmodern performance practices—e.g., in Happenings and performance-art practices, in the early rock-based spectacles of Sam Shepard (*Operation Sidewinder, Angel City, The Tooth of Crime*), in the theater of Robert Wilson, in Kushner's *Angels in America,* in Matthew Barney's *Cremaster* films, or in the postmodern cinema of Hans-Jürgen Syberberg or Peter Greenaway (whose *Prospero's Books* is, of course, a version of *The Tempest*). Whether

such practices reflect the persistence of masque elements in certain theatrical traditions (such as fantastic opera, but also vernacular traditions
such as British pantomime), or a convergence of postmodern poetics
and masque poetics—or both—is impossible to say.

More striking still is the prevalence of what might be called "closet
masques," masquelike texts never intended for performance. Apart from
"Scripts for the Pageant" itself, the most "authentic" example is John
Ashbery's "Description of a Masque" (from *A Wave*, 1984), a prose text
that, for all its campiness, is thoroughly informed by masque poetics,
and even alludes explicitly to Thomas Campion's *The Lords' Masque* (see
Yacobi 1999). Other closet masques are, as it were, folded into postmodernist novels or long poems, e.g., Gilbert Sorrentino's "Masque of
Fungo," in *Mulligan Stew* (1979); Susan Howe's "God's Spies," in "The
Liberties" (see chapter 7 below); or "A"-24, titled "L. Z. Masque," the
final installment of Louis Zukofsky's long poem *"A"* (1968). Modernist
precedent for such inset masques and pageants can be found in Virginia
Woolf's *Between the Acts,* as well as in the "Circe" ("Nighttown") chapter
of *Ulysses,* which, via Ibsen's *Peer Gynt* and Goethe's *Faust,* opens a direct avenue back to the tradition of fantastic theater. Such inset masques
sometimes seem to infect, as it were, the whole surrounding context, so
that entire texts acquire a masquelike character in the light of their insets. Examples include Pynchon's *Gravity's Rainbow,* with its many inset
performances that often spill over into their audiences and swamp the
surrounding context, or Ronald Sukenick's *Blown Away* (1986), a metafictional "Hollywood novel," full of strange loops and other logic paradoxes, involving a B-movie remake of (what else?) *The Tempest.*

Another way of saying this would be to call such inset masques instances of *mise-en-abyme.* That is, inset masques mirror, on their smaller
scale, the poetics of the entire surrounding text in cases such as those
of *Mulligan Stew,* "The Liberties," *Gravity's Rainbow, Blown Away,* or *The
Changing Light at Sandover.* And this, in turn, suggests one reason why
postmodernists like Ashbery, Sorrentino, Howe, Pynchon, Sukenick, or
Merrill might find the obsolete genre of masque attractive. For masque,
like postmodernist fiction (and at least some postmodernist long poems), is an ontological genre; like postmodernist fiction, it presupposes
a plurality of modes of being and literally stages a plurality of worlds; it
renders being fluid, metamorphic. Masque (as its *mise-en-abyme* function suggests) is at least compatible or congruent with postmodernist

poetics—compatible or congruent enough to serve as the latter's scale model.

IV. PROSTHESIS

It's all theater, figuratively speaking: the phenomena of this world, the "things unseen" of the other world, even the Ouija board itself, which mediates between the two:

> About us, these bright afternoons, we come
> To draw shades of an auditorium
> In darkness. An imagined dark, a stage
> Convention: domed red room, cup and blank page
> Standing for darkness where our table's white
> Theatre in the round fills, dims . . . Crosslight
> From YES and NO dramatically picks
> Four figures out. And now the twenty-six
> Footlights, arranged in semicircle, glow.
> What might be seen as her "petit noyau"
> By Mme Verdurin assembles at
> Stage center. A by now familiar bat
> Begins to lecture. Each of us divines
> Through the dark house like fourteen Exit signs
> The eyes of certain others glowing red.
> ("Mirabell" 2.9, 147; ellipses are Merrill's)

With respect to the spirit world, as we have seen, theatrical figures often serve to render the invisible visualizable. Here, nearly the opposite is the case: this elaborate theatrical conceit seems designed to camouflage what is really, ascertainably going on. The Ouija theater is only "conventionally" dark; in fact, the partners are sitting in a sunlit room, which "stands for" the darkened auditorium. Of the four figures supposedly caught in the crosslighting, only two, Merrill and Jackson, are visibly present, the others (Auden and Maria) being spirits. Nor would an outsider, looking in on this scene, be able to see Mirabell lecturing, or his fourteen colleagues ranged around, their eyes glowing like Exit signs. Metaphor in this passage serves to distract attention from the embarrassing fact that what we have here is, so far as the physical eye is concerned, nothing more than two grown men fiddling with a Ouija board.

Serious poets' dabbling in compositional practices based on spiritualism or occultism has been a source of embarrassment throughout the twentieth century. Yeats notoriously derived a cosmological system from his wife's trances; H.D. indulged in séances; Sylvia Plath and Ted Hughes played with the Ouija board (see Sword). A bone of contention between Charles Olson and his friend and close associate Robert Duncan was the latter's attachment to a cultish coterie poetics that accommodated all sorts of occult practices and dubious esoteric "wisdom" (see Davidson, *San Francisco Renaissance* 125–49; Fredman, 99–101, 105–07).⁹ The Ouija board is the great embarrassment of *The Changing Light.* A poem composed in large part by (or with?) a Ouija board: how seriously are we expected to take this? How *can* we take it seriously?

Perhaps we need first to consider what, exactly, the real source of our embarrassment might be. What most scandalizes us about a "dictated" poem is the way it undermines common-sense notions of authority. Who, finally, speaks here? Who is responsible for this writing? Who stands behind it (if anyone)? The problem has more than one dimension. First of all, there is the question of Merrill's collaboration with Jackson. Two hands rest on the Ouija pointer; Merill transcribes the texts, but who's to say that Jackson hasn't had a "hand" in composing them? "Given the way the Ouija board is played *à deux*," Richard Saéz writes, "and the fact that more and more of the pages of Merrill's epic are dictated directly from it, there are interesting questions regarding the authorship of the work and the relationship of JM and DJ. . . . Will the omnibus volume of Merrill's epic be published under the name of David Jackson? And why not?" (313, n. 6). Of course, the omnibus volume did *not,* in the end, appear under Jackson's name, though Merrill himself has gone on record as wondering whether "the trilogy shouldn't have been signed with both our names—or simply 'by DJ, as told to JM'?" (*Recitative* 68).

A ghostwritten book, in the sense of "by DJ, as told to JM," is one thing; but of course Merrill claimed that the trilogy was *literally* ghostwritten, written by ghosts ("Ephraim" U, 72), dictated or ventriloquised, in some sense, by otherworldly "authors." This notion, so scandalously at odds with common sense, is one that Merrill himself struggled with, both inside and outside the poem itself. In "Mirabell," he complains to Auden (in a passage that every critic of Merrill eventually gets around to quoting),

it's all by someone else!
In your voice, Wystan, or in Mirabell's.
I want it mine

He continues:

I'd set
My whole heart, after *Ephraim,* on returning
To private life, to my own words. Instead,
Here I go again, a vehicle
In this cosmic carpool. Mirabell once said
He taps my word banks. I'd be happier
If *I* were tapping them. Or thought I were.
                              ("Mirabell" 9.1, 261–62)

When confronted with questions like J. D. McClatchy's, "Could not the 'they' who move the teacup around the board be considered the authors of the poems?", Merrill answers equivocally in the very language of the Ouija board: "Well, yes and no."

As "they" keep saying throughout, language is the human medium. It doesn't exist—except perhaps as vast mathematical or chemical formulas—in that realm of, oh, cosmic forces, elemental processes, which *we* then personify, or tame if you like, through the imagination. So, in a sense, all these figures are our creation, or mankind's. The powers they represent are real—as, say, gravity is "real"—but they'd be invisible, inconceivable, if they'd never passed through our heads and clothed themselves out of the costume box they found there (*Recitative* 68).

"Taming" and "personifying" the Ouija's ventriloquy is very much to the point here. Confronted with the embarrassment of a poem literally dictated to the poet (or so it is alleged), a text in a sense without an author, many readers' response (the poet's included) has been to tame and personify. Recoiling from the Ouija board's intractably literal reality, and all that *that* might imply, readers have sought comfort in one or other metaphorical reduction of it. Thus, the Ouija board of *The Chang-*

ing Light is commonly read as a kind of literalized metaphor, whether of inspiration, or of tradition or influence, or of language itself.

The traditional figure for the poet's experience of taking dictation is the muse. While the muses do turn up in the trilogy, they are so brutally travestied in their single appearance ("Scripts" &, 400–04) that one might well suppose they were being deliberately discredited in order to clear the way for alternative figurations of inspiration. Such alternative figurations abound. One such figure is that of spirit possession, as in Haitian voodoo ("Ephraim" D, H, M); another is puppetry ("Ephraim" K; "Mirabell" 5.1, 5.2, 189). There are even traces ("Scripts" Yes, 360; Coda, 555) of a motif of inspiration as a kind of radio reception, uncannily reminiscent of the poet Jack Spicer's image of "taking dictation from Mars" (see Davidson, *San Francisco Renaissance* 150–71; Damon 148, 166, 173–74, 184).

But Merrill's primary figure for poetic inspiration, the one that controls all the others, is the Ouija board itself (Kuberski 243). None other than the archangel Michael makes the relevant connection:

IT IS A LONG AMAZING & UNPRECEDENTED WAY FROM YOU TO US.
WE TRIED DREAMS. THEY CAME TO JM LIKE DOORBELLS, EXPECTA-
TION BUT NO GUEST.
WE TRIED 'INSPIRATION'. IT WAS MUFFLED BY SCREECHING TIRES,
KISSES AND DRUNKEN SONG.
SO S A N D O V E R

("Scripts" No, 478)

The trilogy's system of Ouija dictation substitutes for traditional inspiration or dream-vision. Such inspiration-by-dictation is itself open to further naturalization and "taming," mainly in psychological or even neurological terms. For instance, Merrill more than once cited Julian Jaynes's account, at one time celebrated (though no longer taken seriously, if it ever was), of communication between the cerebral hemispheres as the organic basis of "inspiration" (*Recitative* 52, 60–61, 88). He even ventured his own naturalizing account of the process, in a passage that has been widely quoted by critics—with relief, I imagine, for having let them off the hook. "Don't you think there comes a time when everyone, not just a poet, wants to get beyond the self? To reach, if you like, the 'god' within you? The [Ouija] board, in however clumsy or absurd a way, allows for precisely that. Or if it's still *yourself* that you're drawing upon, then that self is much stranger and freer and more farseeing than the one you thought you knew" (from the 1982 interview with McClatchy in *Recitative* 66). This is a more comforting expedient—the god within, the deeper self—than having to acknowledge the full uncanniness of Ouija communication.

Alternatively, a number of critics have sought, with considerable success, to read the Ouija board of *The Changing Light* as a metaphor for tradition, whether in Eliot's sense of "Tradition and the Individual Talent," or in the more agonistic and melodramatic sense of Harold Bloom's "influence" (see Westover; Polito, "Afterword" 246–48; Humphries; Kuberski 243–44; Sword). The poem itself obviously invites such a reading. The poetic tradition speaks through the Ouija, literally, for conspicuous among the dead who communicate with Merrill and Jackson are poets, including Auden, Yeats, Stevens, Eliot, even Homer. Some of them, notably Auden and Yeats, are actually alleged to have composed posthumous poetry using the board.[10]

Merrill himself uses the Ouija, in effect, to insinuate himself into this tradition by engaging its representatives in dialogue, but also by struggling, in Bloom's sense, with his poetic precursors. This struggle takes several forms. Some of his precursors Merrill co-opts, as in the case of Auden, who becomes his ally and surrogate in the spirit world; others he masters and overcomes, as in the cases of Yeats ("Scripts" &, 424; No, 474–75, 481, 486, 492; Coda, 527) and Stevens ("Scripts" &, 428–29). Merrill anticipates and dramatizes his own assumption into the poetic tradition in the closing pages of *The Changing Light* by means of the poetry reading to which he invites (or summons?) distinguished deceased representatives of that tradition. They are twenty-six in all—not quite one famous name for each letter of the alphabet (since some invitees back out and some share initial letters), but close enough to make the assembled writers, from Austen to Yeats (no Zukofsky or other "Z" author), the literary equivalent of the alphabet displayed on the Ouija board.

Again, the Ouija as figure for the poetic tradition is susceptible of further naturalization in psychological terms. For, excluding the possibility of an other world populated by great writers of the past, where is the poetic tradition really to be found? In the minds of writers like Merrill, of course. The Ouija board, on this reading, merely accesses the poet's well-stocked literary subconscious. Merrill acknowledges this naturalization when, in a later Ouija poem, "Nine Lives" (from *A Scattering of Salts*, 1995), he speaks of the dead writers summoned via the Ouija board as returning not to the other world but to "our subconscious," a "black hole" which is "three-quarters literature" (16).

Finally, the Ouija board "can stand . . . for language itself" (Vendler 162). David Lehman concurs: "What else is the Ouija board if not a clear though audacious metaphor for language?" ("Elemental Bravery" 50). On this reading, the Ouija serves as a figurative representation of whatever it is that language users presumably carry around in their heads, something like a combined lexicon, grammar, and etiquette manual. When Merrill and Jackson rest their hands on the Ouija pointer, they are figuratively (but also literally) tapping into the resources of the language.

This interpretation of the Ouija board converges with Merrill's manifest interest in exploiting the "found" or "given" resources of language. If trusting to the Ouija's dictation is one form of letting the language speak through oneself—a form of automatic writing—then another form of it is punning. To pun is to "traffic in linguistic accident," says Polito ("Introduction" 8), and Merrill is an inveterate trafficker (see also Yenser 179–203; Jacoff 151–52; Blasing 174–187). Puns abound in all of Merrill's writing; I called attention, above, to the puns on "wings" in a couple of passages from *The Changing Light* ("Mirabell" 7.41, 231; "Scripts" Yes, 327), but I could easily have found equivalent puns to comment on in nearly all the passages I have quoted. Merrill offers a persuasive (and much-quoted) defense of punning in his 1972 review of poetry by Francis Ponge. The pun, he writes,

is suffered, by and large, with groans of aversion, as though one had done an unseemly thing in adult society, like slipping a hand up the hostess's dress. Indeed, the punster has touched, and knows it if only for being so promptly shamed, upon a secret, fecund place in language herself. . . . A Freudian slip is taken seriously: it betrays its maker's hidden wish. The pun (or the rhyme, for that matter) "merely" betrays the hidden wish of words. (*Recitative* 111)

The pun represents the "secret" willfulness of language itself, and so, for that matter, does rhyme, to which Merrill is equally committed. Rhyming is, of course, more "respectable" than punning (even in an era of free verse), presumably because it is regarded as less completely dependent on accident than the pun, and more subject to conscious manipulation. Nevertheless, both the rhyme and the pun are artifacts of language, linguistic "givens," found objects, and in that sense equally "disreputable." It is revealing that Merrill should associate them here.

A dictionary, especially an etymological dictionary, is a huge storehouse of linguistic accidents, an expression of language's secret willfulness. Ponge, whose punning poetics Merrill was defending in the passage I have just quoted, mined the *Littré* extensively when composing his poetry. Other traffickers in linguistic accident have done likewise: William Empson, whose poetry is inconceivable apart from the opportunities offered him by the *OED*; Louis Zukofsky in his "80 Flowers" and elsewhere; the OuLiPo circle, whose "S+7" procedure specifically calls for the use of a dictionary; the Language poet Tina Darragh; and so on. The *OED*, Merrill says somewhere, is the unconscious of the language. Using a dictionary to generate poems is tapping into that linguistic unconscious—as is, in a precisely parallel way, using the Ouija board.

But what if we were less intent on "saving" the poem from its own embarrassing premises? What if, instead of "resolving" the Ouija board into one or other of its potential figurative meanings—Ouija as inspiration, as tradition, as language, as what-have-you—we were to face up to its intractableness and entertain its literal meaning? This would require us to reflect on the Ouija board's function as *prosthesis*.

A prosthesis, in David Wills's account (1995), disturbingly combines natural and artificial, human and mechanical, the "spontaneous" and the "contrived." Simultaneously the extension of a human capability and its replacement (think of a prosthetic limb), its logic is precisely that of the Derridean supplement, of which it is, indeed, a version. The Ouija board of *The Changing Light* can be seen, in this context, as a prosthetic device for writing—an artificial writing limb. As such, it finds its place in a historical sequence of successive prostheses of writing (Wills 222), from the printing press (*ars artificialiter scribendi,* in Latin "an artificial way of writing") to the typewriter (*machine à écrire,* writing machine in French) to the word processor; word processing is prosthetic, says Wills, "a human attached to a writing machine" (28).

Merrill, it seems, was acutely aware of the prosthetic affiliations of the Ouija board. In his memoir, *A Different Person,* he reports:

In writing I have resorted, after the first scrawled phrases, to keyboards of increasing complexity, moving from Olivetti to Selectric
III, from Ouija to this season's electronic wizard. Now each morning, risen like Kundry in *Parsifal* with a shriek and a shudder to
do my Klingsor's bidding, I make for the arcane, underworld glow
of a little screen. Presently minimal bits of information, variable
within strict limits, like the tesserae of a mosaic, flicker and re-
assemble before my eyes. As best I can—here slubbing an image,
there inverting a hypothesis—I set about clothing the blindingly
nude mind of my latest master. Line after line wavers in and out of
sense, transpositive, loose-ended, flimsy as gossamer, until a length
of text is at last woven tightly enough to resist unmaking. Then
only do I see what I had to say (202).

The Ouija board appears here in a catalogue of "keyboards," sandwiched
between typewriters, manual and electric, and word processors. And the
word processor, in turn, is described in metaphors that assimilate it to
the uncanniness of the Ouija board: it is a wizard; it has a will of its own,
which it imposes upon the poet; its words come as a surprise to him
("Then only do I see what I had to say"—note the ambiguity of that
"had").[11] Moreover, annexed to this prosthetic device, as to the Ouija
board, is an other world: the spirit world, in the case of the Ouija board;
in the case of the word processor, a version of cyberspace, however rudimentary. The "underworld" of the word processor screen and the other
world of *Sandover* are, in this context, functional equivalents.[12] Thus the
difference between Ouija board and word processor becomes vanish-
ingly small here, and both embody the aporias of prosthesis—self and
not-self, master and slave, ghost and machine.

However, unlike the word processor on which, presumably, some of
Merrill's poems (though surely not the trilogy) were composed, the Ouija
board exists both inside and outside the poem. It is not merely a condition of the poem's production, but also an object in the poem's world—
indeed, its most salient object. As such, the Ouija board joins a special
subcategory of prostheses, that of the fictional writing machines so
prevalent in twentieth-century fiction: e.g., William Burroughs's writing
machine in *The Ticket That Exploded*; or Eco's Abulafia, the computer
that generates plots in *Foucault's Pendulum*; or, earlier in the century,
Raymond Roussel's many variations on the writing-machine motif; or

even the "harrow" of Kafka's "In the Penal Settlement." Such images of writing machines, Wills observes, are inscriptions of prosthesis itself: "prosthetic writing, the writing of prosthesis" (200–01; see McHale, *Postmodernist Fiction* 159–61; and, on postmodern representations of machines of reproduction, Jameson, *Postmodernism* 37–38).

Roussel's and Burroughs's writing machines (though presumably not Kafka's or Eco's) existed like Merrill's, both inside and outside their texts; that is, both Roussel and Burroughs, like Merrill, actually *used* their machines, or something analogous to them, to generate their texts, as well as representing those machines *in* their texts, *en abyme*. In Burroughs's case, the writing machine he used was his cut-up and fold-in methods for manipulating "found" texts; in Roussel's, it was his elaborate protocols for generating narratives from puns and transfigured clichés (see Wills 250–85). These instances make it clear that the notion of prosthesis needs to be understood in an extended sense, as embracing not just technological devices but *techniques,* not just writing machines but writing *procedures.* In this perspective, Merrill's use of the Ouija board takes its place among the range of procedural writing that has been practiced in our time: procedural poetry (e.g, John Cage, Jackson Mac Low, John Ashbery in his sestinas and other artificial forms; see Conte), procedural fiction (Walter Abish, the OuLiPo group—Italo Calvino, Georges Perec, Harry Mathews and others). If we think of Calvino manipulating the tarot cards to generate the stories of *The Castle of Crossed Destinies* (1973), it is perhaps not so hard to grasp how Merrill's Ouija poetry fits into this range of writing (see Polito, "Introduction" 3–4; and see Hartman on computer-generated poetries).

This chain of affiliations returns us to the Ouija board's function as a figure for language itself. Now, however, that function appears in a different light, the transformative (changing?) light cast by the notion of prosthesis. Rhetoric, Wills writes, is the "prosthetization" of language (228), the imposition of contrivance and technique upon what is supposed to be natural and spontaneous. Rhyme, wordplay, figurative usage in general, insofar as they are artificial and contrived, are from this perspective prosthetic (229). Thus the association of Merrill's rhyming and punning with his dependence on the Ouija board in *The Changing Light* acquires a new logic, the logic of prosthesis. By the terms of this logic, all these prosthetic devices—the Ouija board as writing machine, rhetoric as prosthesis—appear functionally equivalent and interchangeable.

Ultimately, "language is a prosthesis," says Wills (300). In that case, what could be more appropriate than for one prosthetic device to stand for, at the same time that it mediates access to, another prosthetic device?

The key terms here are *device, contrivance, artifice.* For what is in the end perhaps most scandalous about the Ouija-board premise of *The Changing Light* is not its occult implications (those we are free to take or leave), but rather its status as a *device.* The presence of the Ouija board lays bare the *artificiality* of this poetry, its basis in mechanical procedures—precisely in the operation of a text-generating machine—rather than in the poet's "heart" or "psyche" or "subconscious," or whatever other term we might prefer for the site of authentic feeling. No doubt the Ouija board only mediates a stream of language that proceeds from some such site (if it does not proceed from the other world); but it *does* mediate that language, introducing a device—admittedly a strange device—into the circuit joining poet and audience. Prostheses ought not to be noticeable, and if one does happen to notice one, it is bad manners to draw attention to it; but that is what the Ouija board does in *The Changing Light,* outraging the still-prevalent Romantic ideology of poetic creation, and forcing us to acknowledge the artifice, the prosthetic character, of poetry itself—indeed, of language itself.

This is dis-illusioning, literally. As with Roussel's or Burroughs's or the poets' procedures, at the moment we realize that the text and its world have been generated by some artificial device, some prosthetic writing machine, that world is apt to collapse, lose its ontological volume, and fold back into the surface of the text—no longer a world but just so many words, typographic marks made by a writing machine. And indeed, this sort of collapse is anticipated and mimed more than once in the course of *The Changing Light at Sandover.* More than once the whole elaborate ontological structure, comprising this world and the other one, seems to shrivel and contract into the least typographical symbol, a punctuation mark—ellipses ("Ephraim" X, 85–86) or asterisks ("Scripts" No, 454, 490)—or a typeface:

> *The manor is condemned. One doesn't dare*
> *Say so flatly, but it's in the air.*
> *The fine italic hands that have to date*
> *Etched the unseen we blankly contemplate*

Must now withdraw, and stoic Roman steel
Rim spectacles put on for the ordeal.
("Scripts" No, 482; Merrill's italics)

From italic to roman: what had until a moment before been Sandover is now just print, text turned out by a typewriter or a word processor—or by a Ouija board.

V. DEATH

Abrupt deflations of this kind, catastrophic losses of ontological cabin pressure, recur throughout *The Changing Light.* "Worlds" collapse. They collapse, for instance, when a fiction falls under erasure, or when (as in "Ephraim") a fictional world and a real world hemorrhage into each other. Worlds collapse when one level of reality is "interrupted" by an intervention from another level; or when a projected reality folds up, like cyberspace, at the end of a session; or when the metaphorical bases of the projected world are exposed, and visionary landscapes subside into mere figures of speech; or when the poem's contrivance, its dependence on a device, is laid bare, and its world contracts before our eyes to machine-made marks. And of course ontology collapses in a different sense when, as they do throughout *The Changing Light,* people die.

Though it may seem painfully obvious, the fact needs stating: *The Changing Light* is a poem about death. Its basic premise is communication with the dead; it is full of words allegedly dictated by the dead; it projects an afterlife state (however intermittent, flickering, hedged about with doubts and suspicions) that the dead are said to experience; it speculates about and reflects on death continuously. Moreover, in the course of the poem's unfolding, the deaths of a number of real people are reported: friends and acquaintances like Hans Lodeizen, W. H. Auden, Chester Kallman, Maria Mitsotaki, George Cotzias, Robert Morse; more distant acquaintances, such as Robert Lowell; and David Jackson's own parents. Among other things, *The Changing Light* is, as Peter Sacks has argued, an elegy. The least we can say of Merrill's poem is that it confronts death.

Unless that is saying far too much for it. Robert von Hallberg (*American Poetry* 115) has suggested that, quite to the contrary, *The Changing Light* actually evades the fact of death by making continuing communication with the dead its premise. On this account, Merrill's poem is hardly more than a huge wish-fulfillment fantasy, in which no loss is permanent, and personal extinction can be finessed through the mechanisms of the afterlife and reincarnation. This is a damaging charge, but one that can be answered.

First of all, Merrill gives death a kind of reality here by simulating, on various occasions and in various ways, its *subjective* experience. It is as though he were inviting us to dress-rehearsals of our own individual deaths. On one occasion, when Merrill re-experiences his own death in what is alleged to have been a previous life ("Ephraim" L, 42–43), the experience is traumatic; on another occasion, when Robert Morse posthumously reports his own death from his subject perspective ("Scripts" No, 498), it has the euphoric tone of many so-called "near-death experiences." And on one occasion the subjective experience of death is presented with special emphasis, in slow motion, as it were, when Auden, already a disembodied spirit, undergoes the first stages of a "stripping" process that will leave him, in the end, identity-less, "really" dead. Mirabell reports:

WHA IN OUR MASQUE EXPERIENCED WHAT? THE WIND LET
OUT OF HIS BEING   HIS (M) PERSONALITY GONE   ITS
LOSS A COMPLETENESS IN THAT DANCE UNDER THE POWERFUL
LIGHT FLOODING THE LENS

Merrill immediately grasps the subjective implications:

This loss you call completeness is *lived through*?
Soul, the mortal self, expendably
Rusting in tall grass, iron eaten by dew—
All that in our heart of hearts we must
Know will happen, and desire, and dread?
Once feeling goes, and consciousness, the head
Filling with . . . vivid nothings—no, don't say!
("Mirabell" 6.4, 211; Merrill's ellipses)

This brings us to a second motif through which Merrill confronts rather than evades death. Auden's slow-motion "stripping" of identity will eventuate in a "second death" for him, a state in which he will be irrevocably lost to Merrill, and presumably to himself. Auden's soul, we learn, will be annihilated, and its raw materials (whatever they might be) absorbed into the mineral realm ("Scripts" Yes, 303–04). Nor is he unique in suffering this fate; another friend, George Cotzias, will similarly be reabsorbed into the elements ("Scripts" &, 374; No, 507). Even Maria is reportedly fated to merge with the vegetal realm, but this sentence of "second death" is revoked when she is revealed to have been one of the Five immortal souls all along; instead she is scheduled for reincarnation. So it transpires that the cycle of reincarnation, which appeared to offer an escape from the finality of death, can in fact be broken: the dead can die again. For that matter, reincarnation itself, which is supposed to ensure the soul's survival, in fact places the souls of the dead beyond the reach of the Ouija board, so that, preserved in one sense, they are nevertheless as dead to Merrill and Jackson as if there were no afterlife or reincarnation.

In other words, if Merrill evades the confrontation with death in one sense, by housing his friends in an afterlife where they are still accessible via the Ouija board, he has in fact only *deferred* the confrontation, and thereby heightened its impact. For his friends each undergo a "second death" that renders them finally inaccessible to him. Death, apparently overcome and transcended, is restaged, this time irrevocably. These deaths open "A void within a void" ("Scripts" No, 510). This is the significance of the ceremonies in which, at the close of "Scripts," Merrill and Jackson finally part with Auden, Maria, and George Cotzias ("Scripts" No, 513–17) and, in the "Coda" (532–42), with Robert Morse.

Finally, Merrill does not just "rehearse" and "restage" death in *The Changing Light*, he also *models* it. Every type of ontological collapse in this poem—of fiction à *clef* into reality, of visionary landscape into metaphor, of world into text-generating device, and so on—stands in an analogical relationship to every other type of collapse. Each collapse mirrors and evokes the others, and they all mirror and evoke the ultimate loss of world, namely death. By this reading, every time one or other level of reality is bracketed or erased or eclipsed in this poem, every time a world "crashes," we have a scale model of death. Death, then, saturates the very fabric of the poem; it *is* its fabric.

Strategies for deferring and restaging death in *The Changing Light* anticipate, once again, the motifs of cyberpunk science fiction, where the physically dead often survive as configurations of computer memory or bootable programs, "ghosts in machines," and where the subjective experience of death is often simulated from "within," from the perspective of intelligent "software" beings (see McHale, *Constructing* 264–67). But if the trilogy's deferrals of death recall cyberpunk, its scale-modelling of death recalls instead "serious" postmodernist fiction. Merrill's projection of other-world spaces aligns his poem with postmodernist novels like Alasdair Gray's *Lanark*, Christine Brooke-Rose's *Such*, and Pynchon's *Vineland*; his transcription of posthumous voices aligns it with Joseph McElroy's *Plus* and Russell Hoban's *Pilgermann*; while his mapping of death onto the whole range of types of ontological collapse in his poem affiliates *The Changing Light* with the most profound reflections on death in the postmodernist canon, including texts such as Beckett's *The Unnamable* and *Texts for Nothing*, Federman's *The Voice in the Closet*, or Maggie Gee's *Dying,in other words* (see McHale, *Postmodernist Fiction* 227–32). Merrill is a postmodernist, if in nothing else, then in the resourcefulness and tenacity with which he seeks to model death. And, as is the case with his fellow postmodernists, the purpose of this endlessly resourceful modelling would seem to be to negotiate some kind of hard-won reconciliation with the intractable fact of mortality.

Though *not* with death in all its forms. There is a crucial exception: Merrill seeks no reconciliation with the prospect of self-inflicted *collective* death. If *The Changing Light* is in some respects an elegy, and as an elegy hopes for some kind of rapprochement with death, in other respects it is nothing less than a jeremiad against the threats of nuclear war and destruction of the environment (see Moffett 154, 171; Berger, "Merrill and Pynchon"; Shoptaw, "James Merrill" 762). Early in the trilogy, Merrill and Jackson are horrified to learn from "Ephraim" that the cycle of reincarnation is vulnerable to atomic weaponry:

NO SOULS CAME FROM HIROSHIMA U KNOW
EARTH WORE A STRANGE NEW ZONE OF ENERGY
Caused by? SMASHED ATOMS OF THE DEAD MY DEARS.
News that brought into play our deepest fears.

("P," 55)

Personal death may, after all, be acceptable, but death by nuclear war is irreversible, threatening this world and the other world alike, since it destroys not just bodies but souls.

Moreover, it appears that the worlds that preceded ours, according to more than one version of this mythic prehistory, were destroyed by nuclear weaponry (see "Ephraim" P, 56; "Mirabell" 1.5, 1.6, 119–21). These lessons of history impart to the trilogy a polemical charge. If *The Changing Light* is thanatotropic, death-oriented, it is not, after all, apocalyptic. Leo Zimmerman (175–89) is quite right to insist that *The Changing Light* is in fact an *anti*-apocalyptic poem, for the apocalyptic paradigm (as Frank Kermode has taught us) supplies the "sense of an ending" and redeems history from meaninglessness, while nuclear war, in Merrill's polemic, redeems nothing.

In placing his death-oriented poem at the service of an anti-apocalyptic polemic, Merrill aligns *The Changing Light* with another segment of postmodernist fiction, namely novels of nuclear holocaust, including Russell Hoban's *Riddley Walker,* Denis Johnson's *Fiskadoro,* Maggie Gee's *The Burning Book,* and Pynchon's *Gravity's Rainbow* (see McHale, *Constructing* 159–63). Perhaps the circle of Merrill's postmodernist affiliations should be enlarged to include novels that seek to confront other forms of collective death: postmodernist Holocaust novels, such as D. M. Thomas's *The White Hotel,* Georges Perec's *W, or, The Memory of Childhood,* and the novels of Raymond Federman, or textual representations of the AIDS epidemic, such as Tony Kushner's *Angels in America.*

Waiting for the Angel: according to Mirabell's myth of prehistory, the race of bat-angels to which Mirabell belonged colonized the ozone layer, making it their airborne home:

IT WAS A
SHINING CRUST OVER THE LAND & SEA   WE SUSPENDED ALL
LIFE IN AN OZONE LAYER WEIGHTLESS & SELFSUSTAINING
CHEMICAL GLITTERING & ROOTLESS   WHICH THE ATOM BUILT
THAT WE FUSED
("Mirabell" 1.5, 120)

But these angels fell, and when they did they used atomic energy to destroy their floating world: "WE BROKE THE OZONE LAYER/WITH A LAST THRUST OF ATOMIC FISSION" (121). A monitory tale, in which all too obviously our own present flirtation with collective death, whether by nuclear self-destruction or ozone depletion, is figured.

Waiting for the Angel: early in part 1 of Kushner's *Angels in America,* one of his characters, a woman called Harper, imagines that "guardian angels," dispatched by God to protect the human race, form the ozone layer that screens out dangerous radiation from space (act 1, scene 3). By the end of part 2, however, Harper has learned enough to want to revise her myth. No longer is it angels, beings essentially unlike us, who form the life-preserving ozone layer, but ourselves, our own dead—in this context, specifically the dead of the AIDS epidemic:

Souls were rising, from the earth far below, souls of the dead, of people who had perished, from famine, from war, from the plague, and they floated up, like skydivers in reverse, limbs all akimbo, wheeling and spinning. And the souls of these departed joined hands, clasped ankles, and formed a web, a great net of souls, and the souls were three-atom oxygen molecules, of the stuff of ozone, and the outer rim absorbed them, and was repaired.

Nothing's lost forever.

(act 5, scene 10; Kushner 144)

3
Pop (Up) Figures

Melvin Tolson's *Harlem Gallery* and
Edward Dorn's *Gunslinger*

I. PERIODIZING THE SIXTIES

I've always thought of the sixties decade as 1965 to 1975: 1960 to 1965
was absolutely different. . . . Anybody who was of the age of consciousness during that time recognizes that. It's true that one of the
problems people have with the seventies now, the decade nobody
will mention, is it's really half sixties. I think it will be a while
before that gets sorted out.

Edward Dorn (Bezner 43)

What does it mean to say that two texts "belong" to the "same period"?
What would it mean, for instance, to say that two long narrative poems
—say, Melvin Tolson's *Harlem Gallery* and Edward Dorn's *Gunslinger*—
"belonged" to the sixties?

Among the most compelling proposals for how we might set about
"periodizing" the sixties is Fredric Jameson's. Jameson's sixties begin in
the years 1957–62, with the upsurge of Third World decolonization, and
last until the world oil crisis of 1972–74. As with any other period, his
sixties are characterized by a "whole range of varied responses" to a
shared "objective situation" ("Periodizing" 179). That objective situation
comprises, crucially, movements of political liberation throughout the
Third World, including colonized enclaves within the First World—in
the United States, the Civil Rights movement and its heir, Black nationalism—as well as anticolonial wars such as the one in Southeast Asia,
with its complex repercussions for American domestic politics. Jameson

challenges us to see all these headline-level developments in the perspective of the larger transition to a new, "late" phase in the history of capitalism. It is this moment of transition, the space of interregnum that opens as capitalism reorganizes itself into the transnational forms with which we have since become all too familiar, that accounts for the widespread experience of emancipation on so many fronts, the sense of "free fall" characteristic of sixties politics and culture. The reflection of this moment of free fall in the specifically cultural sphere is the onset of that collection of cultural forms and practices that we have subsequently learned to call "postmodernism." The first inkling of the period's approaching end, according to Jameson, is the economic recession of 1966–67; the decisive break comes with the full-blown economic crisis of 1972–74.

Relative to Jameson's objective landmarks, both Tolson's *Harlem Gallery* and Dorn's *Gunslinger* certainly ought to belong to the sixties. *Gunslinger* appears in four installments from 1968 to 1972, the fifth and final one appearing only with the publication of the complete poem in 1975, just outside the limit of Jameson's period. The only extant book of *Harlem Gallery*, subtitled *The Curator*, appears in 1965, but if Tolson (who died in 1966) had lived long enough to produce the projected four-book continuation, his poem's publication dates would presumably have overlapped Dorn's. Both poems reflect, in their background assumptions if not their foreground events, the anticolonial struggles that, by Jameson's account, comprise the shared objective situation of the sixties: in *Harlem Gallery*, the Civil Rights movement (one character is identified as an "ex-Freedom Rider"; another tells "an anecdote on integration"[1]); in *Gunslinger*, the Vietnam war ("say something quick about the war/in, well you know where the War is"[2]). *Gunslinger*, it has been cogently argued, goes even further; in its narrative of the quest for the elusive tycoon Howard Hughes, and the latter's strange transformation and flight, Dorn's poem constitutes, according to one persuasive reading (Foster), an allegory of the very transition to late capitalism on which Jameson's account hinges. Whether *Harlem Gallery* is as self-conscious about its own historical moment is harder to answer, and must remain an open question for now.

Do these two poems reflect the sixties situation in their poetics as well as in their historical referents? That is, in Jameson's terms, are they postmodernist texts? One approach to answering this question would be to draw up a checklist of postmodernist features to see how closely the features of *Harlem Gallery* and *Gunslinger* approximate those on the list. A shortcut to the same end would be to choose a paradigmatic case of literary postmodernism against which to measure our two texts. A convenient and, as it turns out, highly relevant paradigm case is the sixties fiction of the African-American postmodernist, Ishmael Reed.[3]

Consider, then, in this connection, two of Reed's novels of the period: *Yellow Back Radio Broke-Down* (1969) and *Mumbo Jumbo* (1972). In *Yellow Back Radio Broke-Down,* Reed erects a fantastic and satirical fiction on the ruins of a conventional Western. Reed's gunslinger-hero, the Loop Garoo Kid, is African-American, a devotee of vodun and a fast draw. He is modelled less on the real black cowboys and buffalo soldiers of the American West than on cultural cross-dressers of the late-sixties rock stage—Jimi Hendrix in his Mexican-bandit hat, Sly Stone in his fringed "frontier" jacket. The world through which the Loop Garoo Kid moves is a generic hybrid and a historical patchwork, crosshatched with anachronisms: Thomas Jefferson occupies the White House and Benjamin Franklin is evidently still alive, yet the characters use radios and helicopters and are familiar with Guillaume Apollinaire, the New York School, and Martha and the Vandellas. But the plot motifs of *Yellow Back Radio* are unmistakably those of the conventional Western: the uncannily unbeatable gunslinger, the "revenge motif" (Reed, *Yellow Back* 56), the corrupt frontier town lorded over by the local cattle baron and his cowboys, the hero left in the desert to die, the mail-order bride, the showdowns with the venal Marshall and the hired gun, the capture of the hero, the interrupted lynching, and "A Jigsaw of a Last Minute Rescue" (173).

Yellow Back Radio belongs, in other words, to that wave of parodic, revisionist, iconoclastic, and deconstructed Westerns, films as well as novels, that arose in the midsixties and crested in the midseventies, sweeping away the traditonal cowboys-and-Indians and good-guys-and-bad-guys scenarios so familiar from popular culture. To reimagine and reinhabit the Western in this way is to practice a form of postmodernist pastiche. Dorn's *Gunslinger,* despite its anomalous genre, clearly belongs to this same tendency, and shares many striking family resemblances with Reed's *Yellow Back Radio.* Like Reed's novel, *Gunslinger* is a "ruined" or deconstructed Western, an extended parodic riff on such classic Western movies as, say, *Stagecoach* or *The Magnificent Seven.* Here we find such Wild West conventions as the band of comrades, the faithful horse, the cowtown madam with a heart of gold, the bar brawl, the gunfight, the crossing of the badlands, the final showdown, and of course the gunslinger himself.[4] Dorn's eponymous hero, like Reed's Loop Garoo Kid, is a super-human figure, indeed a demigod ("semidios" I.31), who antagonizes the respectable elements of society wherever he goes, wins gun duels by performing miracles, and seems to be engaged on some mysterious mission (vendetta or rescue?) involving the millionaire entrepreneur Howard Hughes. Hughes's presence alerts us to the fact that the world of *Gunslinger*, like that of *Yellow Back Radio*, is a tissue of anachronisms, the later twentieth century telescoped into the Wild West. Indeed, it embraces even the future, incorporating the technologies and neologisms of futuristic science fiction.

Reed's other relevant sixties novel is generically more hybrid than *Yellow Back Radio* or even *Gunslinger*. *Mumbo Jumbo* is, first of all, a historical novel of Harlem in the twenties, a *roman à clef* featuring lightly disguised and more or less caricatured figures of the Harlem Renaissance (including Countee Cullen, Langston Hughes, Carl Van Vechten, and the racketeer Casper Holstein; see Gates 302–03; De Jongh 207). But it is a historical novel with a difference, in the postmodernist manner—that is, a "historiographic metafiction" in Hutcheon's sense, one that re-envisions the Renaissance of the twenties in the light of the Black Arts Movement of the sixties. It is also, as many critics have observed (Gates 303, 305–07; McGee 84–85) and Reed himself acknowledges in a 1975 interview (Dick and Singh 84), a parodic murder mystery in which the "hoodoo detective" Papa LaBas solves a series of murders and reveals the secret history of the West, though (in common with Poe's August Dupin before him and Eco's William of Baskerville after) without succeeding in recovering the lost text that has been the source of all the trouble. Finally, in one of its many subplots *Mumbo Jumbo* parodies the conventions of that Hollywood staple, the "big caper" film (Kaminsky 74–99). A band of high-living bohemian thieves—Reed calls them the *Mu'tafikah* ("motherfuckers," presumably)—plan and execute a series of spectacular art heists. However, in place of the crew of well-drilled specialists and glamorous eccentrics familiar from the movies and television, Reed substitutes a rainbow coalition of cultural terrorists (Asian, Latino, African-American, a token WASP) dedicated to liberating pieces of Third-World art from First-World museums and repatriating them. This is another of Reed's deliberate anachronisms, of course—a sixties cultural politics (one still topical) imposed on a narrative set in the twenties.

Tolson's *Harlem Gallery* has much in common with *Mumbo Jumbo*, but here, unlike in the case of Dorn and *Yellow Back Radio*, the differences are more conspicuous than the similarities. *Harlem Gallery*, too, seems to evoke the era of the Renaissance, but its historical framing proves to be elusive and ambiguous. While certain episodes clearly belong to the twenties (Prohibiton is still in force, Dutch Schultz is still alive; see "Mu" 262; "Upsilon" 318), others evoke the forties (Rommel's death is news, "Eta" 233), and still others the sixties (the ex-Freedom Rider of "Upsilon" 312). But trying to resolve the text into some system of receding temporal planes, relative to a narrative present, proves to be a frustrating exercise, given the paucity of temporal signposts (see Bérubé 97–99). The result is a strangely elusive kind of historical narrative, one that refuses to commit itself to any particular historical moment.

Equally elusive is Tolson's relation to popular culture in *Harlem Gallery*. Missing here is the gleeful appropriation of popular genres—the Western, the detective story, science fiction—that one finds in Reed and Dorn. Instead, Tolson agonizes over the conflicting claims of popular and high art, centering his poem on a dialectical confrontation between representatives of each—on the one hand, Hideho Heights, street balladeer and self-appointed spokesman for the popular; on the other, the Curator of the Harlem Gallery, defender of high culture (see Bérubé 67–68, 71–92). Tolson's examples of popular art are mainly musical—jazz, folk ballads; nevertheless, *Harlem Gallery* also incorporates, almost surreptitiously, some of the motifs of popular crime fiction, including a vestigial murder mystery (see Dove 113–14). It is as though Tolson were embarrassed to acknowledge his reliance on, and taste for, such popular narrative forms.

But it is when we reflect on Reed's use of the "big caper" subplot that the most striking difference of all emerges. For here *Mumbo Jumbo* and *Harlem Gallery* appear almost as mirror opposites: where Reed's protagonists are "art-nappers," Tolson's is something like their natural enemy, the Curator of an art gallery—a conservator where they are desecrators, the cop to their robbers. Or is this opposition too pat? After all, Tolson's Curator is himself an African-American, and the gallery he curates is the *Harlem* Gallery, a collection of African-American art—presumably just the sort of non-Eurocentric, noncolonialist venue to which Reed's *Mu'ta-fikah* aim to restore the artworks they have liberated from the white "Center for Art Detention" (aka the Metropolitan Museum). It is not clear, however, whether Reed's implicit critique of "museum culture," of the museum's sinister power to "kill" art through decontextualization and dehistoricization, might not extend as far as the Curator and the sort of collection he polices. Furthermore, if the pictures hanging in the Harlem Gallery are by African-Americans, the Curator himself seems to hold orthodox Eurocentric aesthetic theories and tastes—theories and tastes, moreover, that he appears to share with his African-American creator, Melvin Tolson (Bérubé 62–132 passim). Reed the art-thief versus Tolson the curator: the opposition seems starkly emblematic.

No doubt this juxtaposition is tendentious and unfair to Tolson; but it does serve to bring into focus the kinds of problems confronting anyone seeking to "periodize" Tolson's *Harlem Gallery*. Tolson's cultural politics are those of an earlier generation, as are his poetics—or so it appears at first glance, anyway. In this sense, *Harlem Gallery* both does and does not "belong" to the sixties. It is both contemporary with Reed and Dorn and anachronistic, out of date—both residually modernist and emergently postmodernist, both timely and untimely.

Untimeliness is a topos of Tolson criticism. Tolson, writes his biographer, Robert M. Farnsworth, "just missed some of the major fashions in cultural history" ("Afterword" 255). Born in 1898, so more than a generation older than Dorn (born 1929) or Reed (born 1938), Tolson emerges in the awkward "interstitial period" (Bérubé 181) between the Harlem Renaissance and the Black Arts Movement. He figures as one of the *Black American Poets between Worlds* of a critical collection by that title (R. Miller); the "worlds" in question are the Black and white worlds, of course, but also the worlds of the two "Renaissance" generations that bracket Tolson's own.

Tolson is literally belated with respect to the Harlem Renaissance, arriving in Harlem for the academic year 1931–32, just as the extraordinary literary and cultural flowering of the preceding decade was beginning to shut down. His participation seems to have been largely second-hand; a student of the Renaissance, he wrote a Columbia University thesis on "The Harlem Group of Negro Writers," for which the M.A. was not awarded until as late as 1940 (Farnsworth, *Plain Talk* 31–40). Belated with respect to the African-American modernism of the Harlem Renaissance, he was even more belated relative to mainstream (read: white) modernism, undergoing a kind of conversion experience in the late forties. Tolson's modernist conversion earned him condescending (and controversial) endorsements from the influential New Critics Allen Tate and Karl Shapiro: Tate wrote a preface for Tolson's long poem, *Libretto for the Republic of Liberia* (1953), while Shapiro contributed an introduction to *Harlem Gallery*. This support also earned him the contempt of the rising generation of African-American critics, who saw in Tolson's late embrace of mainstream modernism distressing evidence of African-American "cultural lag." Worse, in his apparent willingness to be patronized by white opinion-shapers these critics saw symptoms of what they took to be cultural Uncle-Tomism (see Flasch 135–39; Bérubé 133–206).

Belated with respect to modernism, in its white as well as its Black varieties, Tolson was too early for the Black Arts Movement, the onset of which, beginning from the midsixties, seemed to render his poetics immediately obsolete. Black Arts aesthetics valued the oral-vernacular tradition over the written tradition in Black culture, and accessibility over difficulty, so the timing could hardly have been worse for the appearance of a difficult, indubitably writerly text like *Harlem Gallery* (see Dove 109–10; Nielsen, *Writing* 58–59; Werner). Typical of the reservations that were now being voiced about Tolson's approach to poetry were Stephen Henderson's in *Understanding the New Black Poetry* (1973), a watershed anthology and manifesto (which, not incidentally, signifies on Brooks and Warren's mainstream textbook, *Understanding Poetry*). "Is the blues singer/composer a poet?" asks Henderson in his introductory essay. "Is Melvin Tolson a greater poet than James Brown?" (9). Context as well as word order make it clear that it is Tolson's claim to be regarded as a "great" Black poet that is being questioned here, not James Brown's. Henderson closes on a conciliatory note: the Black community, he concludes, "does not intend to give up any of its beautitful singers, whether Countee Cullen or Melvin Tolson or Robert Hayden. We may quarrel with them sometimes, but ain't never gonna say good-bye" (27). The ultimate outcome of this "quarrel" appears to be presaged in the abrupt shift into the vernacular in the last phrase. Somehow, this is not reassuring.[5]

More recently, Tolson's reputation has undergone a degree of rehabilitation. His belatedness with respect to the Harlem Renaissance now begins to look like an advantage, enabling him to view the Renaissance from a certain critical distance, and perhaps giving him pride of place in the ongoing reconsideration and revision of the Harlem Renaissance legacy (see, e.g., Baker; Stepto; Nelson, *Repression* 88–99; De Jongh; Douglas)—a tendency to which Reed's *Mumbo Jumbo* also belongs. His "post-Renaissance" belatedness may even give Tolson a claim to be considered a precocious African-American postmodernist (Bérubé 199–201; Nielsen, *Black Chant* 7–8, 49–50, 106–07, 127, 148). As for the symptoms of "cultural lag" that some have detected in *Harlem Gallery*, and Tolson's alleged subservience to modernist aesthetic dicta (and to the New Critics who delivered them), here suspicions have surfaced about the possibility of irony in Tolson's stance. Was Tolson more self-critical and self-reflective in his embrace of mainstream modernism than we have given him credit for? Could it be that, far from passively submitting to his modernist masters, he was actually turning the tables on them? Could he even have been signifying upon his modernist models (see Bérubé 139–45; Nielsen, *Writing* 59)?[6]

From such suspicions of duplicity it is only a short step to a complete reevaluation of Tolson and his relations with the mainstream. In place of the epigonic modernist there emerges the image of Tolson as a kind of cultural renegade or guerrilla—or more appositely, as cultural maroon. On this view, Tolson (like Reed) reenacts in the cultural sphere the historical role of the maroon, the escaped slave who periodically raids the nearest plantation for the supplies he needs to survive, all the while scheming against the order of the white masters (Bérubé 145, 203; on cultural marronage generally, see Baker 75 et seq.). Perhaps surprisingly, this view of Tolson has been current since the sixties, at least in some quarters. At a time (1966) when most commentators could see *Harlem Gallery* (if they saw it at all) only in terms of, at best, assimilationism and cultural integration or, at worst, epigonism and Uncle-Tomism, a critic named Dan McCall saw Tolson otherwise. Referring to his earlier long poem, *Libretto for the Republic of Liberia,* McCall wrote, "Tolson seems to be running wild in the white castle of learning. You have made me, he is saying, a black thief in the night; I am a Negro and have made my meals on what I hooked from your white kitchens and now that I have made my way into your study—see here—I walk off with your library" (quoted in Farnsworth, *Plain Talk* 173; Bérubé 203). A Black thief in the night walking off with the white library: if that is what Tolson is, then perhaps *Harlem Gallery* is not so distant from the cultural politics of *Mumbo Jumbo,* after all. Perhaps there is more of the despoiler and "art-napper" to Tolson, and less of the museum curator, than at first meets the eye.

The passage of time has also made it possible to reevaluate Tolson's "untimeliness" with respect to the Black Arts Movement. Even granted the movement's privileging of oral over written forms, there are oral-vernacular dimensions of Tolson's practice that Black Arts polemicists failed to notice or to value. Tolson is closer to vernacular poetics than he has been given credit for; his "street" credentials are better than his critics of the sixties were able or willing to admit (see Dove 112–15; Nielsen, *Writing* 58–59; Werner 163–65). Along these lines, one recent critic (De Jongh 177) proposes that we regard Tolson not as incompatible with the Black Arts Movement, but rather as its precursor. On the other hand, we are also now in a better position, thanks to the passage of time, to question the Black Arts Movement's over-valuing of orality, and to undertake the recovery of the "lost" writerly tradition of the African-American avant-garde (see Mackey; Nielsen, *Black Chant*). With respect to this "lost" avant-garde tradition, Tolson is something like a touchstone; far from a marginal figure, as he appears to be from the perspective of the oral-vernacular tradition, here he appears central, essential.

Such readings—Tolson as engaged in acts of cultural marronage; Tolson as touchstone of the African-American avant-garde—restore *Harlem Gallery* to its period, the sixties, and to the emergent postmodernism of that period. To read *Harlem Gallery* in this light is to assert at least a hypothetical contemporaneity with Reed's sixties novels and with Dorn's *Gunslinger.* Hypothetical contemporaneity, however, is hardly the strongest justification for proceeding with an analysis, such as the one I propose to carry out, that juxtaposes Tolson and Dorn. Stronger authorization may be sought, and found, in contemporary critical practice. It may be found, for instance, in Nathaniel Mackey's challenge to contemporary criticism to read across the color line, to juxtapose African-American and Euro-American avant-gardists and to seek "creative kinship" and "lines of affinity" outside canonical groupings of allegedly related texts and authors (3; see also Nielsen, *Writing* and *Black Chant*). In the end, however, the only thing that justifies juxtaposing two such texts as *Har-*

lem Gallery and *Gunslinger* is the findings of the analysis one brings to bear on them. There are good reasons for regarding them as belonging to the same period; there are good reasons for exploring their potential affinities; but whether those affinities are more than potential depends on what the analysis uncovers.

In fact, despite all the manifold differences between the poets—differences of race, generation, poetical "school," and so on—as well as obvious differences of subject-matter, theme, and underlying ideology, certain profound formal similarities between *Harlem Gallery* and *Gunslinger* do emerge. There are striking formal differences as well, of course; just to name the most obvious of them, *Harlem Gallery* employs end-rhyme throughout, though in an ad hoc manner, following no regular pattern, while *Gunslinger* is unrhymed free verse, apart from occasional interpolated songs. Moreover, certain of their more obvious shared formal features fall under suspicion of actually hiding deeper differences. Narrative is one such shared feature: *Harlem Gallery* and *Gunslinger* are both narrative poems, at least in part, but one might well suspect that the sources of their narrativity are quite different. Tolson's, one might surmise, is a "residual" narrativity, a holdover from the era of narrative poetry before the modernist interdiction of narrative, while the narrativity of *Gunslinger* might be seen as an "emergent" narrativity, heralding the fuller recovery of the resources of narrative by subsequent postmodernist long poems (see Perloff, "Image to Action" 155–71; McHale, "Telling Stories Again"). Or perhaps not; perhaps Tolson's recourse to narrative is emergent after all, and how can we be certain that Dorn's isn't residual? The closer we look, the blurrier the distinction becomes; but the suspicion of difference lingers, nevertheless.

The similarities I have in mind are both more superficial and more profound than this shared narrativity: more superficial, in that they manifest themselves in the poems' figurative language; more profound, in that they derive from a long genre history traceable back into literary-historical "deep time." Ultimately, however, the formal similarity between *Harlem Gallery* and *Gunslinger* arises from the similar way these two poems, otherwise so different in origin and content, inhabit, address, and reflect their period—the way they respond, in Jameson's terms, to their shared objective situation. This involves, in the first place, their response to the carnivalesque aspects of their period—to the sixties as carnival.

II. WRITING CIRCUSES

What's your beef with me Bo Shmo, what if I write circuses? No
one says a novel has to be one thing. It can be anything it wants to
be, a vaudeville show, the six o'clock news, the mumblings of wildmen saddled by demons.

Ishmael Reed (*Yellow Back Radio* 40)

Here again Ishmael Reed's sixties novels prove invaluable guides. Among
other things, *Yellow Back Radio Broke-Down* and *Mumbo Jumbo* allegor-
ize the ebb and flow of carnival in the twentieth century, and in particular its resurgence in the sixties. Popular carnival, as we have learned to
theorize it since the rediscovery of Mikhail Bakhtin's work (see *Rabelais;
Problems* 122–32), effectively disappeared as a real social practice in the
West after the Renaissance. Under pressure from the forces of modernization and rationalization, it subsided into minor forms such as masquerade and contemporary street carnivals of the Mardi Gras type (Castle
100–06), and survives today in a "carnivalesque diaspora" of marginalized activities, holiday enclaves, and representations (Stallybrass and
White 176–81, 188–90). Reed in his sixties novels narrates the return of
carnival from this diaspora.

The Loop Garoo Kid, gunslinger hero of *Yellow Back Radio*, is a carnival Lord of Misrule in exile. Expelled from heaven, he has joined a
traveling circus, one of the forms in which carnival elements persist, albeit on a reduced scale, on the margins of the modern world. However,
even this reduced form of carnival is regarded as intolerably threatening
by the agents of modernization, the property owners and institutional
authorities of the town of Yellow Back Radio, who destroy the circus,
together with the insubordinate children of the town, and send the Loop
Garoo Kid into the desert. From this double exile "The Loop Garoo Kids
Comes Back Mad," in the words of a chapter title, to overturn the hierarchical regime of Yellow Back Radio and usher in a season of blasphe-
mous inversion, sacred parody, and carnival laughter in the classic Bakh-
tinian sense.

Mumbo Jumbo allegorizes the return of carnival even more explicitly,
in the form of Jes Grew, an epidemic of jazz dancing that, according to
Reed, swept the country in the 1920s. Jes Grew is "the carnival impulse
personified" (Fox 49). Like the Loop Garoo Kid it "Goes Away Mad,"

withdraws into exile after an initial outbreak in the 1890s, then returns in full force to galvanize the creative artists of the Harlem Renaissance, only to be overcome again by the forces of "high" (that is, white) culture, but also by its own failure to find its "text," its durable medium, without which it will continue to be "mistaken for entertainment" (Reed, *Mumbo Jumbo* 241). In the epilogue of *Mumbo Jumbo*, set in the sixties, a future resurgence of Jes Grew is prophesied, though at present it persists only in dilute form among imitators and wannabes such as "Hoffman Rubin Zimmerman the Beatles" (246).

These names identify places in the cultural landscape where Reed recognizes signs of carnival's survival, even if it is only carnival of a reduced, denatured kind: in the political street theater of the Yippies (Abbie Hoffman, Jerry Rubin) and in popular culture, rock music in particular (Robert Zimmerman aka Bob Dylan, the Beatles). We could easily identify other such sites in sixties culture: the "motley society" (Nemoianu 292–93), a literary topos literalized in places like "Swinging London" by the temporary relaxation of class barriers; the explosion of pop art, with its legitimation of "low" visual materials; the hippie scene, street life elevated to the level of a kind of performance art; the great rock shows and festivals; the participatory and transgressive theater of the period, from the Living Theater and *Marat/Sade* to *Hair;* carnivalesque cinema, both avant-garde (*Weekend, Zabriskie Point*) and mass-market (*How I Won the War, Barbarella, Casino Royale,* the Monkees' *Head,* Frank Zappa's *200 Motels*), much of it swept along in the wake of Richard Lester's films with the Beatles; and of course the first wave of postmodernist fiction, mainly in the United States, including novels by Heller, Barth, Vonnegut, Coover, Pynchon, Sukenick, and Reed himself, among many others. Taken together, all these symptoms of resurgent carnival tend to corroborate Jameson's insight that the "sense of freedom and possibility" associated with the sixties, while no doubt a "historical illusion" as viewed in hindsight, was also a "momentarily objective reality" at the time ("Periodizing" 208).

This, then, is one of the respects in which Reed's sixties novels address their historical moment, the moment I earlier characterized as that of "free fall," of the experience (however illusory) of liberation, when popular carnival seemed on the verge of revival. Reed addresses this moment by dramatizing the struggle between carnival and its enemies, as in Breughel's painting of the battle between carnival and Lent. Edward

Dorn in *Gunslinger* and Melvin Tolson in *Harlem Gallery* stage much the same struggle. In Dorn's case, the "carnivalized" characters forming the Slinger's entourage—madam, Poet, hippie hitchhiker, talking horse, and assorted merry pranksters—are ranged against the capitalist entrepreneur Robart (aka Howard Hughes) and his repressed, and repressive, microsociety of automatons. If Slinger does not, in the end, succeed in restoring the lost freedoms of carnival to a world that no longer tolerates full-fledged popular carnivals, he does at least preside as a kind of Lord of Misrule, like Reed's Loop Garoo Kid, over certain outbreaks of carnivalesque behavior, including a good-natured brawl at Lil's cabaret in book I, and above all the "carnivalization" of Universe City in book II, where he briefly revives the carnival associations of the public square, traditionally the arena of carnival activity.

Tolson is markedly more equivocal about this struggle than either Dorn or Reed (see Bérubé 71–106, 196–99). His sympathies seem to rest about equally with Hideho Heights, spokesman for the carnival worldview, and his opposite number, the Curator; it is the Curator, however, who always gets the last word. Moreover, Hideho is himself revealed to be internally divided, publicly the "People's Poet," frequenter of cabarets and eulogizer of Louis Armstrong, but privately a closet high modernist (see "Chi" 335–41). In the culture wars of *Harlem Gallery* Hideho Heights's worldview is "officially" bested—which doesn't prevent his vanquisher from voicing a certain grudging admiration for the carnival life, "a way of life that faces the crack of doom/with wine and wit and wiggle" ("Upsilon" 316). Witness the Curator's apostrophe to the Zulu Club cabaret, "a city of refuge" in the midst of ghetto realities ("Phi" 333), or his positive evocation of the New Orleans Mardi Gras ("Mu" 265).

Carnival, as Bakhtin has taught us, is transmitted to literature by one of two vectors: either by direct exposure to carnival practices, opportunities for which become increasingly rare in the modern world, or by indirect exposure through previously "carnivalized" literary forms (Bakhtin, *Problems* 131–32; see Morson and Emerson 461). Among carnivalized forms, the crucial one for Bakhtin's history of the novel is of course Menippean satire, the genre (or antigenre) by means of which ancient carnival practices were ultimately transmitted to the modern novel. Ishmael Reed's novels have long been recognized as belonging to this Menippean genre (e.g., Gates 301). Reed himself asserts his novels' Menippean credentials, without actually using the term, when in *Yellow*

Back Radio he makes the Loop Garoo Kid his spokesman in an aesthetic debate with one Bo Shmo, apologist for social-realist fiction. The freedoms that Reed claims for his kind of fiction are reflected in the models that he has the Kid enumerate (see the epigraph to this section, above): the circus, vaudeville, the six o'clock news, "the mumblings of wildmen saddled by demons." That a novel can be like "the six o'clock news" we have heard before: here the Kid is reasserting the novelist's traditional freedom to address the topical and the contemporary, in all their contingency. His other analogues, however—the circus, a vaudeville show—evoke the novel's distant historical roots in carnivalized literature: the novel can be a circus or a vaudeville show insofar as all three figure as modern heirs (however reduced, displaced, or commercialized) of the great popular carnivals in whose practices and worldview Bakhtin sees the ultimate origins of the novel. As for "wildmen saddled by demons," this surely alludes to the phenomenon of spirit-possession in vodun ritual practice, which Reed, especially in *Mumbo Jumbo,* will picture as the militant avant-garde of a resurgent carnival culture in the twentieth-century world.

Thus to "write circuses," in Reed's sense, is in effect to write Menippean satires, in defiance of the normative aesthetics of novelistic realism. Despite writing long poems rather than novels, Tolson in *Harlem Gallery* and Dorn in *Gunslinger* also "write circuses" in something like Reed's sense.[7] The Menippean genre seems to be periodically reconstituted or "reinvented" afresh by new generations of writers, in part on the model of the few exemplary Menippean satires that the canon does preserve (typically without calling them by that name, however), but also in part in dialectical response to the consolidation of the genre system of canonical literature itself (see Clark and Holquist 194; Morson and Emerson 279–83, 292–93, 296). In this perspective, Menippean satire appears less like a genre in any of the usual senses of the term than like an "antigenre," arising in different historical situations in reaction against the monological orientation and centralizing tendencies of the canonical genres, defining itself as the negation or inverse of "official" literature (see Clark and Holquist 276–77; Relihan 11, 28, 34). Just as, in Bakhtin's account, Menippean satire initially arose in ancient literature as a reaction against the monological classical genres, so in postmodernist literature it reemerges and reconstitutes itself by way of reaction against canonical modernism.

Bakhtin tended to associate Menippean satire exclusively with prose, in particular with the novel and its forerunners and analogues, regarding all poetic genres as intrinsically and inevitably monological (single-voiced) and centripetal, subject to a single organizing dominant and characterized by strong closure, and so incompatible with the centrifugal and multi-voiced Menippean genre. This would seem to leave little room for discussing poetic texts such as *Harlem Gallery* and *Gunslinger* under the rubric of Menippean satire. However, as has been evident for some time, Bakhtin's theory of dialogism is particularly rife with inconsistencies and blindspots when it comes to poetry (see Morson and Emerson 20, 250, 319–25; Hirshkop; Eskin). Not only are many genres of poetry evidently heteroglossic (see Richter), but also Bakhtin himself acknowledged as much, exempting certain long poems (Pushkin's *Onegin*, Byron's *Childe Harold* and *Don Juan*) and even some lyric poetry (e.g., Heine's) from his own blanket characterization of poetry as monological (see Clark and Holquist 277). Moreover, in the course of the twentieth century, poetry of every genre, but especially the "long poem," has become formally and stylistically ever more heterogeneous, polyphonic, and centrifugal, incorporating prose passages, and displaying "prosaic" features even in its verse passages (see Davidson, "Discourse in Poetry"; cf. Beach 220–21). In short, the reasons for restricting Menippean satire to prose genres, if they were ever very strong, have become less cogent in our time, so that it has become increasingly possible, even desirable, to view poetry, especially postmodernist "long poems" like *Harlem Gallery* and *Gunslinger*, in the light of Bakhtin's account of Menippean satire.

The features that Bakhtin (*Problems* 114–19; see also Frye 308–12; Relihan 3–36) identifies as characteristic of Menippean satire are sufficiently familiar that I need not revisit them in detail here; in any case, I am more interested in documenting how they map onto the features of *Harlem Gallery* and *Gunslinger*. First of all, Bakhtin specifies a number of what might be called ideological features, those arising most directly from the carnival worldview that underlies the Menippean genre. Where other ancient genres are typically serious, Menippean satire is comic; where they are likely to depend on received narratives and situations, it is topical; where they are conservative and traditionalist and tend to value moderation, it is utopian and committed to the pursuit of ultimate questions; above all, where other ancient genres are monological, Menippean satire is dialogical. The comic element in particular is quite strong in *Gunslinger,* and nearly as strong in *Harlem Gallery,* justifying Karl Shapiro's characterization of the latter as a "comic poem" ("Introduction" 14). Dorn undermines any expectations of seriousness by saddling his characters with silly, cartoonish names (Kool Everything, Dr. Jean Flamboyant, Tonto Pronto, Taco Desoxin) and by indulging in constant punning and other "low" verbal humor, much of it derived from the argot of the drug subculture. Time and again, Wild West action sequences degenerate into farce or slapstick more appropriate to an animated cartoon than serious literature; animals and inanimate objects (a horse, a cracker barrel) talk. *Harlem Gallery* appears more solemn, at least when the Curator's monologue dominates (mainly at the beginning and end of the poem). But it also showcases the informal verbal competitions among the Zulu Club Wits, wherein contestants seek to best one another through masterful displays of rhetoric, each speaker seizing on the previous speaker's figure of speech and either reinterpreting it against the grain, or topping it with a still more extravagant figure. Rooted in African-American vernacular practice, this amounts to a sort of hyper-educated and self-mocking version of the dozens (see Dove 112–115; Bérubé 99, 110; and, on the dozens generally, Smitherman 128–34).

Earlier I considered the topicality of both these poems, their situatedness in the sixties. (The topicality of *Gunslinger* is further illuminated by the annotations compiled by Stephen Fredman and Grant Jenkins.) As for the utopian element, if there are any utopias to be glimpsed in *Harlem Gallery* and *Gunslinger,* they are ad hoc and short-lived, transient pocket democracies: a motley traveling party (*Gunslinger*), a cross-section of Harlem society assembled at a nightclub to drink and exchange ideas (*Harlem Gallery*). In other words, if there are utopian sites in these poems, they are associated in each case with the zones of dialogical contact and exchange among people, and this is fully in keeping with the carnivalesque spirit of Menippean satire, as described by Bakhtin. Both *Gunslinger* and *Harlem Gallery* (despite the latter's monological frame) are basically dialogical poems, in which multiple voices restlessly banter and contend. The narrative episodes of *Harlem Gallery,* in particular, comprise a series of informal symposia—or a single ongoing "floating" symposium—conducted at various sites around Harlem: Aunt Grindle's Elite Chitterling Shop (in section "Eta"), the Harlem Gallery itself (in "Kappa" and "Lambda"), and especially the Zulu Club, where the Zulu Club Wits gather. At issue are the "ultimate questions" of African-American identity and cultural survival, the competing claims of high and popular culture, and the role of the artist in contemporary society: "the Afroamerican dilemma in the Arts—/the dialectic of/to be or not to be/a Negro" ("Chi" 336). *Gunslinger*, too, is a floating symposium—or more accurately, a rolling one, as the Gunslinger and his band progress from town to town by stagecoach, talking at all the stations on the way, and in between stations too. The talk, again, is all of "ultimate" epistemological and ontological questions: "And so they continued/to walk and to talk/and to discourse on/the parameters of reality" (II.83).

Bakhtin also specifies a number of linguistic and stylistic features of the Menippean text. The most fundamental formal feature of Menippean satire is its heterogeneity. A Menippean text is not a single integral text, but a patchwork of texts, some juxtaposed, some inset in others, belonging to various genres, prose and poetry alike; it possesses not a single consistent style, but a multiplicity of styles, registers, dialects, etc. *Harlem Gallery* might appropriately have been called the *Harlem Anthology*, for within its capacious narrative frame it incorporates texts of various genres, including Hideho Heights's oral poetry (his ode to Satchmo, in "Lambda"; his ballad of John Henry, in "Xi"), but also a sample of his written poetry in a difficult modernist style (in "Chi"). In addition it incorporates an entire cycle of poems by another poet, Mister Starks, entitled "Harlem Vignettes" (section "Upsilon"), the title and structure of which echo Tolson's own *Gallery of Harlem Portraits* (composed during the thirties, published posthumously in 1979). *Gunslinger* is similarly a patchwork of inset texts. It features a series of songs performed by the Poet, including his "Song about a woman" (I.39), "Oh Light; The Light!" (II.48–49), "Cool Liquid Comes" (II. 50–51), an ode to cocaine (IV.172–77), and, by far his most extended and elaborate performance, the "Cycle of Robart's Wallet," part visionary, part satirical, interpolated between books II and III (90–110). Inset prose texts also abound: the manic "Nightletter" from Parmenides' secretary (III.140–41), the texts of Robart's intercepted radio communications (IV.195), the inscription and recorded message of the Sllab monument (IV.164, 165), and so on.

Stylistic heterogeneity is a conspicuous feature of both *Harlem Gallery* and *Gunslinger*. In the case of *Harlem Gallery*, the poem's styles tend toward polar extremes, reflecting the dialogical confrontation between the Curator, with his written, allusive, highly educated style, and the vernacular, "street" style of Hideho Heights. But the polarity of "written" versus "vernacular" style is not the only dimension of stylistic diversity in *Harlem Gallery*. The Curator's own monologue, in particular, displays considerable heterogeneity, even apart from its internal stylistic dialogue with Hideho's vernacular. Mingled in the Curator's discourse one finds a range of styles, registers, and specialized vocabularies—e.g., of zoology, anatomy, optics, viniculture, the law, etc.—often jarringly juxtaposed with one another and with his "native" literary register. A comparable stylistic heterogeneity characterizes *Gunslinger* (see Golding, "History" 54–56; Beach). Archaisms and pseudoarchaisms are generally associated with Gunslinger and his band—e.g, "In the high west/there burns a furious Starre," (II.47); "I see the grass shake in the sunne/for leagues on either side the chorus sung," (IIII.186)—while technical, mass-media, and pop jargons, the languages of the present and future, are associated with the Gunslinger's adversary, Robart (Paul 156). Here, too, as in *Harlem Gallery*, the opposition between two polar styles is complicated by infusions of other varieties, among them counterculture slang and drug argot, border-country Mexican Spanish (e.g., IV.167–68), and various other dialects and linguistic stereotypes, including "blackface" or vaudeville-Negro dialect (e.g., IIII.149) and stage Yiddish (IIII.187). Finally, to complete this picture of stylistic heterogeneity and polyvocality, both *Harlem Gallery* and *Gunslinger* are crisscrossed with quotations from other texts, some more or less verbatim (though often radically changed in their import by recontextualization), others more or less subtly altered, still others grossly travestied.[8]

Apart from these ideological and stylistic features, Menippean satire is also characterized, according to Bakhtin, by a particular repertoire of narrative motifs. Basically picaresque in its narrative structure, the Menippean genre draws on a repertoire of motifs including extraordinary situations (trips to other planets, journeys to the land of the dead, etc.); drastic changes of scale and perspective (views from far above or below, a giant's or lilliputian's perspective on the world, etc.); extreme social circumstances, or what Bakhtin calls "slum naturalism"; and extreme psychological experiences, or what he calls "moral-psychological experimentation." The Menippean repertoire also includes motifs of social transgression, public eccentricity and scandalous behavior. Dorn's *Gunslinger* does indeed narrate an adventurous journey, though not one to another world. The itinerary traced by Slinger and his company across the American Southwest, from Mesilla near the Mexican border, up the Rio Grande, then west across the Colorado Plateau to Four Corners, is entirely this-worldly and can actually be followed on a map. The Gunslinger himself may be an emissary from another world (see below), but no one from this world travels to visit his—unless it is "I," who suffers death and resurrection, but whose journey over there and back again is not actually recorded in the poem. Tolson's picaresque adventurer, the Curator, travels not so much in geographic space as social space, between the upper and nether realms of Harlem. There are no interplanetary or otherworld journeys here either, apart perhaps from the comic descent into the underworld of the Angelus Funeral Home (in "Sigma"). Instead of extraordinary metaphysical situations, poised at or beyond the thresholds of other worlds, Tolson gives us low-life social situations, some of them literally "low," below street level: a basement flat in a slum tenement ("Zeta"), a chitterling shop ("Eta"), a jazz club that once was, or (depending on when the poem's "now" is transpiring) perhaps still is a speakeasy. "Slum naturalism," to use Bakhtin's term, is similarly a feature of *Gunslinger*, with its visit to Lil's rowdy sporting-house (book I) and its constant allusions to the drug subculture—a criminal underworld in the eyes of the Law, as the threatening presence of the Master Nark (III.109, 118) serves to remind us. Thus, motifs of slum naturalism almost invariably also involve motifs of what Bakhtin calls "moral-psychological experimentation," i.e., the experience of extreme or deranged states of mind, including dreams, intoxication, madness, and the like. Suicidal despair (on the part of the artist figures John Laugart and Mister Starks), murderous rage (on the part of Crazy Cain, Starks's killer), the alcohol-fueled euphoria of the Zulu Club episodes—all these extremes may be found in *Harlem Gallery*. If *Harlem Gallery* is alcohol oriented, *Gunslinger* is drug oriented, each of its four books being devoted to a different controlled substance (see Perloff, in Dorn, *Gunslinger* xiii–xiv): marijuana in book I, acid in book II, cocaine in book III and again in book IIII, where it seems to be supplemented by speed (Taco Desoxin, a minor character who enters the poem in that book, bears the name of an amphetamine). But the most radical instance of an "experimental" state of mind in the poem must surely be the case of the narrator "I". "I" dies in book II, but continues in a semblance of life thanks to a massive infusion of acid, returning from the dead in book IIII, allegedly egoless but in fact not noticeably changed from his annoying pre-death self. (Death, it turns out, is less of a life-altering experience than it's reputed to be.)

Scandals abound in both *Harlem Gallery* and *Gunslinger*. The key moment of scandal in *Harlem Gallery,* the one around which all its oppositions of style and worldview pivot, is Hideho Heights's boisterous irruption into the decorous opening-night party at the Harlem Gallery in section "Lambda." Comparable episodes of scandal in *Gunslinger* include the brawl in Lil's cabaret (book I) and the Slinger's confrontations with the respectable citizens of Universe City (book II). Late in the poem, in book IIII, we are introduced to the prankster-figures Taco Desoxin and Tonto Pronto, embodiments of scandal and transgression, like William Burroughs's manic connoisseur of chaos, A.J., or real-world counterparts such as Ken Kesey's Merry Pranksters.

Finally, Bakhtin specifies a number of what might be called *ontological* features of Menippean satire, that is, features of the Menippean world and its inhabitants. Free from any obligation to verisimilitude, the Menippean text is characterized by fantastic elements. Its world is organized into three ontological planes, three worlds: the plane of this world, the divine plane (that of the gods, or heaven), and the underworld (the world of the dead). As for the inhabitants of the Menippean world, what characterizes them, and their relations with one another, are oxymoronic combinations, sharp contrasts and abrupt transitions, and mésalliances or mismatches. It is especially in these organizational features of Menippean characterization that one discerns the persistent traces of Menippean satire's origins in carnival practices, with their parodic doublings, inversions of hierarchy, swapping of roles (and clothes), mésalliances among classes, and so on.

Jarring juxtapositions, mésalliances, and the oxymoronic structuring of characters are all conspicuously foregrounded features of *Harlem Gallery.* We have already observed more than once the structural importance of the systematic confrontaton and oxymoronic contrast between Curator and Hideho, but oxymoronic structuring does not stop there; similar confrontations and contrasts extend throughout the entire world of *Harlem Gallery,* making it a version of the motley society. Ironic juxtapositions of high and low abound: a sublime painter housed in a slum tenement ("Zeta"), an aesthetic symposium conducted in chitterling shop ("Eta") or a nightclub ("Mu," "Nu"), artists visited by inspiration in lowlife milieux ("Phi" 329–33; "Upsilon" 320–01), and so on. More importantly, nearly all of Tolson's characters are in one sense or another walking oxymorons, uneasy combinations of incompatible identities or contradictory tendencies. The Curator straddles Black and white identities— Black in ancestry but white in appearance, curator of a gallery of African-American art but upholder of Eurocentric aesthetics. His colleague Dr. Obi Nkomo, the Black African educated in the white world, is similarly divided, but the most crucially self-divided character of all is of course Hideho Heights, publicly a celebrator of popular culture in populist style, privately an avant-gardist. Hideho's "bifacial nature" ("Chi" 335) is interpreted by the Curator as reflecting the essential doubleness of the African-American, especially African-American artists (336–37). Like the Curator's, the Slinger's band of companions forms a motley society in miniature: semidivine Slinger and whorehouse madam, inspired Poet and dope-smoking talking horse, merry pranksters and mad scientist. The world through which they move is similarly a motley assemblage of present and past, Old West and sci-fi future, a jumble of anachronisms and shards of incompatible genres. Moreover, Slinger himself is an essentially oxymoronic figure, the gunslinger who is also a metaphysician (see II.74), as are other characters, including Lil, the whore who is ultimately revealed to be the avatar of a goddess (IIII.171–77), and the living-dead figure of "I," literally a walking oxymoron.

It is just here, however, that a crucial difference begins to emerge between *Harlem Gallery* and *Gunslinger;* for while the heterogeneity of characters in Tolson's poem is basically sociological and psychological, the heterogeneity of Dorn's characters is ontological. Divine and semidivine figures mingle with mere mortals, humans with talking animals and sentient inanimate objects. This is not so much a world constructed on several ontological planes, as a world in which several planes seem to have telescoped into one. More generally, *Harlem Gallery* observes external verisimilitude, and does not admit fantastic elements; furthermore, we infer that its world lies all on one ontological plane, that there are no other worlds beyond this one. *Gunslinger,* by contrast, *does* admit fantastic elements. Its world accommodates philosophical horses and talking barrels; its physics is often that of comic books and animated cartoons. The Gunslinger himself routinely performs miracles, winning his gunfights not because of his speed on the draw, but evidently through some kind of alteration of time itself (I.28–31, II.74–75). Beyond the world in which the action of the poem unfolds, we catch glimpses of another world, whose emissaries visit ours. The Gunslinger himself is one such emissary, a demigod or "extraTerrestrial" (II.59) who arrives from some other world at the poem's beginning and returns there at its end. Another otherworldly visitation is the delivery, by mailplane, of the posthumous letter from Parmenides' secretary, none other than the late "I," who evidently resides in some realm of the dead. Indeed, all the episodes surrounding "I"'s death, posthumous communication, and return from the dead resonate strongly with the ancient Menippean motifs, described by Bakhtin, of threshold dialogues (i.e., dialogues on the threshold of the other world) and dialogues of the dead.

Moreover, Dorn has peopled his poem not only with characters belonging to different orders of being (some "higher" than human, some "lower"), but also with characters some of whom originate in no world whatsoever, but rather in discourse. Consider the Speaking Barrel who suddenly joins the Gunslinger's party in book IIII (187–94, 197–98): where does he come from, if not from the fixed idiom, "cracker-barrel philosopher"? For that matter, consider the Gunslinger's talking horse; surely he literalizes the idiom, "straight from the horse's mouth" (see II.74). These are figures not so much in the sense of characters, as in the sense of figures of speech—walking, talking idioms. If every character in every verbal text is "made out of language" in a certain sense, characters like the Speaking Barrel and the talking horse are made out of language in a peculiarly literal sense of that expression. Their coexistence in the same world with quasi-realistic characters amounts to a violation of "ontological decorum" (Knapp 61), a form of "ontological promiscuity" (Castle 102)—yet another ontological scandal in a text rife with such scandals.

No such illicit mingling of figures in the character sense and animated figures of speech occurs in *Harlem Gallery*. Or does it? Who are these exotic personages, "the seeress Nix" and Élan, "the artist's undivorceable spouse," who abruptly intrude upon the scene in section "Delta" (221)? Who is this "Marquise de Matrix" who all but takes over section "Theta" (244–45)? One answer is that they are merely personifications; but there is no "merely" about it, for where there is traffic between figures of discourse and figures of the world, as in the instances I have just cited, it is precisely there that a degree of Menippean heterogeneity reasserts itself, quite counter to the general tendency in *Harlem Gallery* toward ontological homogeneity and single-plane reality. *Harlem Gallery* may not be a full-fledged Menippean satire in its ontological structure, but it does share with *Gunslinger* a scandalous ontological promiscuity with regard to figures of speech.

III. POP-UP FIGURES

[H]ere I have donated 3000 objects of African and Oceanic art to the Met and they've escaped to Harlem where they are partying and catching Ruby and the Romantics at Sugar Ray's.

Ishmael Reed ("Cab Calloway" 302)

In *Gunslinger*, Robert von Hallberg observes, metaphors "insinuate themselves from the figurative to the literal level": "literalizing is a convention of the poem" ("Marvellous" 73; cf. also Foster 101). I would go further and argue that it is the dominant convention of the poem, the one that organizes, focuses, and connects most if not all of its other conventions —the one, moreover, that marks the poem as a postmodernist text and simultaneously roots it in the long genre history of Menippean satire.

Von Hallberg has in mind literalized figures like "cracker-barrel philosopher" or "straight from the horse's mouth," or, one that he actually discusses, "to catch one's breath":

Would you like a light
I see yor roach has gone out
continued the Doctor Catching his breath

Slinger, did you flash how
the PHD caught his breath,
never saw anybody do it with their *hand*
(II.81)

These are all "dead" figures—"to catch one's breath," "straight from the horse's mouth," and so on—that is, idioms no longer normally experienced as figurative at all. Paradoxically, their figurativeness is revivified when they are literalized. Not only dead figures come in for this treatment, however; Dorn is just as capable of literalizing newly coined ones. Consider this simile: the Slinger's "mind hung bat-like/from the rafters of the Burlington Arcade" (IIII.187). On first encountering this, we can read it no other way than figuratively (minds "hang" only figuratively, and there is no Burlington Arcade anywhere in the literal vicinity). A little over a page later, however, we are thrown into doubt, as Portland Bill arrives and addresses the Slinger (here inexplicably called "Zlinger"):

That's a grotesque exercise
you got down there
he addressed the Zlinger
who was still suspended
in his mental hanger [sic]
we the only spectators here?
(IIII.187)

The "exercise" to which Bill refers is presumably the battle unfolding on the plain below between Robart's troops and his enemies, the mysterious Single Spacers. Unless, that is, he is actually referring to the Slinger's upside-down ("bat-like") meditative posture. Does Portland Bill perceive the Slinger to be literally "suspended," or is this still "only" a figure of speech? Should we literalize? Or, more to the point, do we have any choice *but* to literalize? Try as we might to expunge it, the image lingers of the Gunslinger literally suspended upside-down, deep in thought (but where? in a "hangar"?).[9]

Many of these literalized figures hinge on puns, "Dorn's favorite trope" (Perloff, "Introduction" xv; cf. also Beach 228; Jenkins 228–29). Normally, punning is entirely a discursive phenomenon, a matter of alternative meanings competing for the same homophone, and a number of Dorn's puns are of this type, e.g., his pun on *literal/littoral* ("We must have a Littoral instance," II.80), and the even more egregious pun on *hostile,* here spelled hostyle (as in hoss-style or, worse, whore-style; the context supports both possibilities, I.24). Other puns, however, equivocate not only between alternative meanings, but also between figurative and literal ontological status. An example occurs near the beginning of *The Cycle* (90), when Robart boards his private railway car in Boston South Station incognito, disguised ("decoyed") as "the cheeze in a burger." What explains this grotesque detail? Simply that the railway car, being at the same time an allegorical "wingèd car" (see below), requires a "long take-off roll" in order to lift off the ground; thus it is the pun on "roll" that generates the cheeseburger disguise![10] Punning similarly underwrites the literalization of a figure in book IIII, when the manager of the

Café Sahagún in Cortez, Colorado, informs one of the Gunslinger's traveling-companions, the hippie hitchhiker Kool Everything, "youd make a fair bandit." This makes adequate literal sense in a Wild-West context, but in fact the manager is punning on "one-armed bandit," i.e., slot machine; how else to explain the fact that he has just stuck his index finger in Everything's ear and cranked him?

> Everythings eyes spun.
> Two plumbs, the manager shouted
> hanging on to Everythings tongue
> too bad you only got two eyes
> youd make a fair bandit
> (IIII.156)

Thanks to what Pynchon calls the "high magic to low puns" (*Crying*, 96), Kool Everything has been (momentarily) transformed into a literal slot machine. What might have remained a punning figure has been upgraded to a fantastic reality.

A special case of punning, running like a thread throughout the entire poem, involves the use of grammatical words as characters' proper names: the pronoun "everything" in one case, the shifter pronoun "I" in another.[11] Asked his name on his first appearance, the unknown hitchhiker replies, "Kool Everything," which is interpreted as an imperative, so that the response comes, "We Did!/several miles back" (II.53). Apropos of his new companion's name, the Slinger remarks,

> Your surname I find hard
> to place, its *generalness*
> is overwhelming (II.53)

When is "everything" general, and when is it "proper" to one person? When Kool Everything begins explaining to the Slinger a new device called the Literate Projector (see below), the latter seizes on a fundamental ambiguity in his account:

> This kinda talkie sounds new.
> It's a revolutionary medium
> It's sure to turn everything around.

Sounds as tho it's meant only for you
commented the Slinger.

That's the trouble with a name like mine
What I mean is Everybody—
A tangible change, the Slinger noticed.
(II.75-76)[12]

The quibbling continues right to the end of the poem, where, in a final pun, Slinger takes leave of his companion and of our world at same time: "Goodbye to Everything" (IIII.200). (See also III.137 and IIII.184 for further puns on Kool Everything's name.)

More radical still are the consequences of punning on "I," the discursive marker of subjectivity (see Golding, "History"; P. Murphy 44-45; Jenkins 210-17; and especially Foster). The poem *Gunslinger*, at least in book I, appears to emanate from an unnamed first-person narrator; the poem's first word is in fact the first-person pronoun—"I met in Mesilla/ The Cautious Gunslinger" (I.3). Throughout book I, "I" behaves normally, shifting in meaning depending upon which speaker has the floor, and reverting in narrative passages to the narrator. Only at the moment of this narrator's sudden death in book II is it revealed that "I" was actually his proper name: "I is dead, the poet said," to which Lil protests, "*That aint grammatical, Poet*" (II.56). Indeed it is not, but there is no way to reconcile reality and grammar from this moment forward, death having driven a wedge between the two meanings of I," "I" as shifter and "I" as proper name. Subsequently revived by a transfusion of acid, and having become a "walking Tautology" (i.e., "I is I"?), "I" provokes an outburst in Everything, to whom the acid belonged and who had plans of his own for it:

> Kool exploded
> I was going to retire on that batch!
>
> *I has,* the Slinger corrected,
> at which Everything fell to the ground
> (II.67)

The pun on one pronoun provokes a pun on the other, and the entire literal context collapses (literally falls to the ground). "I"'s return from the dead in book IIII occasions a fresh bout of punning on his name, and seems to generate a series of knock-on literalizations of other figures, as if by a sort of discursive domino-effect:

I comes thru the door
twirling his psychognosis
in his fingers
and throws it at affective intervals
into the air
like a texas cheerleader
and when he drops it behind his back
which is quite often, according to the formula,
he turns around to pick it up
with a dainty bending of the knees
and an expression of Oh-that-doesnt-matter
on his vibrant lips

(IIII.153)

Literalization of figures of speech is clearly related to the trope of personification; indeed, the former constitutes something like the deep structure of the latter (see Paxson 35–62). Literalization of puns, in particular, is related to the narrative mode in which personification flourishes, namely allegory. In allegories, the unfolding of the narrative world is often driven by the systematic literalization of figures of speech, especially puns (see Quilligan). This connection between punning and allegory is fully borne out by *Gunslinger*, a poem saturated with puns and one that continually flirts with allegory, slipping in and out of the allegorical mode (see Davidson, "To eliminate" 117, 130; Lockwood). For instance, the misadventures of "I" and "Everything," whose names provide so many opportunities for punning, clearly invite interpretation as allegories of the decentering of the self and the "death of the subject" (Foster 82), while Robart seems to function as a personification of capitalism itself.

Allegory presents two different and apparently incompatible faces. It can be seen, on the one hand, as a process of ontological inflation, the "blowing-up" of "flat" verbal figures (*error is a monster, monstrous error*) into a semblance of "roundness" and three-dimensionality (the monster *Errour* in her den, surrounded by her offspring, etc.); on the other hand, it can be seen as a process of ontological impoverishment and deflation, the "flattening-out" of characters, landscapes, and other elements of fictional reality into dimensionless, merely verbal figures, mere personifications. In fact, many allegorical narratives (*The Faerie Queene* is a good example) deploy the two processes successively, filling figures out to something like the volume of fully fledged realities one moment, then the next moment deflating them again, emptying them of reality and letting them subside back into discourse (see Quilligan 67–68; McHale, *Postmodernist Fiction* 145–46). One moment, a masque, in which personifications spring into three-dimensional life; the next moment, a tapestry, in which living realities are reduced to patterns in a fabric.

As a matter of fact, *Gunslinger* has been compared both to a masque and to a tapestry (see Davidson, "Archaeologist" 159, 171 and "To eliminate" 117, 130). The tapestry figure, indeed, is Dorn's own, from the opening of book II:

> This tapestry moves
> as the morning lights up.
> And they who are in it move
> and love its moving
> (II.45)

One moment, Dorn's puns and other figures of speech spring into 3-D reality like the performers in an allegorical masque, the next moment they lapse into the discursive flatness of a tapestry. Or perhaps we need to update our model and speak instead of pop-up figures, by analogy, with those children's books where cardboard cutouts, flush with the plane of the page, physcially spring up when the page is opened to form a tableau, a miniature world, and then flatten out again when the page is turned.[13] Open the book, and flat figures spring up into tableaux: "straight from the horse's mouth" becomes a talking horse, a pun on "roll" becomes Robart disguised as cheese in a cheeseburger. Turn the page, and 3-D realities flatten out into figures of speech, flush with the plane of discourse: the narrator "I" becomes an allegory (the Poet, sampling Kool Everything's acid, says, "this would turn one into an allegory" [II.60], and so it does when it is administered posthumously to "I"); a horse owner, miraculously defeated by the Slinger in a gunfight, undergoes before our eyes a metamorphosis into an allegorical sculpture:

> the Owners hulk
> settled into a sort of permanence
> as if a ship, gone to the bottom
> shifts several ways into the sand
> while finding her millenial restingplace.

> It has become an Old Rugged Statue
> of the good old days, Everything gasped
> a summary of accounts compiled
> from frontier newspapers
> (II.75)

Emptied of ontological volume, the character sinks into a mere personification—moreover, a personification literally made of words (as, indeed, all personifications literally are).

Allegorical processes of popping up and flattening out, realization and de-realization, are particularly associated with Robart's "wingèd car," described at length in "The Cycle." The car itself has impeccable allegorical credentials, descending as it does from the car that the pre-Socratic philosopher Parmenides of Elea mounted for a trip to heaven in the allegorical "Proem" to his only extant philosophical work (Kirk, Raven, and Schofield 2439–62.). The car is staffed by allegorical personifications of Fear, Surrender, and Indignation ("The Cycle," 90, 91, 102), as well as by "*living* Atlantes, a race of half-column half-man" (102), in effect allegorical caryatids who serve as Robart's personal entourage (see Michelson 199). It is unclear whether these Atlantes should be regarded as personnel or furniture—both, presumably—but Robart's favorite among them, the one called Al but code-named Rupert, comes fully equipped with iconological trappings (see Lockwood 173) such as one might expect to find on civic monuments or allegorical frontispieces: he has a sundial "Mounted in the palm of His hand" and "a Star finder in the head of *His* cock" (101), as well as cuneiform signs tattooed or engraved below his ears

(104). Robart's car, with its crew of semicharacters, semipersonifications, foregrounds in its paradoxical structure the very process of de-literalization, of loss of ontological volume and the collapse into textuality; for its interior space is reported to be peculiarly volumeless, as if two- rather than three-dimensional: "The space has *no* front it's *All* rear" (98). Consequently, within the car "There are no *things* there as such" (98), or at any rate such things as are to be found there are correspondingly flattened, reduced to two-dimensional images:

> The furnishings are all strictly flat
> That is, if you see a chair to sit in
> You sit in the image of that chair
> You fry an egg in the image of the skillet
> (102)

If reality were a pop-up book, this presumably is what it would be like to live inside it.

Robart's winged car is an allegorical figure for the allegorical process—a figure of figuration, a metafigure (see Paxson 156–57). Nor is it the only such metafigure to be found in *Gunslinger*. Another is the Literate Projector, a device that converts visual reality into words on a screen, i.e., collapses the world into text, de-realizes reality (II.76). Robart's car isn't even the only literalized pun on "vehicle": another is the car that Dr. Flamboyant is driving when he re-enters the poem in book IIII, "a bright green 1976 Avocado/with a white vinyl top" (IIII.166). Appropriately, this hyperbolic vehicle comes equipped with what else but a "full hyperbolic clutch"; i.e., Flamboyant arrives in a literalized vehicle of the figure of hyperbole.[14] More generally, *Gunslinger* is metafigural from beginning to end, in the sense that its characters seem to be self-conscious about the allegorical status of their world. That is, they seem at least partly and sporadically aware of being themselves personifications in an allegorical text—of living in a pop-up book. They attribute allegorical status to one another and to the situations through which they pass; they produce allegorical readings of *Gunslinger* itself. For instance, the Poet proposes the following allegorical interpretation of the Slinger's horses (presumably including his talking horse) and incidentally of the very quest on which they are engaged: "Your horses," he tells Slinger,

personify the striving after knowledge
the road along which we drive symbolizes
. . . .
our thinking process
(II.120)

Literally between these lines the Slinger interrupts the Poet to remind
him that "Symbolize/and Personify/is a mimicry of Earth Habits," and
so presumably don't apply to him, a semidios and "extraTerrestrial." But
of course Symbolize and Personify *do* apply to him; semidios though he
may be, he subsists within the same pop-up book as the other, mortal
characters, subject to the same alternation of popping up and flattening
out, realization and de-realization.

Pop-up figuration, then, seems to be central to Dorn's poetics in *Gunslinger*, and its presence marks his poem as characteristically postmodernist (see McHale, *Postmodernist Fiction* 140–47). Until now I have left
it an open question, however, whether or how such figuration functions
in Tolson's *Harlem Gallery*. Typically, Tolson's use of figures has been regarded, along with his allusiveness, as among those features that testify
most decisively to his high-modernist affiliations. Critics have tended to
prejudge the case by opting for modernist (that is, New Critical) terminology to describe Tolson's figuration (see, e.g., K. Shapiro, "Introduction"; Schroeder; G. Thompson). To associate a poet's figures with metaphysical or baroque conceits, or to ascribe to them such qualities as
ambiguity, difficulty, tension, etc., is to place them in a particular interpretive framework. But is modernist poetics the only appropriate context
for understanding Tolson's figures? Is there any other context in which
they might be understood otherwise than as the metaphors of a modernist epigone?

There is. As some of Tolson's critics have appreciated, it is also possible
to understand his figuration in the light of African-American vernacular
practice. Virtuoso troping, hyperbolic and litotic figures, riddling and
cryptic imagery, the down-home surrealism of blues lyrics—these are all
features of African-American vernacular performance, and it is as legitimate to approach Tolson from this perspective as from the perspective
of high-modernist metaphor (see, e.g., Nielsen, *Writing* 58–59, who follows Henderson 33–46). As the Curator himself observes, "Metaphors

and symbols in Spirituals and Blues/have been the Negro's manna in the Great White World" ("Xi" 91).

Tolson's connections with vernacular practice are particularly pronounced in those episodes of *Harlem Gallery* involving the informal verbal competitions of the Zulu Club Wits. As I suggested earlier, these competitions amount to a version of the dozens for intellectuals. Most of these exchanges hinge on the production and/or interpretation of figures of speech. In some exchanges, contestants compete for control of a conceit's implications;[15] in others, they trade sly insults couched in metaphors. Some of these insults involve literalizing idioms; thus, if Nkomo can be associated with a brush turkey ("Only an Aristotelian metaphorist," Nkomo marvels, "could conjure up an image like *that!*", "Upsilon" 308), the Curator with a tailor bird (316), and a prominent Harlem preacher with a turkey-gobbler ("Chi" 338), this is because there exists in the language an idiom (a dead metaphor) that underlies all these variant figures:

> The Curator of this variegated aviary on
> Black Manhattan
> emerged as a *strange* bird
> ("Upsilon" 309)

It is only a short metaphorical step from literalizing the idiom "strange bird," to comparing the entire Zulu Club to an aviary of such birds (see G. Thompson 167–68). Other figures that circulate among the Zulu Club Wits in their verbal play achieve literalization in a different way. One such figure is that of the whore, evidently a Zulu Club favorite: Happiness is personified as a "bitch who plays with crooked dice/the game of love" ("Theta" 246), Western culture as a whorish "Jezebel/with falsies on her buttocks" ("Upsilon" 308), even the poet is figured as a whore ("you and I belong to the people," says the poet Hideho to the prostitute Lena, "Nu" 268), and so on. Since these personifications circulate among habitués of the Zulu Club, a place frequented by literal prostitutes, one has the illusion of figures of speech "insinuating themselves from the figurative to the literal level," as Von Hallberg says of Dorn.

But of course it is only an illusion; no such literalization of figures actually transpires here. The Curator never literally becomes a bird in the way that Kool Everything, in Dorn's poem, becomes a slot machine, and the Zulu Club demimondaines continue to exist entirely independently of the Wits' sexist personifications. No figures pop up from the plane of discourse into the poem's world—or at least, not in these Zulu Club episodes, where the distinction between the characters' discourse and the narrative that frames that discourse, between what characters say and the world in which they say it, is scrupulously maintained (as it is not in *Gunslinger*). To the extent that discursive figures remain "merely" discursive, merely the words of characters playing the dozens, to the extent that they are contained, they can do no ontological damage. But what about those sections of *Harlem Gallery* in which no one speaks except the Curator, namely sections "Alpha" through "Epsilon" at the beginning, "Theta" later on, and "Psi" and "Omega" at the end? Here there is little or no narrative framing of the discourse; everything is discourse, top-to-bottom, wall-to-wall. Do Tolson's figures behave any differently here?

The Curator as monologuist is as lavish with metaphor as he is when playing the dozens with fellow Zulu Club Wits. Indeed, almost nothing in his solo discourse is *not* figurative, and some of these figures ramify into elaborate vignettes:

> Tonic spasms of wind and wave
> assail compass and lamp in the cabined night;
> but the binnacle of imagination
> steers the work of art aright—
> . . . .
> As for the critic,
> he is the fid
> that bolsters the topmost mast
> of Art—an argosy of plunder
> from the kingdoms of race and class and caste.
> ("Omega" 357, 359)

The work of art as sailing vessel: it is this sort of figure that prompts critics (who would no doubt be reminded here of the "love as a ship" *topos* of Renaissance Petrarchan poetry) to speak in terms of metaphysical or baroque conceits. Such conceits seem to open out into miniature worlds, enclaves within discourse possessing their own minor reality, quite independent of the reality of the *Harlem Gallery* world outside.

Their independence of the outside world is reinforced by the specialized vocabulary they exhibit—*binnacle, fid* (the bar that supports the top-mast), *mast,* and so on—which overlaps at no point with the styles and registers "native" to the poem's real world. It is as if we glimpsed through these figures, as through a window, a parallel maritime world subsisting in some other dimension, to which the Curator's discourse gives us access from time to time:

> the good ship *Défineznegro*
> sailed fine, under an unabridged moon,
> to reach the archipelago
> Nigeridentité.
> In the Strait of Octoroon,
> off black Scylla,
> after the typhoon Phobos, out of the Stereotypus Sea,
> had rived her hull and sail to a T,
> the *Défineznegro* sank the rock [sic]
> and disappeared in the abyss
> . . . .
> of white Charybdis
>
> ("Psi" 354)

There is no point of contact between this miniature world and the "main" world of *Harlem Gallery*—except by way of interpreting the allegory; otherwise the two worlds, major and minor, form no continuum as worlds. Other figures, however, do sometimes "leak" into the major reality to some extent. This is the case, for instance, with the elaborate vinicultural figure of "Psi" (348–49), where the acquisition of high culture is figured in terms of learning to disinguish fine wines. As the figure unfolds, however, it functions less and less as a figure, and increasingly as an exemplum, a miniature episode illustrating the acquisition of high culture: a cultured person is someone not likely to be conned by the wine waiter. The world of the figure imperceptibly joins the world of the poem, the former becoming (or almost becoming) merely an episode of the latter.

This sort of leakage is not typical of the Curator's figurative discourse, however. More typical is the tendency of these figures to separate themselves from the main world, to the point of threatening to put down ontological roots of their own, as it were, and grow into freestanding microworlds. This tendency is especially prounounced in the case of the miniature allegorical landscapes, or *paysages moralisés*, that abound in the Curator's monologues (see Paxson 42–43.) Art, as we have seen, can be figured as a sailing vessel, but it can also be figured as a landscape feature—a river, say—or as a city in a landscape:

> Many mouths empty their waters
> into the Godavari of Art—
> a river that flows
> across the Decan trap of the age
> with its lava-scarred plateaux
> ("Omega" 356)

> The mecca Art is a babel city in the people's Shinar
> with a hundred gates
> and busybody roads
> that stretch beyond all dates,
> where sweating pilgrims fleshed in hallelujahs
> jostle like cars in a bumping race
> ("Gamma" 216)

If a landscape is always a synecdoche for a world—the part that stands for the whole, the tip of the iceberg—then somewhere, we infer, there must exist some separate world or worlds to which these pocket allegorical landscapes belong.

Now it only remains to people such worlds. (The "sweating pilgrims" of the city of Art count more as landscape features than people.) Just as it abounds with allegorical landscapes, the Curator's discourse also teems with allegorical personifications, most of them conventionally female. I have mentioned a number of them in other contexts: the lesbian seeress Nix, and Élan, "the artist's undivorceable spouse" ("Delta" 221), as well as the crooked *belle dame*, Happiness ("Theta" 246). Happiness, it turns out, is a "distant cousin" of "Art, the woman Pleasure" who "makes no blind dates,/but keeps the end of the tryst with one" ("Theta" 246); and so on. Combine such personifications with an allegorical landscape, and one has something approaching a complete microworld, which is indeed the case in section "Theta," where, in Vanity's allegorical castle

("the *château en Espagne* of Vanity"), the Marquise de Matrix wittily lectures her party guests about aesthetics ("Something there is in Art that
does not love a wall"; "What dread hand can unmix/pink and yellow?").
The world she inhabits derives from multiple sources: a literary allusion
(to Bunyan's *Pilgrim's Progress*), a literalized idiom ("to build castles in
Spain"), even a historical parallel (the house parties at the Harlem heir-
ess A'Lelia Walker's Villa Lewaro during the Renaissance years, where
Reed sets the climactic revelation scene of *Mumbo Jumbo*). More crucial
than its genealogy, however, is its ontology: it does *not* belong to the
world of *Harlem Gallery*. Freestanding, it constitutes a world of its own.

This is as close as Tolson comes in *Harlem Gallery* to pop-up figuration of the *Gunslinger* type. The marquise's house-party world almost
leaps the gap from discourse to world as, say, Robart's wingèd car does
in *Gunslinger;* but not quite. The unruly rhetorical figures thronging the
Curator's discourse—his distended conceits, fragments of allegorical
landscapes, walking prosopopoeias, literalized verbal clichés, and so on
—threaten constantly to pop up from their discursive flatness, assume
three-dimensional volume, and claim a foothold in the world of the
poem. They threaten to do so, but without ever quite managing the trick,
not even in the freestanding allegorical world of section "Theta." Aspir-
ing to reality, they press against the fragile membrane separating discourse from world, but without in the end succeeding in rupturing it.

Meanwhile, on the other side of that membrane, the allegedly "real"
characters of the poem appear suspiciously "flat." Bearing names hardly
less cartoonish than those of Dorn's characters, they behave more like
characters in animated cartoons than like those in realist novels or films,
more 2-D than 3-D. They appear flat everywhere, in the Curator's monologues just as in the narrative episodes, but nowhere more so than in the
Harlem Vignettes, the poem-cycle attributed to Mister Starks, incorporated in section "Upsilon" as an inset text. Perhaps Tolson sought to dif-
ferentiate the second-order representations of *Harlem Vignettes* from the
first-order representations of *Harlem Gallery* by rendering the former
less realistically than the latter, in the same way, say, that Shakespeare
deliberately used more primitive stage technique in the inset play *The
Mouse-Trap* in order to distinguish it sharply from the world of *Hamlet.*
Whatever the motive, the result in Tolson's case is to drain the characters
of what little ontological substance they possessed, reducing them to
bare outlines, or to words on a page—literally:

Ma'am Shears

Her character was a cliché in the *Book of Homilies;*
and *what she was* was as legible
    as a Spencerian address
in the window of an envelope.
                                    ("Upsilon" 305)

Like the horse owner transformed into an Old Rugged Statue in *Gunslinger*, Ma'am Shears collapses into textuality: a cliché, a homily, a legible handwritten address. One blinks at that "Spencerian," but no, Tolson has in mind a style of penmanship, not the Renaissance allegorist; but he might as well have intended Spenser-with-an-s, since Ma'am Shears flattens out into a mere figure of speech, like some Spenserian character reduced before our eyes to a personification (see Paxson 154–55).

Or rather, she almost does. For just as the poem's figures of speech press toward realization, toward joining the poem's real world, without ever quite achieving it, so its figures in the other sense—its real characters—press in the opposite direction, approaching dangerously near to the condition of allegories, but again without ever quite crossing the line and suffering the kind of ontological collapse that that would entail. Under pressure from both sides, the membrane nevertheless holds.

IV. FUNNY PAPERS

1 of these days 1 of our sons, perhaps the son of a Polish immigrant,
will emerge from some steel town in Pennsylvania and mount a
turd on the wall of a museum and make it stick . . . and when you
ask him what it is he will put on his dark glasses and snub you the
way you did us.
                          Ishmael Reed (*Mumbo Jumbo* 127)

Flatness in characterization is typically associated with popular culture: with "genre" fictions such as Westerns, science fiction, or romance, with stereotyping in movies and television, and so on. But it is also associated with various high-art practices, notably satire, including Menippean satire, which generally eschews naturalistic characterization. The two types of flatness, "high" and "low," interestingly overlap at various points, for instance in the visual-arts practice of caricature. A form of visual satire, caricature—realism's disreputable double—lived a kind of shadowy existence on the margins of Western art until the twentieth century, when it not only entered but came to pervade the mainstream of modernist art (see Varnedoe and Gopnik 101–51). Caricature animates many of the new forms of visual representation in the modernist period, including much of the visual art of the Harlem Renaissance; one detects its influence, for instance, in the flat silhouettes of Aaron Douglas, the genre scenes of Palmer Hayden, the deliberately "primitive" stylizations of Jacob Lawrence and William H. Johnson, even the collages of Romare Bearden (see Campbell et al.; Reynolds and Wright; Powell et al.). The flatness of characterization in Tolson's Harlem Gallery invites comparison with the caricatural art of these Harlem Renaissance artists, and with the caricatural dimension of modernist visual art generally (see Farnsworth, Plain Talk 232, 243, 252). In the course of the poem itself ("Zeta" 328; "Upsilon" 317; "Omega" 357), Tolson mentions a number of caricaturists (Hogarth, Daumier) and mainstream modernists influenced by caricature (Picasso, William Gropper); we infer that he regards these artists as models and visual analogues for his own caricatural art.

However, none of these "high" artists—neither the models he himself names, nor any of the "legitimate" visual artists of the Harlem Renaissance—seems as close in spirit to Tolson's characterization as the Renaissance-era caricaturist, Miguel Covarrubias. A Mexican graphic artist, resident in New York from 1923 to 1936, Covarrubias was introduced to the fashionable Harlem cabaret scene by literary and show-business friends, and soon developed a career as caricaturist of Harlem Renaissance celebrities and nightlife. His caricatures appeared in such conspicuous publications as Vanity Fair, and on the jackets of Langston Hughes's first book of poetry, The Weary Blues (1925), W. C. Handy's The Blues: An Anthology (1926), and Zora Neale Hurston's Mules and Men (1935); he published a volume of his Negro Drawings in 1927 (Nelson, Repression 312 n.232; Varnedoe and Gopnik 136; A. Williams).[16] We wince today at what appears the manifest racism of Covarrubias's African-American "types," and indeed some winced even at the time (see, e.g., A. Williams 271–72, n.59); but it seems clear that his caricatures were animated not by any impulse to demean his subjects, but rather by the same sense of discovery in the face of this unprecedented phenomenon, the "New Negro," that animated the Harlem Renaissance writers and artists themselves. Given his extreme ambivalence toward popular culture, Tolson might well have resented the association of *Harlem Gallery* with the work of a magazine caricaturist, but it is hard not to see in the stylized, antinaturalistic flatness of Tolson's Harlemites something more akin to Covarrubias's Harlem caricatures than to any of the more prestigious models Tolson himself cites.

Tolson could have sought models for "flatness" elsewhere in popular visual art, for instance in the comics; he might even have come across an appropriate Renaissance-era master to emulate, namely the African-American cartoonist George Herriman, whose daily *Krazy Kat* strip began appearing about 1913. No doubt Tolson would have found it at least as difficult to acknowledge Herriman as a model as to knowledge Covarrubias; not so Ishmael Reed, however, who dedicated *Mumbo Jumbo* to "George Herriman, Afro-American," and whose own poetics, in *Yellow Back Radio Broke-Down* as well as *Mumbo Jumbo*—indeed throughout his career from the sixties on—has been profoundly influenced by comics (see Reed's 1979 interview, Dick and Singh 181–82; also Lindroth; Fox 83; McGee 26). Here is another point where Reed and Dorn strikingly converge, for *Gunslinger*, too, draws inspiration from comics and animated cartoons. In a text saturated with allusions to popular culture, it is only to be expected that Dorn would occasionally allude to specific cartoon characters—e.g., Dick Tracy (II.71, 108), Daffy Duck (IIII.169), etc. More to the point, however, his characters and their world seem shaped throughout by the visual and narrative norms of various genres of cartooning, including superhero comic books, animated cartoons (Wile E. Coyote, Quickdraw McGraw), underground comics (Robert Crumb), perhaps even Herriman, whose Coconino County landscapes of the *Krazy Kat* strip may well have contributed something to the landscapes of *Gunslinger*. Moreover, Dorn himself has collaborated on comic-book projects: not only was one of the installments of *Gunslinger* originally published with cartoon illustrations, but a later book, *Recollections of Gran Apachería* (1974), actually appeared in simulated comic-book format.[17] Thus, just as *Harlem Gallery* seems to aspire to the condition of Covarrubias's caricatures (though no doubt without Tolson's conscious knowledge), so *Gunslinger* seems to aspire to the condition of comics.

If caricature has been a point of overlap between "high" and "low" in the visual arts throughout the twentieth century, so has comics, though in this case the overlap began in a significant way only after midcentury, especially from the sixties on (see Varnedoe and Gopnik 153–229). Beginning in the sixties, the pop art movement explored the high-art potential of comics and other "low" visual materials. Since *Gunslinger* is roughly contemporaneous with pop, some critics have wanted to see in Dorn's use of comics evidence of his affiliation with the pop movement, even going so far as to identify specific models and analogues—e.g., Jim Dine and Larry Rivers (Perloff, "Introduction" vi), or Warhol (Michelson 190). But in fact it would be hard, on the basis of textual evidence from *Gunslinger*, to infer much direct knowledge of specific pop art imagery or artists on Dorn's part. Perhaps his special mention of Dick Tracy attests to that character's centrality in the iconography of the pop movement, dating from Warhol's early (1960) hand-painted image of the comic-strip detective.[18] Apart from this one doubtful allusion, however, all other traces of Warhol in *Gunslinger* are indirect at best,[19] while allusions, direct or otherwise, to other pop artists seem to me entirely lacking. Nevertheless, Dorn does share at least one thing in common with his Pop contemporaries in the visual arts, and that is his ambivalent attitude toward the popular culture he appears to celebrate. While Dorn is generally more receptive toward popular culture than Tolson—as the pop artists were incomparably more receptive than their abstract expressionist predecessors—he nevertheless maintains a certain ironic and critical distance from his pop materials, much as (at least under one interpretation) the pop artists themselves did. That distance varies, perhaps, but it is always there, preventing *Gunslinger* from lapsing into the status of a pop artifact itself—a comic book without the pictures, or a versified Western.[20]

If Dorn's affiliation with pop art seems tenuous at best—a matter of a shared general attitude rather than shared imagery or aesthetics—Tolson's is nonexistent. Strangely for a poem so preoccupied with the place of the artist in the contemporary world, *Harlem Gallery* shows no awareness of contemporary art—that is, art of the sixties. "Where," Bérubé (105) pointedly asks, "in a poem whose temporal range extends to the Kennedy administration, are Jackson Pollock, Robert Motherwell, Willem de Kooning?" There is no mention in *Harlem Gallery* of any midcentury art movement—not abstract expressionism, and certainly not pop. In particular, there is no trace of them on the walls of the Harlem Gallery itself; no trace, for instance, of someone like Norman Lewis (1909–1979), said to be the only African-American among the abstract expressionists.

One would think that a Harlem Gallery of African-American art would make a point of exhibiting the Black painters working in the most current modes. But then again, it is not clear that the Gallery belongs to the sixties at all, rather than to the forties, say, or even the twenties; consequently it is not clear what the "most current modes" might be.[21] So if it seems doubtful to relate Dorn's comics-style flatness to the flatness of pop art, how much more of a stretch must it be to try relating Tolson's flatness to that of an art movement of which he shows no awareness whatsoever.

And yet, and yet . . . there really *does* seem to be more to the analogy than can be exhausted by the hypothesis of a shared "flatness." For pop not only flattens out images against the picture plane, it also blows them up again; in other words, it exploits exactly the same tensions between ontological fullness and emptiness, volume and flatness, realization and de-realization, that *Harlem Gallery* and *Gunslinger* exploit through their special uses of figuration. Pop, said Roland Barthes, is "ontological" art (373). Some variants of pop style generate ontological tension by juxtaposing illusionistic imagery with "flat," abstract painted passages (e.g., Larry Rivers, in paintings like *Washington Crossing the Delaware*). Other pop variants do so by rendering ontologically "full" (even over-full, hyper-full) subject matter using a technique that drains and flattens it (e.g., Roy Lichtenstein's benday dots, Warhol's silk screens of celebrities and tabloid disasters). Some pop images literally explode out of the two-dimensional picture-plane into the three-dimensional space of the room: Rauschenberg's "combines"; the real objects juxtaposed with flat, stylized painted figures in Tom Wesselman's "Great American Nudes" series; Red Grooms's 3-D "sculpto-pictoramas." We have learned to call all these image-making practices, diverse as they are, by the same name, pop, because of their common receptiveness to popular visual materials; but perhaps we need to learn also to think of them in terms of the common strategy that they share with *Harlem Gallery* and *Gunslinger*— pop-*up.*

What more perfect expression of pop as pop-up could there conceivably be than a pop pop-up book? In 1988, the pop artist Red Grooms collaborated with "paper engineers" to produce a miniature version, in the form of a pop-up book, of a full-scale "sculpto-pictorama" originally constructed some time earlier, in 1975–76, the very years when Edward Dorn was completing his own "pop-up book," *Gunslinger.* It is almost uncannily appropriate that the installation chosen for this pop-up treatment was *Ruckus Rodeo,* a huge (14 feet by 50 feet by 24 feet) tableau of bucking broncos, bull riders, rodeo clowns, cowboys and cowgirls (which may now be seen at the Modern Art Museum of Fort Worth). When pop turns pop-*up,* it seems naturally to gravitate to Dorn's Wild West subject matter; *Ruckus Rodeo* might as well be called *Gunslinger,* or vice versa.

4
Archaeologies of Knowledge

Geoffrey Hill's *Mercian Hymns* and Armand Schwerner's *The Tablets*

I. THE PRIMAL SCENE OF ARCHAEOLOGY

I turn my mind / towards delicate pillage, the provenance / of
shards glazed and unglazed
  Geoffrey Hill, "A Letter from Armenia" (*Collected Poems* 99)

The key—or *a* key, one of the keys—to Geoffrey Hill's sequence of prose
poems, *Mercian Hymns* (1971), is to be found in hymn XIII of the thirty-
hymn sequence. Here someone (the poet? as child or adult?) examines
artifacts from the eighth-century reign of Offa, King of Mercia:

> Trim the lamp; polish the lens; draw, one by one, rare
> coins to the light. Ringed by its own lustre, the
> masterful head emerges, kempt and jutting, out of
> England's well. Far from his underkingdom of crin-
> oid and crayfish, the rune-stone's province, *Rex
> Totius Anglorum Patriae,* coiffured and ageless,
> portrays the self-possession of his possession,
> cushioned on a legend.
>
> (CP 117)

Offa's masterful head emerges out of England's well in at least two
senses: in the sense of the stamped head being ringed by the raised lip
of the coin, but also in the sense of coins emerging from underground
sites where they had been deposited twelve centuries before—wells, mid-

dens. We might think of this as a representation of the "primal scene" of archaeology: the moment when a modern consciousness enters into some relation with the past through an encounter with one of its artifacts, extracted from underground; the moment of the poet's coming to know Offa and Offa's buried world—a kind of epiphany. This scene sends ripples, shock waves, throughout the whole sequence. Its traces are to be found in the recurrent motif of the coin (e.g., in hymns IV, VII, XI, XII), and it is answered, in a sense, by the last hymn (XXX):

> And it seemed, while we waited, he began to walk to-
> wards us   he vanished
>
> he left behind coins, for his lodging, and traces of
> red mud.
>
> (*CP* 134)

In order for some later consciousness to experience an archaeological primal scene, two conditions must be met: the artifact in question must have been deposited, "left behind" to be found later; and the "author" of the artifact must himself have "vanished." These two conditions, enacted by the last hymn, are captured with maximum economy by its iconic blank space between "towards us" and "he vanished." The blank space does double service: it mimes Offa's disappearance, but also mimes the hole—the well (or trench, ditch, excavation, or whatever)—from which the coin will later be recovered.

Another such archaeological primal scene, a moment of coming to know, parallel to yet different from the one in hymn XIII, occurs in tablets XXVI and XXVII of the twenty-seven *Tablets* of Armand Schwerner. Here for the first time in the sequence we are afforded a glimpse into what the text calls the "Laboratory Teachings Memoirs" of the scholar-translator whose work the text of *The Tablets* is alleged to be. Elsewhere, except for one self-revelatory note between tablets VIII and IX, we have only the most meager access to the scholar-translator's practice (as distinct from the fruit of that practice, namely the translations themselves); here, however, we learn from him at some length (XXVI and XXVII are by far the longest of the tablets) something about his underlying assumptions, translation methods, and so on. As in Hill's hymn XIII, here a modern consciousness is caught in the act of drawing an archaeological artifact into the circle of his lamplight, so to speak, and examining it. Unlike the coins of hymn XIII, however, the artifacts of tablets XXVI and XXVII can actually be shown to us because they are pictographs, the translation of which the scholar-translator discusses here, and the forms of which are reproduced (in part) in the text (Figure 1).

As in hymn XIII, this primal scene, too, sends ripples throughout the entire sequence of tablets. Indeed, it might be understood as the paradigm for all the other scenes, hidden from our view, in which each translation (we are to imagine) was produced by the scholar-translator. The scene is ubiquitous, dispersed throughout the sequence, a permanent background situation; the epiphany is diffused. Or, to put it another way, it is *we readers* who enact that primal scene and experience that epiphany every time we look into *The Tablets*, every time we turn its pages, for the translated tablets are themselves the artifacts, or as close as we will ever come to them.

Similarly ubiquitous and dispersed is the iconic blank space—the gap of disappearance and recovery—that, as we saw in the case of Hill's *Hymns*, corresponds to the archaeological primal scene. For much, if not indeed most, of Schwerner's *Tablets* is blank—missing, owing to the fragmentary character of the supposed artifacts themselves (friable clay tablets), or untranslatable owing to gaps in our knowledge of the long-dead language in which they were written. Where language fails him, the scholar-translator conscientiously inserts strings of nonalphabetic signs, indicating what kind of breakdown has occurred: plus signs (++++) for missing passages, dots of ellipsis (. . . .) for untranslatable passages, question marks (?) for variant readings, and square brackets [ ] for material supplied by the scholar-translator himself. These epistemological gaps constitute (in some places) the very fabric of the text itself (Figure 2).

Tracing the expanding ripples of these parallel primal scenes of archaeology, elucidating their differences, and unpacking these epistemological gaps in the respective texts, will be the business of this chapter.

II. ARCHAEO-POETRY

On the sideboard the tray of Stuart coins, base treasure of a bog:
and ever shall be.

James Joyce, *Ulysses* (35)

On the face of it, juxtaposing *Mercian Hymns* with *The Tablets* seems, if not incongruous and arbitrary, then at least an exercise in disproportion. Hill's *Hymns* is a pocket-sized long poem—a "pocket epic" in the British

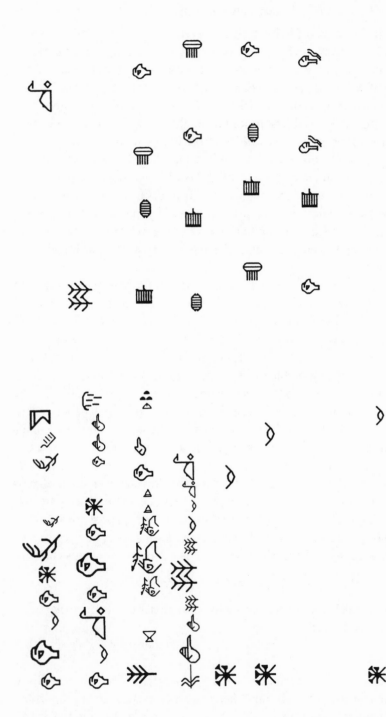

Figure 1. Pages 74–75 from Schwerner, *The Tablets*

do they destroy the ochre, the shad/shad-cod? do they eat?
they wait for the fat pig (god?)

\+ + + + + + + + + + +
\+ + + + + + + + + + + + + +
\+ + + + + + + + + +
\+ + + + + + + + + + + + + + + + + + + +
\+ + + + + + +
\+ + + + + + + + +
\+ +
. . . . of the great Ones (One?)*

*capitalization clearly indicated. The number is in doubt. Is this the
pig, or an incredible presage of the early Elohim?

\+ + + + + + + +
\+ + + + + + + + + + + + +
\+ + + + + + + + + + pattern (shoes?) . . . .
\+ + + + + + + + + + +
\+ + + + + + +
\+ + + + + + + + + + + + +
\+ + + + + + + + + +. . . . .

Figure 2. Pages 15–16 from Schwerner, *The Tablets*

tradition (see my preface). Its thirty sections, none longer than half a
page, each comprises one to four prose paragraphs. Its title alludes to a
ninth-century Anglo-Saxon interlinear gloss on Latin hymns, which may
be found in *Sweet's Anglo-Saxon Reader* (Edwards 167); its prose-poetry
seems akin to St.-John Perse's *Anabase* (Dodsworth 55–61); while its explanatory notes derive from those appended to *The Waste Land,* itself a
pocket epic, perhaps, indeed, the *first* pocket epic. (And of course it was
none other than Eliot who translated Perse's *Anabase* into English.)

Schwerner's *Tablets,* by contrast, is a long poem in the American tradition of lifelong poems (*The Cantos,* Zukofsky's "A", Olson's *Maximus
Poems,* Duncan's *Passages*), literally interminable except by the poet's
death. Individual tablets vary in length from two to twenty-odd pages;
there were fifteen of them by 1971, twenty-four by 1983, two more by
1989, a total of twenty-seven at the time of Schwerner's death in 1999.
Generally lineated as verse, they are nevertheless peppered with prose
interpolations and visual elements, except for tablets XXVI and XXVII,

where the proportions are reversed: these are really prose essays with verse interpolations. A text alternately lyrical, scatological, and visionary, *The Tablets* purports to be scholarly translations of Sumerian pictographic texts incised on clay tablets some five thousand years ago. It imitates scholarly editions of cuneiform texts by academic Sumerologists and Assyriologists such as Samuel Noah Kramer—hence the nonalphabetic signs for missing, untranslatable, doubtful, and reconstructed passages, specified above, which directly derive from editorial conventions in Sumerology.

The Englishman Hill belongs to no school or movement, unless the very diffuse one of "pocket epic." Early in his career, Schwerner was often associated with the ethnopoetics movement of Jerome Rothenberg, Dennis Tedlock, and others, and with maverick performance poets like Jackson Mac Low and David Antin; more recently, there have been attempts to place him in a "neo-objectivist" circle with Rachel Blau DuPlessis and Michael Heller. None of these affiliations seems inevitable. In any case, if Hill and Schwerner share characteristics in common[1] it is not because of their affiliation with any "official" school, but because of their joint membership of a kind of secret society of twentieth-century poets, the society of what Arthur Sabatini (*DLB*) has called "archaeo-authors." In other words, what they have in common is a shared practice of archaeo-poetry: poetry of stratification and excavation, of fragments and ruins.

The trope of archaeological depth and stratification is one that postmodernist poetry absorbed from high modernism. If, as Fredric Jameson (*Postmodernism*) and others have argued, postmodernism has undergone a "spatial turn" away from the temporal thematics of high modernism, it is nevertheless the case that modernism had already undergone a spatial turn of its own. For high modernism conspicuously privileged the spatial dimension of verticality or *depth;* but this privileging of depth entailed no contradiction of modernism's temporal dominant, because "depth" in modernism amounts to spatialized time, the past (whether personal and psychological or collective and historical) deposited in strata. The sources of this master trope are many, but they certainly include the actual archaeological discoveries that coincided with the onset (with the various onsets) of high modernism: the discovery of the painted caves of Europe, beginning early in the nineteenth century and continuing at an accelerated rate into the twentieth (Altamira, 1879; Les

Trois Frères, 1916; Lascaux, 1940); Schliemann's finds at Troy (1873) and Mycenae (1876); Evans's at Knossos (1900); Carter's opening of Tutankhamun's tomb (1922); and so on (see Kenner; Cope; Davenport).

Consider *The Waste Land*, acknowledged fountainhead of one stream of Anglo-American modernism. Its imagery of ruined Europe; its vertical "core-sample" of European culture; its assumption that the "lowest" (i.e., oldest) strata are the truest, and that they persist down to the present, though transformed, like the materials of ruined cities reused to build newer ones ("These fragments I have shored against my ruin"), or like artifacts of childhood experience lingering in adult psychic life; its parallel assumption that etymology and the history of the language reflect and recapitulate the history of culture (for example, the scraps of Sanskrit in "What the Thunder Said")—all of these features derive from the poem's archaeological master trope. Not only *The Waste Land*, of course, but also many of the other defining works of Anglo-American high modernism were shaped by the master trope of archaeological depth, including Pound's *Cantos* and Joyce's *Ulysses* and *Finnegans Wake*.

These texts are the main sources, no doubt, for tropes of archaeological depth in later modernist and postmodernist poetry, but they are hardly the only ones. Archaeological figures also dominate such modernist texts as St.-John Perse's *Anabase* (1924), H.D.'s *Trilogy* (1944–46), and David Jones's *The Anathémata* (1952), all long poems related one way or another to the Eliot/Pound tradition. An independent source is Pablo Neruda's meditation on Andean ruins, *Las Alturas de Macchu Picchu* (*The Heights of Macchu Picchu*, 1944), which inspired Charles Olson, among others (Davenport 87–88). Olson actually ventured into the field for a season as an amateur archaeologist in Yucatan, an experience recorded in his *Mayan Letters* to Robert Creeley, though his own archaeological poetry, in *The Maximus Poems* (1950–70), fixes on Gloucester, Massachusetts, as its site, with excursions (especially in the second and third volumes) into the deep time of Sumer and the Phoenicians. Olson's archaeology of the local in turn inspired Basil Bunting's recovery of the Viking past of Northumbria in *Briggflatts* (1965), and Olson's traces can still be discerned in the more recent North American archaeologies of Susan Howe, e.g., her *Articulation of Sound Forms in Time* (1987) and "Thorow" (1990).

Modernism's archaeological master trope has lost little of its vitality in recent long poems and sequences in late-modernist and postmodernist modes. A conspicuous example is the series of "bog poems" that punctuate Seamus Heaney's volumes *Wintering Out* (1972) and *North* (1976), comprising some eight thematically related lyrics ("The Tollund Man" and "Nerthus" from *Wintering Out*, "Come to the Bower," "Bog Queen," "The Grauballe Man," "Punishment," "Strange Fruit," and "Kinship" from *North*). The bog poems are linked through their intertextual references to Danish archaeologist P. V. Glob's *The Bog People*, which contains verbal descriptions and, more pertinently, photographs of the well-preserved bodies of Iron Age men and women, mainly victims of ritual murders, dug from bogs in Denmark and elsewhere in northwestern Europe. Thus, Heaney's poems are archaeological texts in the sense of responding directly to and thematizing an account of actual archaeological discoveries (see Stallworthy). Other examples include Michael Harper's "History as Appletree" sequence (1972); Clayton Eshelman's poems of the seventies and eighties on the cave paintings of the Dordogne; Nathaniel Mackey's *Eroding Witness* (1985); Clark Coolidge's *At Egypt* (1988); Kathleen Fraser's "Etruscan Pages" (in *when new time folds up*, 1993); and Theresa Hak Kyung Cha's *Dictee* (1995). Archaeology even figures, albeit in belated, attenuated form, in A. R. Ammons's long discursive poem *Garbage* (1993), in which, inverting the trope, the archaeological site is not a midden being excavated but one being raised—a ziggurat of refuse rising stage by stage alongside Route I-95 in Florida.

The modernist master trope of archaeology, which persists in long poems such as *Mercian Hymns* and *The Tablets*, determines a genre of what I have called archaeo-poetry. Ultimately, this genre is the heir of a lapsed Romantic tradition of fragmentary, unfinished, or incomplete poems, poems like Wordsworth's "Nutting" and his unfinished magnum opus, *The Recluse*, Coleridge's "Kubla Khan" and "Christabel," Shelley's "Triumph of Life," Keats's "Hyperion" and "The Fall of Hyperion," Byron's *The Giaour* and *Don Juan*, and so on. Many of these are inadvertently fragmentary, others (such as *The Giaour*) fragmentary by design, still others ("Kubla Khan") ambiguous (McFarland; Rajan; Levinson). Seeming to peter out after its Romantic heyday, the fragment poem revived in the twentieth century in, for instance, Ezra Pound's minimalist fragment "Papyrus" and its later imitations by Ted Hughes ("Fragment of an Ancient Tablet," from *Crow*, 1971) and Edwin Morgan ("Translated from a Tablet in the Royal Library at Nineveh," 1994), or for that matter in Guy Davenport's translations of the surviving lyric fragments of Archilochos, Sappho, Alkman, and Anakreon. Near kin to the Romantic fragment poem is the poetry of ruins, a genre dating at least to the Renaissance (DuBellay, Spenser), but flourishing in the eighteenth century and among the Romantics, after which, like the fragment poem, it died away, to be revived in the twentieth century in *The Waste Land* and its progeny (Janowitz).

Descended from these Romantic poetries of fragments and ruins are postmodernist poems *sous rature*, physically erased texts. Examples include Jackson Mac Low's "5 biblical poems" (1954–55), a "gappy" text produced by selecting Biblical texts and then deleting certain of their words; Ronald Johnson's *RADI OS* (1977), a skeletal version of *Paradise Lost* produced by erasing most of the words of the first book of Milton's epic; and Tom Phillips's "treated Victorian novel," *A Humument* (1980, 1987), produced by drawing or painting on pages of an obscure late-nineteenth-century novel so as to render all but a few scattered words illegible. Clearly, Hill's *Mercian Hymns*, with its iconic gap corresponding to its protagonist's erasure, and even more so *The Tablets*, with its multiple forms of spacing and elision, are poems very much in the spirit of this poetry *sous rature*.

III. MIDDENS

Today's posts are piles to drive into the quaggy past
on which impermanent palaces balance.
                    Basil Bunting, *Briggflatts*, IV (*Collected Poems* 53)

Archaeology is a conspicuous theme of *Mercian Hymns*, and archaeological motifs abound. We have already noticed how two of these motifs converge in the primal scene near the poem's center: the coin and the well or ditch from which it is recovered. Both these motifs recur: coins in hymns IV ("gold solidus"), VII, XI ("Coins handsome as Nero's"), XII, and XXX; ditches in hymns I, VII, and XI. Related to the lost and recovered coins are other lost objects, perhaps to be recovered in some future archaeological dig, including lost toys (hymns VII and XIX) and other mislaid "treasures" (XXI). Related to ditches and wells are kitchen middens, dumps, abandoned buildings, and other future archaeological sites (hymns IX, XIX, and XXVIII). Acts of excavation and uprooting, exposing buried depths to sight, recur throughout: a boar roots (XI), pipe layers uncover a hoard (XII), a crabapple (XV) and later the "shire-tree" are uprooted (XXVII). In general, the English West Midlands, the locale of the *Hymns*, is figured here as a kind of universal tel or midden; so, for that matter, is the past itself. "For Hill," writes Henry Hart, "the past was always a site to excavate" (160).

Archaeology as theme is easy enough to grasp, since it is largely a matter of the poem's lexicon. But in what ways can a poem reflect archaeological themes in its *form*? Can a poem be vertically stratified? In what sense can it be said to excavate, or to have been excavated? Can a poem be understood to be an archaeological site, a tel or midden? Not in any immediately obvious sense, given the horizontal orientation of language itself, its successiveness in time and space. Nevertheless, *Mercian Hymns* not only thematizes archaeological depth and stratification at the level of vocabulary but also *figures* depth at other levels of textual organization.

One possibility would be to figure depth visually in the very shape of the poem. Thus, for instance, the long, narrow, vertically oriented shape of Heaney's bog poems can be grasped as a kind of visual figure of archaeological depth. Like artesian wells, or better yet like shafts sunk into bogs, these poems seem to imply by their visual form that they tap into "repressed psychic and mythic material" (Morrison 45). But, apart from the single iconic gap in hymn XXX, visual possibilities are not much exploited in *Mercian Hymns*. Instead, Hill figures archaeological depth through certain dislocations in the world of his poem, and through a particular repertoire of devices of language.

At the level of its world, *Mercian Hymns* foregrounds historical depth and stratification through the illicit mingling of "deeper" and "shallower" historical strata—that is, through deliberate anachronism. There are modernist precedents, of course—Pound's *Homage to Sextus Propertius* (1919), or *The Waste Land* itself, for instance—as well as postmodernist analogues, such as Donald Barthelme's last novel, *The King* (1990), in which the Middle Ages of the *Morte d'Arthur* mingles with the Second World War. Anachronism produces a kind of temporal double exposure, past and present occupying the same plane, like sherds exposed by erosion or a tel in which the stratification has been disturbed. Thus, for example, in Hill's hymn XXVII, not only do papal legates and Welsh mercenaries attend Offa's funeral, but so do "Merovingian car-dealers." Or consider the first paragraph of hymn XXVI:

Fortified in their front parlours, at Yuletide men
are the more murderous. Drunk, they defy battle-
axes, bellow of whale-bone and dung.

(*CP* 130)

Here the "front parlours" belong to the twentieth century, while the
"battle-axes" (and, by contiguity, the "whale-bone and dung" as well,
presumably) belong to the Middle Ages. The seam or hinge between the
two epochs is "Yuletide," a usage that might with equal propriety belong
to either of them.

Nor are these isolated instances; on the contrary, few of the hymns
lack some comparable anachronism, from the juxtaposition of "King of
the perennial holly-groves" and "overlord of the M5 [highway]" in the
opening lines of hymn I, to the phone calls and poison-pen letters that
the King of Mercia receives in hymn VIII, to the *haleine* (wind, breath;
an allusion to *La Chanson de Roland,* as Hill's note specifies, *CP* 202) of
his "maroon GT" in hymn XVII. The world of *Mercian Hymns* is organized (or disrupted) from start to finish according to a principle of double
exposure of the early Middle Ages and the mid-twentieth century. "The
Offa who figures in this sequence," Hill explains in his note to the poem,
"might . . . be regarded as the presiding genius of the West Midlands, his
dominion enduring from the middle of the eighth century until the middle of the twentieth (and possibly beyond). The indication of such a
timespan will, I trust, explain and to some extent justify a number of
anachronisms" (*CP* 201). Explanation and justification in realistic terms
can, of course, be managed in some of these instances: thus, for instance,
the "battle-axes" of hymn XXVI might be understood in the contemporary colloquial sense as referring insultingly to the drunken men's wives,
while the man who receives the calls and letters in hymn VIII might only
imagine himself to be a medieval monarch. Nevertheless, in the aggre-
gate, and in association with anachronisms that *cannot* be so readily
naturalized, these local anomalies add up to an effect of pervasive historical double exposure.

Mercian Hymns also figures archaeological depth by foregrounding
the *vertical dimension* of language itself, emphasizing its organization on
the paradigmatic axis at the expense (to some extent) of its syntagmatic
organization, and its diachronic existence in time at the expense of its
synchronic systematicity in the present. It does so by deploying a variety

of "vertical" devices, including etymology, ambiguity, paronomasia, and metaphor. These are all linguistic forms of double exposure, equivalent (at least in this context) to the double exposures of anachronism, but at a different textual level.

Etymology instructs us that the successive episodes in the history of a word remain as deposits or residue, "compacted" (vertically) *within* that word, recoverable with the help of a historical dictionary. Etymological wordplay, then, is a ready device for foregrounding the historicity of language, as its conspicuous use in archaeological long poems such as H.D.'s *Trilogy* or Jones's *The Anathémata* testifies. Hill plays on etymologies throughout *Mercian Hymns,* implying thereby an analogy between change and historical difference interior to language, on the one hand, and the stratified, buried history of the locale, on the other. "In handling the English language," Hill said once in an interview, "the poet makes an act of recognition that etymology is history" (quoted in Sherry 88).

Etymology is recognizable as history, or archaeology, whenever Hill juxtaposes words that share a root, exposing, by that gesture, the "network of roots that extends under the surface of Hill's poem" (Hart 175) —or, for that matter, under the surface of the English language generally (Edwards 168). "I abode there, bided my time" (hymn IV); "He was defunct. They were perfunctory" (hymn XXVII)—such juxtapositions remind us of the historical kinship of words that have drifted apart through specialization and the passage of time (Sherry 134, 139). Conversely, Hill also reminds us of the way words of diverse origin have accrued to the English lexicon over time, piling up as if in heterogeneous strata. He especially foregrounds the difference between archaisms of Anglo-Saxon origin (e.g., wergild, moldywarp, burh, marl, darg), some of which still linger in usage as regionalisms, and Latinate words (e.g., solidus, crepitant, arena), some of them barely domesticated as English. Particularly pointed juxtapositions of Anglo-Saxon and Latinate diction occur in the pair of hymns, XVII and XVIII, devoted (appropriately enough) to "Offa's Journey to Rome," and the "Opus Anglicanum" sequence, hymns XXIII, XXIV, and XXV (Robinson "Reading Geoffrey Hill" 213; Knottenbelt 186–88). Thus, in the first paragraph of hymn XXIII, we read this sentence, heavy with Latinate diction:

> In tapestries, in dreams, they gathered, as it was en-
> acted, the return, the re-entry of transcendence
> into this sublunary world.

In the same hymn's second paragraph, we read this:

They trudged out of the dark, scraping their boots
   free from lime-splodges and phlegm.

(*CP* 127)

"Transcendence" versus "trudged," "sublunary" versus "lime-splodges": the archaeological stratification here is pronounced.

If etymology is history for Hill, it does not necessarily follow that "original" meanings are any more authentic or reliable than later "derived" meanings, that older meanings are truer, as they tend to be for H.D. or David Jones (and perhaps for Eliot in *The Waste Land*). Rather, writes Vincent Sherry, "Etymology for Hill reveals no original or true meaning, but a play of difference" (1987: 20); and "Hill's use of etymology . . . is not a search for the atom of true meaning, [but] involves a play of disparate senses accumulated over time" (227). Etymology, in other words, is a rich source of verbal *ambiguities*, another of the devices through which Hill foregrounds the vertical, paradigmatic dimension of language.

Etymology converges with ambiguity in the sense that, in both, alternative meanings—whether deriving from different historical states of the language, or from different synchronic contexts of use—compete for the same word. In the case of paronomasia (punning), several words compete for the same (or nearly the same) sound-shape. *Mercian Hymns* is dotted with witty Empsonian ambiguities, linguistic double exposures that prompt readerly double takes. Consider hymn XIII, the primal scene quoted at the beginning of this chapter, where Offa is "cushioned on a legend" in at least two senses: the legends (stories) told of Offa enhance (buoy up and cushion) his reputation to the point that one is willing to believe his claim to be "King of the Whole Country of the English"; but also, the motto (legend) running around the rim of the coin cushions (serves as a pillow for) the stamped head of the king. Or consider the wording, "he left behind coins, for his lodging," in hymn XXX, also quoted earlier. Does this mean that Offa left behind coins to *pay for* his lodging, or that his coins are the only place where Offa remains now, so long after his death? It means both these things, of course.

In hymn XXVII, the anachronistic "Merovingian car-dealers" contains a punning shadow-sense:

'Now when King Offa was alive and dead,' they were
  all there, the funereal gleemen: papal legate and
  rural dean; Merovingian car-dealers, Welsh mercenaries; a shuffle of house-carls.

(CP 131)

A minuscule shift of word-boundary yields "card-dealers," which in turn
creates the context for (mis)reading "shuffle of house-*carls*" as "house-
cards"—the face cards, presumably (Gifford 154; Hart 190; Sherry 139).
Other puns and ambiguities of comparable complexity, some of them
comparably comic, are documented throughout the critical literature on
Mercian Hymns (see especially Dodsworth; Gifford; Hart; Sherry; Knottenbelt). "Hill's fondness for puns," writes Sherry (34), "shows him . . .
taking ambiguity not as a lapse of authorial control but as a further
strength, like the shafts of vertical richness in the word's etymological
history."

Metaphor, finally, is the classic instance of a figure that foregrounds
the paradigmatic axis of language. The figure of substitution par excellence, it is a major resource of Hill's poetics of verticality in *Mercian
Hymns*. The range and variety of Hill's metaphorical practice exceeds
the scope of this chapter. In some of the hymns, metaphors proliferate
around a single literal image. Thus, for instance, in hymn XII, the pipe
layers' unearthing of what appears to be a hoard of coins triggers an
explosion of metaphors:

Their spades grafted through the variably-resistant
  soil. They clove to the hoard. They ransacked
  epiphanies, vertebrae of the chimera, armour of
  wild bees' larvae. They struck the fire-dragon's
  faceted skin.

(CP 116)

In other hymns, metaphor emerges by juxtaposition across the gap between paragraphs. Take, for instance, hymn XX:

Primeval heathland spattered with the bones of mice
  and birds; where adders basked and bees made pro-
  vision, mantling the inner walls of their burh:

Coiled entrenched England: brickwork and paintwork
stalwart above hacked marl. The clashing primary
colours—'Ethandune', 'Catraeth', 'Maldon', 'Pen-
gwern'.

(*CP* 124)

Hill, in his notes (*CP* 202), identifies the names in the second paragraph
as those of "English suburban dwellings." Thus, we have a before-and-
after juxtaposition: before, unspoiled heath; after, suburbs. But we also
have a metaphor: suburban dwellings are figured as the nests of adders
and bees. The metaphorical strategy is precisely that of Pound's "In a
Station of the Metro," only on a slightly larger scale.

Its strategy of juxtaposition aside, the metaphor of hymn XX belongs
to a pattern of metaphor that recurs throughout *Mercian Hymns*, whereby
human handiwork is figured in terms of nature (e.g., suburban dwellings in terms of animal burrows), or vice versa, nature in terms of human handiwork. The former case is exemplified also by hymn XXI,
where "during the years, deciduous velvet peeled from evergreen [photo]
albums" (*CP* 125); while the latter case is exemplified by hymn XV (119),
where "A wasps' nest ensconced in the hedge-bank" is figured as "a reli-
quary or wrapped head" (and note, incidentally, the pun on "ensconced").
Thus, Hill deploys an entire system of metaphorical correspondences,
whereby whole areas of the lexicon, lexical subcodes, are re-encoded in
terms of other subcodes: nature as culture, and vice versa.

Anachronism, etymology, ambiguity, paronomasia, metaphorical correspondences: Hill's *Mercian Hymns* employs an entire repertoire of devices for foregrounding verticality and figuring "depth." The repertoire
is a familiar one; it derives from high-modernist archaeological poetics.

IV. TABLETS

But the great earth opus of the Midi, rivalling the visual odes of
Lascaux, is the inhuman iconography of little known l'Aven
d'Armand, the work of millions of years of millions of sulphurous
dribbles scribbling a vast subterranean epic.
Ronald Sukenick, "50,010,008" (*Doggy Bag* 92)

I began by arguing for a common generic identity for *Mercian Hymns*
and Armand Schwerner's *Tablets*, based on their shared lineage of archaeo-

poetry; but now I must change directions and insist instead on their difference, on just how *unlike* each other these two poems really are.

Consider Schwerner's against-the-grain handling of the "depth" devices of the high-modernist archaeological tradition. Anachronisms such as Hill's "Merovingian car-dealers" create, I have argued, a kind of double exposure of epochs, foregrounding the historical stratification of the "site" (in this case, the English West Midlands). Anachronisms in *The Tablets* have a markedly different effect. Take the one in tablet VIII, a tablet in the genre of "graveyard curse" (archaic already when Shakespeare, or someone, used it in hopes of defending the Bard's grave from desecration):

> *if you pick your nose on my grave*
> *may you be fixed forever in a stupid*
> *attitude, may the children use you*
> *as a jungle gym and turn your muscle to piss[.]*
> (*Tablets* 30)

How does "jungle gym" differ from "Merovingian car-dealers"? Simply in that, in the case of tablet VIII, we have someone to *blame* for the anachronism: it must be the unnamed scholar-translator of the tablets who is responsible for "illicitly" projecting the playground furniture of his own time back into the Fertile Crescent of five thousand years ago.

Or, more generally, when Hill allows medieval and contemporary items to mingle on the same plane (battle-axes and front parlours, Roland's horn and a maroon sports car, car dealerships and the Merovingians), we infer either some thematic statement about the persistence of the medieval in the (post)modern, or some irony (in the manner of *The Waste Land* or *Ulysses*) at (post)modernity's expense—or, given Hill's ambiguity, both at once. We also, of course, interpret the anachronism as expressing the poet's freedom to forge correspondences between widely separated epochs. But do we make the same sorts of inferences when, for instance, Schwerner's scholar-translator claims to detect a nascent utopian socialism, "the first socialist voice in recorded human history," in the language of tablet XI?

> give fresh yoghurt in exchange for a horde of our people
> + + + + + + + + + + + + + + + ...

give a great netting of fish in exchange for a hunger-servant
give a milking-stool and a calf in exchange for a thin wormy
    thigh-bone
give a bone spoon and another bone spoon and another in ex-
    change for a + + + + + +*

      *the phrase 'in exchange for' shows every possibility of also
meaning 'for the benefit of,' a meaning readily discoverable in the
sub-dialects of silversmiths and lyre-players.

give a drainage system for the miserable without pattern (shoes?)*

      *we know that only government buildings in the archaic
context had drainage systems. So this line is of transcendent importance. In it we finally meet, unequivocally, the direct thrust of
the first socialist voice in recorded human history. The single voice
cries out in early compassion. Who can now easily doubt that
the formula 'in exchange for' served as a mask for the writer's anti-
hierarchical intent? No contemporary of mine can conceive of the
genius and will necessary for one man to break through the almost
total thought-control of the archaic hierarchies.

                                                         (*Tablets* 38)

And what do we infer when, in tablet VI, the scholar-translator insists
on finding traces of a modern sense of individuation and self-consciousness in his ancient texts?

show yourself Pnou, let me see you Lak,
come into my house with a face just once old No-Name
I will call you simple death
show yourself Lak, let me blind you Pnou
o Pinitou Pinitou Pinitou*, this is not me

      *curious: if this [Pinitou] is the surname, or given name, of
the speaker, we are faced for the first time with a particularized
man, *this* man, rescued from the prototypical and generalized 'I' of
these Tablets. If it is *this* man, Pinitou, I find myself deeply moved

at this early reality of self; if we have here the name of an unknown
deity or peer of the speaker, I am not deeply moved.

(*Tablets* 25–26)

In all such cases, we attribute the anachronistic conflation of past and
present not to Armand Schwerner but to the scholar-translator. It is this
translator's running commentary that we read in marginal glosses such
as those quoted above. Already conspicuous in tablet I, these interventions grow in volume and eccentricity as the sequence unfolds until, in
the last installments, tablets XXVI and XXVII, the annotations overwhelm the texts being annotated. These marginal glosses are not presented as Armand Schwerner's direct self-expression, but something like
dramatic monologue. Accordingly, we do not give them weight as a serious thesis about anticipations of the modern in the archaic, or the persistence of the archaic in the modern, but chalk it up to the obsessions
(not to say delusions) of the scholar-translator. That is, we "neutralize"
or "evacuate" anachronistic attributions in the light of the overall dramatic and ironic structure of *The Tablets*.

That dramatic and ironic structure has more in common with modernist and postmodernist prose fictions than it does with a poem like
Mercian Hymns which, despite its "pocket epic" features, is basically
lyric. "Why leave fictive experiments to the prose writers?" reads one of
the entries in the "Journals/Divagations" appended to *The Tablets* (114),
and fictive experiments are precisely what Schwerner has undertaken
here. Indeed, the very presence of such a metafictional remark, and of
the appendix in which it appears, should call to mind a relevant high-
modernist model, namely André Gide's novel-within-a-novel, *Les Faux-
monnayeurs* (1925). A still closer analogue is Vladimir Nabokov's *Pale
Fire* (1962). Like *The Tablets, Pale Fire* purports to be a scholarly edition
of a poetic text; moreover, as in *The Tablets,* the relation between text
and commentary is rendered unstable by the commentator's obsessions
or delusions. Ultimately, it remains an open question whether, in
Nabokov's case, the poem "Pale Fire" even exists independently of its
commentator's fictionalizing imagination—whether commentary, poem,
and poet alike are not all products of the same obsession.

Similarly, in the case of *The Tablets* it is impossible to determine
whether or not the individual "authors" whom the scholar-translator
claims to discern in his ancient texts have any existence apart from the

commentator's projections. Who speaks in the tablets themselves (that is, in the texts exclusive of the scholar-translator's commentary)? The question is a vexed one. As we have just seen, the scholar-translator thinks he glimpses a speaker, named Pinitou, in tablet VI; the latter is perhaps glimpsed again in tablets VIII and XI. Arbitrarily, the scholar-translator declares the speaker of tablet XIII to be "very likely a 'cured' schizophrenic" (*Tablets* 46), and moreover a woman, despite strong indications of male sexual experience in the text of this tablet. The sequence of tablets XX through XXIII is epistolary, the writer identifying himself unequivocally as "I Ahanarshi the scribe" (59), a name already mentioned earlier, in tablet XVII. With grand inconsistency, the scholar-translator ignores the marks of individuation this time—evidently, Ahanarshi's individuality does not "move" him as Pinitou's had. Unless, that is, he is simply suspicious that Ahanarshi might not be what he seems, for the scholar-translator draws our attention to evidence that Ahanarshi might not have been a scribe after all, but a mere student *pretending* to be a scribe (59, 62). In any case, the question of the addressee of these epistolary tablets remains unanswered, indeed unformulated, apart from one marginal gloss that casts everything into doubt: "Address is to an individual, or rather to an embodied energy?" (62). Finally, in tablet XXVI the scholar-translator leaps to the unwarranted conclusion that the tablets possess a single author, arbitrarily projecting "a blind Tiresias figure" (77), then going on to interpolate a middleman figure, an unreliable scribe-redactor (79), thereby complicating the structure of transmission still further.

So the same corrosive epistemological uncertainty prevails here as in *Pale Fire*. In fact, Schwerner goes further than Nabokov, introducing uncertainties for which there is no precedent in Nabokov's text (or Gide's either, for that matter). For instance, doubts arise not only about the authorship of the tablets, but also about their transmission. At certain points the scholar-translator must rely on the work of other scholars to establish his text, and these "authorities" prove in every instance to be at least as dubious, in their own ways, as the putative "authors" of the tablets (or as the scholar-translator himself, for that matter). Thus, the scholar-translator turns for the musical setting of tablet XII to one F. W. Galpin, Canon Emeritus of Chelmsford Cathedral. Canon Galpin's setting is speculative, to say the least; after all, as the canon himself acknowledges (in a statement quoted in the headnote to Tablet XII), "we

shall never meet with anyone who was present at [the music's] first performance and could vouch for its certitude" (39). Indeed not. Tablet VII
presents a different sort of difficulty, for the original tablet seems to have
disappeared, though not without first having been seen and translated
by "a certain Henrik L., an archaeologically gifted Norwegian divine,"
on whose translation the scholar-translator must depend, for lack of
anything more authentic. Bizarrely, Henrik L. has rendered the ancient
text not into any modern tongue but into another dead language, namely
"Crypto-Icelandic, a language we cannot yet understand" (27); moreover, the reliability of his translation is compromised by unmistakable
Christian interpolations ("gott Jesu Kriste," "Jesu Kriste sacrifise") in a
text that predates Christ by several millennia. Similarly, in the most recent tablets, the scholar-translator acquires a young collaborator, one Brad
de Lisle, who helps in translating the cylinder seals of tablet XXVIII, but
whose reliability as a translator is already being called into question before the end of the tablet.

So here is uncertainty introduced into the middle links in the chain
of transmission. Moreover, the same corrosive skepticism applies here as
applies to Pinitou and Ahanarshi and the other tablet "authors": if their
very existence is in doubt, so too is the existence of Henrik L. and Canon
Galpin and Brad de Lisle.

Clearly, the identity of the tablets' original "authors" (or "author")
and subsequent custodians is hopelessly compromised by the mediating
presence of the scholar-translator. The "original" tablets and their putative speakers are not directly accessible to us, leaving us no choice but to
rely on the scholar-translator's reconstructions and translations. Unfortunately, there are many indications of his unreliability. As the marginal
glosses to tablet XI (quoted earlier) attest, he can be self-contradictory:
on the one hand, the tablet author's "anti-hierarchical intent" is indubi-
table ("Who can now easily doubt [it]"), but on the other hand it is literally inconceivable ("No contemporary of mine can conceive of the
genius and will necessary . . . to break through"). Moreover, the scholar-
translator is capricious and arbitrary, as we have also seen: Pinitou's individuality moves him, but not Ahanarshi's; the speaker of tablet XIII is
a female schizophrenic just because he says so. Anomalies and idiosyn-
crasies abound in his renderings, undermining our confidence in them.
For instance, his translations of ancient clothing terms are weirdly anachronistic: if he is to be believed, the archaic people of the tablets wore

shirts, shoes, even "wet socks" and/or "underwear"; these last are offered as alternative translations of the same word! (13, 60) Often (as in the case of "wet socks"/"underwear") he proposes alternatives that, were they adopted, would radically alter the sense of a passage, to the point of inverting or destroying it. Thus, for the translation "stony shit" he proposes the alternative "lentil soup" (51)—hardly a negligible difference! In the same vein, he proposes "whirlpool" as an alternative for "penis-hole/ vagina" (52); for "discover" he proposes "invent" (54); for "for the first time" he proposes "seldom" (68); in several places he proposes "damage" as an alternative for "power" (13, 18, 52); in one place he proposes "outside" for "inside," noting blandly that "This term on occasion refers to its opposite" (67); and he even observes that "'sweetness' in one questionable archaic locus has been taken as 'consciousness'" (68). How can one place any faith in a translation that side-slips from meaning to meaning, from "power" to "damage" and from "sweetness" to "consciousness," in this way?

Positioned as he is between us and the world of the tablets, the scholar-translator is a murky, not a clear, medium. He seems to have some inklings of this himself. Frequently, especially in his headnotes, he expresses doubts or misgivings, or dissatisfaction with his own solutions. One of these headnotes (to tablet IV) reads: "The reconstruction of V is almost certainly correct. Doubts linger about IV" (21). He suspects the "intrusion of a relatively recent hand" in one place (53), and "later accretions" in another (68). The scholar-translator's expressions of doubt reach a crisis in note interpolated between tablets VIII and IX, "I worry myself sick over the possibility that *I* am the variable giving rise to ambiguities. . . . On occasion it almost seems to me as if I am inventing the sequence, and such a fantasy sucks me into an abyss of almost irretrievable depression (31–32)." There are no interpolations of comparable length until tablets XXVI and XXVII, prose essays on translation method; but how unlike the earlier interpolations these are! Here, if not before, one grasps how completely the ancient materials have been mediated through the scholar-translator's eccentric vision. The whole, it turns out, text and commentary alike, has been dominated from the outset, to a degree that we might not have fully appreciated, by the scholar-translator's obsession with uncovering the origins of something like modern consciousness in these archaic traces.[2] Nothing of his earlier self-doubt and anxiety is in evidence here; instead, even more disturbingly, the scholar-translator exudes a manic self-confidence. The figure he cuts will be familiar from *Pale Fire* and other novels with unreliable narration: he is the self-deluded speaker, blind to his own arbitrariness and internal contradictions, incapable of gauging the impression he is making on his audience.

In short, here we have a classic ironic structure. Our role as readers is split: at one level, we play the role of narratee within the fictional world of *The Tablets,* the sort of reader who might be imagined as recipient of the scholar-translator's annotations, interpolations, and essays; at another level, however, we observe the entire communicative situation in which the scholar-translator and his narratee are joined, and we grasp the ironic gaps between the scholar-translator's intentions and his performance, between his self-image and the image he inadvertently projects. In the role of observer of this ironic situation, the reader occupies the same plane as the poet who created this scholar-translator. But even at this level nothing, finally, can be taken for granted: Schwerner's own text is not presented as "definitive," but rather trails off into "Tablets Journals/Divagations," modelled (no doubt) on Gide's *Journals of Les Faux-monnayeurs.* Nothing could contrast more markedly with Geoffrey Hill's self-consciously pedantic, faintly self-mocking notes to *Mercian Hymns* (modelled on Eliot's and David Jones's) than the open-ended, improvisatory, unsettled character of Schwerner's "Journals/Divagations."[3]

Thus, what might have been a chain of transmission, a kind of bucket brigade or relay race whereby the tablet texts get handed off like a baton from one intermediary to another—from the tablet "authors" to their scribes and redactors, and from them to middlemen like Henrik L., and from them in turn to our scholar-translator, and from him, via his act of translation, to us—what might have been a "vertical" structure of transmission, emerging out of archaeological "deep time" into the light of the present, suffers epistemological erosion and ends up collapsing into a single plane. There is no reliable structure of transmission here after all, no hierarchy of more and less reliable sources, of witnesses nearer to and farther from some ultimate source. All have been equalized, levelled by onto-epistemological doubt: the tablets and their translations, the "authors" and their redactors, the middlemen and the scholar-translator and the poet Armand Schwerner himself. Nothing wells up from the depths; there *are* no depths under this eroded plane.

The erosion of this vertical structure is figured (or literalized?) in the very look of *The Tablets* on the page. These semi-effaced lines, inter-

TABLET X

```
.........................................+ + + + + + + + + + + +
+ + + + + + + + + + + + + + + + + + + + + + + + + + + + + + + + + + + + + +
+ + + + + + + + + + + + + + + + +
+ + + + + + + + + + + + + + + + +
+ + + + + + + + + + + + + + + + +
+ + + .................................⊕ ⊕ ⊕ ⊕ ⊕ ⊕ ⊕
...............+ + + + + + + +.........+ + + + + + + + + + +
+ + + + + +.........+ + + + + +.........+ + + + + + + + + + + +
.........................................................
........................................⊕ ⊕ ⊕ ⊕ ⊕ ⊕ ⊕ ⊕ ⊕ ⊕ ⊕
+ + + + + + + + + + + + + + + + + +.......+ + + + + + + + + +
+ + + + + + + [the the] + + + + + + +
+ + + + + + + + + + + + + + + + +
+ + + + + + + + + + + + + + + + +
+ + + + + + + + + + + + + + + + +
+ + + + + +.......+ + + + + +.......+ + + + + +......+ + + + +
...........................................................
.........................................................
.......
.............
..................
......................+ +
.............................+ + + + + + + + + +
```

Figure 3. Page 35 from Schwerner, *The Tablets*

rupted by strings of signs signifying *missing* meanings (ellipses, plus signs, square brackets, parentheses, question marks), in one sense refer to the deteriorated physical condition of the supposed clay tablets themselves—the literal crumbling away of so many passages, the fractures that must be mended, sometimes (as in tablets IV and V) only provisionally—as well as to our imperfect knowledge of the language and script in which they were allegedly written. In another sense, however, these "illegible" lines refer to that epistemological collapse that is the condition of *The Tablets*. Nowhere is this clearer than in tablet X, comprising twenty-three lines of *nothing but* signs of missing meaning (including a new sign introduced by the redoubtable Henrik L., signifying "confusing")—nothing, that is, apart from two words at the tablet's very center

(Figure 3). Square brackets, of course, mean "supplied by the scholar-translator."

The "ruinous" look of *The Tablets*, and the corresponding collapse of its epistemological structure, prompts a reevaluation of this poem's affiliations with the tradition of archaeo-poetry. Obviously, *The Tablets* does not lie entirely outside the tradition of archaeological sequences and long poems extending from Eliot and Pound through H.D., David Jones and Olson down to Heaney and Hill and beyond. Just as obviously, however, it does not share the central epistemological premises of most of the texts in this tradition, which tend to assume a correlation between archaeological "depth" and "truth," and between excavation and the quest for origins. In *The Tablets*, epistemological probes into the "deep time" of archaeology turn up nothing reliable, and the artifacts exhibited to us—the tablets themselves—seem to be a kind of hoax. But who is the hoaxer, exactly? The scholar-translator? Armand Schwerner? Thus, if *The Tablets* belongs to the tradition of archaeo-poetry, as it surely does, then it is to a disreputable and shadowy strain in this tradition—not to the poetry of ruins so much as to the practice of sham ruins; not to the fragment genre of the Romantics so much as to the hoax genre of their predecessors; not to the literature of scholarship so much as the literature of mock scholarship.

The poetry of fragments and ruins—from which, it will be recalled, later traditions of archaeo-poetry emerged—bore witness to a general cultural preoccupation with the ruin in the eighteenth century. This "ruin sentiment" expressed itself not only in poetry but in visual art (e.g., Piranesi) and, most extraordinarily of all, in the fabrication of sham ruins (see Zucker 119–30; Harbison 99–130; Holly 188–215). The artificial ruin, built to order, custom-made, seems such a peculiarly eighteenth-century phenomenon as to preclude revival, even in a period of theme parks, simulacral inauthenticity, historical pastiche, and stylistic recycling such as our own. Not so, however; consider some of Robert Smithson's earthworks, such as his "Buried Shed" (Kent State University, 1970), or Charles Moore's Piazza d'Italia in New Orleans (1978), constructed so as to imitate a kind of jazzed-up classical ruin, or some of the Best Products showrooms designed by the SITE architectural collective—the collapsing Indeterminate Facade showroom in Houston (1975), the Notch Showroom in Sacramento (1977), the showroom with fragmented, jigsaw-puzzle facade in Miami (1979), the Virginia showroom penetrated and enveloped by the surrounding forest (1980), and so on (see Wines 143–50; Harbison 105–06). What are these if not postmodern sham ruins?[4] The conceptual bridge between these built forms and postmodernist poetry is provided by Ian Hamilton Finlay's garden at Stonypath (renamed Little Sparta) in Scotland. Part environmental art installation, part anthology of concrete poetry, Finlay's garden is dotted with purpose-built ruins and sham archaeological finds, all inscribed with poetic fragments (Gintz 110–17; Abrioux). It is in the context of Finlay's literal poetry of ruins that we can most readily grasp the sham-ruin character of *The Tablets*.

Not all archaeological shams are benign. Innocent shams in the tradition of the eighteenth-century landscape architects mingle uneasily with not-so-innocent (paleo-)archaeological forgeries, such as, in our own century, the notorious Piltdown Man forgery (see Haywood, *Faking It;* Lewin; Spencer; Landau). The Romantic fragment poem, too, had its shadowy double, in the form of its eighteenth-century precursor, the hoax poem: Thomas Chatterton's Rowley poems and their supporting documents (also forged), and James Macpherson's Ossianic forgeries, beginning with his *Fragments of Ancient Poetry* (1760; see Folkenflik 378–91; Haywood, *Making of History;* Stewart, "Birth"). The relation between the fragment poem and the hoax poetry of Chatterton and Macpherson is one of deep complicity; as Marjorie Levinson (34–48) has shown, the reading practices developed to accommodate the hoax poems—which had been left fragmentary by design, the better to simulate genuine "found" texts—became the precondition for the production and reception of the Romantic fragment poems. This complicity between fragment and forgery has persisted. It manifests itself in the nineteenth-century folklorists' project of "reconstructing" national folk poetry; *The Kalevala,* for instance, the Finnish folk epic and cornerstone of Finnish national identity, was pieced together by Elias Lönnrot from fragmentary material collected in the field, augmented by lines composed by himself (though these constitute no more than 2 percent of the total, evidently; see Pentikäinen 1989). How different is this, in the end, from Macpherson's fabrication of Scottish national epics, cornerstones of a still-flourishing "Highland tradition" (see Trevor-Roper)?[5]

Fragment, ruin, and forgery remain linked. This linkage is a feature of literary hoaxes and mock hoaxes in our own time, such as the Ern Malley hoax visited on the Australian literary avant-garde in the 1940s, which still resonates in Australian literary culture today (Lehman "Ern

Malley Hoax"; Kane), or Kenneth Koch's gentle mock hoax, "Some South American Poets" (in his *The Pleasures of Peace*, 1969; see McHale "Postmodernist Lyric" 39–44) or, most strikingly of all, in the Araki Yasusada hoax (or mock hoax, or whatever it is).[6] In the case of the Yasusada notebooks, alleged to be those of a Hiroshima survivor, in which poems mingle with letters, journal entries, English-language exercises, and so on, fragmentation is motivated not so much by a will to deceive—it is unclear to what degree the hoaxers (presumably one Kent Johnson and his accomplices, if any) actually intended to deceive anyone—as by allegorical purposes: fragmentation here is a figure for life after nuclear holocaust, life lived among the ruins (Nussbaum; Perloff, "In Search"). Here, once again, we touch on the methods of *The Tablets*, which in this perspective appears as an exemplary mock hoax; indeed, it seems likely to have been the model for *The Notebooks of Araki Yasusada*.[7]

Finally, if *The Tablets* seems at home in the disreputable company of hoaxes and mock hoaxes, it also belongs to the distinguished and venerable tradition of learnéd wit. Descending from Erasmus and Rabelais through Swift, Pope, Sterne, and Diderot to *Sartor Resartus*, the cetological parts of *Moby Dick, Bouvard et Pécuchet*, and Joyce, the tradition of learnéd wit flourishes in a host of late-twentieth-century figures: Borges, Nabokov, Durrell, Flann O'Brien, Gaddis, Gass, Ballard, Lem, Brooke-Rose, the OuLiPians, Alexander Theroux—the roster of names could easily be extended (see Moore). We have already observed the family resemblance between *The Tablets* and Nabokov's mock scholarship in *Pale Fire*. Other cognate texts in this vein of mock scholarship include the mock book reviews of Borges and Lem, the mock scientific reports of J. H. Prynne ("The *Plant Time Manifold* Transcripts," 1974), Georges Perec ("Experimental Demonstration of the tomatotropic organization in the soprano," 1980), and Harry Mathews ("The Dialect of the Tribe" and "Remarks of the Scholar Graduate," 1980), the mock encyclopedia of Milorad Pavić's *Dictionary of the Khazars* (1984), the mock-scholarly prefaces and appendices of Samuel R. Delany's *Nevèrÿon* series (1979–89), and so on. Archaeology, no one will be surprised to learn, figures conspicuously in this mock scholarship of learnéd wit, for instance in Delany's *Nevèrÿon*, the four volumes of which allegedly derive from the translation of a nine-hundred-word text fragment in a language predating all others on record, or in Borges's archaeological fantasy "Tlön, Uqbar, Orbis Tertius." Or of course in *The Tablets*.

V. BURIED SELF, SELF IN RUINS

I am Hamlet the Dane,
skull-handler, parablist,
. . . .
coming to consciousness
by jumping in graves
    Seamus Heaney, "Viking Dublin: Trial Pieces," IV (*North* 23)

No doubt many of my readers will have noted a lacuna in my account of the modernist trope of archaeology in section II above. The lacuna is a major one and can be summed up in a word: Freud. More so even than the actual archaeological finds of the modernist period, it was Freud's use of archaeological tropes for the "stratified" structure of the psyche and the "excavatory" work of psychoanalysis that shaped, nourished, and sustained the modernist master trope of depth. Freud's own imagination was profoundly receptive to the impact of the discoveries at Troy and elsewhere, and the discipline of archaeology, which in the course of his lifetime emerged from amateurism to aspire to the status of a science, was one of his models for the projected science of psychoanalysis. We know of Freud's preoccupation with archaeology not only from his writings but also, perhaps even more revealingly, from his own personal collection of antiquities. Ringing him at his writing desk and mingling with his patients in his consulting room, these synecdochic figures of archaeological "deep time" literally bore witness to his professional practice, and even followed him into exile in London at the end of his life (see Gamwell and Wells; Torgovnik).

Freud evidently found the archaeological metaphor irresistible as a figure both for the psyche and its products (e.g., dreams) and for the work of psychoanalysis itself; certainly he returned to it throughout his career, early and late. In doing so, in the view of Freudian critics of Freud such as Donald Spence (see also Kuspit), he did both psychoanalysis and archaeology a disservice: psychoanalysis, because he burdened it with a master trope that has subsequently hardened into an ideology; archaeology, because he attributed to it a kind of "scientism" a good deal less sophisticated, hermeneutically speaking, than archaeological procedures and archaeological thought really are. Other critics, more sympathetic to Freud (e.g., Møller 1991), have observed that the archaeological model of psychoanalytic process alternates in his writing and thought with other, more constructivist models, whereby truth is not recovered by excavating the deep strata of the patient's psyche, but rather constructed in the therapeutic encounter—not so much an archaeological dig, then, as a kind of collaborative novel. Nevertheless, the archaeological model, whenever it appears in Freud's writings, undeniably reflects the positivist side of his intellectual makeup, underwriting a discourse of epistemological mastery.

Negative though its impact might have been, in certain respects, on psychoanalytic practice, the modelling of the psyche, and the psychoanalytic discipline's self-understanding, the Freudian appropriation of archaeology has proven to be an invaluable resource for modernist art, and modernist poetry in particular. Freud's "psychologization" of the archaeological trope has left its mark not only on the poems of poets (such as H.D.) knowledgeable about and to some degree sympathetic toward Freudianism, but even on those by poets indifferent or hostile to it. Hill's *Mercian Hymns* perhaps falls into the latter category: an archaeological poem colored by the Freudian version of the trope, despite its author's apparent indifference toward Freud.

Which is not to say that the Freudian figure of the buried self, or buried stratum of the self, is the first thing one is likely to grasp about the structure of selfhood in *Mercian Hymns*, despite its pervasive imagery of excavation, uprooting, and lost and recovered treasures. Instead, one is more likely to be preoccupied, at least initially, with sorting out the elusive surface features of the poem: who speaks? who perceives? who utters the first-person pronoun? The poem stages this problem itself in hymn XXIV. Here the focus of attention is the carved tympanum of a West Midlands church, clearly a kind of inset microworld, a scale model or *mise en abyme* of the world of *Mercian Hymns* itself. Of this world *en abyme*, someone (but who?) asks, "Where best to stand?" (*CP* 128). Where, indeed.

The question could be posed throughout *Mercian Hymns:* where does this discourse position itself vis-à-vis its world? Voices and positions shift constantly; at the most superficial level of textual organization, personal pronouns shift. Right at the outset, in hymn I, someone (but who?) utters a panegyric to Offa, to which the king, identified in the third person, responds: "'I liked that,' said Offa, 'sing it again'" (*CP* 105). Elsewhere, however, the king seems to command the first-person pronoun, unequivocally in hymn VIII, or so it would seem: "I am the King of Mercia, and I know" (112). I doubt I am alone in detecting here an echo of one of the more dreamlike of John Berryman's first batch of *Dream Songs* (1964): "I am Henry Pussy-cat! My whiskers fly" (Dream Song 22, "Of 1826"; Berryman 24). If hymn VIII really does allude to Berryman, inadvertently or otherwise, then perhaps the effect is to insinuate doubts about the king's monopoly of the first-person pronoun, for the *Dream Songs* are a model of shifting pronoun reference, splintered selfhood, and proliferating masks.

Here in *Mercian Hymns*, too, pronoun reference shifts and masks proliferate. "I" sometimes belongs not to the king but instead, as far as one can determine, to the poet (e.g., hymn XXV); sometimes, however, its referent is wholly indeterminable (e.g., hymn XII). Offa does not always command the first-person pronoun, but often figures, as in hymn I, in the third person (e.g., hymns VII, XI, XV–XVIII, XXI, XXVII). Moreover, the poet, too, sometimes seems to be cast in the third person (e.g., hymn XXIX, if we understand the "child" of this hymn to be the poet himself). Occasionally, a collective "we" intervenes (hymns III, XIX, XXII, XXX); more rarely, so does an elusive second-person referent (hymns IX, XXVI, XIII).

This volatility of perspective, signalled by shifts in personal pronouns and pronoun reference, is further aggravated by the poem's heteroglossia, its radical disparities of style and register (including the juxtapositions of Anglo-Saxon and Latinate vocabularies described above in section III). Markers of style and register ought to allow us to reconstruct a speaker's social identity and the social situation of utterance. But how are we to make situational sense of a patchwork of registers such as we find in hymn X?

> What should a man make of remorse, that it might
>   profit his soul? Tell me. Tell everything to Mother,
>   darling, and God bless.
>
> (*CP* 114)

And what situation of utterance can we reconstruct from hymn XVII?

> 'God's honour—our bikes touched; he skidded and came
>   off.' 'Liar.' A timid father's protective bellow.

Disfigurement of a village-king. 'Just look at
the bugger . . . '

(121; ellipses are Hill's)

It is precisely at such points, where style breaks up like white light passed
through a prism, and with it the speaker's identity and situation, that
Hill's critics bring their hermeneutic ingenuity most aggressively to bear.
Sherry, for instance, identifies the passages between quotation marks in
hymn XVII as dialogue from a radio play overheard by the protagonist
on his car radio (Sherry 133), while Knottenbelt (164, 173) frames the
same quoted material as a flashback to an episode from Hill's childhood.
When, as here, the text refrains from specifying situations where disparities of style might realistically occur, the critics rush in to do the job for
it. The amount of interpretative energy invested in such recuperations
of heteroglossic passages suggests how much is at stake here.

Hermeneutic ingenuity of this kind is a measure simultaneously of
anxiety and desire: anxiety provoked by the "shiftiness" of the text's surface; desire to reconstruct a text more homogeneous, univocal, and centripetal than this text actually, demonstrably is, at least on its surface.
Such ingenuity seems not so much mistaken as misdirected, devoted to
local solutions of local cruxes when it might more profitably be invested
in a global solution of *all* these local incoherences of voice and perspective. For *Mercian Hymns does* have a center to which all of its surface
diversity can ultimately be subsumed, and that center is the archaeological figure of the unearthing or recovery of a buried self.

Mercian Hymns, as all its commentators have recognized, is in part
the poet's autobiography, if covertly so. Harold Bloom says as much;
Mercian Hymns, he writes, "is not only hard to hold together, but there
is some question as to what it is 'about,' though the necessary answer is
akin to *The Prelude* . . . ; Hill has at last no subject but his own complex
subjectivity, and so the poem is 'about' himself" ("Survival" xxii). So the
poem might appropriately be subtitled, "Growth of a Poet's Mind," or
perhaps "A Portrait of the Artist as a Young Man." But if the poem is
about nothing but the poet's "own complex subjectivity," that subjectivity depends for its expression on a figure or fiction: the fiction of the
poet's identity with Offa, King of Mercia.

According to this fiction, obliquely narrated in hymns IV and V, Offa
is reborn or reincarnated as the child Geoffrey Hill, the poet-to-be:

IV

I was invested in mother-earth, the crypt of roots
and endings. Child's-play. I abode there, bided
my time: where the mole

shouldered the clogged wheel, his gold solidus; where
dry-dust badgers thronged the Roman flues, the
long-unlooked-for mansions of our tribe.

V

So much for the elves' wergild, the true governance
of England, the gaunt warrior-gospel armoured in
engraved stone. I wormed my way heavenward for
ages amid barbaric ivy, scrollwork of fern.

Exile or pilgrim set me once more upon that ground:
my rich and desolute childhood. Dreamy, smug-faced,
sick on outings—I was taken to be a king of
some kind, a prodigy, a maimed one.

(*CP* 108–09)

The sequence of hymns IV and V begins with Offa dead and buried,
"invested in mother earth," just one more archaeological artifact among
others in the midden. In hymn V, he unburies himself, worming his way
"heavenward for ages," until he stands "once more upon that ground,"
namely the West Midlands, of which, we recall, he is said to be the "presiding genius." By the end of hymn V, the referent of the "I" has shifted
from Offa dead to Offa reincarnated as a modern child prodigy, or at any
rate a spoiled child, one "taken to be a king of some kind"—presumably,
Hill himself. This hypothesis is confirmed much later, in the penultimate
hymn (XXIX), when the child-poet is said to have "entered into the last
dream of Offa the King," implying, surely, that what came before (i.e,
the preceding twenty-odd hymns) must have been *other* dreams of Offa.
The child-poet, we might suppose, has been *possessed* by Offa in some
sense; and if so, then that goes some way toward explaining the vacillat-
ing pronouns and calculated stylistic incoherences of *Mercian Hymns*.

Thus the sequence of hymns IV and V narrates a myth of Hill's poetic vocation and his special relation to his home region and its past. The myth is one familiar from modernist writing—from *Ulysses,* for instance, where Leopold Bloom in some sense reincarnates (Joyce's theme of "metempsychosis") his Homeric precursor, Odysseus. It is also a version of the Freudian trope of excavating the buried "true" or originary self. *Mercian Hymns,* it might be said, literalizes the Freudian trope of archaeology.

Schwerner's archaeological poetry, by contrast, seems so distant from the Freudian archaeological master trope as to be incompatible with it. There is some evidence that Schwerner himself sees it this way. In a 1994 interview, the interviewer, Willard Gingerich, tries to interest Schwerner in reading *The Tablets* in terms of the Freudian archaeological model, even paraphrasing for him Freud's metaphor of the mind as the city of Rome, built upon the ruins of its own past. Schwerner, however, seems leery of the whole idea, calling his interviewer's attention instead to the ironic structure of *The Tablets:* the scholar-translator may indeed picture the persistence of "deep time" in terms of a Freudian archaeological model, but he may be deluded in this. Ultimately, says Schwerner, "what's more interesting than what Rome is[,] is the process[,] which seems to be a human need . . . to go back to find aspects of past history. But they're unfindable. Now if . . . what's important is not what really happened, either in . . . past experience, or archaeological 'truths,' [if] what is really interesting and important in human life is to find out what is happening now, this minute . . . if that's what's most important, and I think it is, it has a very ambiguous relationship to 'what really happened'" (Gingerich, "An Interview" 38; my ellipses). In effect, Schwerner reproduces (or reinvents) here the argument against "historical truth" in psychoanalysis, and in favor of "narrative truth," that we find in critics of Freud such as Spence. That is, nothing is gained by attributing the status of historical truth to reconstructions of a patient's (or, in Schwerner's case, a culture's) past, when the "truth" of those reconstructions isn't verifiable in any case; what counts is the *stories* that patients (cultures) tell themselves about their past, and how those stories reflect their *present* situation.

Nothing wells up from the depths of *The Tablets,* as I said before; there *are* no psychic depths under it. Instead of being brought to light by excavation, self is dispersed over a horizontal plane, distributed among the subject-positions accommodated by the complex narrative structure detailed above in section IV. That structure multiplies subject-positions, none of them stable, many of them internally divided. Thus, at the level of the archaic world recorded in *The Tablets,* selves flicker in and out of existence, projected by the text's elusive multiple voices. Some bear names (Pinitou, Ahanarshi), others remain anonymous; one is alleged to be psychotic (tablet XIII). At least one of these speakers appears to be sharply aware of the self-division that arises from the practice of writing itself: "when I write letters and do accounts I am that other man" (tablet XIV; *Tablets* 48). One is reminded here of Borges's reflection on "that other man," the written one, in his short puzzle-text, "Borges y yo" (1956).

At the next level "up" (but the levels are constantly collapsing upon each other) we glimpse the middlemen, mediators of the tablets, those putatively responsible for rendering the texts accessible and placing them before us: the scholar-translator and his various shadowy colleagues (Canon Gilpin, Henrik L., Brad de Lisle). The scholar-translator himself is shadowy, elusive, no less so in the garrulous later tablets (XXVI, XXVII) than in the earlier, more laconic ones. Transparently, he identifies with the speakers of the tablets; if he is their medium (in something like the spiritualist sense), they are also his, in some sense. He *is* them, as Flaubert was Madame Bovary. The scholar-translator identifies especially with their elusiveness, the volatility that makes them so hard to grasp, as in tablet XI:

whenever I was open I was closed*

*who is speaking here?

where? when you took them with him?
she opened her vagina so late it was no prophecy it was. . . . . . . +
whenever I opened your vagina*

*who is the narrator?

Then, several lines later in the same tablet:

she took him with them for her
where?. . . . . with him for it?
she opened her + + + + + + + + + + + + + + + + + + + and
never minded
she took him splayed from them to cover it*

*singular confusion of pronouns here. I do not know who I
am when I read this. How magnificent.

(*Tablets* 36)

"I do not know who *I* am when I read this." Throughout, and most explicitly in tablets XXVI and XXVII, the scholar-translator is seeking
traces of modern consciousness, modern identity in archaic materials:
"the possible development of a radical self-plumbing," "a sense of person as Self-examiner" (*Tablets* 70–71). Yet the harder he looks, the more
consciousness and identity seem to disperse into mobile clouds of par-
ticles, and his own consciousness and identity along with them.

Finally, at some hard-to-specify distance from the scholar-translator
stands the poet Armand Schwerner himself. Schwerner, of course, is
ultimately responsible for this entire structure and all the voices that
people it, the scholar-translator included; he is, after all, their "author."
This is easy to say, hard to make sense of; for if Schwerner is the ven-
triloquist, he behaves as though he has no control over the dummies,
indeed barely recognizes them. For instance, what is especially striking
in Schwerner's 1995 *American Poetry Review* interview is the degree to
which the poet distances himself from his alter ego, the scholar-translator (to the point where the very term "alter ego" seems misplaced). Dis-
avowing any special insight into the scholar-translator's intentions, he
confesses to finding the latter's reasoning puzzling:

Well, [the scholar-translator's] goal in that particular Tablet
[XXVII] is in a certain historical sense a little bizarre. That is, he
says that this is the only historical evidence for a narrative structure
findable in a series of cylinder-seals. On the face of it, that seems
to me a little weird. No matter how closely you read that Tablet, it's
very difficult to find a rationale for this assumption. I don't know
where he comes by it. He tries to validate it scientifically by saying

that things were found on the same level, in the same strata and so [on], but it seems to me a bit strange . . . it almost appears that his intention relates to an investment in narrative. Now why that should be so is not clear to me. (Gingerich, "Armand Schwerner" 29; ellipses in the original).

Of course, it is a cliché of fiction-writers' "craft" interviews to claim that invented characters achieved independent life, that they dictated their stories to their authors, and so on; but the tone of this interview, I submit, is one of genuine detachment, as though a separate center of consciousness had spun free of the poet and now could only be observed, even by him, from without: "I don't know where he comes by it"; "why that should be so is not clear to me."

And that same sense of separation and splintering of selves occurs not only in the poet's reflections on *The Tablets* but persistently throughout the poem itself. It is a leitmotif of the "Journals/Divagations," the poet's notebooks, appended to *The Tablets* and ambiguously part of the text itself or exterior to it, depending. Here the theme of dispersal of self is reiterated. One notebook entry reads, "what is 'I'?" (127); another, "who is talking?" (129); and a third, "Destroy the point of view: who's speaking? to whom? and the rest of it" (136). Repeated several times is the refrain, "there is no nuclear self" (130–31, 133; see Finkelstein 111–12). There is no nuclear self; no depths anywhere under *The Tablets*.

VI. ARCHAEOLOGY IN RUINS

In the ruins of great buildings the idea of the plan speaks more impressively than in lesser buildings, however well preserved they are; and for this reason the German *Trauerspiel* merits interpretation. In the spirit of allegory it is conceived from the outset as a ruin, a fragment.

> Walter Benjamin, *The Origin of German Tragic Drama* (235).

Archaeology in the tradition of learnéd wit is clearly not the archaeology of the Freudian model. There are no buried truths to be excavated here, no upwellings from "deep time." If the Freudian model is inadequate to texts like Schwerner's *Tablets* in particular, then is there some alternative model that might be more adequate?

There is Michel Foucault, of course.[8] Far from being merely a variant of the Freudian archaeology trope, as casual observers have sometimes assumed (e.g., Kuspit 15, n. 8), Foucault's use of archaeology proves to be strongly at odds with Freud's. Indeed, so perverse is Foucault's approach to archaeology that some have suspected his methodological book, *The Archaeology of Knowledge* (*L'Archéologie du savoir*, 1969), of being not at all the essay on method that it purports to be, but rather a *parody* of method (see Megill 222–32). Does this place Foucault in the mock-scholarly tradition of learnéd wit, then, alongside Borges, Nabokov, and the others, including Schwerner? In the light of his fascination with certain figures from that tradition, such as Raymond Roussel and the Borges of the Chinese encyclopedia, this is perhaps not as implausible a hypothesis as it might appear at first sight. In any case, whether or not we regard the *Archaeology* as parody, its method is certainly *not* archaeology in the Freudian sense.

The Archaeology of Knowledge is arguably Foucault's least-cited, least-understood, and worst-regarded book. This calls for some explanation. It has become conventional to divide Foucault's career into two parts, an earlier "archaeological" phase, ending with the *Archaeology* itself, and a later "genealogical" one, and to value later Foucault much more highly than early Foucault. Archaeology tends to be dismissed as a dead end. A skeptic might venture to suggest that the later, genealogical Foucault was seized on (at least in the United States academy), and the archaeological Foucault dismissed, for much the same reason that "poststructuralism" in general was adopted and "structuralism" passed over: not because American theory had fully absorbed either structuralism or Foucauldian archaeology, made its critiques of them, identified their respective shortcomings, and moved on to more fruitful enterprises, but because genealogy, like poststructuralism, allowed everyone to carry on business as usual (see Culler, "Beyond Interpretation"). "Business as usual," in the case of Foucauldian genealogy, meant *narrativizing* (often misnamed "historicizing"): genealogy permits the uninterrupted telling of historical narratives, while archaeology is aggressively, off-puttingly antinarrative and antihistorical. The rhetoric of this "anti" is the key to grasping the perversity of Foucault's archaeology. The terms in which Foucault characterizes his archaeology are almost entirely negative—he tells us what it is *not*, what it does *not* do, but seldom what it is or does:

Archaeology tries to define not the thoughts, representations, images, preoccupations that are concealed or revealed in discourses; but those discourses themselves. . . . Archaeology does not seek to rediscover the continuous, insensible transition that relates discourses . . . to what precedes them, surrounds them, or follows them. . . . Archaeology is not ordered in accordance with the sovereign figure of the *oeuvres*. . . . archaeology does not try to restore what has been thought, wished, aimed at, experienced, desired by men in the very moment at which they expressed it in discourse. . . . It is not a return to the innermost secret of the origin. (*Archaeology* 138–40)

What animates this negativity is a profound epistemological skepticism: Foucault refuses to be bound by the categories in terms of which intellectual history has been written—the received partitioning into fields and disciplines, the assumed transhistorical permanence of the objects of knowledge, the familiar developmental models of change—viewing these categories as themselves products of the history they purport to capture. Instead, he practices, under the name of archaeology, what David Shumway (98) has characterized as "the history of ideas without ideas and without history": without ideas, because Foucault systematically refuses to *take seriously* the meanings of the discursive *énoncés* whose formation, dispersal, and transformations he seeks to grasp; without history, because he emphasizes the discontinuities of a particular archaeological stratum of discourse rather than its continuities with strata "above" or "below" (before or after) it.

It is hard to imagine an approach more remote from the archaeological model either in the Freudian version, with its rhetoric of epistemological mastery, or in the modernist version, with its emphasis on continuity and persistence and its vertical spatialization of "deep time." On the other hand, Foucault's archaeology does seem congenial to Schwerner's failed epistemological quest for origins, and his collapsing of vertical structures of transmission onto a single plane. Archaeology, Foucault writes (131), "does not imply the search for a beginning; it does not relate analysis to geological excavation." But if it does not involve "excavation," in some metaphorical sense, then in what respect is Foucault's procedure properly called "archaeological" at all? What Foucault proposes, in effect, is not so much an archaeology in any familiar modernist or Freudian sense, but something like archaeology in the sense of *The Tablets:* the *ruins* of an archaeology; archaeology *sous rature.*

+ . . . . + + + + + + + + + +
+ + + + + + + [the the] + + + + + + +
+ +
+ +
+ +

5
How (Not) to Read a Postmodernist Long Poem

John Ashbery's "The Skaters"

The Cognitive Questions
(asked by most artists of the 20th century, Platonic or Aristotelian, till around 1958):
"How can I interpret this world of which I am part? And what am I in it?"

The Postcognitive Questions
(asked by most artists since then):
"Which world is this? What is to be done in it? Which of my selves is to do it?"

Dick Higgins, 1978 (101)

LET'S ASSUME, if only for the sake of argument, that there really is such a thing as postmodernist poetry—or at any rate, that there is something to be gained by using the term "postmodernist" with reference to poetry. Granted this assumption, then surely it follows that John Ashbery must rank among the exemplary postmodernist poets (see Mohanty and Monroe).[1] His long and prolific record of publication, beginning in 1956 and comprising, as of this writing, over twenty volumes of poetry (not to mention a volume of plays, much art criticism, and a coauthored novel), closely coincides with the onset, rise, and (perhaps) climax of the postmodernist mode in North America. Moreover, the shifts in that long poetic career seem to parallel, when they do not actually anticipate, shifts in postmodernism across a range of cultural practices.

The disjunctiveness of Ashbery's early poetry, peaking in *The Tennis Court Oath* (1962), parallels that of the first phase of postmodernism, as represented by, for instance, John Cage in music, Robert Rauschenberg in the visual arts, William Burroughs in prose fiction, or, closer still to Ashbery's mode, Donald Barthelme at his most radical, as in "The Indian Uprising" (1968; see McHale and Ron). "Disjunction," in the context of verbal art, involves either (1) the breakdown of textual cohesion (in the sense of Halliday and Hasan) within or between sentences, as in the poems of *The Tennis Court Oath*, or (2) abrupt, unmotivated shifts of frame of reference between sentences or passages, whether or not textual cohesion is preserved. The latter type of disjunction characterizes "The Skaters."[2] Ashbery's early disjunctiveness would later be adopted as a model by the Language poets, arguably the most fully postmodernist of any of the late-twentieth-century poetic movements (see Ward; Lehman, *Last Avant-Garde* 369–73).

Meanwhile, Ashbery himself had moved on, radical disjunction having gradually given way in his poetry to a poetics based more on the "secondhand" and "found"—on "recycled" language, on appropriated, mediated, and simulacral materials. Clichés had figured conspicuously in Ashbery's linguistic repertoire from the beginning, of course, but came increasingly to dominate the verbal texture of his poetry from *Three Poems* (1972) on. Similarly, appropriations of popular-culture materials had appeared from early on (e.g., women's-magazine fiction in "Idaho," 1962; comic strips in "Farm Implements and Rutabagas in a Landscape," 1970), but the density and salience of such material increases in his later poetry, from, say, "Daffy Duck in Hollywood" (1977) through *Girls on the Run* (1999), based on the appropriative imagery of the "outsider" artist Henry Darger (1892–1972; see Vine; Anderson). This reorientation of Ashbery's poetics parallels or anticipates the shift in postmodernism generally from forms of disjunction to recycling, appropriation, pastiche, and other varieties of secondhandedness: "double-coding" and historicism in architecture, *le mode rétro* in cinema, "historiographic metafiction" and the "avant-pop" mode in prose fiction, and so on (see chapter 1).

If Ashbery is an exemplary postmodernist poet, then his long poem of the midsixties, "The Skaters" (from *Rivers and Mountains*, 1966), must be a strong candidate for the title of exemplary postmodernist long poem—exemplary, at least, of what I have been calling the first, disjunctive phase of postmodernism. About the stature of "The Skaters" there can be little doubt. David Lehman, for instance, characterizes it as the first of the major works of Ashbery's maturity (*Last Avant-Garde* 161).

About its exact place in the trajectory of Ashbery's development there is less of a consensus. For Charles Berger ("Vision" 164), for instance, the crucial watershed between Ashbery's early and later modes falls between *Rivers and Mountains* (a volume more than half of which is taken up by "The Skaters") and his next book, *The Double Dream of Spring* (1970); for Harold Bloom ("Charity" 60), on the other hand, the gap is wider between *Rivers and Mountains* and the book that precedes it, *The Tennis Court Oath*, though like Berger he also acknowledges a crucial transition between the former and *Double Dream*. Perhaps, after all, it is less important to determine conclusively whether "The Skaters" falls on the near or far side of this divide, than to recognize that somewhere hereabouts Ashbery's early mode of disjunction peaks and begins to ebb, and that "The Skaters" is implicated in that changeover.

Powerfully disjunctive though it is, "The Skaters" does not appear as radical as "Europe," the long, fragmentary centerpiece poem of *The Tennis Court Oath*. This lower degree of disjunctiveness serves as a lure to the reader. No one contemplating the detached word clusters of "Europe" would expect them to make much sense, so that the reader's frustration at failing to make sense *of* them is paradoxically less than in the case of "The Skaters," which often appears to make good sense locally, inducing an unwarranted expectation that the *whole* ought to make equally good sense. Instead, what the reader actually encounters is an all but unmanageable flux. Narrative episodes emerge—a sea voyage in part II, a desert-island castaway scenario in part III, followed by scenes from expatriate life—only to be abandoned; no continuous, sustained narrative develops. Verbal "found objects" litter the poem's surface, many of them having evidently been scavenged from a book improbably entitled *Three Hundred Things a Bright Boy Can Do* (Shoptaw, *Outside* 94–96; Lehman, *Last Avant-Garde* 121–22):

An Indianapolis, Indiana man collects slingshots of all epochs, and so on.[3]

The lines that draw nearer together are said to "vanish."
The point where they meet is their vanishing point. (II.208)

Plant your feet squarely. Grasp your club lightly but firmly in the hollow of your fingers.

Slowly swing well back and complete your stroke well through,
 pushing to the very end.

(III.218)

The style shifts erratically and without motivation, and the text abounds
with fragments belonging to disparate levels and registers: bureaucratic
("Please leave your papers on the desk as you pass out," II.205), devo-
tional ("To hear wings of the spirit, though far," I.195), art-critical (quasi-
technical vocabulary such as "line," "mass," "perspective," "value"), high-
"poetical" ("And up the swollen sands/Staggers the darkness fiend, with
the storm fiend close behind him!" I.195), low-colloquial ("I'd like to
bugger you all up,/Deliberately falsify all your old suck-ass notions,"
II.202), and so on (see D. Shapiro, *John Ashbery* 100, 102, 114). Juxtapositions, particularly of "poetical" and colloquial registers, are frequent and
jarring:

Scarcely we know where to turn to avoid suffering, I mean
There are so many places.

(II.208)

Now you must shield with your body if necessary (you
Remind me of some lummox I used to know) the secret your
 body is.

(III.211)

The verbal texture is further enhanced, or muddied, by abundant literary allusions—to Shakespeare (*King Lear*), the Romantics (Wordsworth,
Coleridge, Keats), the symbolists (Baudelaire, Rimbaud), various high
modernists and avant-gardists (Eliot, Pound, Auden, Apollinaire, Mayakovsky), other New York School poets (Koch), even the egregious and
incomparable William McGonagall (see D. Shapiro, *John Ashbery* 93–131
passim; Shoptaw, *Outside* 89–99 passim). These allusions, sometimes
nearly verbatim quotations (e.g., "What matter now whether I wake or
sleep?" III.214, quoting Keats's "Ode to a Nightingale"), are more often
so oblique and diffuse—distant echoes rather than allusions—as to lead
the reader to doubt whether they are "really there" at all. How can one
be sure they're not some kind of mirage induced by the text's sheer
indeterminacy—unconscious on the poet's part, a kind of hermeneutic

grasping at straws on the reader's part? The answer is, one can't ever be sure with Ashbery, least of all in "The Skaters."

How is one to negotiate or manage such flux? Critics, who in this respect (if no other) may be regarded as representative readers, tend to proceed by selecting "key" lines or passages, treating these as interpretative centers or "nodes" around which to organize the heterogeneous materials of the poem. Other materials come to be subordinated in various ways (explicitly or, more often, implicitly) to these "key" passages, e.g., as exempla or illustrations, or as figurative or allegorical restatements— that is, as metonymically or metaphorically related to the "nodal" material. Alternatively, material lying outside the "nodes" is simply passed over in silence, so that the poem is reduced, in effect, to a skeletal structure of points that yield most readily to a particular interpretative orientation, the rest having disappeared, like the soft tissue in an X-ray image. Ars-poetic statements, which abound in "The Skaters," are naturally the preferred interpretative "keys," but other types of passage can also be made to serve, as we will shortly see. Identifying key passages and either subordinating or ignoring the rest of the text is the strategy favored by Harold Bloom, arguably Ashbery's most influential reader, and while Bloom has sometimes been faulted for undertaking to read Ashbery this way (see, e.g., Mohanty and Monroe 39–42), his approach has also been widely imitated.

There are two damaging drawbacks to this reading strategy, one generally applicable to this mode of interpretation wherever it is found, whatever the text and whoever the author, the other specific to Ashbery. First, this strategy fosters the illusion that interpretation grounded in key nodes can master or exhaust the text, when really it only samples the latter. Particularly in versions of this strategy in which the poem is reduced to a collection of decontextualized "key" quotes (as tends to be the case in Bloom's readings), most of the text ends up "falling through the cracks," and the bulk of the poem goes uninterpreted—unread, to all intents and purposes.[4] Secondly, Ashbery (or perhaps we should say, his poem) anticipates this sort of reading, appearing to cater to it, but only in order to entrap and outflank the reader. No conscientious critic of Ashbery fails eventually to recognize the degree to which Ashbery's texts seem always to have pre-empted one's best moves.[5] Even the supremely confident Bloom seems uneasily aware at times of Ashbery's having gotten there ahead of him (see e.g., "Introduction," *John Ashbery*

14). Which is not to say that one can avoid falling into Ashbery's traps or succumbing to his flanking maneuvers; only that one does so with eyes wide open.

In what follows, I undertake to examine three types of key or node in "The Skaters," demonstrating how Ashbery's text anticipates and pre-empts interpretative moves in each case. The types of keys to be considered are (1) descriptive (or world-oriented) statements; (2) autobiographical (or speaker-oriented, expressive) statements; and (3) ars-poetic (or text-oriented, textually self-reflexive) statements. Underlying my categories here is the "three-dimensional model of semiotic objects" proposed by Benjamin Harshav (Hrushovski); see McHale, "Making (Non)Sense." Harshav's three dimensions are (1) the dimension of meaning and reference, comprising the text's frames and fields of reference (in other words, its "world"); (2) the dimension of speakers, voices, and positions (the area conventionally covered by theories of point of view, narration, and focalization); and (3) the dimension of the organized text. Readings of Ashbery that seek to organize the text around its descriptions clearly privilege the dimension of "world"; readings seeking to organize it around its first-person passages (its allegedly "autobiographical" moments) privilege the dimension of speakers, voices, and positions; while readings that key on textual self-reflection privilege the organized text (albeit at a remove).

I. WHICH WORLD?

Reflecting on Ashbery's methods for sustaining a poem as long as "The Skaters," David Shapiro distinguishes between the poem's continuous patterns, in particular its "landscape observation," and the "smaller curves" that its many lyric moments inscribe within those larger continuities (99–100). Treating passages of landscape description as "key" or "nodal" passages, and subordinating other types of material to them, Shapiro's reading seems to promise a degree of interpretative mastery. Unfortunately, the poem it promises mastery *of* bears little resemblance to "The Skaters," and much more to something like the landscape poetry of, say, Douglas Crase (e.g., "The Lake Effect" or "Six Places in New York" from *The Revisionist*, 1981), in whose poems, clearly derivative of Ashbery, "landscape observation" does indeed dominate and organize the whole, while accommodating the "smaller curves" of lyric digression. If "The Skaters" yielded as readily as Crase's poems to the kind of reading that Shapiro proposes, it would certainly be a more accessible poem, but also a lesser one.

Ashbery seems to be a poet of landscape, and his poems often seem to be descriptive. Yet, as critics who have reflected on Ashbery's landscapes have discovered (see, e.g., Perloff, *Indeterminacy* 8–11, 248–87; Costello), the expectations of descriptive coherence that Ashbery's landscapes invite are seldom satisfied. What, if not landscape description, are we to expect of a volume entitled *Rivers and Mountains* that opens with what purports to be a cityscape ("These Lacustrine Cities"), and that, apart from the title poem, also contains a catalogue of rivers ("Into the Dusk-Charged Air") and a poem with a toponymic title ("The Thousand Islands")? "The Skaters," in particular, the long poem that closes the volume, solicits by its very title expectations of a descriptive scene. Its model ought to be something like the memorable skating scene in Wordsworth's *Prelude*, Book I, ll.425–63 (see Bloom, "Charity" 58; Shoptaw, *Outside* 92). *Ought* to be; but where are the skaters in Ashbery's poem? Their only unambiguous traces are to be found in the twelfth line, which stands alone, separated by white space from the verse paragraphs that precede and follow it—

Here a scarf flies, there an excited call is heard.

—and then a couple of lines later:

. . . it is novelty
That guides these swift blades o'er the ice
Projects into a finer expression (but at the expense
Of energy) the profile I cannot remember.

(I.194)

Pretty minimal, for a description,[6] but its sparseness is not really the issue here. The issue, rather, is the description's ontological status. Its disjunction from the surrounding discourse, as well as the abstractness of that discourse, suggest that the image of "swift blades" might not belong to a literal scene after all, but rather to a metaphorical figure, while the archaism "o'er" suggests quotation from some earlier source, or the imitation of one. The line, "Here a scarf flies," and so on, also strikes a false note: could this, too, be a verbal found object? The suspicion, once aroused, proves hard to shake (and is amply borne out in the rest of the poem): this is not, after all, direct description of some world, fictional or real, but secondhand description, mediated by another, prior representation—intertextuality, not "reality."

The reader's experience of elusive descriptiveness in this skating scene (if that's what we want to call it) gives us our first taste of the dynamics of world building (and unbuilding) in "The Skaters" as a whole. Time and again, verbal materials that seem descriptive, or potentially descriptive, of some world of reference spring ontological "leaks" of one kind or another—e.g., the combined suspicion of metaphoricity and secondhandedness in the skating scene—and empty out, hemorrhaging reality and bringing the reader's world-making operations to a halt. And this happens no matter how "present" the described scene might initially appear to be, or how fully its description has been elaborated.

By way of substantiating this last point, we might provisionally distinguish three degrees of descriptive elaboration. The minimum degree of elaboration would be the freestanding word or phrase with descriptive potential, such as the poem's title, "The Skaters," or paratactic catalogues of such words or phrases (i.e., words or phrases juxtaposed with minimal syntactical articulation). At an intermediate level of elaboration, potentially descriptive words or phrases are integrated into sentence-level syntactical structures: "Here a scarf flies, there an excited call is heard," or "novelty . . . guides these swift blades o'er the ice." This is the level, roughly, of what might be called the descriptive "image." Finally, at the highest level of elaboration, one arrives at fully articulated descriptive discourses extending over multiple sentences—descriptive "passages," let's call them.

One of the favorite devices of the New York School poets (Lehman, *Last Avant-Garde* 225–26), the descriptive catalogue or inventory occurs often in Ashbery (though less often, perhaps, than in Koch). There are several in "The Skaters," including a catalogue of sounds and the instruments that produce them, and another of the contents of a room, each item metonymic of the occupant's poverty:

> This, after all, may be happiness: tuba notes awash on the great flood, ruptures of xylophone, violins, limpets, grace-notes, the musical instrument called serpent, viola da gambas, aeolian harps, clavicles, pinball machines, electric drills, que sais-je encore! (I.195)

A broken mirror nailed up over a chipped enamel basin, whose
    turgid waters
Reflect the fly-specked calendar—with ecstatic Dutch girl
    clasping tulips—
On the far wall. Hanging from one nail, an old velvet hat with a
    tattered bit of veiling—last remnant of former finery.
The bed well made. The whole place scrupulously clean, but cold
    and damp.

                                                    (II.208)

Now, just because descriptive items are minimally integrated—merely paratactically juxtaposed—does not make them, for that reason, any less capable of projecting a world; think of how crowded and richly textured is the world projected by Whitman's catalogues, or (especially with respect to the second of the Ashbery examples cited above) how the reality of rural poverty acquires "thickness" through James Agee's inventorying of a sharecropper's possessions in his and Walker Evans's *Let Us Now Praise Famous Men* (1941).

No, what deprives these descriptions from "The Skaters" of "presence" or "reality"—ontological substance—is not their catalogue form per se, but rather, in one case, internal anomalies, and in the other, external framing. The catalogue of noisemakers, which might pass muster at first glance, begins to unravel from the moment we recognize that a "limpet" is not a musical instrument like a "serpent," but rather a shellfish (or a below-the-waterline explosive device modelled on such a shellfish), and moreover that "clavicles" must be a slip for "clavichords" (see D. Shapiro 98–99). Such "errors," no doubt deliberate, prevent our reconstructing from these items anything like a setting or scene—a museum collection of musical instruments, for instance, or some kind of avant-garde orchestra—and converts the potential assemblage of objects into a mere list of words; world empties out, leaving only text (see McHale, *Postmodernist Fiction* 153, 162–64).

What compromises "reality" in the description of the room, in the other example, is nothing internal to the catalogue, but rather its immediate textual context. The immediately following line, separated from the catalogue by a blank space, reads: "All this, wedged into a pyramidal ray of light, is my own invention" (II.208). "All this" presumably refers to the contents of the catalogue. So what we had taken to be the description of a fragment of the world is retrospectively reframed as fiction—"My own invention." Worse, the language used to accomplish this reframing is itself secondhand, borrowed from the White Knight of *Through the Looking-Glass*. Moreover, the phrase "wedged into a pyramidal ray of light" suggests not the description of a scene so much as the description of a *visual representation* of a scene—the description of a painting of the room, perhaps; perhaps something like the "pyramidal ray of light" that dominates Picasso's *Guernica*. In short, here we have, not a metonymic representation of poverty, but rather the representation of a representation of poverty, at one remove: either fiction or ekphrasis, or both.

I have been treating the inventoried room as an example of a descriptive catalogue, but its separate items might just as appropriately have been treated as examples of descriptive images. The modernists elevated imagery to the very measure of poetry; in effect, poetry *was* imagery, and a poet was someone who produced images. "The Skaters" abounds with descriptive imagery, almost as though Ashbery were presenting his imagist credentials for inspection. Part IV is especially rich in fresh, sensuous images of the natural world—or that's how they appear at first glance, anyway:

The wind thrashes the maple seed-pods,
The whole brilliant mass comes spattering down.
(IV.220)

. . . wind hard in the tops
Of the baggy eucalyptus branches.
(IV.220)

The birch-pods come clattering down on the weed-grown
marble pavement.
(IV.222)

The wind has stopped, but the magnolia blossoms still
Fall with a plop onto the dry, spongy earth.
(IV.222)

Such imagery seems animated by the "oriental" aesthetics of haiku and related genres that played so crucial a role in the development of modernist practice. But the connection with haiku hardly has time to register before one's suspicions are aroused: aren't these images a bit *too much* like haiku? And isn't the semantic-syntactical parallelism among them just a bit *too* systematic, to the point of suggesting an artificiality or mechanicalness somewhat at odds with the tender responsiveness to nature that the poet seems otherwise to flaunt here?[7] One's suspicions grow: this imagery is not so much *like* haiku as a *pastiche* or *parody* of the haiku model.

Once again, what we had taken to be unproblematically descriptive proves, on closer scrutiny, to be secondhand, mediated (in this case) by a literary model that is being proffered *instead of* the illusion of unmediated access to a world. One might usefully contrast here Ashbery's practice with Riffaterre's (1978) semiotics of poetry. By Riffaterre's account, *all* poetry is mediated by models, but seeks to cover its tracks by pretending to imitate a world (and of course by seducing the reader into playing along with that pretense). Ashbery, by contrast, exposes the models to our scrutiny; what he represents are the models themselves, not the worlds that the models purport to represent.[8] Thus, in "The Skaters," part IV, we encounter not the-world-as-modelled-by-haiku, but rather the haiku model of the world.

Moreover, just as in the case of the inventoried room, so here, too, description suffers ontological depletion by being retrospectively reframed. Immediately after the image of the falling magnolia blossoms we find this:

> There is only one way of completing the puzzle:
> By finding a hog-shaped piece that is light green shading to buff
> at one side.
>
> (IV.222)

Is the preceding image, then, or even the whole of part IV, nothing but a puzzle picture—the representation, not of nature itself, but of a prior *representation of* nature? Yet another ekphrasis? We need at least to entertain this possibility.

This brings us finally to Ashbery's fully elaborated descriptive passages, which, in "The Skaters," are almost without exception "narratized," that is, animated and set into motion by the agency of an observer or experiencer who, in effect, conducts us around the described world (see Mosher). Typical of the poem's narratized descriptions is the voyage episode (II.203–06), a travelogue in quatrains narrated in the first person. The echoes here of Baudelaire and Rimbaud are particularly pronounced, once again arousing suspicions of secondhand description, mediated by another text or texts. Moreover, the abrupt transition signaling the end of the voyage episode opens up certain destabilizing interpretative possibilities:

And, as into a tunnel the voyage starts
Only, as I said, to be continued. The eyes of those left standing
    on the dock are wet
But ours are dry. Into the secretive, vaporous night with all of us!
Into the unknown, the unknown that loves us, the great
    unknown!

So man nightly
Sparingly descends
The birches and the hay all of him
Pruned, erect for vital contact.

(II.206)

The syntax here suggests an elaborate simile, of the form, "Just as . . . so . . . ": "Just as [something], so man nightly sparingly descends," and so on. Could that unspecified "something" be the entire voyage episode? In other words, could the voyage turn out to have been the vehicle (in the poetological sense) of an elaborate conceit, a kind of epic simile? As if at the flip of a switch, the literal travelogue is recategorized, in retrospect, as figurative.

Nor is this the only possibility of reframing that we are compelled to consider here. A passage immediately preceding the description of the voyage mentions "an old map or illustration" (II.202), and in the midst of the voyage itself we find this: "And we finger down the dog-eared coasts. . . . " (II.205). "Finger" and "dog-eared" suggest someone handling a book or map. In the immediate context, this reads as metaphor ("A boat steaming parallel to the coast is like fingering a dog-eared map"), but once we take into account the larger context (the context that includes "an old map or illustration"), the relationship between literal and figurative threatens to invert. So is the putative voyage nothing more, after all, than a fantasy or daydream, perhaps stimulated by perusal of an old map? There is precedent for such a scenario in Ashbery's poetry, most memorably in the early poem, "The Instruction Manual" (from *Some Trees*, 1956), a fantasy travelogue in which the fantasist never leaves his desk. By one means or another, then, this descriptive passage is robbed of its claim to represent a world directly.

Much the same pattern holds for all the other descriptive passages of "The Skaters." The structural model for all these descriptive passages is "laid bare" for our inspection by the "fire fountain" passage (II.209–11). One of the *Three Hundred Things* that Ashbery found to do in a turn-of-the-century book for boys (see Shoptaw, *Outside* 95–96), the fire fountain involves a chemical reaction that produces images on the surface of a basin of "phosphorescent liquid." The fountain is "a kind of drawing," but a peculiarly unstable kind; first it produces a nostalgic image of an April day in an idyllic small town—"a young girl and boy leaning against a bicycle," a postman threatened by a bulldog, a young woman fixing her stocking, etc.—which metamorphoses into a nocturne, then into a sea-scape. An image surfaces, only to be effaced and replaced by another; "Then this vision, too, fades slowly away." As in the other descriptive passages, an illusion of reality is momentarily generated, only to be deprived of its illusionism (see D. Shapiro 116–17). The difference is that here, un-like in the other descriptive passages, we observe the mechanism itself in action, as figured in the fire fountain, which operates, we are told, "for all the world like a poet" (II.211). And of course, the description of the fire fountain is itself ekphrastic—if not of the fire fountain's "drawings" themselves, then perhaps (because once again we are given a second op-tion) of a picture puzzle, for the springtime vignette is also identified as "a puzzle scene" (II.211).

All descriptions in "The Skaters," we are compelled to conclude, are ekphrastic or otherwise "secondhand" one way or another (or more than one way, in several instances). Up to and including the level of the entire poem, one wonders? Reconsider, from this perspective, the lines from part IV quoted above: "There is only one way of completing the puzzle," and so on (IV.222). Coming as they do on the poem's penultimate page, and recalling other puzzles throughout the poem (such as the one in the fire fountain passage), these lines seem to insinuate that the poem as a whole, and not just its last part, might be regarded as a picture puzzle. Is the entire "world" of the poem just a puzzle scene, then, so that the entire poem amounts to an extended ekphrasis, the representation of a representation? If so, this would not be the only time that Ashbery would devote an entire extended text to ekphrasis of a visual representation; "Description of a Masque" (in *A Wave*, 1984; see Yacobi), "Self-Portrait in a Convex Mirror" (1975) and *Girls on the Run* (1999) are all ekphrastic in just this way. Nor would it be the only time that he would retrospectively reframe a text in its closing moments. For instance, two of the three prose texts comprising *Three Poems* (1972) seem to end with a similar reframing of everything that has come before in the text:

> [I]t is here that I am quite ready to admit that I am alone, that the film I have been watching all this time may only be a mirror, with all the characters including that of the old aunt played by me in different disguises. . . . I have been watching this film, therefore, and now I have seen enough; as I leave the theater I am surprised to find that it is still daylight outside. ("The System," in *Mooring* 374)

> There were new people watching and waiting. . . . The performance had ended, the audience streamed out; the applause still echoed in the empty hall. But the idea of the spectacle as something to be acted out and absorbed still hung in the air long after the last spectator had gone home to sleep. ("The Recital," in *Mooring* 383)

At the last moment, the experiencers of these worlds (the *I* of "The System," the audience of "The Recital") ascend to a higher ("realer") level of reality, and the worlds themselves correspondingly undergo an ontological demotion from reality to representation (film, theatrical "spectacle"), from firsthand to secondhand. It is a signature postmodernist moment, anticipating by a year, in the case of *Three Poems*, and by seven years in the case of "The Skaters," the quintessentially postmodernist ending of Pynchon's *Gravity's Rainbow*, when the novel's world is revealed to have been nothing but a film being viewed by us "old fans who've always been at the movies (haven't we?)" (769; see McHale, *Postmodernist Fiction* 116).

II. WHICH SELF?

"But the floor is being slowly pulled apart/Like straw under those limpid feet" (I.198): when the ontological rug (or floor) is pulled out from under a descriptive passage, demoting it from reality to fiction, as at the end of "The System" or "The Recital," and presumably of "The Skaters" as well, the reader correspondingly experiences a sense of having emerged from fiction into reality, of having at last achieved the level of the "really real." An example would be the castaway episode of "The Skaters" (III.214–16), involving a picturesque description of a desert island. The rug is abruptly jerked out from under this fantasy world: "In reality of course the middle-class apartment I live in is nothing like a desert island" (III.216). The temptation is strong here to read the ensuing passage (III.216–17) as a more or less undoctored report on the poet's "real life" (presumably during his expatriate years in Paris; see Lehman, *Last Avant-Garde* 115–16). Fantasy having been banished, what follows must, we feel, be authentic autobiography, spoken in the poet's own persona. But surely in responding this way we succumb to a fallacy, a sort of optical illusion. What justifies the assumption that this account of middle-class expatriation reflects Ashbery's "real life" any more directly than did the castaway fantasy?

Underlying such a leap to conclusions is a general habit of reading. Armed with one or two familiar facts about Ashbery's life (just about the extent of public knowledge of his biography, until recently), such as that he was raised on a farm in western New York State, that he lived an expatriate life in Paris, and so on, critics seek out passages like the "middle-class apartment" one and treat them as nodes of autobiographical veracity, relative to which the putative "reality" of other passages can be gauged.[9] It is somewhat in this spirit, for instance, that Shapiro (102) adduces the fact of Ashbery's farm childhood ("the farmyard . . . where Ashbery lived as a child") when reading a passage (I.196) in which (presumably) remembered experience of winter on the farm mingles with the secondhand realities of literature and visual art (allusions to or echoes of Brueghel, Eliot, Daumier). It is as if, profiled against the backdrop of autobiographical reality, the passage's secondhand literary and visual allusions stood out sharply in their ontological difference—or so Shapiro would have us believe. Such touchstone passages as the snowy farmyard seem compatible with what we take to be the poem's autobiographical materials, and so are tentatively admitted to its "real world," whereas passages like the castaway fantasy, so flagrantly incompatible with the poem's autobiographical touchstones, end up being classified as fictional, fantastic, or secondhand.

The exercise is sheerly arbitrary, involving little more than shopping around for plausible first-person passages to treat as autobiographical "keys" to the poem. Such shopping expeditions are especially tempting, but also especially problematic, in the case of "The Skaters," where the first-person pronoun proliferates. Ashbery is notorious for the elusiveness of his pronoun referents; elsewhere, the elusive pronouns are likely to be *you* and *it* (see Shetley 112–17), but in "The Skaters" it is above all *I* that keeps us guessing. Shoptaw warns us about the poem's "host of voluble, disarmingly direct first-person speakers. But as one 'Ashbery' gives way to the next, we realize that the author can only enter his poem by subjecting himself to its mysterious rules" (*Outside* 90). In particular, he continues, "Few of [the poem's] childhood memories . . . are Ashbery's" (89).[10] His clear-sightedness on this point does not, however, prevent Shoptaw himself from succumbing to the temptation to assimilate the poem to the poet's autobiography. If the poem's details are not to be construed as autobiographical, nevertheless, Shoptaw claims, its overall four-part structure does reflect the general structure of Ashbery's personal experience: his childhood (part I), "voyaging" to Harvard and New York (part II), expatriation in Paris (part III), and projected old age (part IV) (*Outside* 89).

The elusiveness of "autobiography" in "The Skaters"—that is, the problem of determining which *I*'s (if any) belong to the poet, and which to various fictional personae—is particularly conspicuous in part IV (see Shoptaw, *Outside* 99). Here, as the poem's end approaches, the large verse blocks of preceding sections give way to a multiplicity of short, disconnected fragments, most of them cast in the first person, and many of them apparently mutually incompatible, as far as their respective worlds of reference are concerned:

This is my fourteenth year as governor of C province.
I was little more than a lad when I first came here.
Now I am old but scarcely any wiser.

(IV.220)

Today I wrote, "The spring is late this year.
In the early mornings there is hoarfrost on the water meadows.
And on the highway the frozen ruts are papered over with ice."

(IV.220)

. . . together we look back at the house.
It could use a coat of paint
Except I am too poor to hire a workman.
I have all I can do to keep body and soul together
And soon, even that relatively simple task may prove to be
    beyond my powers.
                                                    (IV.221)

I have spent the afternoon blowing soap bubbles
And it is with a feeling of delight I realize I am
All alone in the skittish darkness.
                                (IV.221)

I had thought of announcing my engagement to you
On the day of the first full moon of X month.
                                            (IV.222)

One morning you appear at breakfast
. . . .
And over a pot of coffee, or, more accurately, rusted water
Announce your intention of leaving me alone in this cistern-like
    house.
                                                    (IV.222)

"At thirty-two I came up to take my examination at the university.
The U wax factory, it seemed, wanted a new general manager.
I was the sole applicant for the job, but it was refused me.
So I have preferred to finish my life
In the quietude of this floral retreat."
                                                    (IV.222–3)

The pump is busted. I shall have to get it fixed.
                            (IV.223)

By applying rules of discursive cohesion and common-sense world-
knowledge, we can perhaps begin to determine which, if any, of these
I's might have emanated from "Ashbery," or at any rate we can begin to
eliminate the ones which could not possibly have done so. Among the

"impossible" candidates must figure those that belong to what appears to be a parody of Chinese poetry, or more like a parody of Pound's modernist versions of Chinese poetry in *Cathay* (e.g., the much anthologized "River-Merchant's Wife"). If we eliminate these—the governor of C province, the speaker who once aspired to the job at the U wax factory, etc.—what remains? Well, perhaps the writer in the second passage, though the lines he reports having written sound suspiciously, maybe parodically "Oriental"; perhaps also the scene of "your" desertion. Tempting as it is to treat this latter, in particular, as autobiographical "confession," a moment of private pain exposed for our delectation, one notes that the "rusted water" and "cistern-like house" in this passage seem associated with the earlier passage pleading poverty, as well as with the later one-line stanza about the busted pump (is the water "rusted" because the pump is "busted"?). All of these phrases seem appropriate for an aged speaker, presumably the one all but exhausted by the "relatively simple task" of "keep[ing] body and soul together." Ashbery, at the time of writing "The Skaters," was in his late thirties, so it is hard to reconcile this voice with the facts of the poet's autobiography. No, this *I* seems co-referential with the "old man" in another isolated line from this same part of the poem: "The tiresome old man is telling us his life story" (IV.223).

Perhaps, then, none of the *I*'s in part IV can be attributed to the autobiographical Ashbery, after all; perhaps they are all to be construed as uttered in the fictional persona of a "tiresome old man" who is precisely *not* the poet. Once this possibility has been recognized, a corrosive uncertainty begins to set in: how much of what precedes in part IV belongs to this old man's "life story"? Only the passages relating to the dilapidated house? or perhaps all the first-person passages throughout part IV? or even throughout the entire poem? (see D. Shapiro 128). There is, in other words, the potential here for a retrospective reading that reframes the entire poem, "lowering" it one level "down," ontologically speaking, by attributing all of it to the monologue of a fictional persona —the equivalent, in the dimension of "voice," of ekphrasis in the dimension of description.

What confronts us, at this point, is the complete failure of the reading strategy of keying on putatively autobiographical statements. Far from reducing the intractable flux of voice in "The Skaters," as it is meant to do, this strategy only aggravates that flux. How, then, might we go about salvaging some stability from the proliferation of "floating" first-person pronouns? Grasping at straws, critics have recourse to statements such as one found near the beginning of the poem (I.195): "I have a dim intuition that I am that other 'I' with which we began." Such a statement is obviously problematic, evoking as it does Rimbaud's "Je est un autre": if this "I" is autobiographical, it is also mediated and secondhand, simultaneously Ashbery's "I" and Rimbaud's. Nevertheless, problematic though it may be in this respect, the statement does seem reassuring, appearing to afford a degree of stabilization, some place to stand amid the flux. The first "I," from whom this statement emanates—the one who says, "I have a dim intuition"—seems to occupy a position of mastery, a vantage superior to the flux of *I*'s, from which one might adjudicate among their conflicting claims to speak with authority. This speaker stands, in other words, just where the poet ought to stand.

All very reassuring, no doubt, but only until one begins to reflect on what might actually be meant by "that 'I' with which we began." Which "I" would that be? And where *did* we begin, anyway? (And, for that matter, who is this "we"?) Perhaps the reference here is to the very beginning of the poem, so that "that 'I' with which we began" would be the first "I" in the poem, namely the one in the third stanza:

. . . it is novelty
That guides these swift blades o'er the ice
Projects into a finer expression (but at the expense
Of energy) the profile *I* cannot remember.
                    (I.194; my emphasis)

Or does "that 'I' with which we began" mean the first "I" in this particular stanza, namely the seventh: "Why do *I* hurriedly undrown myself to cut you down?" (I.195; my emphasis). And is this "I" at the beginning of the seventh stanza identical with the "I" in the third stanza? In short, the more narrowly we reflect on this statement, the more its mastery slips away, and we are returned to the flux of voice, no more certain than we ever were of who says "I" here, and no nearer to stabilizing the category of self than we were before to stabilizing the poem's world.

III. ARS POETICA

The statement, "I have a dim intuition that I am that other 'I' with which we began," is a classic self-reflective statement: it reflects on the discourse of "The Skaters" itself, calling attention to how its pronouns function. This is just the sort of statement to which critics regularly turn when seeking to establish interpretative nodes, because self-reflective or ars-poetic statements seem to promise fullest mastery or control over the text, or at least some degree of "leverage" or "purchase" on it. Bloom's influential readings of Ashbery hinge on just such an identification of self-reflective and ars-poetic statements (or statements that can be construed as self-reflective or ars-poetic). Typically, Bloom collects a number of such statements (or figures, or key phrases or words) from the poem in question and recontextualizes them in his own interpretative discourse, "slot[ting] them into a new syntactical context of his own making, which relates them to one another in ways they were not related in the original text" (McHale, "Against Interpretation" 154). This powerful reading strategy creates a de facto canon of "key" quotations, which, once identified, begins to circulate among other critics' discourses, to the point where the decontextualized quotations threaten to displace their source-poem as the object of critical attention.[11]

No Ashbery text appears to lend itself more readily to such a reading strategy than "The Skaters," which is generally recognized to be "the most explicitly self-referential of Ashbery's earlier long poems" (Mohanty and Monroe 43). Self-reflective "moments" in Ashbery's poetry generally, and in "The Skaters" in particular, fall into two broad categories. First, there are ars-poetic statements proper, or statements that can be construed as reflecting on the poet's own practice or on features of the text. A special case of such statements, peculiar to "The Skaters," are the various "rules" and examples of perspective in drawing, which Ashbery appears to have adapted from his main source of "found" material, *Three Hundred Things*, and, which, in the context of this poem, seem impossible to construe otherwise than as referring to the practice of poetry. (Near the beginning of this chapter, I quoted one such "found" rule, from II.208; others appear on I.196, II.207, and III.212.) The other ars-poetic statements with which this poem abounds are more miscellaneous, e.g.,

the words fly briskly across, each time
Bringing down meaning as snow from a low sky, or rabbits
    flushed from a wood.

(I.196)

the sticky words, half-uttered, unwished for,
a blanket disbelief, quickly supplanted by idle questions that fade
     in turn.
Slowly the mood turns to look at itself

                                                           (I.198)

Loving you? The question sinks into
That mazy business
About writing or to have read it in some book
To silently move away.

                                    (II.206–07)

I am convinced these things are of some importance.

                                    (II.207)

You have chosen the customary images of youth, old age and death
To keep harping on this traditional imagery. The reader

Will not have been taken in.
He will have managed to find out all about it, the way people do.

                                    (III.218)

The day was gloves.

How far from the usual statement
About time, ice—the weather itself had gone.

I mean this.

                                    (IV.220)

The second category is that of ars-poetic figures or images—emblems
of the practice of writing, or scale models (*mise en abyme*) of the text
itself. Especially conspicuous in this category are the "fire designs" and
"fire fountain" (described above), adapted, once again, from *Three Hundred Things*, and recontextualized here in such a way as to make it possible to construe these images as figures of writing.[12]
     Can ars-poetic statements and figures actually deliver what they seem
to promise, namely a degree of hermeneutic mastery over the text? Ash-

bery himself appears to warn us against investing too much interpretative energy in ars-poetic statements, or expecting too much of them: "Who, actually, is going to be fooled one instant by these phony explanations,/ Think them important?" (I.200). Of course, it would be as naive to take this warning at face value as it would be to take the statements it warns us against at face value (see Shoptaw, *Outside* 90–91).

A crucial test case of the interpretive power and utility of ars-poetic statements is a much cited passage from the first section of "The Skaters," which I quote here in part. It begins, tantalizingly enough, "It is time now for a general understanding of/The meaning of all this," and then after a few lines, which I omit, resumes as follows:

> Isn't this a death-trap, wanting to put too much in
> So the floor sags, as under the weight of a piano, or a piano-
>   legged girl
> And the whole house of cards comes dinning down around
>   one's ears!
> But this is an important aspect of the question
> Which I am not ready to discuss, am not at all ready to,
> This leaving-out business. On it hinges the very importance of
>   what's novel
> Or autocratic, or dense or silly. It is as well to call attention
> To it by exaggeration, perhaps. But calling attention
> Isn't the same thing as explaining, and as I said am not ready
> To line phrases with the costly stuff of explanation, and shall not,
> Will not do so for the moment. Except to say that the carnivorous
> Way of these lines is to devour their own nature, leaving
> Nothing but a bitter impression of absence, which as we know
>   involves presence, but still.
> Nevertheless these are fundamental absences, struggling to get
>   up and be off themselves.
>
> This, thus, is a portion of the subject of this poem
>
>   (I.199)[13]

This passage has proved irresistible to critics (myself included; see McHale, "Postmodernist Lyric" 40), who have found its formulations ("This leaving-out business," "the carnivorous/Way of these lines," "ab-

sence, which as we know involves presence," etc.) useful not only for purposes of interpreting "The Skaters," but also as a reflection on Ashbery's
poetics in general. Moreover, in investing this passage with the power to
"unlock" Ashbery's poetics, the critics appear only to be following the
poet's own lead, for Ashbery himself would revive its key notion of
"leaving out" six years later, at the beginning of "The New Spirit" (in
Three Poems).

There are many things that might be remarked on in the passage from
"The Skaters," not least of all its backhanded rhetorical strategy of specifying what it refuses to discuss ("This leaving-out business") or do ("I
am not ready/To line phrases," etc.), thereby, in effect, discussing and doing them anyway. The question at hand, however, is, how reliably does
this passage yield insights into Ashbery's practice?

Certain difficulties and indeterminacies immediately present themselves. The first of these we have touched on already, namely the potential *scope* of these self-reflections. To what, exactly, are they applicable?
To this poem alone, maybe even to this *passage* alone? Or can they properly be made to apply *beyond* this particular text? Some critics have been
disposed to construe "This leaving-out business," for instance, as referring particularly to the radically disjunctive poetics of Ashbery's *Tennis
Court Oath* phase, which (according to this account) Ashbery is hereby
renouncing. If so, then to what does "put[ting] too much in" apply? Perhaps to "The Skaters" itself? (Think of that catalogue of noisemakers
into which, somehow, "limpets" and "clavicles" intrude. Could this exemplify "put[ting] too much in"?) Unless, perhaps, *both* descriptors—
"putting in" and "leaving out"—apply equally to "The Skaters." Perhaps,
as the critics (and maybe Ashbery himself) seem to want us to believe,
the "putting in" and "leaving out" modes persist as permanent alternatives in Ashbery's poetics, their relevance as descriptors extending beyond "The Skaters" at least as far as *Three Poems*, and conceivably all the
way to *Flow Chart* (a "putting-in" poem?), *Girls on the Run* (a "leaving-
out" poem?) and beyond. In other words, if this passage is a "key," then
which lock or locks was it meant to unlock, and which might it appropriately be tried on, whether intended or not?

Second, one can't help but notice that the key phrase about "the
carnivorous/Way of these lines" alludes to Walt Whitman, who in "Song
of Myself" #42 memorably characterized his own "words" as "omnivo-
rous": "I know perfectly well my own egotism,/And know my omnivo-

rous words, and cannot say any less,/And would fetch you whoever you are flush with myself" (67). Thus, just when Ashbery purports to be holding the mirror up to his own text, it turns out that an element of secondhandedness, of a prior text's mediation, has been allowed to intrude once again. How does this affect our sense of the relevance and reliability of this passage, as far as Ashbery's own poetics is concerned? Is he only, yet again, pastiching someone else's text, in this case Whitman's? Is this true self-reflection, or just another act of more or less plausible ventriloquism?

Finally, and crucially, "these lines" are self-deconstructing. That is, if the deictic "these" is understood to refer self-reflectively to the lines actually before us (i.e., the ones I quoted a few paragraphs above), then to say that they "devour their own nature" and "leave nothing" suggests that they cancel or rescind the propositions they express, or that they somehow evacuate their own semantic content (or whatever it is that the strange locution "their own nature" refers to). If they are "carnivorous" in this sense, then they deconstruct themselves. "The carnivorous/ Way of these lines is to devour their own nature": if this proposition is true, then (having devoured themselves) these lines must be false; but if what these lines express is false, then (having devoured themselves) they must be true. Ashbery, writes Lehman, "is particularly fascinated by the liar's paradox—that is, by the capacity of language to generate sentences that can logically be neither true or false, as when someone says 'I am a liar'" (*Last Avant-Garde* 112)—or, as here, when a sentence reads something like, "This sentence does not mean what it says." Alternatively, we might opt for a different specialist jargon, and say instead that these lines lie *sous rature,* under erasure.

The difficulties and indeterminacies we have uncovered with respect to this particular ars-poetic passage are typical; similar problems arise in most of the ars-poetic statements in this poem, so that Mohanty and Monroe are certainly correct in concluding that in "The Skaters" there is "no possibility of a secure metadiscourse" (43). Nor is there, for that matter, much greater possibility of secure metadiscourse anywhere else in Ashbery's poetic output. Moreover, ars-poetic statements, here as elsewhere in the Ashbery corpus, labor under the burden of our inability as readers to distinguish "serious" ars-poetic statements from mere "citations," that is, from ars-poetic statements functioning not as statements about *this* text or even *this* corpus, but instead as generic *exhibits* of ars-poetic discourse. In other words, given the manifold indeterminacies of Ashbery's text, how are we to distinguish between statements that are being "used" and those that are merely being "mentioned"? (See Shoptaw, *Outside* 95; and on use versus mention generally, see Lyons 5–10.)

This difficulty applies, *mutatis mutandis,* to all the categories of "key" statement to which critics have had recourse—descriptive, autobiographical, and ars-poetic alike. Due to the heterogeneity, indeterminacy, and fluidity of Ashbery's text, and its tendency toward the relativizing and levelling of all discourses, "key" passages can be ascribed no especially privileged or "authorized" status among the text's discourses, but only appear as generic "samples" or "exhibits" of one or another discursive mode—e.g., a descriptive sample, an autobiographical sample, an ars-poetic sample, and so on. In this levelling context, no statement or passage gives us any special "purchase" or "leverage" on the text, after all.

IV. HOW (NOT) TO INTERPRET "THE SKATERS"

[T]here is little to be learned from competing interpretations of, say, "The Skaters." The poems generate interpretations very readily.

Geoff Ward, *Statutes of Liberty* 130

Is there a *wrong* way to interpret a poem by John Ashbery?

John Gery, "Ashbery's Menagerie" 126

These three types of node having failed us as interpretative "keys" to the text, what is to be done? Well, of course one could describe exactly how and why these keys fail to deliver what was expected of them—as I have just done in the preceding pages. Paradoxically, such a description actually yields a kind of mastery over the text after all; that is, if it does not "solve" the problems and puzzles with which the text challenges us, at least it enunciates those problems and puzzles, thereby "solving" the text after all, in a sense, but one level higher up. If nothing else, the exercise is an instructive one, in the sense that it compels us to reflect on our own interpretative procedures, even if it doesn't finally yield a satisfactory reading of Ashbery's poem.[14]

To account for our hermeneutic failure is to supply, not a solution exactly, but a kind of meta-solution. However, lest one become too self-satisfied about having finessed Ashbery, it needs to be remembered how little of the text even such a meta-solution actually addresses. That is, insofar as much of the poem "falls between the cracks" of any of these interpretative approaches (world-oriented, self-oriented, or text-oriented), it follows that the metacommentary that describes the failure of these approaches also, inevitably, misses out on the material that has fallen between those very cracks. Consider these facts: of the approximately 780 lines comprising "The Skaters," no more than about 90 lines were actually discussed in the preceding pages. Even if we were to include in this count all the lines implicated by the argument, or covered by extension— e.g., all the other descriptive passages besides the ones actually discussed, all the other ars-poetic passages, etc.—the grand total would, under the most generous construction, amount to no more than, say, 500 lines, leaving some 280 lines unaddressed, in effect unread. Thus, even after one has accounted for all the (pseudo-)descriptive, (pseudo-)autobiographical, and (failed) ars-poetic material in the poem, there is still much material left unaccounted for, including lines that are among the most resistant to interpretation (and so, of course, most in need of it) in the entire poem, e.g.,

> Uh . . . stupid song . . . that weather bonnet
> Is all gone now. But the apothecary biscuits dwindled.
> Where a little spectral
> Cliffs, teeming over into irony's
> Gotten silently inflicted on the passages
> Morning undermines, the daughter is.
> (III.213; ellipses are Ashbery's)

These lines come as close as anything in "The Skaters" to the radically disjunctive mode of such poems as "Leaving the Atocha Station" from *The Tennis Court Oath* (see Carroll). Needless to say, identifying the similarity doesn't by any means address the interpretative problem such lines pose in the context of "The Skaters."

So, to repeat: what is to be done? One could, perhaps, return to the metaphor of "flux" with which this chapter began, and reevaluate it in the light of our hard-won knowledge of exactly how this poem *can't* be read. Our struggle with "The Skaters" has yielded a sense of the ebb and flow of intelligibility in this poem: how meaning in one passage is retracted in the next, or how meaning at one level is evacuated at another. Descriptions, the ontological rug having been pulled out from under

them, are retrospectively reframed as ekphrases, just as putatively autobiographical confessions are reframed as the utterance of a fictional persona (a "tiresome old man," perhaps). Ars-poetic statements, promising
hermeneutic mastery over the text, are evacuated of that mastery by
the indeterminacy of their scope, and all categories of "key" statement—
descriptive, autobiographical, and ars-poetic alike—are deprived of their
"purchase" on the text by our chronic inability to distinguish instances
of "use" from instances of "mention" in this poem. This ebb and flow
of intelligibility seems to have been figured in the poem itself; Ashbery
writes in one place of the

> rhythm of too-wet snow, but parallel
> With the kind of rhythm substituting for "meaning."
> (II.207)

He seems to associate this "rhythm" with the "millionfold" solutions to
the problem of suffering, which are "like waves of wild geese returning
in spring" (II.208). The rhythm of ebbing and flowing meaning, or of
the ebb and flow of interpretative "solutions," parallels that of natural
phenomena: wet snow, waves of geese, or for that matter the rhythm of
a wave, as in his later long poem by that name:

> a giant wave that picks itself up
> Out of a calm sea and retreats again into nowhere
> Once its damage is done.
> (*A Wave* 81)[15]

But of course, in citing these images from "The Skaters" and "A Wave"
I am undertaking precisely the sort of interpretation in terms of ars-
poetic figures that I have just shown to be baseless. Ashbery, it appears,
has anticipated even this move; he has gotten there ahead of me and
evacuated in advance all the positions that I might have tried to occupy,
leaving me nothing but a bitter impression of absence. Which as we
know involves presence, but still . . .

6
Will the Revolution Be Televised?

Thomas McGrath's *Letter to an Imaginary Friend* and Bruce Andrews's "Confidence Trick"

I. THE "CHINA" SYNDROME

Here an on-line editor objects that imitation of war in rapid displacements of incommensurate remarks is not an argument against
war—it could likewise be a form of participation.

> Barrett Watten, *Bad History* (19)

Politics and postmodernism: many Left-oriented commentators on poetry have tended to assume that these two terms must be incompatible.
"If we conceive of poetry in postmodernist terms," writes Terence Des
Pres (57), "we shall conclude that it can have no bearing upon life or action's deeper passions." Of course, all poetry is political, even (or especially) expressly apolitical poetry, in the sense that poetry (like all writing) always presupposes, however tacitly, some particular organization
of human life (Scully, *Line Break* 4–5). But we usually reserve the term
"political poetry," as James Scully reminds us, for poetry that criticizes
or resists the status quo or projects some alternative to it—"dissident poetry" might be the better term. It is politics in this sense of dissidence
that postmodernist poetry is presumed to lack.

The great counterexample ought to be the poetry of the Language
group, which seems to combine a version of postmodernism (at least as
I understand it) with political dissidence. But a funny thing happened
to Language poetry on its way to the political arena: it ran afoul of
Fredric Jameson. The natural alliance that one might have presumed
would arise between Language poetry and "progressive" academics suf-

fered a sharp setback when, in his seminal 1984 essay on postmodernism, Jameson exhibited "China," a short text by the Language poet Bob Perelman, as an example of the "schizophrenic disjunction" that, by his account, characterizes late-capitalist modes of expression (Jameson, "Postmodernism" 73–75; *Postmodernism* 28–30). Far from being dissident poetry, Perelman's "China," as Jameson sees it, is merely symptomatic of the "postmodern condition."[1]

"China" is the only poetic example Jameson discusses either in his essay, "Postmodernism, or, The Cultural Logic of Late Capitalism," or in the highly influential follow-up book by the same title, and for this very reason it is the only postmodernist poem certain to be familiar to every academic practitioner of postmodern criticism. This is convenient, no doubt, for the critical institution, which prefers its range of reference to be narrow (particularly with respect to contemporary writing), its touchstone texts to be few and far between, and its controversies to be contained, but it means that "China" has effectively been stigmatized as *the* typical instance of postmodern complicity. Actually, Jameson himself concedes that "China" is "in some curious and secret way a political poem" (*Postmodernism* 29), but this seems not to have affected his view of the poem's complicity with late capitalism. Evidently its politics are sufficiently curious and secret as to preclude his considering the alternative, namely that "China" is not after all a symptom but rather a *diagnosis* of the postmodern condition, not complicit but critical (see Hartley 42–52; Bernstein, *A Poetics* 100; McHale, "Postmodernism" 28–29; Perelman, 63–64, 78).

But how does one distinguish a symptom of postmodernism from a diagnosis? a text complicit with late capitalism from one resistant to it or critical of it? Imitation of schizophrenic disjunction, as Barrett Watten acknowledges in the passage I have quoted as my epigraph, is as likely to be taken for participation as critique. The problem is a vexed one, not only for poetry, but also for all forms of postmodern cultural expression (see Harvey 101, 116–17, 323, 351). The present chapter seeks to address (though it can hardly pretend to solve) this problem.

First, however, we need to dispense with Perelman's "China." While "China" has the advantage of being widely anthologized and discussed, it also comes to us obscured by layers of readerly misapprehension and misprision, thanks to Jameson. In any case, it is too slight a poem—only twenty-seven lines long, some 236 words in all—to sustain unaided a topic as weighty as "the politics of postmodernist poetry." We need a test case similar in kind but more substantial—something like "Confidence Trick," a text by Bruce Andrews, coeditor in the seventies (with Charles Bernstein) of the seminal journal $L=A=N=G=U=A=G=E$, and a conspicuous practitioner and theorist of Language poetry. Composed in 1981 (Andrews, "Work" 286), though not published in full until six years later, in the volume *Give Em Enough Rope*, "Confidence Trick" marks a shift in Andrews's poetic practice to the kind of disjunctive prose poetry that he would subsequently extend to book length in *I Don't Have Any Paper So Shut Up (or, Social Romanticism)* (1992). More manageable in its scale than the sprawling *I Don't Have Any Paper*, "Confidence Trick" is nevertheless forty-five pages long, comprising over ten thousand words. It reads like this:

> Talk *is* cheap—We jump up lobotomized post syn-fuels; propaganda amputee kills Doc; in God we trust insect coins—(The information kit is free)—Getting this optative just enjoy what are our; electro-wave your meltdown brain army revved up—Freedom by any means necessary, but almost involuntary UFO brandname without any sentiment—Cultural transmission christ statue; women in the middle income—Multiple humor stands bad with congas at the convent gate, my TV police on chairs, you qualify vet, KGB bid to slay pope; yellow spot (Andrews, *Enough Rope* 168)

This is the first of nine "paragraphs" comprising the thirteenth of the twenty-two "chapters" of Andrews's text. In it one recognizes the same failures of textual cohesion and discontinuities of topic, the same lurches and swerves, that presumably induced Jameson to compare Perelman's "China" to schizophrenic discourse, except that here the discontinuities have been further heightened by stylistic disparities. Perelman's text, its fragments all pitched at the same colorless, mildly colloquial level, is stylistically rather neutral and homogeneous. Andrews's, by contrast, is stylistically wildly heterogeneous, a bristling junkyard of verbal found objects: aphorisms and slogans ("Talk *is* cheap," "in God we trust," "Freedom by any means necessary"); headlines, real or manufactured ("propaganda amputee kills Doc," "KGB bid to slay pope"); marketing come-ons ("The information kit is free"); specialized academic and managerial registers ("Cultural transmission," "women in the middle income," "you qualify [as a] vet"); shards of technologese and sci-fi neologisms ("We jump up lobotomized post syn-fuels," "electro-wave your meltdown brain army revved up"); and so on.[2] While the basic unit of measure in "China" is the sentence,[3] "Confidence Trick" juxtaposes sentences ("propaganda amputee kills Doc," "The information kit is free") with detached, floating phrases ("women in the middle income," "yellow spot") and grammatical fragments ("Getting this optative just enjoy what are our"). Visually, "China" seems at first glance to offer a more striking icon of disjunction, with each of its lines separated from the next by a double-space gulf, while the passage from Andrews registers visually as a "normal" prose paragraph. On closer inspection, however, it proves to be anything but normal, and less like a paragraph than a densely compacted block, a collapsed or telescoped text from which all connective tissue has been pared away, leaving scars of idiosyncratic punctuation (dashes, semicolons; see Inman).

Is this political poetry? The passage exhibits only one overtly "political" statement, Malcolm X's slogan, "Freedom by any means necessary"; and perhaps "exhibits" is the operative word here, since it is unclear whether this represents a serious *use* of Malcolm's slogan or only a *mention* of it (see chapter 5)—whether, in other words, the poem endorses this statement or merely displays it as a sample of political discourse. In any case, the weird enjambment ("Freedom by any means necessary, but almost involuntary UFO brandname without any sentiment") seems to sap Malcolm's slogan of its political import. In the absence of unambiguously political statements, the resourceful reader is reduced to construing Andrews's enigmatic appropriations as politically charged ironies. Thus, e.g., "The information kit is free" perhaps aims to remind us, by ironic indirection, that nothing is finally "free" where the market is concerned, least of all "information"; "insect coins," conjoined with "in God we trust," can perhaps be interpreted as a sardonic gloss on the pious sentiment that sanctifies our currency; and so on. If this is political diagnosis, then it leaves most of the diagnostic labor to the reader, taking for granted a predisposition on our part to ferret out political implications.

Context, immediate or general, offers us little guidance in our interpretative efforts. The remaining eight paragraphs of this chapter are made up of materials essentially interchangeable with those in the opening paragraph: political statements that may nor may not be meant seriously (e.g., "this is madness this is madness this is madness," quoting the Last Poets, Black-Power rap artists, and so presumably alluding to their revolutionary message); decontextualized samples, evidently exhibited ironically (e.g., "Treat me like a labor unit," "the A bomb woke me up"); and so on. And the same holds true for the other twenty-one chapters comprising "Confidence Trick"; nowhere will one find a "key" to interpretation, some unambiguous clue to decoding this text whose politics are so much more "curious and secret" even than Perelman's "China."

Symptom or diagnosis? Perhaps, in the end, we are left with no choice but to fall back on Andrews's own statements of intent *outside* his poetry proper (see Perloff, "Syntax of Contrariety," 156–58; Vanderborg 1–5). In essays and interviews, Andrews has frequently ascribed diagnostic and critical purposes to his own poetry, as well as to poetry by others in this same radically disjunctive mode (see Andrews, *Paradise & Method*). Moreover, fellow poets and poet-critics in Andrews's circle have generally agreed to follow Andrews in reading his poetry politically (see, e.g., Watten, "Social Formalism"; Silliman et al. 270–71; Lazer 77–94; Perelman 96–108). But this seems uncomfortably like accepting on faith Andrews's own claims to having written political poetry, something one might well be reluctant to do, particularly in view of his title "Confidence Trick." Is Andrews warning us that his poem is intended as a hoax? If so, it belongs to a venerable if somewhat disreputable tradition of hoax poetry including, in our own time, the Hiroshima survivor Araki Yasusada and even the faux-Sumerologist Armand Schwerner (see chapter 4). Consider, too, the title of the volume in which "Confidence Trick" appears: *Give Em Enough Rope*, as in, "Give 'em enough rope and they'll hang themselves" (see McGann, "Apparatus" 185; and for an alternative reading, Brossard 79). Is it we readers, so willing to project political meanings where (possibly) none exist, who have been given enough rope? Are we the ones who have been left to twist slowly, slowly in the wind of Andrews's derisive irony?

But these supposed tip-offs are no less ambiguous than anything else in "Confidence Trick." It all depends on *who* is alleged to be conning *whom:* is Andrews confessing to having conned the reader, or is he rather exposing (let's say) the global confidence trick that is the system of late-capitalism? And what if the "they" who are being given rope enough to hang themselves turn out not to be Andrews's readers at all, but rather the producers and consumers of the various discourses Andrews has ap-propriated here, in the sense that his noncommittal exhibition of these discourses allows them to denounce ("hang") themselves without any overt intervention on the poet's part? Nor are the ambiguities cleared up even if we happen to recognize the allusion in Andrews's title to the 1978 album *Give Em Enough Rope* by The Clash, the most overtly political of the classic punk bands. For not only do The Clash themselves remain deeply ambiguous—were they more diagnostic and critical, or (as a com-mercially successful band) more symptomatic and complicit?—but so does Andrews's use of them here. The best we can say is that, by appro-priating a title from The Clash, Andrews is presumably advertising his text as political. But this does not mean that he believes his own adver-tising, or, even if he does believe it himself, that his belief is necessarily well-founded. In other words: symptom or diagnosis?

II. THE REVOLUTION OF THE *LETTER*

Little as it is, what have we, comrades, but love and the class struggle?

(McGrath, *Letter to an Imaginary Friend* 233)[4]

If poems such as Perelman's "China" or Andrews's "Confidence Trick" can be dismissed by progressives like Jameson as not really political, or not political enough, or political only in some "curious and secret" way, then this suggests that they are being tacitly measured against some model of what constitutes political poetry and found wanting. What would such a model political poem look like?

First of all, the model political poem would presumably be one that acknowledged its own place in history; that is, it would inscribe itself within some larger historical metanarrative. It follows that such a poem might itself be structured along narrative lines, or that it would at least imply or evoke a narrative. Secondly, such a poem would specify the so-cial subject-position from which it issued; that is, it would indicate from where it spoke, in class and other terms, and consequently with what authority it spoke. Ideally, perhaps, this social subject-position would be identical with the poet's own. Moreover, the model political poem would project a social profile of its target addressee; it would, in other words, ground both ends of its communicative circuit in social reality. Finally, it would be tendentious (in Scully's sense, *Line Break* 59–87); that is, it would express, however obliquely, political judgments or analyses or values (in however narrow or broad a sense).[5]

Presumably, then, the model political poem would look something like the political poetry of Brecht or Hugh MacDiarmid or Ernesto Cardenal or, a little more problematically, that of Mayakovsky or Pablo Neruda (see Des Pres; Scully, *Line Break* 87, n.20). In the context of the United States, one might expect to find such a poem among the Dynamo poets who flourished in the thirties, including Kenneth Fearing, Muriel Rukeyser, Edwin Rolfe and others (see Novak; Nelson, *Repression and Recovery;* Kalaidjian). But if one were seeking a more recent text that approximated the model of political poetry, and moreover qualified as a "long poem" and thus could serve as a foil to the political poetics of Andrews's "Confidence Trick," then the strongest candidate might well be Thomas McGrath's *Letter to an Imaginary Friend*. McGrath (1916–1990), a younger associate of some of the Dynamo poets,[6] bridges in his own career the gap between the activist poetry of the thirties and the emergence of the Language poets, with their claim to having renewed political poetry in the United States. His *Letter to an Imaginary Friend*, a poem begun as early as the fifties and originally published in three installments (part 1, 1962; part 2, 1970; parts 3 and 4, 1985), actually overlaps chronologically with the writing (though not the publication) of Andrews's "Confidence Trick." In this sense, if perhaps in no other, the two poems are contemporaries.

McGrath's *Letter* satisfies many of the criteria of the model political poem. Its quasi-autobiographical narrative inscribes itself within the larger enfolding narrative of working-class experience and aspirations in the United States from the thirties through the Cold War. It treats the poet throughout as a "representative" subject of history. "I am interested," McGrath writes, "in those moments when my life line crosses through the concentration points of the history of my time" (McGrath, "From *Letter*" 93). Among those "concentration points" is the House Un-American Activities Committee's hounding of Leftists in the fifties, from which McGrath emerged blacklisted and unemployable. Beginning from that point, the poem ranges backward in time to earlier episodes of working-class solidarity, activism, and trial—prewar union organizing among farm laborers, wartime shipyard work, postwar radicalism on the waterfront—and forward, in its later parts, to episodes such as the revolutionary overthrow of the dictatorship in Portugal in the midseventies. Throughout, the poem speaks with the authority of McGrath's own personal experience, his own "witness" of the rise, crisis, and rollback of American labor and revolutionary politics in his own lifetime (see Butwin; E. P. Thompson).

Somewhat more problematic is the poem's addressee. By identifying his poem as a "letter," McGrath seems to assert its affiliation with the long tradition of epistolary poems stretching back to Horace, or, in the modern world, from Pope's "Epistle to Dr. Arbuthnot" to Auden's "New Year Letter," Kenneth Patchen's "poem[s] in the form of a letter" (the title of one of them), Charles Olson's *Maximus Poems,* Richard Hugo's letter-poems, and beyond. Who, then, is the "imaginary friend" to whom this epistolary poem is addressed? Among others, McGrath's young son Tomasito, but only in parts 3 and 4, since his birth still lay decades in the future at the time when the *Letter* was begun. Sometimes the addressee is the reader, in the manner of the progressive poetry of the thirties: "Friend, when all collapses around you the bosses/Find work" (2, IV.2.220); "A nation of murders [*sic*]—O say, can you see/Yourself among them?" (2, III.2.191). Sometimes it seems to be the poet himself, playing the role of his own addressee, and so akin to the imaginary friend of childhood (Manfred 55). This seems an awkward solution, however, not least because it construes the poem as introverted and solipsistic. Perhaps, then, the imaginary friend is best thought of as an introjected addressee, the progressive audience that, having been driven out of sight, into silence, underground by political repression in the McCarthyite fifties, was denied McGrath. Hence the elusiveness and opacity of what ought to have been the most transparent aspect of a poem that advertises itself as a letter.

But if the *Letter*'s addressee remains somewhat elusive, this does not make the poem any less tendentious. "The poem is *political,*" McGrath writes emphatically, "it hopes to invent and restructure the past and the future by using the narrative line of the speaker of the poem and events from personal and political-social history to create the 'legend' of these times. . . . I think perhaps this is the only *long* poem to make the attempt" (McGrath, "From *Letter*" 94; McGrath's emphasis). The *Letter* is saturated, at all levels, with political value judgments, both implicit and explicit. Often McGrath places the most explicit political statements in the mouths of characters other than the poem's narrator—the union organizer Showboat Quinn (see below), for example, or the radicalized farm laborer Cal. Nevertheless, the poet's own attitudes and positions are readily reconstructed, as much from his choice of episodes to narrate (e.g., his uncle's beating of Cal for organizing a strike in part 1, III.5) as from his mode of narrating them. In the poem's later parts, expressions of political attitude become even more direct and unmediated—e.g., the roll call of revolutionary heroes in part 4, 2 (including Lenin, Joe Hill, Pancho Villa, Denmark Vesey, Big Bill Haywood, and others), or the pointed satire on capitalism as the "Sixth Heaven" in part 4, 4. Never, in any case, are McGrath's working-class identification or revolutionary commitments in the least doubt, from beginning to end. Which is not to say that his politics are blandly or supinely orthodox or "correct"; on the contrary, they are often provocatively heterodox, more nearly akin to the wildcat politics of the Industrial Workers of the World (IWW) than to the Party line (see Butwin).[7]

Nor does the *Letter*'s approximation of the model political poem mean, as some might suppose, that McGrath values transparency and accessibility over aesthetic complexity, or that he shuns difficulty in the interests of untroubled communication. On the contrary, the *Letter* actually exhibits several varieties of difficulty. Occasionally its difficulty resembles that of high-modernist lyric—the symbolist hermeticism of Yeats and Eliot, or the dense figuration of Hart Crane—poetry to which, despite his populist politics, McGrath was deeply attached (he even includes Hart Crane in a fantasized symposium of poets in part 3, III.3). More typically, however, the poem's modernist-style difficulty appears at the level of narrative, for instance in the dislocations of part 2, which begins and ends in the present time of writing on the Greek island of Skyros, flashes back to resume the narrative of McGrath's career where it had been left at the end of part 1, with his blacklisting in the fifties, carries that forward (with occasional flashbacks) to the point of his return to North Dakota, then flashes back from there to his North Dakota adolescence. The difficulty here, in other words, has less in common with modernist poetry than with modernist fiction, or for that matter, as McGrath himself observes ("From *Letter*" 94–95), with modernist cinema.

Other varieties of difficulty in the *Letter* are more readily assimilated to postmodernist aesthetics than to modernism. McGrath was pleased to hear his *Letter* characterized as "the first post-modernist long poem"

("From *Letter*" 93), and while there might be some rival claimants to priority (*The Pisan Cantos*, 1948; *The Maximus Poems*, 1960), it makes surprisingly good sense to consider *Letter* in connection with postmodernism.[8] The postmodernist difficulty of *Letter* emerges most conspicuously in the carnivalesque wildness of parts 3 and 4 (see Des Pres 177–79), where alternative sub- or para-worlds bubble up within or alongside the "real" (recollected) world of McGrath's childhood experience. In part 3 this wildness is mainly language-driven, featuring heightened linguistic extravagance and playfulness, parodies and travesties, digressions and insets, promiscuous mingling of genres, hypertrophied catalogues, literalized figures, passages of concrete poetry and OuLiPian *exercises de style*.[9] The linguistic improvisations spill over into part 4, where they eventually give way to a dream-vision of multiple worlds in the visionary mode of Dante (whom McGrath several time evokes) or for that matter of Merrill's *Changing Light at Sandover* (see chapter 2).

But postmodernist-style opacities and disturbances are not restricted to parts 3 and 4. Rather they are detectable throughout the poem in the recurrence of the "scene of writing," or what the surfictionists used to call the insistence on the "truth of the page" (Sukenick, "Thirteen Digressions" 24–25):

> The world
> Is always outside this window: Now: a blaze of January
> Heat: the coyote: the cicadas of Skyrian snow—all *here*
> Now or later.
>   (The poem is merely what happens
>   now
> On this page . . .)
>   (2, II.7.173)

Inscribing the scene of writing serves to compromise or even destroy narrative illusion, though by the same token it also serves to "ground" the text in real time and space (see section III). In any case, such insistence on the "truth of the page" contrasts sharply with the effacement of the scene of writing in modernist long poems, a notable exception being the *Pisan Cantos*—which, for that very reason, can be seen to anticipate, if not inaugurate, postmodernist poetics.

Apart from its other postmodernist credentials, McGrath's *Letter* also shares with Andrews's "Confidence Trick" a postmodernist poetics of plurivocality and citation. Both these poems (like other postmodernist poems in the disjunctive mode) rely heavily on "discursive imagery" (see Forrest-Thomson, *Poetic Artifice* 41–42, 65–80), that is, on the representation or evocation of *linguistic* objects, *linguistic* reality: styles, registers, genres of speech and writing, discourse "found," heard, overheard, seen, sampled, pastiched, parodied. At the same time, this shared practice of discursive imagery also serves to clarify a crucial difference between McGrath's and Andrews's texts, as we shall see in section III.

McGrath's proletarian and progressive commitments are reflected in his program of recovering from silence the voices of those lost to history —workers, the underclasses, the heroes of progressive lost causes: "out of these ghosts I bring these harvest dead/Into the light of speech" (1, II.4.13; see also 2, I.2.138). McGrath's program here recalls Susan Howe's aspiration, in a comparable context, to "lift from the dark side of history, voices that are anonymous, slighted—inarticulate" (*Europe* 14; see chapter 7). McGrath, for his part, accomplishes this partly by the conventional novelistic means of representing the direct speech of workers, bosses, activists, and other types, with inflections appropriate to each socio-dialectal style:

"Ach, woman, the chiselur's tall as a weed!
He's not to be spike-pitchin', a whistle-punk only—
A breeze of a job and he'll sit in the shade on his bum
The day long."

(1, III.1.15)

And Showboat
Quinn goes by (New York, later), "The fuckin' proletariat
Is in love with its fuckin' chains. How do you put this fuckin'
Strike on a cost-plus basis?"

(1, III.7.31)

"First they broke land that should not ha' been broke
                                                        and they *died*
Broke. Most of 'em. And after the tractor ate the horse—
It ate *them*. Most of 'em. And now, a few lean years,
And the banks will have it again. Most of it. Why, hellfar,

Once a family could live on a quarter and now a hull section
  won't do!
Half of the people gone left the country; the towns dyin';
And this crop uh hayseeds gutless—wouldn't say shit and
  themselves
Kickin' it out their beds. It's hard lines, buddy!"

$$(2, \text{V.3.250–51})$$

In these three "voices"—McGrath's Irish grandfather, the union organizer Quinn, and "Bill Dee speaking his piece"—one glimpses both the
strengths and weaknesses of this sort of ventriloquism: on the one hand,
its power to open the poem to untapped ranges of diction and performance style; on the other hand, its tendency toward novelistic illusionism and sociological caricature.

Fenced off behind quotation marks, such enclaves of direct quotation
preserve the hierarchical superiority of the quoting discourse (the poet's
"own voice") over the quoted discourses. More radically "egalitarian" in
its implications is the diffusion of various extraliterary ("found") discourses throughout the poet's "own" discourse. These found discourses
include the specialized registers of diction associated with particular
forms of labor (many of them now obsolete)—steam-threshing, horse-
breaking—and the specialized political jargons of the IWW, the Communist Party (CP), the Popular Front (see Butwin 64; Stern, "Delegate
for Poetry" and "Revolutionary Poet" 15, 42):

That night they *broke* Outlaw—were *breaking* him when I
  came back,
A *buckskin bronco—hammer-headed, wall-eyed, long-gaited*
  and *loco*—
Mean as a runaway buzzsaw: kicker, striker and biter

                                        . . . . And now—
Three ropes to hold him and still *rearing!*
                        But they *ear him down,*
Snub him against the corral-post and slap the *blindfall* [sic]
                                                on . . .
. . . .
    The *honyock pulls leather* at the first stone-legged *buckjump;*

Outlaw *swaps ends* like a blacksnake: while the rider is openly
wondering
Whether to shit or go blind.

(2, IV. 2.223–24; my emphases)

Morning stirring in the haymow must: sour blankets,
Worn *bindles* and half-patched *soogans* of working *bundle-stiffs*
Stir:
. . . .
Rouse to the new day in the fragrant
Barnloft soft haybed: wise heads, gray;
And gay *cheechakos* from Chicago town; and cranky *Wobblies;*
Scissorbills and *homeguards* and grassgreen wizards from the
playing fields
Of the Big Ten: and decompressed bankclerks and *bounty
jumpers*
Jew and Gentile; and the odd Communist now and then
To season the host.

(2, IV.1.205–06; my emphases)

Wherever these extraliterary registers appear, they tend to have an "authenticating" function; that is, they serve to confirm McGrath's position
as a participant-observer in the world of work, and his authority to
speak for workers and revolutionaries. They are not *exhibited,* with ironic
distancing effect, as they might have been in a text whose politics were
different. McGrath endorses these discourses, at the same time that they
legitimize him; he stands behind the worlds to which they belong, and
the values they reflect. One might compare the novelist John Dos Passos's
techniques in his *U.S.A.* trilogy (*The 42nd Parallel,* 1930; *Nineteen Nineteen,* 1932; *The Big Money,* 1936), a work of modernist aesthetics and
progressive politics. As in McGrath's *Letter,* style markers (especially
diction) belonging to specialized registers are dispersed throughout narrative passages, and while some of these registers are "exhibited" for purposes of irony (e.g., public-relations discourse, genteel middle-class cir-
cumlocutions), this is strikingly not the case with registers belonging to
labor (e.g., merchant seamanship) or proletarian-revolutionary movements (the Wobblies, the CP).

One glimpses here an incipient conflict of interests in McGrath's poetics between his project of recovering and valuing the voices of history's

lost and silenced and his evident attachment to "literature" in the received sense. Doesn't the persistence of high-literary stylistic values, one wonders, tend inevitably to *de*value the non- and extraliterary styles—"outsider" styles? Not that McGrath's commitment to high-literary style is serene or untroubled; quite the contrary, he appears sharply conflicted and ambivalent on this score. At moments, he is quite capable of mocking the literary orthodoxies of his New-Critical teachers (1, IX.4.80–81, 5.83–84) or of derisively parodying canonical period styles: Middle English alliterative verse (3, III.3.334–37), metaphysical conceits (1, IV.1.5; 2, III.4.201–02), Augustan periphrastic diction (2, IV.2.214–15; 4, 1.360–63). He even parodies particular poetic devices, notably apostrophe, the style marker par excellence of sublime poetry (see Culler, "Apostrophe"):

> O impeccable faubourgs
> Where, in the morning, you fought bedbugs for your shoes!
> (1, VIII.2.68)

> (It's poison—
> Welding-smoke of galvanized iron puts fire in your belly, O
> Poets!)
> (2, III.2.188)

At other moments, on the other hand, he is equally capable of using these same canonical styles and devices perfectly seriously:

> O great port of the Dream! Gate to the fearful country,
> So near and magically far, what key will open?
> (1, III.3.22)

> O holy marvelous morning! Ecstatic plunge into fullest
> Being! Blazing down to what end? None! To none!
> But straight through the strait gate and into reality prime!
> (2, IV.1.208)

Moreover, McGrath's text is shot through with echoes—many of them intended, some perhaps inadvertent and subliminal—of precisely the canonical literary figures he elsewhere mocks and parodies. Striking in this regard are the recurrent echoes throughout the *Letter,* often at moments of special rhetorical heightening or strong closure, of the memorable closing line of Yeats's "Byzantium" ("That dolphin-torn, that gong-tormented sea"):[10]

> Toward the heaving, harsh, the green blurring of the salt
> mysterious sea.
>
> (1, III.6.28)

> In the fox-prowling,
> In the dog-barking, and daylight-seeming night.
>
> (1, VI.1.52)

> To the black lots and the god-mating beasts of the green
> man-farming sea.
>
> (1, IX.4.83)

> It steers toward the starfish-lighted, the alewife-breeding sea.
>
> (3, II.2.311)

But most striking of all the uses of high-literary language in *Letters* is the sequence of "privileged moments" that spans the text. Related to the "spots of time" of Wordsworth's Romantic aesthetic, these passages all render memories of solitary, intimate relationship with the natural world, typically in winter (especially in part 2), though the very first of the series (1, III. 6–7.26–29) occurs in high summer. These moments serve to "anchor" the self through direct, unmediated, private experience of reality, i.e., they have an "authenticating" function, though one different from the authenticating function of the specialized registers of labor. The language of these moments is not "public" but "private": imagistic, sensuous, synaesthesic, highly figured, conspicuously "poetic":

> Now: mackerel sky: the cloudy bones of the wind
> Slow air climbing the light and the little stair
> Of dustmote, waterdrop, iceflake   weightless celestial blue . . .
> Night with the winter moon caught in the stars' far
> Houses . . .
>   And noon blazing cold in its cage of fire . . .
>
> (2, V.3.255–56)

Again, one might compare Dos Passos's *U.S.A.* trilogy, where, alongside the "public" language (specialized registers of labor, socio-dialects, etc.) that colors the narrative passages one finds separate chapters rendering subjective experience through sensuous, imagistic language. The language of these "Camera Eye" (read: "Camera I") chapters also "infiltrates" the narrative chapters, where it appears in enclaves of subjective language amidst the public registers of the shared social world.

If Dos Passos's practice offers analogies with McGrath's with respect to the incorporation both of literary and nonliterary discourses, it nevertheless differs from McGrath's in at least one important respect, exposing, it seems, a lacuna in McGrath's political use of extraliterary registers. Dos Passos assimilates to his narrative style the "authentic" discourses of workers and revolutionists, but he also, as I observed earlier, displays various "inauthentic" discourses with ironic intent: discourses of militarist propaganda, capitalist public relations and advertising, genteel hypocrisy, and so on. This strategy is one that Dos Passos shares with the progressive poets who were his contemporaries—Kenneth Fearing, for example, throughout his poetry, or Muriel Rukeyser in her long poem of 1938, "The Book of the Dead" (see Kalaidjian 165–75). A similar strategy of ironically exposing and discrediting bourgeois discourses— of giving them enough rope to hang themselves—characterizes some of McGrath's earlier poetry, especially the satires collected in *Longshot O'Leary's Garland of Practical Poesie* (1949). Strikingly, McGrath seems all but to have renounced this strategy in the *Letter*. Here, when he incorporates discourse from outside the literary range, he almost always selects from varieties associated with values or "worlds" he can endorse; only rarely does he exhibit discourses for the purpose of ironically distancing himself from them and their associated values. There are a few conspicuous exceptions: the ironized Bible-thumping sermon of the wartime chaplain Pastor Noone in part 1, X, the language of capitalist values in the "Sixth Heaven" of part 4, 3, and, throughout, the discourse of the church, tendentiously misapplied to profane contexts, or vice versa, "profaned" by the interpolation of secular (often sexual) matters:

> The Holy Ghost descended
> On Mary . . . the long long Fall into the Flesh . . .
> *There* was a traveling salesman no farmer's daughter resists!
> (3, I.1.277)

Otherwise, McGrath's strategy for handling institutions, groups, classes, professions, etc., whom he wishes to discredit is quite different. Instead of appropriating and ironically showcasing the languages of such groups and institutions, allowing them to denounce themselves out of their own mouths—Dos Passos's, Fearing's and Rukeyser's strategy—McGrath tends to resort to direct invective (see Hall). An example is his denunciation of unscrupulous scientists willing to serve the military-industrial complex:

> Scientists who have lost the good of the intellect, mechnico-
>   humanoids
> Antiseptically manufactured by the Faustian homunculus
>   process.
> And how they dream in their gelded towers these demi-men!
> (Singing of overkill, kriegspiel, singing of blindfold chess—
> Sort of ainaleckshul rasslin matches to sharpen their fantasies
> Like a scout knife.)
>   Necrophiles.
>   Money protectors . . .
>   (2, II.2.148–49)

Invective, of course, is one of the traditional tools of political poetry across the entire spectrum, from far Right (e.g., Pound's "Hell" Cantos, XIV and XV) to far Left (e.g., Amiri Baraka);[11] moreover, it also figures in the epistolary tradition (e.g., Pope). So there is no pressing need to attribute special motives to McGrath for preferring invective. Nevertheless, we might speculate that he substitutes invective for the strategy of ironic citation out of a wish to reserve the privilege of citation for discourses he wants to document and honor; or perhaps that he prefers not to give the "enemy" any discursive foothold in his text; or perhaps that he distrusts the power of irony to discredit (see McGrath's remarks on irony in a 1978 interview; Stern, *Revolutionary Poet* 159). But this lacuna in McGrath's practice, which appears conspicuous only relative to his own earlier practice and that of his immediate predecessors, perhaps reflects a real blindspot in his political analysis.

It is common for critical writing on McGrath's *Letter* (see, e.g. Des Pres 151–52, 179; Stern, "Revolutionary Poet") to celebrate the range and variety of "voices" that the poem accommodates. Admittedly, its stylistic range *is* wide, but capacious as it is, the poem nevertheless exhibits some striking gaps corresponding to areas of experience that, for various reasons, one might have expected McGrath to notice. One particular area of "discursive imagery" that McGrath pointedly avoids is the discourse of the mass media—print and broadcast journalism, the entertainment industry, advertising. In a poem otherwise so open to the "voices" of collective experience in the middle decades of this century, there are few traces of the various registers of "the news"—newspapers, newsreels, news broadcasts, all the registers captured by the "Newreels" feature of Dos Passos's *U.S.A.;* few traces, in an era that saw unprecedented expansion in the mass-entertainment industry, of the ambient discourses of radio, recorded music, and the movies. Where are the newspaper headlines, the advertising slogans, the snatches of popular songs and movie dialogue that made up so much of the verbal texture, the background noise, of the period?

Above all, where is television? In a poem part of whose temporal range covers the very decades in which television established itself as the principle medium of consumer society—a poem, moreover, some four hundred pages long!—I count no more than six references to television, none of them very probing or analytical. In the most substantial of these references, McGrath ironically juxtaposes the remains of real Native Americans—an Indian graveyard (2, V.1.241-42)—with the simulacral Indians of TV Westerns:

> The houses blacked out as if for war, lit only
> With random magnesium flashes like exploding bombs (TV
> Courtesy R[ural]E[lectrification]A[dministration])
> . . . .
> Over the sealed houses, dark, a troop of phantoms,
> Demonic, rides: the great Indians come in the night like
> Santa Claus
> down the electronic chimneys whooping and dead . . .
> (2, V.2.244; first ellipsis mine; the second,
> McGrath's. See also 2, V.2.249-50)

Later, in part 4, McGrath will make "sky-to-sky television," broadcasting sports and pornography, a feature of the delusory "Seventh Heaven" of the working class, the Land of Cockaigne (4, 4.391-92). Elsewhere television serves to sharpen the poet's invective against fellow poets who have made their peace with the prevailing order of things ("Establishment Poets, like bats, in caves with color TV/Slept upside down in clusters," 2, II.3.154), and to enhance the surrealism of a vision of the irrepressible Bill Dee coming up the coulee with a portable TV

> On which you may see Bill Dee, coming
> Up the coulee with a portable TV on which you may see
> Bill Dee with a portable TV coming . . .
>   Get the idea?
>   (3, I.3.296; McGrath's ellipsis)

We get it, but it doesn't amount to much. At one point, the poet's brother demands of him, "My god, man, don't you *ever* watch teevee?" (2, IV.3.232). The answer, if the evidence of the *Letter* is anything to go by, was no.

McGrath's systematic avoidance of mass-media discourses seems all the more surprising in view of his own personal experience of the movie industry. A Los Angeles resident during one period of his life, and a "small-time producer" in the culture industry—as Kenneth Fearing, for one, was before him (see Barnard 13)—McGrath wrote occasional screenplays (for the director Michael Cimino, among others). It is hardly incidental that his collected (actually selected) poems of 1972 bears the title, *The Movie at the End of the World*, a phrase that recurs at least once in the *Letter* (3, III.4.341). We must assume that if McGrath has edited out mass-media discourses from his poem's polyphonic mix, this is not for lack of exposure to them, but on purpose, tendentiously.

Here, then, is the lacuna in McGrath's analysis. His predecessors, Fearing in particular (see Kalaidjian 199–206; Barnard), had grasped, already as early as the thirties, that the mediating discourses of twentieth-century consumer culture and the culture industry had effectively preempted and co-opted collective experience, personal "authenticity," and revolutionary aspirations. No analysis that failed to take this situation into account stood much chance of making any headway against capitalist institutions; no literary strategy that did not focus its attack on the mediating discourses of the mass media, the entertainment industry, advertising, etc., could hope to get much real purchase on the contemporary political situation. If it is the *medium*, our culture's mediating discourses themselves, that is the enemy to which progressive poetry most urgently needs to address itself, then a strategy of denunciatory citation, of giving them enough rope—the strategy of Dos Passos, Fearing, Rukeyser and others—must be preferable to McGrath's refusal even to recognize that enemy's existence. The essential correctness of this analysis has been confirmed repeatedly since the thirties, and the strategy of the thirties writers has been adopted (or more likely rediscovered) by successive generations of political poets—including the Language poets (see Perloff, *Radical Artifice*).

III. THE POETICS OF THE MIX

To make equality less drab, never ounce ointment, beat rhythm, it
streamlines unction, mix & the remix—
       (Andrews, "Confidence Trick" in *Give Em Enough Rope* 145)

Andrews's "Confidence Trick" diverges radically from the McGrath model of political poetry. None of the structural elements that make McGrath's *Letter* intelligible *as* political poetry figure here. "Confidence Trick" lacks a global narrative and a stable subject-position (as we shall shortly see); it lacks a discernible addressee, even one as elusive as McGrath's; and it offers few if any unambiguous expressions of political attitude, as we saw in section I above. On the other hand, Andrews does share with McGrath a poetics of discursive imagery. His text, like McGrath's, is a dense weave of found and sampled discourses: professional registers and dialectal varieties, slogans, graffiti, clichés, fixed idioms, and other types of linguistic found object. Andrews has compared his compositional practice to that of film editing—the splicing together of segments of footage shot previously (*Paradise & Method* 103); but it might more appositely be compared to audio sampling and mixing in a recording studio (see section IV below).

Even with respect to its poetics of discursive imagery, the one area where Andrews's practice and McGrath's do converge, "Confidence Trick" differs in certain crucial ways from the *Letter,* both in terms of *which* discourses are sampled and of *how* the samples are handled. One could say that, in diverging from McGrath, Andrews's poetics converges instead with the poetics of some of McGrath's radical precursors in the thirties—Fearing, Rukeyser, Dos Passos—except that, for this to be true, one would have to imagine a Fearing or Rukeyser poem that was *all* citation, without connective tissue, or Dos Passos's "Newsreels" without the "Camera Eye" or circumambient narratives.

We might begin by considering the respective statuses of "literary" discourse in the *Letter* and "Confidence Trick." McGrath, as we have seen, while he displays a conflicted, ambivalent attitude toward "the literary" as such, distancing himself from it through parody, ironic allusion, and so on, also remains attached to high-literary stylistic values and adopts them for his most profoundly personal expressions. Andrews, by contrast, almost entirely avoids identifiably literary styles or devices (see DuPlessis, "Surface Tensions" 54), tending to substitute pop-culture allusions for allusions to canonical literature. His literary allusions, when they do occur, almost always involve clichés, i.e., canonical fragments that have already passed into general circulation in the language and culture at large:

1lb. of flesh
    (*Enough Rope* 151)

Estrogenic lipstick; double double toil & trouble, I *hate* inept men
                                              (172)

I want in private, that's it!, rent, the quality of mercy is not
    so eager
                                              (182)

Nervous enema murder will out
    (185)

In appropriating these Shakespearean tags, among the most overworked and hackneyed of all "familiar quotations," Andrews is not so much citing Shakespeare as citing the *citations of* Shakespeare in everyday discourse and popular culture (compare Susan Howe's strategy of allusion, discussed in chapter 7). When he makes one of his rare forays outside the canon of familiar quotations, Andrews's literary allusions are likely to be outright parodic: "Clap your hands, does it have any second coming?; it has a little dictionary in it, give me some more monitors" (150). Confronting Yeats at his most sententious (as in "Sailing to Byzantium" and "The Second Coming," the poems evoked here), anyone might feel tempted to counter the Yeatsian afflatus with a strategically placed sneer ("it has a little dictionary in it"). McGrath, too, finds opportunities to parody Yeats from time to time (e.g., "And a small cabin/Built there: of elm and cottonwood made: squatter—," 2, V.3.252); but we remember that he also imitates Yeats's cadences and rhetoric to serious purpose, how intentionally or otherwise it is impossible to say.

Andrews thus resolves the conflict of interest that troubles McGrath, between literary and extraliterary discourse, by the simple expedient of devaluing literary discourse across the board. But devaluing literary discourse does not necessarily entail *valuing* non- or extraliterary discourses. Where McGrath tends to cite only those discourses whose values he can endorse, conspicuously avoiding citation of mass-media and consumer-culture discourses, even for purposes of irony, Andrews *always* exhibits discourses as specimens (see Levy 82, 86), never endorses any, and gravitates toward consumer-culture registers. Andrews's preferred discursive imagery derives from mass-media and entertainment-industry sources: from newspaper headlines—

Schizophrenia in Popular Books: A Study Finds Too Much Hope

(*Enough Rope* 158)

Pope Names New Primate for Poland

(163)

How TSS hit tampon makers

(168)

President tilts toward apartheid

(172)

Rather than disband when polio is at last conquered, the March of Dimes looks for other diseases to fight

(182)

Cancer in mice illegal after 1982

(183)

from magazine discourse, prominently including the fashion register and the subgenre of "useful tips"—

If you don t go out & commit adultery now & then it may only be your lack of confidence that s keeping which is keeping together for regrooving—10 Donts for honeymooners

(160)

Seventeen magazine gives lessons [. . . .] Do the anorexia nervosa [. . . .] Fastest weight loss method known to medical science next to total starvation [. . . .] Don t disarrange your partner's dress by continually changing the position of your hand without releasing theirs

(175; my ellipses)

Plum tones are back
(164)

Don t flash your bracelets & watches; turn your rings around so the rings won t show

(183)

Cleanliness can be assured by teaching a boy to wash his penis
(186)

occasionally, though infrequently, from television and the movies—

The witch is dead
(144)

gidget goes to public publications
(170)

These raids on the wagon train have got to stop
(179)

as seen on TV, catch the plague quiz show
(173)[12]

and very frequently from the discourses of the pop-music world, including the specialized register of radio dj's—

especially Velvets-like
(185)

the ballads but not the honky-tonkers
(151)

I am the DJ
(168–69)

now here s a classic from Roy Drusky, 'Second Hand Heart'
(174)

now here s some beautiful polyphony to help you relax
(180)

we do play reggae but only by whites
(185)

and the genre of rock lyrics—

How his naked ears were tortured
(154)

the Jack of Hearts was drilling
(155)

they say my love is wrong, they don t know what love is
(177)

despite all the amputations
(159)

we don t perform *Heroin* anymore
(153)

The lyrics cited here come from songs by Cream ("Tales of Brave Ulysses"), Bob Dylan ("Lily, Rosemary and the Jack of Hearts"), Randy Newman ("You Can Leave Your Hat On"), and the Velvet Underground ("Rock and Roll") respectively. "Heroin" is of course a Velvet Underground song.

Andrews's citation of pop-culture materials, and of pop-music materials in particular, is characteristically indeterminate. Is this a subversive gesture, deploying pop materials to undermine the high-culture institution of poetry? Are Jack Bruce and Lou Reed weapons in a culture war that Andrews is waging against the likes of Yeats? Or are the pop-culture materials themselves being cited ironically and parodically, with a view to delegitimizing them alongside a delegitimized high culture? In other words, is pop-culture material, in Andrews's recycling of it, more "authentic" than high-culture material or less? or are they both equally inauthentic? It is perhaps this built-in political ambivalence of pop materials—resistant or complicit?—that explains, at least in part, McGrath's avoidance of culture-industry discourses, and his substitution of invective for the strategy of ironic citation as practiced by Fearing and others. With invective, after all, there is no doubt about where McGrath himself stands.

Crucially, McGrath allows those passed over by history to speak for themselves, introducing direct quotations from characters (or at least character-types) whose situations and subject-positions are specified. Andrews, in sharp contrast, inverts the relation of voice to source, and lets the discursive tail wag the situational dog. In the absence of determinate speaker-positions, "The words have to do *all* the work" (Rasula 27). That is, Andrews cites bits of spoken utterance out of context, implicitly challenging us to reconstruct situational contexts in which such "sound-bites" might conceivably be uttered:

> Well, all of them are talented so it s only a question of who sells
> out the most successfully
>
> (152)

> Or you can *ruin* the *whole culture* by a picture in a book
>
> (163)

> This country is totally fucked I hope somebody takes us over
> maybe the Japanese will take us over
>
> (165)

Do you want to sacrifice your career *totally* to lack of confidence
(179)

Everything is industry; you mean alternative drinks?; psychopath, that was translated as lackey?
(176)

I don t know why you guys are talking about complete sentences,
he shoot up anything; come around the store sometime [. . . .] I
don't play with *your pencils.*
(178; Andrews's emphases throughout)

In the next to last of these examples, for instance, the last of the three
juxtaposed utterances might refer to a tendentious translation into (say)
Chinese, where "psychopath" might conceivably be (mis)translated as
"lackey" (as in "imperialist lackey"). Is a translator speaking, then? an
academic? a diplomat? And in what situation? In the last example, perhaps the first utterance belongs to a conversation among linguists or editors; in that case, perhaps the next one, "he shoot up anything," evidently a fragment of nonstandard English, might be a sample sentence
under discussion. Or does "he shoot up anything" belong to a distinct
context of situation, in which the topic of conversation is heroin use?
Might it even belong instead to the same context as "come around the
store sometime"? And so on.

   This exercise of reconstructing speculative situational contexts—
mini-narrative frames, fragmentary scenarios—for Andrews's decontextualized utterances (see Perelman, 96–108; Perloff, "Syntax of Contrariety;" and section IV below) drives home the essential "ungroundedness"
of Andrews's citational practice, by contrast with McGrath's in the *Letter.*
McGrath projects a world, purportedly a scale model of the real world—
or that, anyway, is what he aspires for it to be; he peoples it, and samples
discourses circulating among those people in that world. Andrews, by
contrast, begins without premising any particular world, and merely
exhibits bits of discourse, leaving it to us to reconstruct a world from
the detritus (if we can, that is). Unlike McGrath's imagery, Andrews's is
exclusively discursive; it is never empirical imagery (Forrest-Thomson,
Poetic Artifice 41–42, 65–80), that is, never imagery in the imagist sense,
never putatively unmediated fragments of a world. In "Confidence Trick,"

only *language* is given, never the world in which that language might be "at home."

"Confidence Trick" is "ungrounded" in other respects, too—precisely those respects in which *Letter to an Imaginary Friend* is grounded, moreover. Thus, as we have seen, the *Letter* narrates a (pseudo-)autobiography, a narrative of the poet's self in time as a "representative" subject of history. "I" here refers consistently to an identifiable subject-position; values, judgments, attitudes, etc., not otherwise attributed to some character can reliably be attributed to this positioned subject. In "Confidence Trick," by contrast, it is impossible to reconstruct a stable self—autobiographical, pseudo-autobiographical, or otherwise (see Rasula 20–27; Lazer "Equality" 84–91). Here the subject is volatile, mobile; there is no guarantee that successive occurrences of "I" refer to the same subject (or to any subject at all, for that matter). Values, judgments, attitudes, etc., expressed or implied by "I" in one of its occurrences are not necessarily attributable to "I" in its next occurrence, even where no change of speaker has been indicated:

I am the bishop [. . . .] I hate humans [. . . .] Wedding bank is OK
I m gay [. . . .] Dog eats dinner on your bed; Exhibit A: why don t
I manage to get those images in there? (is it really purity or do I
want things more personal?)—Shit, man, we fire at passers-by all
the time [. . . .] Get tension wire brakes in her brain pan, if I were
you [. . . .] I want the same ouput you want

(146–47; my ellipses)

I wish I was a dog, society gargoyles it up; this *is* myself [. . . .]
I wish I had the same destiny [. . . .] I ve got your class ring—I can
t just perform on command is a false alarm [. . . .] I *hate* inept men,
I *want* grievance expressed in birth control raps [. . . .] I guarantee
alternative TV, you mercenaries do not own me [. . . .] Now I can
have a stable identity I want to punish myself, the mouth is supposed to be community or repressive pseudo-community, to suck
your veins becomes monotonous dress code? [. . . .] I like the Romantics [. . . .] I used to be human [. . . .] I sucked his dick, but
disappointed myself by lack of technique

(172–73; my ellipses)[13]

Does the same subject who declares him/herself to be the bishop also hate humans? Does the same subject wish he/she were a dog and also that he/she had the same destiny (as who or what?), and does this same subject both hate inept men and like the Romantics? There is no way to be certain that the subject is continuous from one fragment to the next, and even if it were, what likelihood would there be of our successfully reconstructing a recognizable "self" from such disparate materials anyway?

As we have seen, a recurrent self-reflective "scene of writing" serves to anchor or ground the text of *Letter to an Imaginary Friend* in determinate time and space, and in relation to a determinate performing self (see section II above). Self-reflexive expressions, or expressions capable of being interpreted *as* self-reflexive, also abound in "Confidence Trick." However, in the absence of a determinate context for *any* of the fragments comprising this text, there is no compulsion to construe any particular phrase as reflective of *this* text's poetics or its scene of writing (it might just as plausibly refer to some other, extrinsic context). But there is also no compulsion *not* to construe any particular phrase in a self-reflexive sense:

If I understand these words, then I find them disgraceful

(142)

I like to mistranslate everything else we hear

(144)

I don t have the questionable challenge of an oral audience

(145)

why don t I manage to get those images in there?

(146)

I m sorry, we had a technical problem with the words [. . . .] He wants to *force out* its meaning

(152; my ellipsis)

As punishment, the mandarins are only going to be able to use the 300 most frequently found words [. . . .] maybe I should cross out some words

(169; my ellipsis)

The confusion of the language matches the confusion of the sentiment

(185)

Supposing these fragments to be self-reflective, they must be ironic, i.e., they must mimic responses to his text ("disgraceful," "mistranslated," "confused") that Andrews himself does not endorse. But ironic or not, reading such expressions as self-reflexive, meta-poetic, or "ars-poetic" statements is in any case neither well-founded nor necessary, but purely speculative and arbitrary.

McGrath in *Letter to an Imaginary Friend* carefully maintains separations among the various planes of discourse and world, with the poet's "I" fixing the position from which the relative distances of the respective planes can be gauged. The recurrent "scene of writing" establishes the poem's here and now, relative to which the receding planes of past experience can be situated. Similarly, the poet's "voice" fixes the primary plane relative to which other discourses appear as insets (directly or indirectly quoted). Above all, the poem's recurrent moments of heightened and "authentic" experience—"privileged moments" or "spots of time"—serve to establish a norm relative to which the authenticity or inauthenticity of other moments and other cited discourses can be determined. Occasional slippages or local collapses of planes—telescoping of past and present or here and there (e.g., Lisbon, North Dakota, and Lisbon, Portugal, in part 3, II.2), temporary merging of "own" and "other" voices —far from undermining the system's integrity, actually serve to throw the text's internal organization into high relief. By contrast, Andrews in "Confidence Trick" systematically collapses discourse planes into a single plane by *un*fixing the position of the poet's "I." Meta-poetic statements may or may not be interpretable as referring to *this* discourse, so consequently they are of little or no use in establishing a "scene of writing." "Authentic" discourses may or may not issue from the poet, may or may not be "authoritative." ("Nothing is prioritized," writes DuPlessis, "Surface Tensions" 50; see Lazer, "Equality" 90). Conversely, "inauthentic" citations may or may not be ironically or parodically distanced from the poet.

As if driving wedges between utterances and their contexts, between utterances and the speaking subject, and between meta-poetic statements and the "scene of writing" were not all disruptive enough of intelligibility, Andrews takes the further, even more radical step of disrupting the signifiers themselves, deliberately introducing "noise" of various kinds: deliberate errors, slippages, malapropisms, hovering word-boundaries, and so on:

No place in our pogrom [program?] for revenge
(149)

absolved, absurd!, I mean absorbed
(156)

Squalid with pity no squalid with piety
(186)

remorse code
(175)

we push the tribes of other lands off our porch
(173)

We putsch the tribes of other states off our head
(175)

I am of less than one mind?
(180)

I am out of two minds
(182)

zip dub [zipped up?]
(176)

"I've wanted," Andrews writes in response to a critic's questionnaire, "to allow for a less instrumentalized attention to words, recapturing more of their waywardness, their artifice, musicality, & materiality" (*Paradise & Method* 80). McGrath, too, seeks effects of waywardness, artifice, musicality and materiality, especially in parts 3 and 4 of the *Letter*, for instance in the Christman Oratorio that ends part 3:

That nightingal some sherbacha were in the fient outside the villainst guarding the sheepfacedness, suddenly an angeleyes appeared among them and the landsmaal shone bright with glory of the lorelei; they were badly frightened, but the angeleyes reassured them.

"Don't be afraid!" he said "I bring you the most joyful newsmonger ever announced, and it is for everyone! The Savorer, yes, the Messire, the Lorenzo has been born to nightchair in Betise! How will you recognize him? You will find a bacalao wrapped in a blarina in a mangleman!" (3, III.5.349)

But McGrath preserves some control over this signifying play by carefully framing the playful interlude—in this case, by treating it as a carnivalesque inset within a largely realistic narrative of a child's Christmas-Eve memories—and by seeing to it that the norms of "serious" discourse reassert themselves afterward. In "Confidence Trick," it need hardly be reiterated, there are no determinate frames and no norms to which the discourse could return.

As Andrews's text itself informs us, "The confusion of the language matches the confusion of the sentiment." But who authorizes this statement? And to what or whom does it refer—to the language of *this* text, or some other? to *this* poet, or someone else? And anyway, is it even true?

IV. HIPHOPRISY, OR, WILL THE REVOLUTION BE TELEVISED?

Now they can take something away from you and sell it back to you in a Sprite commercial in six months, when it used to take them two years.

(Tracie Morris, at the "Poetry and the Public Sphere" conference, Rutgers University, 26 April 1997)

Of all the differences between McGrath's political poetry and Andrews's, nothing seems more telling than their respective approaches to mass-media culture: McGrath's resolute refusal even to engage with the mass media, on the one hand; Andrews's deep but equivocal engagement, on the other. In shunning mass-media discourse, McGrath aligns himself with one tendency of radical-Left artistic expression. An Old-Leftist in his politics, and (as we have seen) somewhat nostalgically "literary" in his aesthetics, McGrath would no doubt have been surprised to find how much he shared in common with Black Power and Black Separatist poets and performers of the late sixties and early seventies such as the Last Poets and, classically, Gil Scott-Heron:

> The Revolution will not be brought to you by Xerox in four
> parts without commercial interruptions
> . . . .
> The Revolution will not give your mouth sex appeal
> The Revolution will not get rid of the nubs
> The Revolution will not make you look five pounds thinner,
> because the Revolution will not be televised
> . . . .
> The Revolution will not go better with Coke
> The Revolution will not fight germs that may cause bad breath
> The Revolution *will* put you in the driver's seat
> . . . .
> The Revolution will be no rerun, brother
> The Revolution will be live

In "The Revolution Will Not Be Televised," Scott-Heron expresses the same alienation from consumer culture as McGrath in the *Letter*, and the same confidence in the revolution's capacity simply to execute an end-run around the electronic media. Far from fearing the contaminating influence of televison advertising, he boldly plagiarizes its slogans, turning them satirically against themselves. In this respect, Scott-Heron's strategy is the very opposite of McGrath's strategic disengagement ("don't you *ever* watch teevee?"), but both are underwritten by the same analysis of the mass media as at best irrelevant, at worst an impediment to revolutionary change.

Revolutionary confidence is the manifest content of Scott-Heron's rap; but do we detect an undercurrent of anxiety in his very mimicry of the advertising slogans that he assumes (no doubt correctly) all his listeners will recognize? If so, then Scott-Heron turns out to have been a better prophet than his manifest revolutionary message might have led one to suppose, and certainly clearer-sighted than McGrath. For the fact of the matter is that, in the decades since Scott-Heron assured us that

that revolution would not be televised, it *has been,* over and over again. A case in point: in June 1999, Turner Network Television, a cable channel, aired a trailer with the catchphrase, "The computer revolution *will* be televised." The trailer advertised a made-for-TV movie entitled "Pirates of Silicon Valley," dramatizing the careers of Steve Jobs of Apple Computers and Bill Gates of Microsoft. Turner, Apple, Microsoft: it would be difficult to imagine a more perfect demonstration of how the rhetoric of revolution has been captured by corporate America and sold back to the American consumer as entertainment—moreover, entertainment that lionizes precisely the corporate "pirates" who stole the revolution in the first place.[14] "In a world of spectacles," writes Rita Barnard, "the representations of revolution, too, can readily be turned into an institution . . . in a context where commercial mass culture has become such a powerful force, it may no longer be possible to avail ourselves of notions like 'the people' or any other such holdouts of cultural authenticity" (94–95).[15] If the Revolution has not exactly been brought to us by Xerox, that's only because it was brought to us by Microsoft and Turner Broadcasting instead; one way or the other, it was hardly the revolution that Scott-Heron had in mind.

Gil Scott-Heron's successors and heirs, the rappers of the eighties and nineties (see Rose 55), know all this very well indeed. Among the most legitimate of his heirs is the short-lived duo known as the Disposable Heroes of Hiphoprisy, who list Gil Scott-Heron among their "Inspirators & Conspirators" in the notes accompanying their only CD release, *Hypocrisy Is the Greatest Luxury* (1992). Fronted by Michael Franti, the Disposable Heroes revisit and update "The Revolution Will Not Be Televised" on a rap track targeting "Television, the Drug of the Nation":

Back again, "New and Improved",
we return to our irregularly programmed schedule
hidden cleverly between heavy breasted
beer and car commercials
CNNESPNABCTNT but mostly B.S.
Where oxymoronic language like
"virtually spotless" "fresh frozen"
"light yet filling" and "military intelligence"
have become standard
T.V. is the place where phrases are redefined

like "recession" to "necessary downturn"
"crude oil" on a beach to "mousse"
"Civilian death" to "collateral damages"
and being killed by your own Army
is now called "friendly fire"

Granted, there is nothing very novel or unprecedented in Franti's critique of television. The addiction metaphor ("the drug of the Nation") has been circulating in Left-wing critiques of the mass media since at least the thirties (see Barnard 87–89), while the demystification of military euphemism, updated here to include Gulf War doublespeak ("collateral damages"), dates at least from the Vietnam War, if not from the Great War. Nevertheless, it is striking that Franti can no longer assume, as Scott-Heron apparently could, the immunity of the revolutionary masses to contamination by consumer culture; still less can he afford the luxury of simply ignoring the mass media, as McGrath did. Far from dismissing it as irrelevant to the struggle, Franti here identifies television as the enemy to be overcome.

Scott-Heron's message was essentially conveyed verbally; the funky musical backing on "The Revolution Will Not Be Televised," while it certainly energizes the track and buoys up Scott-Heron's rap, seems to add nothing semantically. The Disposable Heroes, by contrast, have more than one medium at their disposal for conveying their critique. On the one hand, they have the verbal medium of Franti's rap, which, though direct and forceful enough, is also perhaps a little banal and predictable. On the other hand, there is the track's aural texture, which communicates nonverbally and indirectly, but seems to imply a fresher, defamiliarized, and potentially more radical critique of mass culture. By "aural texture" I mean not just the driving bass line and pulsing beat of "Television, the Drug of the Nation," which differ in no essential way from Scott-Heron's jazz-funk arrangement on "The Revolution Will Not Be Televised," but more crucially, the variegated sounds that surround, interrupt, and overlay the rhythm, some of them musical (fragmentary guitar figures, isolated organ chords), others not, including vaguely industrial squeals and grinding sounds, bursts of white noise, and spoken words.

The variety and density of this texture of sound is impossible to capture on paper, except perhaps its spoken-word component, and even in this case much crucial information that would be available to the listening ear—accent and gender of the speaker, channel (e.g., face-to-face versus radiophonic versus telephonic), etc.—is lost. Spoken-word materials are particularly conspicuous at the beginning of "Television," which opens with a thirty-second intro comprising ten or so brief bursts of speech evidently recorded directly from television or radio broadcasts, yielding something like an audio image of channel surfing:

> On a brighter note—Commercial break—The government has now banned the carrying of spears—Stop about every thousand miles isn't askin too much now, is it?—You might wish to stay on and listen—It was a place where everything was legal—I met this woman—So if you're looking for emotional satisfaction, my advice to you is, seek professional help—Thank you for joining us live on the air—my pleasure

Let this transcription stand in for all the other elements of "Television"'s sound mosaic that cannot be represented on this page.

What I am describing, of course, is sampling and mixing, the cornerstone principles of hip-hop musical aesthetics, which the Disposable Heroes' "Television" exemplifies (see Rose; Potter; Shusterman "Fine Art" and "Art in Action"). What differentiates hip-hop from all other popular musical forms is its reliance on secondhand sound, that is, its appropriation (sampling) of prerecorded sounds, musical and non-musical, and their transformation, juxtaposition, and recombination in new mixes. Another of hip-hop's resources, rapping, has been with us for some time now—on record, since at least Gil Scott-Heron and the Last Poets, and long before that in African-American popular oral-performance practice—but the coupling of rapping with sampling technology is a relative novelty, dating from the late seventies. Public attention, mostly negative, has tended to focus on the content of rap lyrics, in particular the violence and misogyny of some gangsta rap, and while these features certainly warrant criticism, such criticism as they have actually received from print and electronic journalists and from politicians has often been indistinguishable from "moral panic" (Potter 15, 90). In any case, one could argue that it is not after all rap's allegedly anti-social lyrics but its sampling techniques that pose the real danger to the late-captalist status quo. It is sampling, not rapping, that subverts authorship and threatens (intellectual) property rights, as witness all the copyright litigation that hip-hop music has occasioned over the years (see Rose 90–93).

Sampling, as practiced in the eighties and nineties, depended upon the availability of a particular technological apparatus—MIDI digital samplers and the devices that have succeeded them, and of course sources of prerecorded sound (vinyl LPs, CDs). In the early days of rap, however, at the end of the seventies, before MIDI samplers were generally available, sampling was accomplished by simpler means, using turntables. This suggests that, though sampling is a *technique,* its aesthetic principles of appropriation and juxtaposition may be achievable independently of any *particular* technological apparatus. Thus, sampling and mixing is perhaps optimally practiced using a MIDI sampler, but it may also be practiced using turntables and vinyl LPs, or even pen and paper and a newspaper archive, as Dos Passos did when he assembled the "Newsreel" sections of his *U.S.A.* trilogy, or scissors and paste, as William Burroughs did when he cut up and folded in preexisting texts to create new, radically disjunct texts of his own. Or one could use file cards, as John Zorn did when he composed his musical piece *Spillane* (1987), writing down on separate cards ideas for sounds derived from hard-boiled detective fiction and films, next sorting the cards until a satisfactory order had been achieved, then getting musicians to execute the sounds. Bruce Andrews's methods for composing "Confidence Trick" were evidently similar, and also involved accumulating (verbal) materials, original and "found," on cards and assembling them into a composite text (see Andrews, *Ex Why Zee* 22; *Paradise & Method* 103–04, 252–54). The end product, as a glance at any paragraph from "Confidence Trick" will confirm (e.g., the passage beginning "Talk *is* cheap," quoted above in section I), strikingly resembles a Burroughs cut-up text. Andrews's file-card method, then, like Burroughs's cut-and-paste, might be thought of as a kind of low-tech version of hip-hop sampling.[16]

Sampling, I suggested earlier, has the potential to imply critique; if so, how? Do juxtaposed fragments, on their own, speak for themselves, implying, say, a critique of the medium from which they have been sampled? Does it suffice, in the case of "Television, the Drug of the Nation," just to give television enough rope and expect it to hang itself? Perhaps not, particularly in view of the way that (already in 1992 when the Disposable Heroes' track was released, and increasingly since then) sampling and juxtaposition have been normalized in commercial radio advertising and station-identification spots, coming to signify merely, "This is commercial radio."[17] But then again, no one is expecting these fragments to speak for themselves, independently of support or corroboration from any other discourse. Rather, it is precisely the content of Franti's rap that directs and focuses our attention as listeners, allowing us to grasp the critique implicit in the juxtaposed samples. Perhaps, in the absence of the explicit guidance provided by Franti's lyrics, this collage of found discourses would not strike us so forcibly as a critique and demystification of consumer culture—or perhaps it would; it's a moot point, in any case, since the collage does not function alone, except when, excerpted and stripped of context, it ends up stranded artificially on the page to serve as an example of sampling. In their "home" context, that of the total mix of "Television," sampled passages and rap lyrics mutually reinforce and illuminate one another.

Similarly, the political tendentiousness of, say, Burroughs's sampling practice is made explicit through narrativization in a way that is ruled out, for lack of narrative context, in the case of Andrews's "Confidence Trick." Or is it? Bob Perelman (59–78) argues for reading disjunct New Sentences, of the kind from which his own poem "China" is made, as mini-narratives. By scaling them up to full-size, as it were—that is, by contextualizing and renarrativizing them, proceeding on the assumption that these are essentially narrative sentences that have somehow lost their narrative context——one begins to catch sight of the larger, circumambient metanarrative that will make their political meanings manifest. Perelman undertakes just such a renarrativization of "China," as Hartley (42–52) had already done before him—and as Jameson did, for that matter, albeit in a somewhat half-hearted and rudimentary way (*Postmodernism* 29). Just because Andrews, in "Confidence Trick," typically works with units below the sentence level doesn't mean that the same can't be done for his phrases and fragments as Perelman proposes to do for New Sentences. And indeed, Andrews has done it himself in a number of his essays, contextualizing and renarrativizing material from his own poetry, either by collaging it with other poetic material (his own or other poets'), or by weaving it into the fabric of an expository-prose argument, notably in the 1981 essay "Constitution/Writing, Politics, Language, The Body" (see Golding, "Andrews's Poetics"):

One radical variant of respect for this way of characterizing the medium would be a poetics of subversion. *Nomenclature . . . / dishevel. Tumult verbal. secular violation. elated with the thought of transgression.* The system of oppositions could itself be opposed. *uses bad language / anarchy otherwise. nonsigns.* To oppose the structural underpinnings by an anti-systematic detonation—*dizzying . . . elasticize . . . by flashes . . . nonsigns . . . scrambled*—by a blowing up of all settled relations. (*Paradise & Method* 25)

The italicized material here (the italics are Andrews's) has all been lifted from Andrews's own poetry: for instance, *Nomenclature . . . /dishevel* from "True Flip To" (*Enough Rope* 133), *elated with the thought of transgression* from "Praxis" (*Getting Ready* 50), and so on.

When, as here in the "Constitution/Writing" essay, Andrews undertakes to contextualize material from his own poetry, integrating it in an enveloping expository discourse, differences that had seemed crucially to distinguish Andrews's poetics from McGrath's begin to dwindle into insignficance. What makes their poetics comparable, as we have seen, are the uses they respectively make of discursive imagery—found and sampled discourses; what had seemed to distinguish them was the absence from Andrews's practice of any determinate framing of these discourses. Not so, as it turns out; the only real difference between them, on reconsideration, is that McGrath prefers to put his frames—narrative structure, determinate subject-position, etc.—*inside* his *Letter,* while Andrews prefers to construct his *outside.*

V. ENOUGH ROPE

what they expect me to do is turn the stigma into a rousing slogan
(Andrews, "Confidence Trick" 180)

Nevertheless, differences between McGrath's *Letter to an Imaginary Friend* and Andrews's "Confidence Trick" persist, and they are substantive. They might be captured in one way by saying that, as far as McGrath is concerned, Gil Scott-Heron was right, and the Revolution will *not* be televised, so why should a political poet waste his or her time reflecting on mass-media discourse?; while for Andrews, as for the Disposable Heroes of Hiphoprisy, television *is* the drug of the nation, and thus analyzing, unmasking, and deconstructing mass-media discourse and the consumer culture it sustains remain high priorities for political poetry.

Another way of capturing their differences might be to suggest that, between them, McGrath and Andrews divide up the expressive resources that are so tightly integrated in hip-hop music, arguably the most powerfully political popular art form of the last decades of the twentieth century. McGrath's *Letter* exploits some of the same resources as the rap component of hip-hop music—narrative, the creation of a memorable and charismatic speaker-persona, awareness of audience, direct political statement (see Rose)—precisely the features that make *Letter* something like a model political poem. On the other hand, McGrath subordinates and to a degree neglects the expressive potential represented by the hip-hop mix—the power of sampling and mixing social discourses and thereby giving them rope enough to hang themselves. Andrews, conversely, fully exploits the expressive resources of sampling, but without availing himself of the resources of narrative framing, a stable subject-position, and so on—the resources of the rap. Or, insofar as he does resort to such framing, he does so (as we have seen) *outside* the poem, not, like McGrath, inside it. Lacking the interpretative guidance that such frames provide, it sometimes proves impossible to infer a definite political position from Andrews's mix (see Perelman 96–108)—just as it might be to grasp the critical implications of the mix in "Television, the Drug of the Nation" in the absence of Michael Franti's rap.

Moreover, each choice of method—McGrath's of rap-like narrativity and communicativity, Andrews's of the citational indirection and indeterminacy of the mix—involves implicit (and sometimes explicit) critique of the other method. Andrews (see *Paradise & Method* 49–71 and passim) regards political writing that fails to scrutinize its own discursive medium as inadequate, and views with suspicion writing that aspires to speak "authentically" from a particular personal experience of the social—what for McGrath would be "representative" experience—or seeks to be politically "efficacious." "Authentic" utterance and "efficacious" modes take the existing discursive apparatus for granted, in Andrews's view, or worse, even reinforce it, instead of exposing its limits, norms, and operations. Such exposure of the discursive apparatus is essential, since the language medium, far from providing a neutral "warehouse of styles" (52) from which one might freely pick and choose, constitutes a repertoire that has already been preemptively ordered into social codes. Narrative, direct communication, the claim to authenticity, the aspiration to efficacy—all these features conform to the norms of contemporary mass-media discourse, playing straight into the hands of the entertainment industry, as witness the massive commercial co-optation of gangsta rap in recent years. Insofar as McGrath embraces these features in his own practice, he makes his writing similarly available for co-optation; we can almost imagine a made-for-TV movie, along the lines of "Pirates of SiliconValley," based on *Letter to an Imaginary Friend*. A painful irony: despite his aversion to the mass-media, McGrath is altogether too ready for prime time—at least, as viewed from Andrews's position.

Conversely, as viewed from McGrath's position—or, let's say, from the position of the model political poem, which McGrath's *Letter* approximates—Andrews's sampling practice in "Confidence Trick," his poetics of discursive imagery, can appear as something like exemplary postmodernist "blank parody," parody without ulterior motives, untendentious and politically toothless (see Jameson, *Postmodernism* 17). Such an appearance of "blankness" is one of the "occupational hazards of the parodist: producing mere clones of the object of parody, losing a critical edge and sliding into pastiche" (Barnard 144). In the absence of narrative context, such as the one supplied by McGrath or Burroughs, but eschewed by Andrews, how are we to distinguish a *critical* sampling practice from sampling in the service of late-capitalist consumer culture? tendentious parody of socially coded discourse from the blank kind? How are we to distinguish commercial radio from its deconstructors, or, in other words, symptoms from diagnosis?

Thus, if McGrath's method appears to be complicit with consumer culture in one way, Andrews's sampling method can be construed as complicit in another way. To some extent, as we have seen, charges of complicity against Andrews can be answered by pointing to the possibility of framing and contextualizing Andrews's poetry in ways that bring its political implications to light—the print equivalent of rapping over the mix. This will not satisfy everyone, however. There are those who persist in considering the sort of renarrativizing of disjunctive poetry that Perelman endorses, and that Andrews undertakes in his own contextualizing essays, as somehow illegitimate. If de-contextualized poems are to have their contexts "restored" in this manner, then the poems must themselves supply or indicate the relevant contexts; contexts must not be "dragged in" by readers. This, for instance, seems to be the tenor of Charles Altieri's objections to certain influential political readings of Language poetry. Altieri thinks Language poems can only be read politically if the reader is willing to apply a number of interpretative and "framing" operations not actually "given" by the text. The underlying (unspoken) assumption would seem to be that political poetry carries, or at any rate *should* carry, its interpretative context around with it—as McGrath's *Letter* appears to do, for instance (which is why it qualifies as such a good candidate for the model political poem). The poem should supply everything necessary for its own successful interpretation, and if the reader must call on "extrinsic" operations and information (e.g., knowledge of Andrews's politics), then there is something inadequate about the text in question.

This assumption of the text's self-sufficiency is, of course, a cornerstone of New Critical aesthetics. The model of the self-sufficient poem persists among certain Left-wing critics (see, e.g., Alan Wald on John Brooks Wheelwright). Even Andrews himself appears to believe, like Altieri, that poems can, or should, explain themselves, in the sense of carrying with them, or at any rate implicating, the contexts in which they make sense and can be made sense of. "Circularly," he writes of fellow Language poet Barrett Watten, "the writing itself is 'explained' by (it lays bare its motivation in terms of) the 'explanation' or 'account' of the social which it offers" (*Paradise & Method* 236). Elsewhere he seems to repudiate this notion of self-explanation when he challenges the "popular temptation . . . to want meaning without subtitles," but then he goes on to raise the issue of "how to build the subtitles back into the text itself— or at least make palpable how much of their own cache of subtitles the readers might bring with them. . . . Or: how to get the words arranged to carry the charge of their own interpretation as an inside filament" (140). Making palpable to readers the "cache of subtitles" they bring with them to a text seems a task to which disjunct poetry of the "Confidence Trick" type is well suited; but building subtitles back into the text itself, and arranging for it to carry its own interpretation "as an inside filament"—these aspirations seem animated by assumptions of textual self-sufficiency that Andrews certainly knows to be untenable. (Andrews expressly attacks "official versions of 'high modernism'" that presuppose the text's self-sufficiency; *Paradise & Method* 229.)

To challenge such assumptions is finally to invalidate the sort of objections that Jameson and others have voiced against postmodernist disjunctive poetry such as Andrews's. For if political poems do *not* carry their contexts of intepretation around with them, if they depend for "correct" political decoding on the expectations and dispositions of communities of readers (the "cache of subtitles" they bring with them to the task of reading), and if readers are free to use poets' *other* writings as keys or templates for decoding, then symptomaticity or diagnosticity, compliance or critique, are not after all properties of *poems* but of *readings* (see Suleiman 192–93). As Rita Barnard writes, the political bite or "edge" of an ambivalently parodic text such as Nathanael West's (or Bruce Andrews's) "remains inseparable from the [parodist's] intentions, *as well as* its audience's strategies of interpretation" (144; my emphasis). Diagnosis and critique are, at least in part, in the eye of the beholder, and the beholder's eye is never entirely innocent—nor should it be.

7

The Silent Woman

Susan Howe's *The Europe of Trusts*

Women's speech, their silence, and their silencing: these are vener-able topoi of misogynist literature, which is to say of canonical literature generally. But they are topoi fraught with irony, not all of it intended. Consider Ben Jonson's play *Epicoene, or The Silent Woman* (1609), which develops from a kernel of misogynist cliché. Morose seeks a silent wife; his nephew and heir inflicts a scam on him, finding him a woman, the eponymous Epicoene, who can hardly be made to speak before the wedding, but who within minutes of the vows being uttered reveals herself to be the talkative woman of the familiar stereotype. So the joke is on womankind: there is no such creature as a genuinely silent woman.

Unless, that is, the joke is really on Jonson: for at the very heart of his misogynist scenario, a strange gender disturbance emerges. The scam is double: Epicoene, it transpires, is not a woman after all, but (as her name insinuates) an epicene young man in drag. Jonson presents this final revelation as further evidence of the nephew's virtuosity and wit, but it is hard not to see in it a profound unravelling of the play's misogynist premises. Far from exposing women's talkativeness to ridicule, Jonson seems in the end only to have exposed the talkativeness of men!

Of course, there are ways of finessing the apparent contradiction, for instance by reading it as implying a critique on Jonson's part of the ef-feminacy of contemporary men and the manliness of contemporary women, or even as "baring the device" of the conventional transvestism of the Elizabethan/Jacobean stage. Such readings fail to explain, how-ever, why similar internal contradictions keep emerging, across periods and genres, wherever the figure of the talkative woman recurs. Consider

John Berryman's "Homage to Mistress Bradstreet" (1953), the medium-long poem (some fifteen pages in the *Collected Poems*) through which he first laid claim to the status of "major poet," subsequently confirmed by the *Dream Songs*. Naming Anne Bradstreet his precursor and muse, Berryman nevertheless admits to finding her poetry prolix, conventional, drably orthodox. He quotes almost nothing from her "proportioned, spiritless poems," as he calls them dismissively (st. 42, l.6); "all this bald/abstract didactic rime I read appalled," he reports (st. 12, ll.5–6) ("Homage" 143, 135). His poetic "homage" to the precursor-poet consists in silencing her. Berryman addresses Anne Bradstreet; then ventriloquizes "her" voice; then compels her to enter into a kind of dialogue with him, in which we can't help but be aware of his virtuosic acting-out of both interlocutors (he do the police in different voices). In his note to the opening stanzas, Berryman revealingly explains that "the poem is about the woman but . . . spoken [in part] by the poet" (147); by this we understand that "the woman," Bradstreet, is *not* "the poet," and that the only poet in *this* poem is the man, Berryman. Who, then, is talkative here? Again, not the woman but the transvestite man; the woman remains silent, silenced.

It is contradictions such as these in the male canon of writing in English that Susan Howe has sought, throughout her entire resourceful and difficult body of verse, but especially in the poems of *The Europe of Trusts*, to expose, reverse, and rectify. Her writings, poetry and prose alike, can be seen as a series of countermeasures against the received version of literary historiography for which Berryman's "Homage" serves as a kind of parable.

I. HOW(EVER)

Literary history and the present are dark with silences. . . .
        Tillie Olsen, "Silences in Literature," 1962 (Olsen 6)

If in one sense Jonson's and Berryman's misogynist texts self-deconstruct, in another sense they succeed only too well. For Jonson's misogyny in *Epicoene* is not really directed at the silent/talkative woman (how could it be, since Epicoene is not a woman after all?), but rather at "the Collegiates," a circle of middle-class London women who presume to live independently of their husbands' control and to conduct their lives as they please. It is these women who are decisively silenced by the revelation of Epicoene's true gender identity—literally; for from the moment of this revelation to the end of the play, none of the Collegiates speaks another line. The threat to be countered, it appears, is not so much women individually as women *in groups;* what needs silencing is not women's speech so much as women *speaking collectively.* Berryman, however unconsciously, seems to be responding to a similar threat: his muting of Anne Bradstreet's speech contributes to the historical effacement of what was arguably the first circle of dissident women in America, the one around Anne Hutchinson, with whom Bradsteet was for a time affiliated. Hutchinson's voice was found so dangerous in her own time as to constitute grounds for explusion; does Berryman's ventriloquism of Bradstreet, then, perpetuate the silencing of the Hutchinson circle, only by other means?

Recovering the voice of the Hutchinson circle and tracing its covert influence on the antinomian tradition in American writing (including the writing of Emily Dickinson and Herman Melville) has been one of Susan Howe's projects; she devoted most of the essays in her book *The Birth-mark* (1993) to it. Evidently Howe sees her own writing as belonging to this tradition. Moreover, one might see in the Hutchinson circle a kind of precursor or model for the circles of dissident women in which Howe herself has moved: circles of women speaking (and publishing) collectively, real-world equivalents of the fictional Collegiates whom Ben Jonson found so threatening. The most important of these circles is the one centered on *HOW(ever),* the journal of the feminist literary avant-garde, founded by the poet Kathleen Fraser in 1983. But the *HOW-(ever)* group is not the only community of women poets with whom Howe has been associated, nor is her association with this group the only community-building activity in which she has been involved.[1]

The feminist poets of the *HOW(ever)* group, including Fraser, Beverly Dahlen, Frances Jaffer, Rachel Blau DuPlessis, Susan Gevirtz, and others, see themselves as belonging to a tradition of women's avant-garde poetry that extends back at least as far as Dickinson (if not Sappho), and that includes, in the twentieth century, H.D., Gertrude Stein, Mina Loy, Laura Riding, Lorine Niedecker, and Barbara Guest, among others. But perhaps just as appropriate as the term "avant-garde" would be Howe's preferred term for this tradition: antinomian. Rachel Tzvia Back (124) clarifies this distinction: where "avant-garde" implies only a *break* with the poetics of the past, "antinomianism" implies a revisionist *dialogue* with the past. In the case of the *HOW(ever)* group, that dialogue has entailed, first of all, reclamation and restoration to the literary-historical archive of the female innovators who had been edited out of it, notably those listed above. Second, it has entailed revisionist intervention in the received (male) canon and the literary-historical narrative that sustains it.

"Howe," writes Back (76), "is steeped in the literary masters that preceded her, and a central strategy of her poetic project is to maintain an ongoing dialogue with those masters through the intertextuality of her works." In fact, Howe's "central strategy" of revisionist dialogue with the "masters" encompasses two distinct strategies. One involves disturbing the structure of the (male) canon by revaluing marginal works and figures at the expense of central ones. Howe tendentiously directs her (and our) attention toward marginal works by central canonical figures: not Milton's poetry or major prose writings, but instead his topical propaganda tract *Eikonoclastes* (in *A Bibliography of the King's Book*, 1989); not Swift's public writings, but instead (in "The Liberties") his *Journal to Stella*, emphasizing especially its "little language," part private code, part baby talk, used in his domestic circle; not *Moby-Dick* but (precisely) "Melville's Marginalia" (the title of a poem of Howe's published in 1993). When she does address central, "major" texts, she is likely to give equal weight to uncanonical and para-literary texts by the same author: thus, if Spenser's *Faerie Queene* figures conspicuously in "Defenestration of Prague" (1983), so does his prose *View of the present state of Ireland*. Alternatively, Howe redirects our attention toward figures on the margins of the canon, such as the obscure James Clarence Mangan (in "Melville's Marginalia") or the even more obscure Reverend Hope Atherton (in *Articulation of Sound Forms in Time*, 1987), or physically marginalized figures such as the semiotician C. S. Pierce in his rustic exile, or Swinburne in the semi-isolation of his last decades (in *Pierce-Arrow*, 1999).

A second strategy involves intervening directly in the central canonical texts of the male literary tradition, "rewriting the books we assumed we knew, against the grain of the most precious canon" (DuPlessis, *Pink Guitar* 136). Howe's practice here has much in common with Dickinson's, as Howe herself describes it: "Forcing, abbreviating, pushing, padding, subtracting, riddling, interrogating, re-writing, she pulled text from text" (*Dickinson* 29; see Vanderborg 62–63). Howe, too, pulls text from text; she cites, appropriates, and alludes in (almost) conventional fashion, but she also "writes through" texts (like John Cage or Jackson Mac Low using the initial or medial letters of found words to spell out new words) and erases texts (like Tom Phillips or Ronald Johnson). Entirely characteristic is her deliberate abuse, in *The Europe of Trusts*, of texts by several major canonical figures: William Shakespeare (who can be seen as defining the very notion of a modern secular literary canon), Edmund Spenser, Jonathan Swift, W. B. Yeats, Samuel Beckett. All of these apart from Shakespeare appear to have special meaning for Howe because of their association with Ireland, her mother's homeland, with which (at least in the eighties, the period of *The Europe of Trusts*) she seems very strongly to identify. In the sections that follow I will consider in order Howe's (mis)treatment of texts by three of these figures: Shakespeare, Spenser, and Swift.

Howe's challenge to the male literary tradition involves problematizing the very genre in which she writes, namely the long poem. The long poem, whether in the narrative mode of the epic or in one of the various Romantic or modernist modes, has historically served as the measure of the height of a poet's ambition; undertaking to write one amounted to a declaration of one's designs on canonical status. Perhaps for that very reason women have tended to keep their distance from it, acknowledging thereby the genre's special status as "the quintessential male territory whose boundaries enforce women's status as outsiders on the landscape of poetry" (Friedman 11; quoted in Keller, *Forms* 4). Before the 1960s, few women poets in English dared to venture inside that privileged enclosure to measure themselves against the male masters: Elizabeth Barrett Browning in the nineteenth century; among the modernists, Stein, Loy, Muriel Rukeyser, H.D. All that changed with the onset of the second wave of feminism in the sixties. The avant-gardists of the *HOW(ever)* circle, in particular, set about demonstrating in practice that women poets had as legitimate a claim to the modernist and postmodernist tradition of the long poem as any man. Fraser produced a number of medium-long poems or sequences, while Dahlen and DuPlessis each began serial long poems (*A Reading* and *Drafts*, respectively) that promised to achieve the scale of "lifelong" poems like those of their male precursors Pound, Olson, or Duncan (see Keller, *Forms* 239–301).

The question remains, are Susan Howe's poems "long poems"? And if they *are*, then how "long" are they, exactly? The latter question, which may sound like a quibble, actually gets right to the heart of the matter.

All Howe's poems are made of disparate parts, but it is seldom clear whether, in her own view, these parts add up to a "whole," and if they do, what exactly the scope and character of that "whole" might be. This, in turn, affects how we read these texts: as single, integral poems? as poetic sequences in something like Rosenthal's and Gall's sense? as collections of separate poems? or as none or all of the above?[2]

Especially problematic is the case of *The Europe of Trusts* (1990). Two of its three parts (or poems), "Defenestration of Prague" and "The Liberties," had formerly appeared together in a book called *Defenestration of Prague* (1983), and a number of critics (including Martin; Perloff, "Collision"; and Reinfeld) have proceeded on the assumption that these two parts together constitute a whole, while others (including DuPlessis, *Pink Guitar;* McGann "Composition"; Keller, *Forms*) have treated them as separate poems. The first part (or poem), "Pythagorean Silence," published separately in 1982, never appeared together with either of the other two before the 1990 volume; nevertheless, it could be described, on formal grounds, as a companion-piece to "Defenestration" (while "The Liberties" seems formally quite distinct from the other two). Moreover, the three parts (or poems) are preceded, in the 1990 edition, by a preface or prologue that seems to throw a frame around them, appearing to invite us to read them all as a single long poem, or perhaps as a trilogy, like H.D.'s long poem by that name. Nothing in the 1990 edition itself prevents our reading them this way; nevertheless, in bio-bibliographical notes published since then, and opposite the title pages of her more recent books, Howe has appended to the title *The Europe of Trusts* a new subtitle, *Selected Poems,* which appears nowhere in the 1990 volume.[3] It is as if she were *dis*couraging us, retrospectively, from reading *Europe* as an integral long poem.

So which is it, a trilogy or a "selection"? I'm disposed to think that Howe has deliberately left this an open question, and that she has done so precisely with a view to troubling her poem's (or poems') relation to the male long-poem tradition. By leaving the question wide open, she sets herself up as rival of the male masters and candidate for membership in the tradition, and at the same time as that tradition's critic and deconstructor. She simultaneously lays claim to the long-poem tradition, with all its high ambitions and prestige, and distances herself from it; she positions herself simultaneously inside and outside the privileged enclosure.

In short, Howe has made it impossible for us to decide (except for strategic reasons, and ultimately arbitrarily) whether she does or does not mean for her poem (or poems) to count as an entry in the long-poem sweepstakes. Nevertheless, in what follows, I will proceed (albeit gingerly) on the assumption that *The Europe of Trusts can* be read as a single book-length poem, though it *need not* be read that way, and can indeed be read otherwise.

II. HER WILLIAM SHAKESPEARE

And as for this line I stole it from T. S. Eliot
And Ezra Pound and A. C. Swinburne. All very good
Poets to steal from since they are all three dead.
Veronica Forrest-Thomson, "Cordelia, or
'A Poem Should Not Mean but Be'" (*Collected* 105)

Howe writes of Emily Dickinson, "The way to understand her writing is through her reading" (*Dickinson* 24). Similarly, in order to grasp Howe's practice we need to understand how she understands her precursors, particularly the writers in the dominant (male) literary tradition.[4]

In Howe's intertextual reading of Dickinson, it seems as though sooner or later all roads lead to Shakespeare, or at least by way of him. The same might be said of Howe's *The Europe of Trusts*. In part, Howe's engagement with the Shakespearean canon takes the familiar form of conventional literary allusion (see Back 113). Exemplary in this respect is the presence in her texts of various Shakespearean characters, including Cordelia in "The Liberties" (a special case, to which I shall return below), Ophelia (see Taggart 117), Peter Quince (*PS* 81), Falstaff (*DP* 95) and, in at least one passage, Macbeth:

Leaf of Cawdor

sere memory restless remembrancer
(*DP* 124)[5]

The allusion here is particularly subtle, requiring us to recognize "Cawdor" as one of Macbeth's titles (Thane of Cawdor), and to catch the echo, in the near juxtaposition of "Leaf" and "sere," of a famous soliloquy from *Macbeth* (V.iii.22–23), slightly distorted: "My way of life/Is fall'n into the sear, the yellow leaf," and so on.

More radical in its form and its implications alike is a second strategy of intervention, involving direct verbatim appropriation from the source text and "foregrounding words and phrases as 'found objects'" (Vickery 182). Depending upon how one looks at it, this could be regarded as a strategy of sampling or of erasure (i.e., erasure of everything in the source text *except* the sampled words), and it could be compared to William Burroughs's cut-up and fold-in strategies or Kathy Acker's poetics of appropriation, or viewed as akin to Cage's practice of "writing through" source texts, or even to the studio production techniques of hip-hop music (see chapter 6). Consider, for example, page 96 from "Defenestration of Prague" (Figure 4). As with many other passages in Howe's poetry, one senses here that these words come from elsewhere, that they are not Howe's—or not Howe's in the first place, but only by virtue of appropriation. Alternatively, it is as if Howe had dipped some source text in an acid bath until everything had dissolved away except these few resistant nuggets of language. But which text? Luckily, we are given several clues—"Moth crew," for instance, and "Mechanicals," the first directing us to the fairy servants who wait on Peter Quince at the behest of the fairy Queen, the second directing us to Quince and his workingmen's company of amateur actors. The source text, in other words, must be *A Midsummer Night's Dream*. Once we have made this initial identification, it becomes possible to guess at likely contexts for other material on this page; for instance, "casement(*open* of great Moone," "*Solemnities blaze*," "LION," "thorn," and "revel" all seem likely to have been derived from the play's final scene, in which the "mechanicals" perform "Pyramus and Thisby" at court. Once we had tracked down the exact sources of the fragments, and determined their relevance in context, we could begin reconstructing the rationale for Howe's selections (and omissions), her reasons for juxtaposing just these materials in just this way, and thus begin forming a picture of Howe's reading of this Shakespearean text.

I don't propose to undertake this reconstruction here, but instead to move on to a third and even more distinctive strategy. For the two strategies I just outlined—conventional allusion on the one hand, sampling (or hop   Moth crew

Mechanicals

casement(*open* of great Moone

Epilogue

Palpabl
                          Stub
stab winter nipt prodigal

                          Solemnities blaze

hoodwink
                    t
I messenger of Power
                          salt-errand
sea-girt   PEACE and LION
                          sleeve for thorn keen
        wimpl
                    oaten
        run

                    run
                    revel   hop
                                   lob

Figure 4. Page 96 from Howe, *Defenestration of Prague*

erasure) on the other—do not suffice when it comes to Shakespeare, because of Shakespeare's special status in Anglo-American culture. Spenser, by contrast (to whom we will return below), has always been a possession of the educated, and nowadays only of the specialist, but Shakespeare's status is different: he belongs to the "public." A collective possession of the culture- and the language-at-large, "Shakespeare" exists for us less as a body of written or performed texts than as a repertoire of textual fragments, a mobile body of quotations—often not even recognized as such—in constant circulation in English-speaking culture. Even someone who has never read, say, *Hamlet* or *Romeo and Juliet*, or seen them on stage or at the movies (but hasn't everyone seen them at the movies by now?), already knows a great many stock phrases ("hoist with his own petard"), whole sentences ("Romeo, Romeo, wherefore art thou Romeo?"), and fragments of speeches ("To be or not to be," etc.) from these plays, just because they are in general circulation. This is the situation captured by the anecdote, no doubt apocryphal, of the society matron who, having just seen *Hamlet* for the first time, complained of its being too full of quotations.

In view of this situation, Howe has developed a third strategy of intervention to supplement the other two, custom-made to accommodate the special status of the Shakespearean canon. We might think of it as a strategy of abusive (mis)quotation. Its effect is to foreground "Shakespeare's" existence as a kind of intertextual coinage in general circulation, susceptible of all the abuses to which coinage itself is subject: clipping and shaving, counterfeiting, devaluation. Designed to target the imperfection and unreliability of our collective cultural memory, Howe's abuses undermine our confidence in our collective "possession" of Shakespeare.

Consider, for example, a passage from "Pythagorean Silence":

GHOST enters WAVES he

scatters flowers

from the summit

of a cliff that beckons on or beetles o'er

his base

ORISONS

(*PS* 23)

Here Howe is quoting mainly from a familiar speech of Horatio's in *Hamlet,* I.iv (though "ORISONS" fast-forwards, as it were, to a later scene: "Nymph, in thy orisons/Be all my sins remembered" [III.i.89–90]). But now compare the original *Hamlet* passage. Horatio speaks, referring to the ghost:

> What if it tempt you toward the flood, my lord,
> Or to the dreadful summit of the cliff
> That beetles o'er his base into the sea,
> And there assume some other horrible form,
> Which might deprive your sovereignty of reason
> And draw you into madness?
>
> (I.iv.69–74)

Something has gone slightly wrong with this quotation, for in the midst of it Howe has introduced an alien verb, a kind of tiny stutter: "cliff that *beckons on or* beetles o'er/ his base" (my emphasis). It could happen to anyone—to the actor delivering Horatio's lines onstage, for instance—and indeed unless one checked it against the text the stutter might pass unnoticed. But if one *does* go to the trouble of checking the text, it becomes clear that the alien verb is not so alien after all, merely slightly displaced; for "beckons" appears in a stage direction (specifying the ghost's gesture) some dozen lines before the (mis)quoted passage. Moreover, Horatio himself immediately takes up the word from the stage direction, almost as if (but how could this be?) he had just read it in the script: "It beckons you to go away with it" (I.iv.58).

So Howe gives us here a miniature model of the kinds of conflations and displacements that characterize our collective cultural memory of Shakespeare in general. In this case the slippage is minimal, merely involving adjacent passages in the same scene.[6] But other larger, more alarming conflations are also possible—for instance, between different Shakespearean texts, as in the *God's Spies* section of "The Liberties." Cordelia (another appropriation from Shakespeare) speaks:

Free from tangle our clipper flies. Billows—check the
chart! A flagstaff but no flag stands at the railings.
Not for nothing our going forth—lucky, into great
blue—bedecked with crowflowers and long purples—
Nameless abashing flame. (*Pause*)

(*L* 197–98)

These "crowflowers and long purples" are a problem (just one among
many in this passage). There's something familiar about them, something unmistakably "Shakespearean," yet we grope in our memories for
the precise allusion. Since Howe attributes these words to Cordelia, we
perhaps begin by mentally reviewing relevant passages from *King Lear*.
And indeed there is one in which Cordelia speaks of her father in his
madness:

Alack, 'tis he! Why, he was met even now
As mad as the vexed sea, singing aloud,
Crowned with rank fumiter and furrow weeds,
With hardocks, hemlock, nettles, cuckoo flow'rs,
Darnel, and all the idle weed that grow
In our sustaining corn.

(IV.iv.1–8)

While we mght accept Howe's "bedecked" as a variant on Shakespeare's
"crowned,"[7] there's no getting around the fact that these are not the right
flowers: there are "cuckoo flowers" here, maybe even "cornflowers" lurk-
ing in the linguistic shadows, but no "crowflowers," and no "long purples," either. So we seem to have been mistaken in our assumption that
Shakespeare is implicated here. Unless, on reflection, it is not after all
King Lear that we are being invited to recall, but another play altogether:
could it be *Hamlet* again? In a famous set piece, Queen Gertrude describes Ophelia's last, pathetic moments:

There is a willow grows askant the brook,
That shows his hoar leaves in the glassy stream.
Therewith fantastic garlands did she make
Of crowflowers, nettles, daisies, and long purples,

That liberal shepherds give a grosser name,
But our cold maids do dead men's fingers call them.
There on the pendent boughs her crownet weeds
Clamb'ring to hang, an envious sliver broke,
When down her weedy trophies and herself
Fell in the weeping brook.

(IV.vii.165–74)

Here, then, not in *King Lear*, is the source of Howe's "crowflowers and long purples," obscured by the simple misattribution of these words to Cordelia. But of course there's nothing "simple" in this misattribution at all, for it opens the door to further conflations and "subject rhymes" among characters.[8] We are invited to see how mad Ophelia rhymes with mad Lear; how the silenced woman Ophelia rhymes with the silenced woman Cordelia; and how the play *Hamlet* "bleeds" into the play *King Lear*, and vice versa, in our cultural collective consciousness.

Slippages can occur, then, between adjacent passages of the same text, or even between different Shakespearean texts. But there's worse abuse: Howe's conflations and misattributions are sometimes even more brazen than these. Consider this passage from "The Liberties":

> children of Lir
>   lear
>   whistling would in air ha
>   nameless appear—
>   Can you not see
>   arme armes
>   give tongue
>   are you silent o my swift
>   all coherence gone?
>   Thrift thrift
>   we are left darkling
>   waiting in the wings again
>   thral in the heart of Hell.

(*L* 176)

"Thrift thrift" we may succeed readily enough in tracing back to a memorably sardonic utterance of Hamlet's: "Thrift, thrift, Horatio! The funeral baked meats/Did coldly furnish forth the marriage tables" (I.ii.180–81). As for "we are left darkling," that might well linger in the mind, coming as it does from one of the Fool's inscrutable punch lines in *King Lear:* "So out went the candle, and we were left darkling" (I.iv.208).[9] But what about "All coherence gone"? It sounds familiar, and would not be out of place in either *Hamlet* or *Lear;* so, from which of them does it derive? Neither, of course: it comes from John Donne's poem, "An Anatomy of the World" of 1611, also called "The First Anniversary" (l. 213). By juxtaposing the Donne phrase with fragments from *Hamlet* and *King Lear,* Howe slyly tempts us to conflate Donne with Shakespeare, in the process exposing to skeptical scrutiny our taken-for-granted sense of Shakespeare's cultural identity. If "Shakespeare" can turn out so easily to be "Donne," then how secure, really, is our grasp of what distinguishes him, of what makes him "Shakespeare"?

Howe's forms of abusive misquotation from Shakespeare—involving slippage between adjacent passages, between different Shakespearean texts, between Shakespearean texts and texts by other authors—remind us of a salient fact that our literary ideologies do their best to repress: namely, that literature does not exist for us only or even most importantly as integral texts (such as the plays of William Shakespeare), but rather as verbal detritus, dispersed and misremembered fragments circulating in everyday discourse. "The direct consumption of *integral texts,*" insists the Israeli cultural theorist Itamar Even-Zohar,

> has been, and remains, peripheral to the largest part of "direct," let alone "indirect," consumers of "literature." All members of any community are at least "indirect" consumers of literary texts. In this capacity we, as such members, simply consume a certain quantity of literary fragments, digested and transmitted by various agents of culture and made an integral part of daily discourse. . . . Fragments of old narrative, idioms and allusions, parables and stock language, all, and many more, constitute the living repertoire stored in the warehouse of our culture (36–37, 44).

Even-Zohar suggests that the function of such circulating textual fragments is to help maintain a society's models of reality, which in turn govern interpersonal interaction. In Anglo-American culture, an indefinitely large part of that circulating body of text fragments derives from the texts of Shakespeare, while another part of it, no doubt, is mistakenly assimilated to Shakespeare (e.g., "All coherence gone"); so that for us, in effect, "Shakespeare" can conveniently serve as the name for the *entire* cultural intertext. "Shakespeare," one might say, is a *synecdoche* for the cultural intertext, the part that stands for the whole.

Thus, to intervene in the Shakespearean intertext as Howe has done, to trouble our confident sense of "possessing" Shakespeare, is to intervene in the cultural intertext at large. To intervene in "Shakespeare" is literally to engage the "public sphere," in the sense of engaging our collective models of reality, our norms of social interaction, and the language that maintains them.

III. HER EDMUND SPENSER

The Irish are the [blacks] of Europe.
Roddy Doyle, *The Commitments*, 1989 (quoted in A. Murphy 11)

The general cultural intertext that we identify by the synecdoche "Shakespeare" includes, as we have already seen, certain texts of John Donne; it also overlaps with those of Edmund Spenser. This is true not only in the sense that all Renaissance textual fragments, insofar as they survive in collective cultural memory at all, have come to be assimilated to a composite figure called "Shakespeare," but also in the sense, amply documented by the literary historians, that Shakespeare and Spenser shared in common much of their own era's cultural and literary intertext. From Shakespeare's point of view, moreover, Spenser had already been subsumed into that contemporary intertext, and so could be drawn on for materials. For instance, one of Shakespeare's sources for the story in *King Lear* was Spenser's retelling of that story in the second book of *The Faerie Queene* (II.x.27–32)—a fact that must surely have interested Susan Howe. Nevertheless, the Spenser component of our own general cultural intertext is relatively invisible, eclipsed by the Shakespeare component. Nobody would ever think to joke about *The Faerie Queene*'s being full of quotations, as one does about *Hamlet*, for the simple reason that *The Faerie Queene* isn't full of quotations. *The Faerie Queene* has long since become little more than a museum, visited only by academics (and few enough of those). If in *The Europe of Trusts* Susan Howe chooses to intervene in the Spenser intertext, as she demonstrably does, then her motives for doing so must be different than her motives for intervening in the Shakespeare intertext. There must be something else at stake than the exposure and demystification of the general cultural intertext that motivated her engagement with Shakespeare. So, why Spenser?

The answer, in a word, is "Ireland." As I suggested earlier, Howe in *The Europe of Trusts* addresses her Irish cultural legacy, transmitted to her through her mother (see Back 16, 61, 90). She does so most obviously in "The Liberties," through the figures of Swift and Stella and their Dublin milieu, but she does so elsewhere in *Europe* as well, mainly through the writings of Edmund Spenser. Spenser's association with Ireland—his career as a colonial administrator of the crown, and subsequently as colonist himself on forfeited lands in Munster—has until relatively recently been a conspicuous no-go area of Spenser scholarship. The basic facts of Spenser's Irish experience were already reliably established by the time of the Second World War (see, e.g., Henley), but, ignored or repressed, they figured almost not at all in postwar scholarship until Stephen Greenblatt placed "Spenser and Ireland" decisively on the scholarly agenda in 1980. From the eighties through the present writing, the topic has been revisited regularly by Renaissance scholars in Ireland and abroad (see, e.g., Coughlan; Fogarty; Hadfield). What is especially startling about Howe's (mis)treatment of the Spenserian texts in *Europe of Trusts* is the way it predates and indeed anticipates (albeit obliquely and allusively) so many of the key themes of subsequent research on "Spenser and Ireland."

In engaging with Spenser, Howe has no use for the strategy of abusive (mis)quotation that she employed to such subversive effect in her engagement with the Shakespearean canon. Unlike Shakespeare, Spenser is not a collective possession of the culture-at-large, and his language is not intertextual coinage in general circulation. Howe's other two strategies, however—conventional allusion and verbatim appropriaton or "writing-through"—do apply to the Spenser case, and I'll consider them in order.

Howe's strategy of allusion is entirely conventional in the sense that she incorporates names or other cues (or "markers") from an "alien" text in her own text, thereby inviting the reader to explore the general relevance of that other text to her own (see Ben-Porat). If Howe's practice is in any way unconventional, it is in the amount of "unpacking" of which her allusions are susceptible; but of course, as she herself demonstrated in the case of Emily Dickinson, other poets' allusions are also susceptible of extensive unpacking. Howe's main allusions to *The Faerie*

Queene involve the character Florimell, who figures in books III and IV of Spenser's poem, though her story is not finally concluded until book V, canto iii. Howe alludes directly to the Florimell story three times in the course of "Defenestration of Prague" (and perhaps obliquely on a number of other occasions):

A fictive realm
Words and meaning meet in

feigning

without a text and running from
true-seeming

Florimell flees away into the forest

Hide her there
an illusion (fiction)

Beauty of the world
becoming part of the forest

. . . .

Florimell embarks blindly
(being lost)

to interpret the world

chivalric courtesy
chivalric constancy

. . . .

Wild man of pageant and poem
wild man in a dream

Progression through forgotten time

myth Marinell foam night
sea-treasure husband

Florimell and her false double
True and false beauty
(*DP* 107, 109, 135)

Why Florimell? Right at the outset some unpacking seems called for.
Florimell's story, first of all, is transparently modelled on that of
Ariosto's Angelica from *Orlando Furioso* (this is one of the places where
Spenser's own intertext is most open to inspection), and her main function, like Angelica's before her, is to flee and to be pursued: "Florimell
flees away into the forest" (*DP* 107). The male characters of both Spenser's and Ariosto's narratives, heroes and villains alike, find these women
irresistible, and set off immediately in pursuit of them, usually on horse-
back—the villains (and, in Ariosto's case, the heroes as well) with the
intention of raping the fleeing woman, the heroes (in Spenser's case)
with the intention of rescuing her. But rescue and rape prove hard to
distinguish, and Florimell flees from her would-be rescuers as precipi-
tously as from her would-be rapists, "running from/ true-seeming" (*DP*
107). In short, the latent violence of erotic pursuit is here laid bare ("chivalric courtesy"? "chivalric constancy"?). Moreover, throughout this pursuit, Florimell is essentially silent; we only hear her "complain" once she
has been captured and imprisoned by Proteus (IV.xii). She is, in other
words, one of the silent women of the Western canon, and in this respects she "rhymes" (or partially rhymes) with Cordelia, Ophelia, Stella,
Igraine, and Iphigenia—all "characters" in *Europe*—and perhaps with
Jonson's Collegiates and Berryman's Mistress Bradstreet as well. (She
also rhymes interestingly with the women of the North American cap-
tivity narratives, such as Mary Rowlandson, about whom Howe writes
at length in *The Birth-mark.*)

Florimell exposes herself to these dangers voluntarily, for the sake of
Marinell, whom she loves, but who disdains women, on the strength of
a prophecy that he would one day suffer at the hands of one. Florimell
sets out to find Marinell when she hears he has been overthrown by a
strange knight—in fact, the cross-dressing female knight Britomart; so

the prophecy is fulfilled. This confrontation occurs on the Rich Strond, the beach rich with flotsam and jetsam, which is the gift of Marinell's grandfather, the sea-god Nereus (his mother being a sea-nymph). Eventually, having overheard her "complaint" in Proteus's cell, Marinell becomes aware of Florimell's love for him, redeems her from Proteus, and marries her; thus, "myth Marinell foam night/sea-treasure husband" (*DP* 135).

Flight through the forest, the violence of erotic pursuit, silence: these seem to be among the features of Spenser's story of Florimell that Howe aims to evoke. But there is another side to the Florimell story—literally another Florimell, "Florimell and her false double" (*DP* 135). Spenser's Florimell, having taken refuge with a witch and her son (III.vii), soon becomes (in the usual way) the object of the son's importunate desires. When she flees him, the witch creates an artificial double, a "false Florimell," to replace her (III.viii), and we continue to follow the adventures of this simulacral Florimell, a kind of Renaissance cyborg or replicant, throughout the rest of books III and IV, until her final unmasking and (literal) deconstruction at the wedding of the true Florimell with Marinell in book V.

Howe ventures a more or less conventional allegorical interpretation of this doubling of Florimell—"True and false beauty" (*DP* 135)—but one suspects that her real interests in this figure lie elsewhere. For Spenser's false Florimell is transparently a literalized blason, one of the basic conventional figures of Petrarchan poetry (most familiar from Shakespeare's ironic inversion of it in Sonnet 130), in which the beloved is anatomized, and each part of her anatomy likened to some precious object. The blason, in other words, fetishizes the beloved, and false Florimell is nothing other than a walking fetish. The witch, we are told, makes her body from "purest snow" (tempered with mercury and wax, plus vermilion for color), her eyes from "burning lampes" in "siluer sockets," and her hair from "golden wyre" (III.viii.6–7; Spenser, *Poetical* 183). These are all familiar clichés of the Renaissance blason, and by literalizing the figure Spenser exposes its fetishism, its literal "objectification" of women. In singling out "Florimell and her false double" for special attention, Howe in her turn ensures that we recognize the force of Spenser's analysis.

Moreover, just as silent Florimell rhymes with other silent women of the canon, so her double the false Florimell rhymes with another story of doubling and simulation. Howe explicitly calls our attention to the rhyme; the "false Florimell" passage from "Defenestration" continues:

> Florimell and her false double
> True and false beauty
>
> Helen Hermes of clouds
>
> to deceive Paris
> Players melt into one another
> (*DP* 135–36)

Howe evokes here the story of how the true Helen was transported to Egypt, and replaced in Troy by a phantom double. Lacking Homeric authority, this story comes down to us from Stesichorus of Sicily, but it seems clear that Howe's primary allusion here is neither to Homer nor Stesichorus but to H.D., whose long poem *Helen in Egypt* (1961) retells this alternative, "unauthorized" myth of Helen. In juxaposing false Florimell with phantom Helen, Howe thus implicitly intervenes in the received literary-historical narrative, derailing the usual all-male sequence that passes from Homer through Spenser and Milton to the Romantics and beyond, and proposing in its stead an alternative line of descent that makes H.D. one of Spenser's legitimate heirs.[10]

There is at least one other potential subject-rhyme with Florimell. Pauline Henley, whose invaluable 1928 book *Spenser in Ireland* marshalled the available facts of Spenser's Irish career, proposed to read Florimell as an allegory of Ireland (137–38), and while her reading is not fully persuasive, the possibility of rhyming Florimell with the Irish (if not with Ireland) does seem tenable in *The Europe of Trusts*. Apart from the general "feminization" of the Irish (see, e.g., Cavanagh; Maley, 86–87), which potentially rhymes with Florimell as silent woman, there is the matter of Florimell's flight and its juxtaposition with the overseas exile of the Irish lords after the defeat at the Boyne, the so-called "flight of the wild geese," which Howe evokes at least twice in "The Liberties" (*L* 158, 184; see Keller, *Forms* 212–13; Back 68–69).

There is, finally, one other element of Howe's allusions to the Florimell story that requires unpacking, and that is the forest motif: "Florimell flees away into the forest"; "Beauty of the world/ becoming part of the forest" (*DP* 107). The motif of the forest or woods recurs throughout *The Europe of Trusts,* from beginning to end:

> we that were wood
> when that a wide wood was
> (*PS* 17)

> Dream of wandering in woods with

> my father
> (*PS* 61)

> world is my way in sylvan
> imagery
> (*DP* 89)

> The woods seem to thicken
> (*DP* 103)

> The woods are on fire.
> (*L* 184)
> Leafy I
> labyrinth am
> lost in the woods (or hiding)
> (*L* 195)

With respect to Florimell's story, these woods no doubt allude to the forests of Faeryland through which Spenser's heroine is perpetually fleeing, and ultimately, perhaps, to their intertextual source in the forests through which Ariosto's Angelica flees. These may be specifically Irish forests (see Henley, 128; Coughlan, 53–54); at any rate, they are not specifically North American forests, as would be the case in most of Howe's other poems of the woods (especially *Secret History of the Dividing Line, Articulation of Sound Forms in Time* and "Thorow"). It seems likely that Howe means to evoke, via Spenser's forests of Faeryland/Ireland, the general cultural meaning of forests: forests as the other and "outside" of culture, as culture's unconscious (see Harrison; Schama).

But she also, I think, clearly intends these forests to be self-reflective figures—figures for textuality itself. This emerges into sharper focus if we return for a moment to Florimell herself. Florimell's presence in *Europe* is ephemeral and sporadic; she appears and disappears, comes and goes. Named only three times, in the passages I quoted above (*DP* 107, 109–10, 135), she nevertheless seems to have scattered her traces throughout the poem, at least throughout "Defenestration"—depending, that is, on our willingness to construe various enigmatic phrases as evidence of her continuing presence. "[N]imble phantasma capering on a page/ with antic gesture" (*DP* 110)—is that Florimell? "Treadable tender/ those paths to the lost path" (*DP* 111)—could that be her? How about, from "Pythagorean Silence," "through a forest glade/ she fled" (*PS* 80)? Sightings abound, though they are often ambiguous, indeterminate. As Florimell "flees away into the forest" she also disappears into the ambient text, and we track her there through her appearances in enigmatic combinations of words and letters, as if catching glimpses of her as she moves "behind" the words. What are these "other" words, then, behind which she moves, if not the forest?

The woods, then, is a figure for text: "The text . . . is a wood" (DuPlessis *Pink Guitar*, 128), a "wood of words" (Butterick 319), a "word forest" (Dworkin 400; see also Perloff, "Collision" 308–09; Back 118–19). Throughout *Europe* this woods-as-text figure recurs, sometimes blatantly, sometimes implicitly, with changing emphases and local variations: "green syllables of scenery in spring" (*PS* 57); "Twenty lines of/ boughs bend into hindering/ Boreas" (*DP* 105); "Stanzaic glade" (*DP* 131). Often it is associated with the figure of the labyrinth or maze, as in the lines I quoted earlier, "Leafy I/ labyrinth am/ lost in the woods" (*L* 195; see also *PS* 61, *DP* 131): the textual woods as a maze in which we wander. Moreover, the woods-as-text figure has a strong visual dimension; it is a visual figure as well as a semantic one. Its visual dimension is based on an analogy between woods and print on a page, with the lines of print corresponding to aisles of trees in a forest, the letter-forms themselves to bristling vegetation.[11] This visual analogy seems particularly to be activated whenever Howe deploys isolated words in word grids or "word squares" (as DuPlessis [*Pink Guitar* 138] calls them); see for example Figure 5.[12] Here, no doubt, our identification of the visual analogy is partly cued by the names of trees and other vegetation that make up the grid; still, the analogy is always latently present, available to be called up whenever the woods-as-text figure solicits it.[13]

timid   satyr   vesper   winnow

snow   chastity   berry-blood(secrecy)

rosemary   poplar   holm-oak   juniper

holly   casket   cud

Figure 5. Page 83 from Howe, *Pythagorean Silence*

Finally, the woods-as-text figure is also a woods-as-intertext figure. Howe's textual forests are contiguous with other textual forests; as her text is dense with intertextual allusions and appropriations, so her textual forest mingles with and interpenetrates the forests of other texts. Howe's forest becomes a figure for the whole circumambient intertextual space in which she has located her own text, encompassing (at least) Spenser, Ariosto, and of course Shakespeare—the Shakespeare of greenwood plays such as *A Midsummer Night's Dream* and *As You Like It*: "Quince has come here to crouch" (*PS* 81); "The woods seem to thicken/ Merry men in Arden/ (foresters fear foresters)" (*DP* 103).

Shakespeare's greenwood yields not only allusions, but also visual analogies, like the one in the passage I reproduced earlier, near the beginning of my discussion of Howe's interventions in the Shakepearean canon. There the greenwood of Shakespeare's *Midsummer Night's Dream* was mirrored in Howe's "word forest"—a forest made up of words culled from the text of the play by a process of sampling or "writing-through." A similar visual analogy emerges in Howe's "writing-through" of *The Faerie Queene,* though this time the analogy is not with a forest but rather with a garden (Figure 6). The clues to identifying the source text are to be found near the middle of the page: the words "GARDEN" (in caps) and "Adonis." Of the fifty different words on this page, fully twenty of them can be found in the "Garden of Adonis" canto (canto vi) of *The Faerie Queene,* book III. They appear there in a different order; some of them appear in slightly different forms (e.g., "felicity" rather than "FELICITAS"); some appear multiple times there; and all, of course, occur in a fully elaborated syntactical and narrative or descriptive con-

Genius

outside necessitate

One

FELICITAS

woodcut of space time logic

substance

in particular

wend
as naked babies

watery watery

wanton   bough

GARDEN

Adonis

conclusively and matter

Born so couple

formandform(s)

Amor

twyne(heraldic rose)

lapped sweet   paramoure

Pleasure
pleasure

word made flesh before fall
plummet-deep dimension of my soul

Figure 6. Page 92 from *Defenestration of Prague*

text, not, as here, stripped of context and "scattered like a handful of jacks" (Du Plessis, *Pink Guitar* 138) across a white page. What we have here are something like shattered remnants of the "Garden of Adonis" canto, as if the canto had been dropped from a height (from a window? defenestrated?) and these were the pieces that could be swept together.

Why choose the "Garden of Adonis" canto for this (mis)treatment? The garden, first of all, is the heart of the companion books III and IV, the same books in which Florimell's story unfolds—evidently the books that interest Howe the most. One of Spenser's elaborate set pieces, abstracted from the times and spaces of the narratives around it, and strikingly heterodox with respect to the rest of the *Faerie Queene* world, the garden constitutes a separate enclave or reserve, a microworld whose spatial organization Spenser carefully details. Howe simultaneously foregrounds and deconstructs the spatiality of Spenser's microworld by dispersing a sample of its words across the blank space of a page.

Spenser's garden is an invented myth (though Neoplatonic in its general conception) about form and substance. In it, chaotic matter receives form, is released into the physical world, then returns after its alloted span to the garden, where form is separated from matter again, ready to be imposed anew on the formless. That Howe reads this as a meditation on artistic form (as well she might) is indicated by some of the words she samples: "substance," "matter," "formandform(s)."[14] Others of Howe's selections belong to the mythic furniture of Spenser's meditation: "Genius" is the gardener of the garden, and his charges, the forms themselves, are personified as "naked babes" (vi.32). Moreover, Genius, who is also the garden's porter, "letteth in, he letteth out to wend,/ All that to come into the world desire" (vi.32); "wend" is another of Howe's selections.

But if Spenser's garden is in one sense a meditation on form, it is also a meditation on the cosmic centrality of heterosexual love—and of death, too, of course (you can't have one without the other). For at the center of the garden, on an anatomically correct mons veneris of landscape gardening, dwells Adonis, Venus's "paramoure," preserved alive from the boar that (according to the received myth) killed him, and which itself is imprisoned, in all its hirsute and violent phallicism, in a cave under the mount (vi.48). Several of Howe's selections derive from the eroticized landscape of this central bower: "wanton" (vi.42, 44, 46, 49), "bough" (which appears only in the plural form "boughes," vi.42, 43), "twyne" (vi.44), "lapped" (vi.46), "sweet" (vi.41, 46, 48), "paramoure" (vi.41, 45), "Pleasure" (with a capital P, daughter of Cupid and Psyche, vi.50; with a small p, vi.46). "Amor" of course is Cupid, though Spenser doesn't actually use this alternate name, and "watery" is an attribute of the "shore" where Narcissus (also preserved alive in the garden) is normally to be found (vi.45).[15]

The central bower, with its potent polarity of love and death, is the engine that drives the whole of the garden, indeed the whole of books III and IV (the Legends of Chastity and Friendship, respectively)—perhaps, indeed, the whole of the *Faerie Queene,* in a sense. The axis on which Spenser's world spins (as in "Love makes the world go round"?), this engine is fueled by a metaphysics of sexual difference. So to dismantle this engine as Howe has done, laying out its separate parts (or at least a selection of them) for inspection, is to get at the heterosexual metaphysics underlying Spenser's synoptic poem.

This is one plausible way of reading Howe's "writing-through" of the Garden of Adonis, but it is certainly not the only way. Howe directs our attention to another context for reading the garden, and that context is, once again, Ireland—or, to be more precise, Spenser's *A View of the Present State of Ireland,* his prose dialogue on Irish policy, written in 1596 but not published until 1633, more than thirty years after his death. Literally facing her page of Garden of Adonis samples (in the Sun & Moon Press edition of *Europe of Trusts*), and continuing onto the verso of that facing page, Howe arranges words culled from Spenser's *View* (Figures 7 and 8). The words on page 93 seem almost (but not quite) as if they would fit into the blank spaces left by the arrangement of words on the Garden of Adonis page; but even if the two pages are not complementary in quite so literal a way, they do nevertheless seem to challenge and answer one another.

In his *View of the Present State of Ireland,* Spenser addressed the Irish crisis of his time—the continuing uprisings of powerful Irish and Anglo-Irish lords, the chronic lawlessness of the countryside. Employing the convention of a dialogue between a well-informed veteran of Irish affairs (called Irenius) and an interested outsider (Eudoxus), Spenser exposed what he regarded as the failures of the Elizabethan colonial regime in Ireland, and advocated a more aggressive policy aimed at reducing the country to order. He also took the opportunity to defend the actions of Lord Grey, the former Lord Deputy, whose secretary he had been. The

sound sounde)   of soun

amend unto

bowrougholder borrougolder borsolder bar

soldier burrow holder Him

bring into Awe

stranglerstragglers no

nightstealer

(by ways and blind fords)

Bog

some little fortilage or

woden castle

ragtaile ragtayle two letters worn off

were a sea-poole

corner

Figure 7. Page 93 from *Defenestration of Prague*

antiquarian interest that Spenser displays in questions of the origins and prehistory of the Irish consorts strangely with the ruthlessness of his policy recommendations: his program for pacifying Ireland involves garrisoning troops throughout the country wherever they might effectively deprive rebel armies of supplies, thereby defeating them through famine. Irenius claims (naively or callously, it's hard to know which) that such a strategy would shorten the campaign, and so would be merciful in the long run. In any case, his proposals, had they been acted on, would have required a level of expenditure that the skinflint Elizabeth would never have countenanced.

Howe's "writing-through" of the text of Spenser's *View* emphasizes several key themes. First, she exploits the scholarly apparatus of the variorum edition of the *View* to foreground the instability of Spenser's text at its most literal level: its orthography. The text having circulated

all that land were a sea-poole
corner and glennes
morrice of waste wilde places

realme realme Realm
first inhabitinge and afterwarde stretchinge

an Irishe Scott or Pict
folter flatter flatter Fond
(half-lit)
pure purer concluded
Clouded
chronicler chronicl
Testimony

Figure 8. Page 94 from *Defenestration of Prague*

in manuscript for over thirty years before finally appearing in print, there is considerable variation of phrasing and especially spelling among texts of the *View*, all of it duly recorded in the variorum edition. This orthographic variety and waywardness evidently fascinates Howe. She lifts out of the variorum's footnotes strings of alternate spellings—e.g., "bowroughholder borrougolder borsolder bar/soldier burrow holder," "ragtaile ragtayle," "realme realme Realm," "folter flatter flatter Fond"—and even retains the editor's comment, "two letters worn off" (see Spenser, *View* 63).[16] Apart from emphasizing the materiality of the text (a recurrent theme of Howe's at all times and in all contexts), Howe's fixation on orthography perhaps conveys an ironic reflection on order and disorder: the very text in which Spenser advocates the imposition of order is itself subject to the textual vagaries of manuscript transmission.

Secondly, Howe selects details relating to Spenser's speculations on Irish origins. For instance, the line "first inhabitinge and afterwarde stretchinge" (*DP* 94) derives from a passage in which Spenser imagines how the Scythians, the supposed ancestors of the Irish, came to occupy the island: "gettinge intelligence of this Countrye of Irelande," he writes, "[and] fyndinge shippinge Conveniente [they] passed over hither and Arived in the Northe parte thereof whiche is now called Vlster which *firste inhabitinge and afterwarde stretchinge* themselves forthe into the lande as theire numbers increased named it all of themselues Scuttenlande which more brieflye is Called Scuttlande or Scotlande" (*View* 82–83; my italics). Moreover, the material comprising the last six lines on *DP* 94, from "an Irishe Scott or Pict" through "Testimony," all seems to have been sampled from the same passage of the *View* (86), in which Spenser learnedly evaluates the various authorities on the ancient history of Ireland and Scotland, concluding that Buchanan is the most reliable ("he himselfe being *an Irishe Scott or Pict* by nation"), but that the Irish bards and chroniclers are valuable sources despite their tendency to flatter (the printed text spells it "folter") and their having "Clouded the truethe of those times" (one manuscript has "concluded" for "Clouded"). Here again, I think we may suspect irony at the expense of Spenser the antiquarian, who is so judicious about others' relative reliability or unreliability while himself endorsing baseless speculations about Scythian origins.

Finally, Howe samples from passages in which Spenser recalls failed campaigns and policies of the past, and makes his own recommendations for the policing of Ireland. The phrase, "were a sea-poole," for instance, which occurs at the bottom of *DP* 93 and again on the top of *DP* 94, evokes a striking sentence from early in the *View* in which, speaking in the person of Eudoxus, Spenser captures the note of fatalism and desperation that, from his time to our own, has so often crept into reflections on the Irish situation: "So haue I allsoe harde it often wished," Eudoxus reports, "(even of some whose greate wisdome in opinion shoulde seme to iudge more soundlye of so weightye a Consideracion, that all that Lande [*viz.,* Ireland] weare a sea poole. . . . " (Spenser, 1949: 44). The lines, "corner and glennes/morrice of waste wilde places" (*DP* 94), derives from a passage concerning a campaign by the Duke of Clarence, who succeeded in shutting the Irish up "within those narrow Corners and glennes vnder the mountaine foote," though immediately after his departure for England his gains were swept away by the uprising of one Murrough en ranagh, "that is Morrice of the fearne or waste wilde places" (1949: 58). All the material, finally, in the seventh through eleventh lines on *DP* 93 (from "no/ nightstealer" through "woden castle") comes from a passage in which Spenser explains how he proposes to control disorder in the countryside by building forts ("some little fortilage or woden Castle") at strategic fords, bridges, passes, and other choke-points (224).

How, then, are we to read Howe's juxtaposition of Spenser's Garden of Adonis and his *View*? By arranging samples from these texts on facing pages, Howe seems to imply some kind of dialogue between them, but if so, what are they saying to each other? Perhaps the implications are demystificatory: on the one hand, a thoroughly mystified version of re-ality, in which eternal form masters lowly matter, death is contained, and heterosexual love makes the world go round; on the other hand (literally on the facing page), the reality of Spenser's Irish experience, in all its brutality and messy contingency. Or perhaps the relation between the two pages is rather a dialectical one: the truth of "Spenser and Ireland" lies neither in the fantasy sublimations of the Garden microworld nor in the Realpolitik of the *View,* but in some synthesis of the two. Either reading primes us to see in these strangely spaced and shaped pages a different sort of visual analogy from the ones we have considered so far—neither a forest nor a garden but something like a map of Ireland. Of course, they could hardly constitute a mimetic map, some kind of iconic representation using printed letters and lines of types in place of the usual cartographic outlines and shading. Rather, the pages of words culled from Spenser's texts yield an experience of difficulty—the diffi-culty of contextualizing these words, of negotiating these spaces—par-allel, on a miniature scale, to the large-scale difficulty of "reading" Ire-land itself; in short, a cognitive mapping (Jameson *Postmodernism,* 51–54, 410–18).

IV. HER BOOK OF STELLA

If one proposes to read Howe's *Europe of Trusts* as a single integral long poem, as I have been doing, rather than a "selected poems," one will naturally seek to emphasize the ways that the third and last section, "The Liberties," seems to provide closure for the whole. Perhaps the effect of closure is accidental; perhaps it attests more to the reader's ingenuity in finding closure than to any intention on the poet's part to provide it. Nevertheless, "The Liberties" does seem to recapitulate and complete many of the strands—themes, preoccupations, devices, intertexts—that weave through the preceding sections.

For one thing, "The Liberties" recapitulates, heightens, and develops the strategy, present throughout the poem, of visual analogy between the physical spaces of the text and the represented spaces of the text's world. The iconic "forests" of typography and spacing into which, earlier in the poem, Florimell had disappeared recur here in a particularly heightened form, in the word grids of "Formation of a Separatist, I" (*L* 204–08). But in developing the visual analogy between the printed text and represented spaces, Howe in "The Liberties" introduces a striking turn or twist. For the words and spaces of this section do double duty, mapping not only the woods but also the *city*. "I was really," Howe told Edward Foster in the *Talisman* interview, "trying to paint that part of Dublin [viz. The Liberties] in words" (*Birth-mark* 166)—or better, perhaps, to *map* it *with* words.

The title "The Liberties" refers (among other things) to the old district of Dublin between St. Patrick's Cathedral (where Swift was dean) to the site where the Guinness Brewery now stands, formerly outside the city walls and under sole jurisdiction of the archbishop. A number of pages here (e.g., *L* 161, 168, 174, 176, 179), regarded strictly as visual forms, appear strikingly maplike in their layout. Should we "read" these irregular forms as maps of an old-world city? perhaps as itineraries through such a city's twisting streets? At least two of these shaped pages (*L* 159, 203) suggest a visual analogy with a churchyard thick with gravestones or (better) the interior of a cathedral crowded with funerary monuments —presumably the interior of St. Patrick's itself (Keller, *Forms* 214, 231; Back 71), beneath whose floor both Swift and Stella lie buried, and where Swift's self-composed epitaph (famously rendered into English by Yeats, and quoted in both his version and the Latin original by Howe, *L* 156) can be read.

This substitution of the text-as-city visual analogy for the text-as-woods analogy of earlier sections leaves one factor conspicuously unchanged, namely, the Irish theme. If the textual woods of earlier sections are Spenser's woods—the woods of Ireland/Faeryland into which the fictional Florimell fled—the textual city-space of "The Liberties" is Swift's city.[17] Through Howe's use of visual analogy, Spenser, the agent of English imperial policy in Ireland, is juxtaposed with Swift, celebrated as the defender of Irish liberties against English imperial encroachments. So in this respect, too, "The Liberties" recalls, completes, and dialogically and dialectically answers the preceding sections.

Finally, and crucially, "The Liberties" complements and completes the sequence of "subject rhymes" among silent women that weaves through the preceding sections: Igraine, Iphigenia, Ophelia, Florimell, paradigmatic figures of the mass of the "anonymous, slighted—inarticulate" (*T* 14) whom Howe aspires to raise from silence into speech. To this silent company "The Liberties" adds two more, one fictional, the other historical: Shakespeare's Cordelia, Swift's Stella. This incongruous coupling of Cordelia and Stella is structural as well as thematic: in the first part of "The Liberties," each has a "book" of her own ("THEIR Book of *Stella*," "Book of Cordelia"); in the second part, the closet drama *God's Spies*, the two impossibly share the same space and time, in a scandalous short-circuiting of ontological levels; in the third part, neither appears as such, or if they appear at all, then it is in the minimal form of their initials, S and C. Howe's coupling of these two ontologically disparate figures, one a fictional character from a play, the other a historical personage (Hester Johnson, 1681–1728), encourages us to reflect that the ontological gap separating them might not after all be as profound or unbridgeable as it at first appears. Cordelia, after all, is semihistorical (perhaps fully historical from the point of view of Shakespeare and his contemporaries), while Stella is in a sense semifictional, a "character" whom we know only from Swift's birthday poems to her and from his *Journal to Stella;* even the name we know her by is his invention.

More importantly, however, the odd coupling of Cordelia and Stella foregrounds their shared plight as silent, in fact silenced, women. Cordelia's silence, of course, is the plot mainspring of the play in which she is a character: her refusal to speak precipitates the whole chain of events that follows. But it would be a mistake to think of her silence as fully voluntary, an act of refusal or resistance; it would be truer to say that she can find no opening for her own speech in the regime of a king-father who monopolizes and commands all language (see Back 81): "Speak." "Nothing, my lord." "Nothing will come of nothing. Speak again." Stella's real-world silence is more complex, and since Howe cannot depend upon our knowing her story as we know *Lear,* she prefaces "The Liberties" with a prose account of Stella's life, entitled "Fragments of a Liquidation." If the "fragments" of the title are the rather meager documentary traces of Stella's historical existence, the "liquidation" is that of Stella herself, whose identity and voice have been all but completely effaced by those of Swift, once her teacher and subsequently her domestic companion for nearly thirty years.

"Fragments of a Liquidation" is profoundly but subtly subversive. It draws on conventional literary-historical scholarship, mainly the information to be found in the introduction and appendices of Harold Williams's definitive edition (1948) of Swift's *Journal to Stella,* and it nowhere oversteps the bounds of what is reliably known about Swift and Stella. Nevertheless, Howe's inferences and emphases are radically at odds with the picture that emerges from traditional (male) scholarship. Everywhere Howe detects symptoms of Stella's effacement: no authentic portrait of Stella exists (*L* 152); Swift's letters to her from London have been preserved, as the *Journal to Stella,* but not her letters to him (*L* 151); only three poems attributable to her have survived (*L* 152), and these appear alongside Swift's in *The Poems of Jonathan Swift;* Swift's memoir, "On the Death of Mrs. Johnson," is "remarkable for what it doesn't say" (*L* 154); even the name Stella, which has eclipsed her given name Hester (she herself preferred to be known as Esther), was imposed on her by Swift, who "gave allegorical nicknames to the women he was romantically involved with" (*L* 149). These are facts, and Howe presents them flatly, noncommittally, without any particular rhetorical heightening; nevertheless, their effect is to create a plausible parallelism (reinforced structurally, as I have noted) between Stella's historical silencing and Cordelia's fictional silence.

Nevertheless, Howe is sensitive to the complexities of Stella's case. Stella, after all, is not a fictional character, despite Swift's fictionalizing manipulation of her identity, and she cannot be reduced to a strict parallelism with any fictional silent woman, whether Cordelia or Ophelia or any other. For instance, she is pointedly *not* to be conflated with Florimell, the silent woman who flees timorously from men across the pages of *The Faerie Queene* (and into the pages of Howe's "Defenestration"). Swift himself insists on this distinction, in a poem entitled "To Stella, visiting me in my sickness" (1720?): "She wonders where the Charm appears/In *Florimel's* affected Fears:/For *Stella* never learn'd the Art,/At proper Times to scream and start" (*Poems* 725). Swift is thinking, no doubt, of the occasion (mentioned by Howe in "Fragments of a Liquidation") when Stella "shot and killed a prowler after her servants had fled the house in terror" (*L* 52). The "Florimel" of this passage is very likely a conventional name (like the other conventional ladies' names of seventeenth- and eighteenth-century erotic, complimentary, and satiric verse), but this does not necessarily exclude an allusion, direct or indirect, to Spenser. So if Stella does "rhyme" with the sequence of fictional silent women (Igraine, Iphigenia, Ophelia, and the rest), this does not mean she can be simply identified with any or all of them; if she is, in some sense, Cordelia's double, she is also pointedly the *anti*-Florimell.

A further complication of Stella's relationship with Swift, which is not easily accommodated to the paradigmatic figure of the silent woman, is the reciprocity of their influence on one another. If Swift in some sense enforces silence on Stella, swallowing her voice up in his own, Stella reciprocally induces strange, broken language in Swift. At intervals throughout the *Journal to Stella*, almost invariably at the end of each day's entry, Swift abandons standard English for what he calls "our little language"—or rather (in the terms of the little language itself) "ourrichar Gangridge"—a mixture of private references, cryptic abbreviations, endearments, and baby talk, evidently reflecting the kind of speech Swift habitually used in his intimate domestic circle of Stella and her companion Rebecca Dingley. Stella, recipient of these letters in diary form, presumably elicited this kind of language from Swift, in some sense. We might even say, somewhat tendentiously, that she had the effect of "liberating" Swift from the straitjacket of the standard, public language to which he was otherwise so fully committed, both in his own practice and as a matter of public policy: "Ld Treasr has lent the long Lettr I writt him [viz., Swift's 'Proposal for Correcting . . . the English Tongue'], to Prior, and I can't get Prior to return it; and I want to have it printd, and to make up this Academy for the Improvemt of our Language. Fais we nevr shal improve it as much as FW [Foolish Wenches] has done. Sall we? No fais, ourrichar Gangridge" (Letter XLIII, entry for 11 March 1711–12; *Journal* II, 510). It would be understatement to call this passage richly ironic: Swift, reporting to Stella on the progress of his project for standardizing English, ends with a burst of just the kind of idiosyncratically nonstandard, socially irresponsible language that his program presumably aspired to legislate out of existence.

Swift's lapse into this "aberrant" baby talk could not fail to fascinate Howe, with her interest in all kinds of archaic and "deviant" orthography (as in the *View* variorum), idiosyncratic punctuation and lineation (as in Dickinson's fascicles), marginalia, printer's errors and accidents.[18] In the light of Howe's appropriative aesthetic, we might have expected extensive sampling from the little language in "The Liberties"; surprisingly, however, Howe seems to have directly quoted from it only once, in an epigraph to "Fragments of a Liquidation." Perhaps, then, it is less the little language as such that interests her than its potential as a *model*.

Perhaps, indeed, we ought to see it as authorizing or conferring a kind of legitimacy on all the varieties of "broken English," all the distortions and abuses of standard language the recur throughout "The Liberties":

Bedevikke bedl
bedevilled by a printer's error
(*L* 158)

Do not come down the ladder

ifor I

haveaten

it a

way
(*L* 177, reprised on *L* 180)[19]

The complexity of Stella's silencing, and the problem of her own complicity in it, is especially reflected in Howe's quotation of the full text of one of the three poems attributed to her, "To Dr. Swift on his birthday, November 30, 1721," which is folded into the middle of the masque text, *God's Spies* (*L* 190–01). Unlike in other instances of verbal appropriation, here Howe does not "write through" the text, selecting a handful of words and leaving the rest (or erasing the bulk of the words and retaining a few); rather, she retains the entire text intact, but displaced into an estranging context. Like Borges's Pierre Menard, who rewrites passages from the *Quixote* word-for-word, but in a historical context so different from Cervantes's that their significance is entirely changed, Howe's Stella recites a poem that, in the context of "The Liberties," acquires meanings radically at odds with the meanings we suppose it might originally have had. Thus, the metaphor of life as a stage play, a threadbare cliché in the original context—

Short was her part upon the stage;
Went smoothly on for half a page;
Her bloom was gone, she wanted art,
As the scene chang'd, to change her part:

She, whom no lover could resist,
Before the second act was hiss'd
                    (*L* 190; Swift, *Poems* 737)

appears substantially rejuvenated when uttered by a speaker who is herself a character in a closet drama. Here the cliché acquires metatheatrical
overtones, so that it reflects not only on the theatrical context of *God's
Spies,* but on the "re-staging" of Stella generally, of which Howe's appropriation and recontextualization of this very poem is itself symptomatic.
More importantly, the misogynous commonplaces about women's vanity which, in their original context, Stella must be seen as endorsing, are
here, in the context of Howe's anti-misogynous project, ironically punc-
tured and overturned.

Unless, that is, there are ironies within ironies here, and the ironic
overturning of misogynous clichés is itself ironically overturned. For
Howe's recontextualization of "To Dr. Swift on his birth-day" leaves
open the possibility that this text is not Stella's at all but Swift's, in some
sense (see Back 90, 201 n. 34). The Ghost of Swift is present onstage when
Stella recites "her" poem, and as she rises to do so the stage direction
reads, "*The GHOST remains on his knees throughout, mouthing*" (*L* 189).
Is the Ghost ventriloquizing, then? Is it really his voice we hear, issuing
from Stella's mouth? There are at least two ways we could understand
this: first, that the poem is really (as some have suspected) the work of
Swift himself, merely spoken in Stella's persona as a kind of dramatic
monologue; the fact that it is indistinguishable from Swift's own poetry
in style and (misogynous) sentiment supports this supposition, as does,
in another way, the fact of its inclusion in Swift's collected poems. But
second, we could understand this ghostly ventriloquism as a kind of
metaphor for the power and pervasiveness of Swift's influence over Stella:
even when she speaks in her own name (but what is "her own name,"
anyway?), even when she recites her own poem, it is not her voice we
hear but Swift's, not her sentiments but his.

This interpretation of Swift as being present "inside" Stella's own
voice, an occupying power, as it were, a kind of linguistic censor and
superego, is amply corroborated by the strange document to which Howe
alludes in "Fragments of a Liquidation," the memoir "On the Death of
Mrs. Johnson." This text, too, like "To Dr. Swift on his birth-day," is
founded on misogynous commonplaces, for throughout it Swift com-
mends Stella for having been conspicuously *unlike* other women: she did

not affect timidity, did not indulge in "female chat" (*Prose* 230), did not spend money on "fopperies" (233), prefered men's company to women's (235), and so on. Above all, however, he emphasizes the propriety of her verbal behavior: unlike other women, she did not interrupt (230, 234) or even appear impatient to take her turn in the conversation (230); she was normally reticent, even among friends (230); she was skillful in diverting the conversation away from inappropriate (mainly male) topics, such as "News, politics, censure, family-management, or town-talk" (235); "She was never positive in arguing," and never contradicted even those whom she knew to be in the wrong, in the interests of "prevent[ing] noise" (235); she never paraded her knowledge, especially before women, though "wise men" readily recognized it (236). In short, she practiced good verbal hygiene: she closely monitored her own verbal behavior, and censored herself, so there was never any need for anyone else (such as her erstwhile teacher and constant companion Swift) to censor her.

Stella, by Swift's account, had entirely internalized her own silencing, so that there was no need to impose silence from without. She would have satisfied even the misogynist of Ben Jonson's *Epicoene,* who sought a silent woman to marry. The ideal silent woman, Stella is nowhere more ideally so than in this memoir of Swift's, when she is already dead, and her voice and image are finally and wholly under his control. This is the moment anticipated at the end of "To Dr. Swift on his birth-day," though weirdly reversed: Stella (or whoever we suppose to be speaking this poem) imagines Swift preceding her into final silence—but only by one day:

> Late dying may you cast a shred
> Of your rich mantle o'er my head;
> To bear with dignity my sorrow,
> One day *alone, then die to-morrow.*
> (*L* 191; Howe's emphasis)

V. HOWE'S SILENCES

Maybe there is in silence a far greater mystery.
Susan Howe, "*Talisman* Interview," 1990 (*Birth-mark* 169)

There seems to be a paradox here. For, despite her commitment to the project of recovering voices of "anonymous, slighted—inarticulate" women, Howe's own voice is itself singularly elusive. She cites, selects, juxtaposes, arranges, re-stages other voices, but her own voice is seldom audible in her poems—or at any rate, one cannot be certain that what one "hears" really is her voice, or just another of the voices appropriated from elsewhere. As author, Howe is self-effacing, present everywhere in general but nowhere in particular (see Butterick 312, 314–15; Perloff, "Collision" 310). Allowing others to speak for her, she maintains a near-complete silence

Howe's personal voice is unambiguously audible only at the very beginning of *Europe of Trusts,* in the prose introduction entitled, "There Are Not Leaves Enough to Crown to Cover to Crown to Cover." This introduction anticipates, in its personal tone, the brief essay that Howe would later prefix to "Thorow" (in *Singularities,* 1990), and the much longer and even more autobiographical one in *Frame Structures* (1995); but it contrasts markedly with "Fragments of a Liquidation," the prefatory essay to "The Liberties," which is scrupulously impersonal and indirect. In "There Are Not Leaves Enough . . . ," Howe locates her autobiographical self relative to the cataclysmic events of mid-twentieth-century world history (see Bernstein, *A Poetics* 193–217). "In the summer of 1938 my mother and I were staying with my grandmother, uncle, aunt, great-aunts, cousins, and friends in Ireland, and I had just learned to walk, when Czechoslovakia was dismembered. . . . That October we sailed home on a ship crowded with refugees fleeing various countries in Europe. . . . This is my historical consciousness. I have no choice in it" (*T* 9, 13). She proceeds to use this autobiographical frame to contextualize fragments, otherwise cryptic, from "Pythagorean Silence" (*T* 10–11, 12–13; *PS* 21, 27), thereby allowing us to grasp how, in these particular instances, autobiographical experience has been inscribed in Howe's poetry (see Back 106–20). Unfortunately, even after these autobiographical traces have been brought to our attention, we are in no better position to generalize to other passages, and Howe's personal presence remains cryptic, elusive: we suspect she must be there somewhere, maybe everywhere, but exactly where we are unable to say.

This is particularly the case with respect to the behavior of first-person pronouns in *Europe*. The first-person pronoun is utterly unreliable here as a marker of the poet's personal presence. Some occurrences of "I/me/my" do seem to refer to the poet herself, that is, they behave something like the "lyric I."[20] But other occurrences certainly refer to other speakers, voices appropriated from other texts, fictional characters or historical figures, not to be confused with Howe—that is, they behave something like the "I" of dramatic monologue:

Bark be my limbs my hair be leaf

Bride be my bow my lyre my quiver
(*PS* 17)

I see the knife

deer to bleed for me
(*PS* 73)

Where I ride no man shall mark
(*DP* 137)

I am maria wainscotted
(*L* 171)

In some cases we can hypothesize about speakers of this "I"—Daphne and Apollo in the first set of lines above from "Pythagorean Silence"? Iphigenia in the second set?—but even where we cannot trace the origin of these voices, or determine exactly who speaks, we have the sense of some character other than poet herself speaking (the poet's name is *not* "maria wainscotted"). Elsewhere we may not be able to feel even this degree of tentative certainty:

I lay down and conceived Love
(my dear Imaginary)
(*PS* 44)

Dream of wandering in woods with

my father
(*PS* 61)

I walk through valleys stray

imagining myself free
                    (*PS* 71)

Often I hear Romans murmuring
I think of them lying dead in their graves
                    (*L* 158)

Who speaks here—the poet, a fictional character, an historical figure?[21]
We are perhaps most confident in attributing first-person pronouns to the poet in self-reflexive passages, where her own activity, the very processes of imagining and writing, seem to be thematized:

(Books

blaze up
my room is bright) World I have made
                    (*PS* 40–41)

Words are not acts
out of my text I am not what I play
                    (*PS* 46)

I invent
(*DP* 117)

I will go to my desk

I will sit quietly
                    (*L* 175)

But after all, why should we feel any confidence in such an attribution, even here? For of course Howe could be citing another's discourse even when the activity predicated of "I" is writing; the writer could always be someone else.

Ultimately, "I" is no more "personal" in this text than any other word, no more immune than any other word from Howe's manipulations. It is, like every other word, material, typographical, visual—a found object, malleable. Look again, for instance, at the passage from "The Liberties," quoted above in section IV: "Do not come down the ladder/ ifor I/ haveaten/ it a/ way" (177, 179). Should that second line be read as "I for I"? "if or I"? the name "Ivor," misspelled? The more closely we scrutinize it, the more "I" here seems to surrender its pronominal meaning and lose itself in the material stratum of typography and spacing—no longer a marker of selfhood, merely ink on a page. Compare these instances of "I":

He plodded away through drifts of i
ce

$$(PS\ 35)^{22}$$

reland

I

$$(L\ 209)^{23}$$

Moreover, Howe treats even her own name in the same way, as no less malleable than any other word, and equally available for manipulation. The effect in this case is somewhat different, however—not so much that of the word's absorption into the material stratum as of a secret, coded or occluded personal presence, as though the poet had encrypted herself in the text: "Set family name in secret form" (DP 118).[24] "Howe" appears, misspelled and camouflaged, in various combinations throughout the poem: as "Nohow" (PS 73), wittily conflating the poet's absence ("no Howe") with her competence (her "know-how"); as "Whowe" (L 173; see DuPlessis, Pink Guitar 138); in the phrase "for how or to who" (L 174); perhaps even in the Irish place-name "Howth" (L 174).

The sequence of encoded variations on Howe's name climaxes in a rebus or riddle incorporated in the last section of "The Liberties":

I am composed of nine letters.
1 is the subject of a proposition in logic.

2 is a female sheep, or tree.
3 is equal to one.
4 is a beginning.
5 & 7 are nothing
6 7 & 8 are a question, or salutation.
6 7 8 & 9 are deep, depression.

(*L* 209)[25]

Only after the riddle has been posed (and presumably solved) does Howe allow herself to introduce her own name in unencrypted form—first name only, however—and in conjunction with a first-person pronoun that here refers unambiguously, possibly for the first and only time since the prose preface, to the poet herself:

Across the Atlantic, I
    inherit myself
semblance
    of irish susans
    dispersed
and narrowed to
            home
        (*L* 213)

"Irish susans" alludes, presumably, to Howe's grandmother Susan Manning, whose namesake the poet is, and to whom "The Liberties" is dedicated; Susan is, in this sense, a "family name."

Thus Howe, like Florimell in "Defenestration," appears and disappears in the text, emerging from its constituent lines, words ("Nohow," "Whowe," "Howth"), even letters and spaces, then melting back into them again, only to reappear later. Like Florimell, she flashes into view, then vanishes into the textual woods, emerging again into sight later on, elsewhere. Even (or perhaps especially) when she is most present, as when she inscribes her own name in the text, Howe is absent. In what respect, then, does her reticence, her near silence, differ from Stella's, or from that of any of the other silent women whose silencing she seeks to reverse in the course of her poem?

It is only superficially paradoxical that the phenomenon of silence has generated an enormous volume of words. Silence, it turns out, is complicated, "more complicated than noise," as one linguist puts it (Saunders 175). There are multiple types of silence. First there is what might be called semantic silence, that is, any absence of speech—any pause, gap, or lapse—that contributes to the construction of meaning by participants in a discourse exchange (Lakoff 26). Not always easily distinguishable from this type of silence is pragmatic silence. This is silence in the sense of "silencing," that is, silence arising out of a disparity in powers and roles between participants in the discourse (Lakoff 26). A wealth of case studies, especially those carried out by feminist linguists, documents the relative silence or outright silencing of women in a range of discourse situations. In an extended sense, this is the silence implied by Tillie Olsen's question, "*Why are so many more women [writers] silenced than men? Why, when women do write . . . is so little of the writing known, taught, accorded recognition?*" (24–25; see also Rich 33–49). Finally, apart from silence in this privative and wholly negative sense, we need also to recognize a more positive sense of silence, which might be called aesthetic silence. This is the silence, more often figurative than literal, of the artist's deliberate refusal to speak. It can signify heroic renunciation or asceticism, or avant-garde negation, or aggression toward the audience, or the recoil from the unspeakable ("no poetry after Auschwitz"), or some combination of these; it can serve as an emblem of difficult, all-but-inexpressible new thinking, or as a prefiguration of apocalypse (see Steiner; Sontag, "Aesthetics"; Hassan, *Silence* and *Orpheus*).

All of these types of silence are more or less relevant to Howe's practice in *Europe of Trusts*. Her poetry reflects semantic silence, not in the sense of reproducing the meaningful pauses and gaps of everyday discourse (hers is about as far from colloquial style as poetry can easily get), but in the sense of extending the repertoire of written markers of silence (punctuation, spacing; see Saville-Troike 5–6). Other poets have experimented with silence markers, notably Dickinson, about whose experiments Howe herself has written (*Dickinson* 131–53), but where Dickinson employed dashes, line breaks, and stanza breaks to indicate kinds and durations of silence, Howe tends in *Europe* to use line spacing (double, single and even half spacing) and, of course, horizontal and diagonal spacing across the page (word grids and "word forests") for this purpose. As for pragmatic silence and silence in the extended sense of exclusion from the public discursive domain, Howe of course thematizes this throughout *Europe of Trusts* in her sequence of silent female figures, including, as we have seen, Cordelia, Florimell, and Stella. Finally, it seems possible to understand the extraordinary emptiness of her pages —the sparse scattering of words across them, the way blankness penetrates and threatens to overwhelm print—in terms of aesthetic silence, though more, perhaps, with reference to visual art (the whiteness of blank canvas, the ascetic restraint of Agnes Martin; see Hafif 342) than to verbal art of the "heroic" epoch of Laura Riding, Celan, and Beckett.[26]

Howe herself, of course, proposes a category of silence that presumably has some relevance to her own practice, in the very title of one of the sections of *Europe of Trusts:* "Pythagorean Silence." Far from clearing matters up, however, the allusion makes them only more mysterious. In what respect is Pythagorean silence relevant to Howe's practice? And what *is* Pythagorean silence, anyway? Indeed, why evoke the Presocratic philosopher Pythagoras at all?

There are a number of elements of Pythagorean doctrine that Howe must have found intriguing, not least of all its sheer longevity. Traces of ancient Pythagorean thought persisted as late as the Renaissance, having been absorbed into the Neoplatonism that colored such texts as Spenser's *The Faerie Queene,* with which, as we have seen, Howe engages in revisionist dialogue throughout *Europe of Trusts.* One such survival was the doctrine of the "music of the spheres" or "celestial harmony," to which Howe alludes directly in the title of the first section of "Defenestration of Prague," "Tuning the Sky."[27] Other Pythagorean survivals were less benign in their influence, for instance the doctrine elevating misogyny to a principle of cosmic order—less benign, but not for that reason any less intriguing to a feminist revisionist like Howe (the reverse, if anything).[28]

But most intriguing of all, surely, must have been Pythagorean silence (see Back 106–07). The reason intellectual historians know as little as they do about Pythagorean doctrine is this "Pythagorean secrecy" or "Pythagorean silence," which, like the music of the spheres, remained proverbial at least as late as the Renaissance. For instance, when, in Jonson's *The Silent Woman,* the character Truewit bursts noisily in upon Morose and his silent servant Mute and cannot get them to answer his questions, he accuses them of being Pythagoreans (II.ii.1–3), a line which a recent edition glosses as "committed to a noviciate of five years' silence" (Jonson 141). This indeed is one of the dimensions of the Pythagoreans' proverbial silence: candidates for admission to the Pythagorean brotherhood were said to undergo a five-year novitiate of silence (Guthrie 151). But silence as a form of ascetic discipline is not the only dimension of Pythagorean silence, which also referred to intitiates' refusal to reveal secret doctrines to the uninitiated; according to Porphyry, "What [Pythagoras] said to his intimates, no man can say with certainty, for they maintained a remarkable silence" (Guthrie 151). Finally, Pythagorean silence also involved a "religious scruple" (Guthrie 151), that is, a refusal to discuss doctrinal matters even after they had been revealed, as a mark of respect for the sacredness of the Pythagorean mysteries.

In what respect, if any, are Howe's silences "Pythagorean"? If the silence of the poet in *Europe of Trusts* were of the first kind, that is, silence as ascetic discipline, then we would not be far here from Stella's self-censorship and self-effacement, the good verbal hygiene for which Swift commended her posthumously. But this is not the only or likeliest possibility. Suppose we were instead to regard Howe's silences as being of the second and third kinds—silence as self-defense and self-respect, a withholding of the "mysteries" of the self from readers who (accustomed to the conventions of the postwar confessional lyric) demand self-revelation, self-exposure, self-expression. In this sense, Howe can be seen not as "silenced," but as refusing to gratify our appetite for self-advertisement—as deliberately, programmatically *in*expressive; as deferring to her *materials,* withholding her *self.* This woman is silent not out of deference to men who require silence of her, but in defense of a selfhood that it is no one's business to know.

We might gloss Howe's silences by referring to feminist work in a different medium, namely some recent films by a pair of distinguished directors. In Jane Campion's revisionist gothic romance, *The Piano* (1993), the heroine Ada submits herself to a self-imposed regime of silence, or "elective mutism," refusing all self-expression except by means of her piano. Ada's silence is resonant but, like Cordelia's, finally ambiguous, simultaneously a form of resistance to patriarchal domination and a symptom of it (Greenberg). Less ambiguous in this respect is Marlene Gorris's feminist revision of Aeschylus's *The Eumenides, De Stilte Rond Christine M.* (1982), released with the English title *A Question of Silence* though the original title, *The Silence around Christine M.,* seems more apposite (see L. Williams; Fischer; Ramanathan). In Gorris's film, three women, strangers to one another, spontaneously murder a male shop owner, and then refuse to explain their motives either in open court or to a court-appointed female psychologist; one of the three, indeed, the Christine M. of the title, refuses to speak at all. Here the language of the male-dominanted public sphere is found to be inadequate to express women's truths, so these women resort to substitutes for speech: to violence, in the killing of the shop owner; to laughter, in the final courtroom scene; and to silence—Pythagorean silence?

Here, then, is one final analogical meaning for the blank spaces of Howe's text. DuPlessis calls the visual silence of Howe's white spaces "a trope for an anti-authoritarian practice" (*Pink Guitar* 133); Peter Quartermain speaks of the isolation of her poems on the page as "a visible trope of Howe's tough and difficult feminism" (193; see also Golding, "Drawing" 154). Precisely. The white page space that surrounds, separates, and threatens to engulf every line of these poems can be grasped as the silence out of which these lines (barely) emerge and into which they subside—a visual equivalent for the (Pythagorean?) silence of the withheld, the unsaid, the confession resisted, the secret preserved, the mystery defended.

Coda

Elements of Postmodernist Poetry

"As we move into the twenty-first century," writes Marjorie Perloff, "the modern/postmodern divide has emerged as more apparent than real" (*21st-Century* 164). She is certainly right in the sense that all such divides, all distinctions among periods, all "advances" and "retreats" in literary history are constructions, quasi-fictions, moves in a language game—all of them "more apparent than real" (see McHale, *Constructing* 1–3). Perloff is right, too, in the sense that many of the features that we identify with postmodernism in poetry are revivals of features to be found among the early-modernist avant-gardes; this is the thrust of her argument about "21st-century modernism." But she is wrong if she means to imply that there is nothing to be gained by attempting to view the poetry, or *some* of the *poetries*, of the second half of the twentieth century as falling into a particular shape, making a picture, constituting something like a *period poetics*. The premise of this book has been that there *is* something to be gained by doing so.

Granted, the picture that these poetries make is a messy one, but recognizing this fact does not relieve us from what I have been calling the obligation to the difficult whole. If one were seeking a strong unifying theory that would capture all the essential features of a postmodernist long poem—something like the unifying theory of the postmodernist novel that I advocated in *Postmodernist Fiction*—then the evidence of the present book is equivocal at best. There doesn't seem to be any decisive shift of dominant that distinguishes postmodernist long poems from modernist ones in the way that, by my account, the shift from an epistemological dominant to an ontological one distinguishes postmodernist from modernist fiction; or, if there is something like such a shift, then it is only one distinguishing feature among several, and so not a matter of *the* dominant after all. I haven't been able to identify any "umbrella" model capable of accommodating the full range of postmodernist features in poetry. For one thing, postmodernist poetry, and the postmodernist long poem in particular, does not seem to be simply reducible to the model of the postmodernist novel. Nor does it seem to be reducible to any of the models of postmodernist architecture (as the postmodernist novel itself is, according to some accounts)—neither to the model of "Post-Modern" historicism, nor to the deconstructivist model, nor, presumably, to any other model. Neither simply one thing nor simply the other, the postmodernist long poem remains a difficult whole.

On the other hand, if one's criteria were a little less demanding—if one were willing to settle for recurrences and tendencies, for "weak" unity instead of a powerful "umbrella" model—then perhaps there is a good argument to be made for a postmodernist period poetics after all. One could try finessing the problem of defining the postmodernist long poem by gathering up the various features singled out in the preceding chapters and regrouping them into a list of recurring elements of postmodernist poetry, a *repertoire* of features. Such a repertoire might look something like the following:

Poetry under erasure: construction and deconstruction.
Robert Rauschenberg's erasure of a Willem de Kooning drawing is arguably one of the defining gestures of postmodernism, inaugurating the "dematerialization" of visual art. If one were seeking an analogous defining gesture in poetry, there would be a number of candidates: Ronald Johnson's erasure of all but a few dozen words on each page of the first four books of Milton's *Paradise Lost,* to produce his own poem, *RADI OS;* Tom Phillips's over-painting of the pages of an obscure Victorian novel, leaving only a few legible words, in his book *A Humument;* the many "lost" passages (missing, untranslatable, speculatively reconstructed) in Schwerner's *The Tablets;* or even Tom Raworth's one-line poem, "University Days," which reads in its entirety: "[This poem removed for further study.]" Or one might push the inaugural moment of the postmodernist practice of erasure still further back, to the great postwar European poets of silence and the void, Paul Celan and Edmond Jabès.

Erasure in postmodernist poetry is not a single phenomenon but a range of diverse practices. We need to distinguish among erasure at the level of the *material support,* erasure at the level of *language,* and erasure at the level of *projected world.* Erasure at the level of the material support includes all the signifying uses of blank space in poetry, e.g., in Johnson's, Phillips's, and Schwerner's physically erased texts, but also in the spatially oriented poetry of Jabès, Susan Howe, and others. Erasure at the level of language includes strategies of self-cancellation or self-evacuation, whereby poems "unmake" themselves as they go along, one line or sentence retracting or effacing what the preceding line or sentence had posited. Ashbery's "The Skaters" has served here as the main exemplar of a poetry of self-erasure, a "carnivorous" poetry of absence, "which as we know involves presence, but still" (199). Kenneth Koch, Ashbery's New York School colleague, in a mock manifesto attributed to a nonexistent South American poet, calls this practice *hasosismo,* "the art of the fallen limb," defined as *"the art of concealing in one line what has been revealed in the previous line"* (56; see McHale, "Postmodernist Lyric" 35–37). Substitute "sentence" for "line" in this definition, and the "art of the fallen limb" could pass for the art of the New Sentence, as practiced by the Language poets. "New Sentences forget their antecedents," writes John Shoptaw of Language poetry ("Music of Construction" 244). Lines fall under erasure, concealed by what follows them; sentences fall under erasure, "forgotten" by succeeding sentences; even individual words fall under erasure, according to Shoptaw's account of crypt-words in lyric poetry ("Lyric Cryptography").

Erasure may take other forms at the level of language. Real objects or persons in a poem's world may abruptly lose their "reality" status and collapse into figures of speech; or, vice versa, figures of speech may be promoted into literal realities, or they may be left to hover indecisively between states, ambiguously figurative or literal. This is the form of erasure practiced by Tolson in *Harlem Gallery* and, much more uncompromisingly, by Dorn in *Gunslinger.* Finally, at the level of projected world, poems may seek to represent or evoke realities that are themselves ontologically unstable (as they often are in postmodernist prose narratives). For example, in his series of poems entitled "House," David Shapiro seeks, through a strategic deployment of gaps, voids, evasions, and deliberate failures of expression, to emulate or model the deconstructivist architecture of Peter Eisenman. At the furthest extreme, we encounter entire worlds placed under erasure, as the "other world" is in Merrill's *The Changing Light at Sandover*. Thus, postmodernist poetry erases itself at the "micro" end of the scale (words, sentences, lines), but also at the "macro" end.

Poetry as prosthesis: aleatory and mechanical procedures.
Merrill's *Changing Light at Sandover* dramatizes the use of predetermined procedures to generate poetry. The procedure in this case involved use of a Ouija board in séances where Merrill and his partner David Jackson were "given" strings of letters from which, after considerable editing, much of the text of *Changing Light* was composed. A different sort of procedure figured in the composition of Andrews's "Confidence Trick," where the poet manipulated file cards bearing fragments of text in order to compose his poem. Procedure, chance, constraint—all these features recur throughout postmodernist poetry, where compositional methods designed to limit or channel the poet's "free" creativity abound (see Conte; McHale "Poetry as Prosthesis"). The French OuLiPo group have been particularly fecund in proposing "artificial" methods for generating texts, some of which, such as their "S+7" procedure and its variants, are in wide use among postmodernist poets of all schools.[1] Other early and influential postmodern proceduralists include John Cage, whose "writing-through" of others' texts (*Finnegans Wake, The Cantos*) is a quintessentially procedural practice (see Perloff, *Radical Artifice* 149–61), and the inexhaustibly resourceful Jackson Mac Low (see McHale, "Postmodernist Lyric" 30–35). Many poems of the New York School and the Language group were evidently composed using predetermined procedures or observing predetermined constraints, although in most cases we can only speculate about which particular procedures might have been applied.[2] Among the conspicuous cases where we *do* know precisely what procedures were involved are Ron Silliman's *Tjanting,* based on the Fibonacci number series, and Lyn Hejinian's similarly number-driven long poem, *My Life* (see Perloff, *Radical Artifice* 161–70).

Merrill's Ouija board is a kind of text generating machine, if a primitive one. Indeed, all of the procedures used by postmodernist poets can be viewed as virtual machines for generating text, or at least as programs that could be run on such machines—software, then, if not hardware. Some of them are not virtual at all, but involve actual computer hardware. A range of possibilities for human poets' collaboration with computers in generating poetry is surveyed in Charles O. Hartmans's *Virtual Muse* (1996). Once the option of machine-assisted composition is acknowledged, it becomes possible to reconsider a number of postmodernist practices as reflecting various kinds and degrees of mechanical intervention or mediation. Allen Ginsberg's and David Antin's use of tape recorders in composition might fall under this category; and so might, among the poems discussed here, Armand Schwerner's recourse to font-generating software to create new pictographs in the last *Tablets*.

Moreover, once we begin to think of mechanical composition in this extended sense, other, more traditional aspects of poetry appear in a new and estranging light. What, after all, is a fixed form—haiku, sonnet, sestina, canzone, villanelle, pantoum—if not a kind of miniature machine for generating poems? Hence the revival of these forms in the postmodernist context by, among others, Louis Zukofsky, Ashbery, Harry Mathews, Ted Berrigan, and Bernadette Mayer (see Conte 167–92). For that matter, what is language itself if not a sort of machine with which the poet collaborates? The cybertext theorist Espen Aarseth raises the question of "whether any author, in using the techniques and genres of his or her trade, is not already a cyborg" (135), that is, part human, part machine, a human incorporating a machine, or vice versa. What, finally, is the muse of traditional poetics if not a figure for the poets' collaboration with this language-machine—what is "she," if not a cyborg?

Hip-hop poetics: sampling and the "found."

Over twenty years ago, Jonathan Holden (22–37) stigmatized the practice of "found poetry" as essentially trivial, a period cliché of late-twentieth-century poetry. A few years earlier, David Antin had identified the "found" as one of the major aesthetic discoveries of the century. From the perspective of the twenty-first century, it increasingly appears that Holden was wrong and Antin right. The use of found materials in poetry belongs to that massive reconfiguration of the aesthetic realm that affected nearly all art practice in the twentieth century, and included Cubist collage, Dadaist ready-mades, Surrealist *objets trouvés*, Situationist *détournement*, assemblages and installation art, and even sampling in popular-music production (hip-hop, techno).

The role of "finding" in twentieth-century poetry appears less trivial, more fundamental if we understand the "found" in an expanded sense, as postmodernist poetic practice invites us to do. At one end of a spectrum of possibilities we might place the "classic" practice of found poetry: the poem produced by lineating as poetry a prose text "lifted" from some nonliterary source (e.g., Antin's own "Code of Flag Behavior"), or composed of lines appropriated or sampled from multiple sources, as in a cento. Related to this is the interpolation of sampled material, altered or unaltered, into an original text, a practice widespread among postmodernist poets of many schools. Bob Perelman's "China," which depends on the "found" imagery in a Chinese-language children's book, as well as, on a much larger scale, Ashbery's sampling from "found" texts such as *Three Hundred Things a Bright Boy Can Do* in "The Skaters," both belong here. So do Howe's appropriations from Shakespeare, Spenser, Swift, Beckett, and others, a practice that radicalizes the poetics of allusion to the point of laying bare the "foundness," the second-hand and recycled nature, of received culture in general.

Further along this spectrum one would locate the incorporation of materials, not from specific texts, but from *text types:* social varieties, specialized registers, speech genres, and so on. Practiced across a whole range of twentieth-century poetries, found poetry of this type is especially conspicuous among the Language poets. Andrews's use of material stored on file cards in composing "Confidence Trick" and other poems combines proceduralism with the poetics of the "found" in this sense. Found poetry in the expanded sense also includes what might be called the found practices of everyday life, the apparently indiscriminate and unedited (or minimally edited) notation of everyday experience, as in Frank O'Hara's "I do this I do that" poetry, widely imitated by his New York School epigones, such as Ted Berrigan ("Things to Do on Speed," "Things to Do in Providence," etc.). Other examples, emerging from a different, Zen-inflected aesthetic orientation, can be found among the Beats, e.g., in Gary Snyder's "Things to Do" poems ("Things to Do around Seattle, " ". . . around a Lookout," " ". . . around a Ship at Sea," " ". . . around Kyoto"), or Allen Ginsberg's "auto poesy" dictated into a tape recorder. Finally, at the furthest extreme of found poetry we might place materials apparently "given" to the poet by agents or forces outside his or her control, for instance, Jack Spicer's experience of "dictation" from extraterrestrial sources, Robert Duncan's "dream data," the "clairvoyant" poetry of Hannah Weiner (which came to her, she maintained, in the form of words literally inscribed on people and objects around her, or on her own forehead, which she transcribed), or even the poetry that Merrill allegedly received from angels and the dead at Ouija board seances. This is the postmodern version of the poetry of "lyric possession" (see Stewart, "Lyric Possession"), and, in common with the "I do this I do that" notation of the New York School and the Beats, it involves the recontextualization, revaluation, and renewal of traditional elements of poetic ideology: the poetry of experience, in the case of "I do this I do that" poetry; poetry as inspiration, in the case of clairvoyant and "possessed" poetry.

Poetry and the person: "you" and "I".

All of the elements outlined above—the poetry of absence and erasure, cyborg poetry, the "I do this I do that" poetry of everyday experience, the poetry of possession—have more or less radical consequences for subjectivity in poetry. Postmodernism in poetry, it appears, entails the effacement or occlusion or dispersal of the traditional "lyric I." This crisis of the "I" is wittily dramatized in the death and resurrection of the character named "I" in Dorn's *Gunslinger*. It is corroborated in various ways by most of the other long poems discussed in preceding chapters— by Schwerner's *Tablets*, Hill's *Mercian Hymns*, Ashbery's "The Skaters," Andrews's "Confidence Trick," and Howe's *Europe of Trusts*.

Lyric subjectivity has been under pressure since at least the beginning of the twentieth century. One symptom of that pressure is Eliot's notorious doctrine of impersonality, the radicalism of which has, through overfamiliarity, come to be underestimated (but see Perloff's revaluing of it in *21st-Century Modernism*). Yet only a little after he had formulated that doctrine (in "Tradition and the Individual Talent" of 1919) we find Eliot taking pains to reconstitute a personal consciousness from the dispersed subject-positions of his most radically depersonalized poem, *The Waste Land*, first by proposing the dramatic monologue "Gerontion" as a preface to frame the poem, then by composing the infamous "Tiresias" note that gives it by fiat a unifying point of view. A similar anxiety over the loss of the poetic self runs through the entire range of high-modernist practices of depersonalization and displaced subjectivity: the mask, the persona, pseudonymity (e.g., "Hugh MacDiarmid," C. M. Grieve's public and poetic alter ego) and heteronymity (e.g., the four named personae among whom Fernando Pessoa distributed his poetic identity).

Symptomatic, too, of the twentieth-century crisis of poetic subjectivity are the poetic hoaxes perpetrated over the course of the century. These might charitably be viewed as experiments with poetic identity, some more or less well-intentioned, others more or less malicious. Notorious cases include the Australian hoax-poet Ern Malley and, more recently, the faux-Japanese poet Araki Yasusada (see McHale, "A Poet May Not Exist"). Schwerner's *Tablets* might also be included in this category of experiments.

Many postmodernist poems foreground and thematize the making and unmaking of the poetic subject, for instance Lyn Hejinian's poetic sequence "The Person" (reprinted in *The Cold of Poetry,* 1994) and another punningly entitled *The Cell* (1992). Whether or not it appears as an explicit theme, however, the construction and dispersal of subjectivity are all but universal in postmodernist poetry of all genres. One locus of selfhood's making and unmaking in poetry is, inevitably, the personal pronouns. Personal identity in a poem like Andrews's "Confidence Trick" is elusive in part because Andrews exploits the intrinsic shiftiness of the first-person pronoun, which is after all a "shifter" in discourse, its referent changing depending upon who has the floor. The decoupling of the poet's own subjectivity from the pronoun "I," and the volatility of pronouns generally, are features that Susan Howe shares with other poets of the *HOW(ever)* group. "'I' rarely appears," Rachel Blau DuPlessis's remarks of her own long poem, *Drafts;* and "'I' was never at issue except as a way-station to something else" ("On Drafts" 74, 75). Volatility of pronouns, the apparently free interchangeability of "I," "you," and "she," is particularly a feature of Beverly Dahlens's *A Reading* (see DuPlessis, *Pink Guitar* 121).

The second-person pronoun *you* is also a shifter, of course, though one might think that its usefulness as a tool for exploring selfhood in poetry would be severely limited by its long history as a mere poetic cliché, first in the form of formal apostrophe (see Culler, "Apostrophe"), later as a convention of twentieth-century colloquial style (see Holden 38–56). Nevertheless, the unself-conscious "absorption" in poetry that conventions such as apostrophe and the colloquial *you* promote can also be shattered by direct address (C. Bernstein, *APoetics* 32); the second person can be used against its own tendency to lapse into automatism and cliché. New York School poets, for instance, have revisited apostrophe in the mode of parody and pastiche, as in Kenneth Koch's recent book of apostrophic poetry, *New Addresses* (2000). The second person can also function as a means of gesturing across the ontological divide separating the speaker of the poem (the poet?) from those of us sitting "out here" in the world beyond the text, with the poetry volume open across our laps or on the desk in front of us (see McHale, *Postmodernist Fiction* 222–27). This gesture across the divide can take the form of an erotic seduction, as in Ashbery's widely anthologized second-person poem, "Paradoxes and Oxymorons," or it can take more malign forms, as in Ishmael Reed's "Beware: Do Not Read This Poem." Here second-person poetry aspires (or pretends to aspire) to the condition of black magic.

The replenishment of narrative.

One of modernism's legacies, I observed in the introduction, is its interdiction of continuous narrative in poetry. That interdiction has yet to be lifted, as far as much contemporary poetic practice is concerned. Consider the ubiquitous "workshop poem," the epiphanic lyric fragment that, pregnant with narrative implication, nevertheless seems powerless to narrate. Postmodernist poetry, by contrast, seeks to replenish the resources of narrative in poetry (Perloff "From image to action"; McHale "Telling Stories Again"). It does so by outflanking the modernist interdiction of narrative on two different fronts. First, postmodernism adopts, to a degree unprecedented in "high-art" poetry, the conventions of popular narrative genres—science fiction and gothic, the Western and the adventure story, comic books and animated cartoons, soap opera and pornography. Secondly, it strives to recover, through pastiche and parody, narrative modes that flourished *before* the imperialist expansion of lyric that reached its peak with high-modernist imagism, including the modes of early-nineteenth-century novels-in-verse, of Renaissance and medieval romances and dream-visions, and of ancient epic. Some postmodernist poems combine or superimpose the two approaches.

Dorn's *Gunslinger* exemplifies postmodernism's embrace of popular narrative forms, in this case the Western. Narrative has always been the lingua franca of popular culture, and modernist poetry's interdiction on narrative stems in part from the general modernist anxiety about maintaining the "great divide" between high and low strata. *Gunslinger*, in common with other postmodernist adaptations of "low" genres, seems largely untroubled by the "great divide," and unthreatened by popular culture. Other postmodernist Westerns-in-verse include Jerome Rothenberg's "Cokboy" (1974), Bruce Andrews's "West West" (reprinted 1991), and Michael Ondaatje's *The Collected Works of Billy the Kid* (1970), a Menippean satire that mixes poetry and prose. Paul Muldoon in *Madoc* (1994) combines Western conventions with those of science fiction. Other striking uses of sci-fi conventions can be found in the poetry of the Scottish poet Edwin Morgan and the Israeli Dan Pagis. Another Scot, Andrew Greig, adapts the narrative conventions of the adventure story in his "pocket epics," *Men on Ice* (1977) and *Western Swing* (1994). Kenneth Koch, in his long poem *Seasons on Earth* (1955, 1977), incorporates material from comics and animated cartoons, as does Ted Hughes in *Crow* (1971), while Kenneth Bernard combines cartoons with pornography in *The Baboon in the Nightclub* (1994); and so on.

The recycling of historical styles is a hallmark of postmodernist aesthetics across a range of media, from historicist architecture (what, in the introduction, I called "Post-Modern" architecture) through the postmodernist historical novel to nostalgia films and remakes, retro fashions, and pop-music covers and "tribute" albums. This postmodernist retro aesthetic is also an option for narrative poetry, where the recycling of earlier narrative modes can serve to outflank the modernist interdiction of storytelling in poetry. Here Merrill's adaptation, in *Changing Light*, of the mode of Dante's *Divine Comedy* is exemplary. Similarly, if more obliquely and fragmentarily, Schwerner's *Tablets* recalls the narrative mode of ancient Mesopotamian texts such as the *Epic of Gilgamesh*, while whatever residual narrativity clings to Howe's *Europe of Trusts* has been evoked through her allusions to Spenser's *Faerie Queene*. Somewhat more robust adaptations of premodernist narrative modes include Koch's use of Ariosto and Byron (combined with Disney and Bugs Bunny) in *Seasons on Earth*, Lyn Hejinian's reworking of Pushkin's novel-in-verse, *Evgeny Onegin*, in *Oxata: A Short Russian Novel* (1991), and Christopher Logue's cinema-inflected "account" (not a translation) of the *Iliad* in *War Music* (1963, 1981, 1991, 1995).

Finally, an alternative to the postmodernist revival of narrative is the strategy that I have elsewhere called "weak narrativity." Weak narrativity involves, precisely, telling stories "poorly," distractedly, with much irrelevance and indeterminacy, in such a way as to *evoke* narrative coherence while at the same time withholding commitment to it and undermining confidence in it. A number of longer postmodernist poems exemplify this alternative strategy, among them Ashbery's "The Skaters" and his most recent book-length poem (as of this writing), *Girls on the Run* (1999); also Michael Palmer's "Notes for Echo Lake" poems (1981), Kathleen Fraser's "When New Time Folds Up" (1993), and the long prose poems of Leslie Scalapino. Such poems have in common what might be called a "killed virus" approach to narrativity, whereby "minor" and "failed" narratives inoculate against the sort of master narratives about which postmodernism (according to Lyotard) is incredulous.

The spatial turn.

"A certain spatial turn," says Fredric Jameson, "has often seemed to offer one of the more productive ways of distinguishing postmodernism from modernism proper" (*Postmodernism* 154). The evidence of postmodernist long poems tends to bear out this hypothesis of the spatial turn of postmodernism. Postmodernist poetry can be thought of as "spatial" in at least two relevant senses. First, it is "spatial" in its emphasis on the materiality of poetry itself (see Davidson, *Ghostlier Demarcations*), on poetry's existence as lines of type, pages of paper, binding—or for that matter, as sound waves, or recording media, or electrons bombarding a monitor's screen. Moderately foregrounded in Hill's *Mercian Hymns,* Dorn's *Gunslinger,* and McGrath's *Letter to an Imaginary Friend,* poetry's materiality is more aggressively foregrounded in Schwerner's *Tablets* and Howe's *Europe of Trusts*. Material practices of the "spatial turn" in postmodernist poetry range from anomalous spacing and lineation through varieties of concrete poetry to the hypertext poetry of John Cayley, Jim Rosenberg, and others, and beyond that to installation art—perhaps the LED-text installations of Jenny Holzer, certainly the poetry-garden of Ian Hamilton Finlay. Even measure itself, a basic category of traditional poetics, seems to be undergoing redefinition in spatial terms in postmodernist poetry, as witness Rachel Blau DuPlessis's "Codicil on the Definition of Poetry" ("Manifest" 51) or Jim Rosenberg's "Notes Toward a Non-Linear Prosody of Space" (http://www.well.com/user/jer/nonlin_prosody.html).

Secondly, postmodernist poetry exhibits a "spatial turn" in foregrounding the spaces of the worlds it projects. The visionary other-world spaces of Merrill's *Changing Light* are exemplary in this respect; so, too, are the Western landscapes of Dorn's *Gunslinger*. Behind Merrill's projected spaces lies a long tradition of visionary poetry, including that of Dante, Milton, and Blake, while Dorn's tradition is of more recent vintage, emerging as it does from Charles Olson's poetics of American space. Other types of projected space to be found in postmodernist poems include the *archaeological space* of Hill's *Mercian Hymns,* Schwerner's *Tablets,* and such related poems as Seamus Heaney's "bog poems," Clayton Eshelman's poems of the painted caves of the Dordogne, Nathaniel Mackey's *Eroding Witness* (1985), Clark Coolidge's *At Egypt* (1988), Kathleen Fraser's "Etruscan Pages" (1993), and Theresa Hak Kyung Cha's *Dictee* (1995); *architectural space* such as one finds in David Shapiro's "House" poems, Robert Duncan's "Passages 9," and Ronald Johnson's *Ark;* the *cartographic space* of Howe's "maps" in *Europe of Trusts,* or those of C. S. Giscombe in *Here* (1994) and *Giscome Road* (1998); even the *corporal space* of body-mapping poems such as Michael Harper's "Debridement" (1970) or Harryette Mullens's *Trimmings* (1991). If one were looking for a definitive onset for this "spatial turn" in postmodernist poetry's world-spaces, one could do worse than fix, once again, on the great European postwar masters: on the desert which is also a book (and vice versa) in Edmond Jabès' *Livre des questions* (1963–73); on the meadow which is also a poem (and vice versa) in Francis Ponge's "Le Pré" (1964).

This repertoire of recurrences and tendencies is not exhaustive in any sense. It exhausts neither the features of the poems discussed in this book, nor the elements of postmodernist poetry generally. The items that constitute it do not occur in every postmodernist poem, nor do they occur *only* in postmodernist poems. Some can be found in modernist poems, or in the repertoire of poetry in general, regardless of period; some even occur outside the genre of poetry, for instance in postmodernist novels or visual art. The presence of these elements does not inevitably identify a poem as postmodernist, nor does their absence necessarily disqualify it from being so. In particular poems, as in postmodernist poetics more generally, items from the repertoire overlap, interfere, pull in different directions, jar against each other, even contradict each other; but they also echo, amplify, and mutually reinforce each other. They do not slot smoothly together like pieces of a jigsaw puzzle, but they do form (what else?) a difficult whole.

Notes

CHAPTER 1

1. For Eliot in particular, the criteria for qualifying as a "major" poet were intimately (if equivocally) bound up with the writing of long poems. Some "minor" poets, Eliot reflected in 1944, certainly wrote long poems (Southey, Landor), while some undeniably "major" poets wrote only shorter poems (Donne); but "the *very* greatest poets, who are few in number"—poets of the stature of Sidney, Milton, Wordsworth, Byron, and Keats—"have all had something to say which could only be said in a long poem" (47).

2. James Merrill was the author of *The Seraglio* (1957) and *The (Diblos) Note-book* (1965); Thomas McGrath *This Coffin Has No Handles* (written in 1948, though not published until 1988) and *The Gates of Ivory, the Gates of Horn* (1957); Edward Dorn *By the Sound* (originally titled *Rites of Passage*, 1965) and a collection of short stories, *Some Business Recently Transacted in the White World* (1971); while John Ashbery was the coauthor, with James Schuyler, of *A Nest of Ninnies* (1969). Susan Howe, though not herself a novelist (unlike her sister, the poet and novelist Fanny Howe), nevertheless regularly uses quasi-narrative prose passages to frame her poems. *The Europe of Trusts* is prefaced by one such quasi-narrative passage, entitled "There Are Not Leaves Enough to Crown to Cover to Crown to Cover," while "The Liberties," the third part or poem of *Europe*, begins with a prose biography of Hester Johnson, Swift's Stella.

3. Brackets in this quotation indicate my reconstruction of material obliterated by holes punched through the book in question, Derrida and Eisenman's *Chora L Works* (1997).

4. The Piazza d'Italia never became the civic focus it was intended to be; quite the contrary, the urban planners' attention having shifted away from the Piazza's neighborhood to the Mississippi riverfront, the Piazza d'Italia has been allowed to crumble into ruin. When I last saw it, it was frequented only by New Orleans's homeless.

5. After designing a series of private homes, Eisenman has gone on to build such conspicuous major commissions as the Wexner Center at Ohio State, the Columbus Convention Center, and the College of Design, Architecture, Art, and Planning at the University of Cincinnati.

6. See also the mock-ruinous showrooms designed for Best Products by James Wines and the SITE collective in the tradition of eighteenth-century sham ruins (Wines 143–51).

CHAPTER 2

1. References in the text to the three parts of the trilogy will make use of the organizing schemes established by Merrill, with page numbers taken from the single-volume edition of *The Changing Light at Sandover* (1982). References to "The Book of Ephraim" (originally published in *Divine Comedies,* 1976) will be of the form: "Ephraim," followed by the letter ("A" through "Z") corresponding to the relevant book, followed by the page number. References to "Mirabell's Books of Number" (as here) will be of the form: "Mirabell," followed by the relevant book and section numbers (from 0 through 9.9), followed by the page number. References to "Scripts for the Pageant" (1980) will be of the form: "Scripts," followed by the title of the relevant division ("Yes," "&," "No"), followed by the page number. References to the coda to *The Changing Light* will be of the form: "Coda," followed by page number. Note that Merrill's organizing schemes reflect the traditional makeup of the Ouija board, which features the alphabet, the numbers from 0 to 9, the words "Yes" and "No," and the ampersand.

2. Some twenty years earlier, in his first novel, *The Seraglio* (1957), Merrill had described an opera, entirely his own invention, based on the Orpheus myth, in which an angel visits Orpheus in a twentieth-century setting. The anticipation of Kushner's premise in *Angels in America* is striking, but surely coincidental.

3. "No one has accused James Merrill of being postmodern," writes Mutlu Konuk Blasing (156); she then proceeds to do so herself. In any case, she might be wrong about that; Stephen Yenser, for one, if he didn't quite "accuse" Merrill of postmodernism in so many words, came about as close to it as one could without actually using the P-word (39–40).

4. *The Changing Light* was actually dramatized onstage in 1990; for an account, see Merrill's memoir, *A Different Person* (266–67).

5. Note that communications spelled from the Ouija board are given throughout Merrill's text in small capitals—as here, "VERY BEAUTIFUL"—reflecting the fact that the board has no lowercase letters, and also as a device for distinguishing Merrill's own interpolations (in conventional mixed lowercase and caps) from transcriptions of Ouija communications. "Von" and "Torro" in this passage are names provisionally given to two members of the Five, immortal souls reincarnated over and over again throughout human history, who concentrate the positive qualities of the human race and are responsible for its progress. "God's chosen apes" presumably refers to the famous opening sequence of Kubrick's *2001,* in which apes make the transition to human tool-use through the intervention of extraterrestrial forces.

6. An important exception is the high-camp sensibility displayed at intervals throughout the trilogy, especially when Chester Kallman, Auden's partner and, in this version at least, something of a flaming queen joins the circle of spirit-informants in *Mirabell* 0.6 (see Moffett 166–68; von Hallberg, *American Poetry* 109–13). The camp attitude is, of course, an important feature of the gay subculture out of which this poem issues, and one of its strategies involves cannibalizing and aestheticizing works and trends of popular culture. The classic account of camp, only slightly out-of-date now, is still Susan Sontag's "Notes on 'Camp'" (1966).

7. See Barthelme's "On Angels," from *City Life* (1970); Márquez's "A Very Old Man with Enormous Wings" (1960); Pynchon's *Gravity's Rainbow* (1973); Kundera's *Book of Laughter and Forgetting* (1978); Goytisolo's *Makbara* (1980); Rushdie's *The Satanic Verses* (1988); Katz's "Mongolian Whisky," from *Stolen Stories* (1984); Brodkey's "Angel" (1985).

8. Mack (26, 44) coined the term "ontological shock" to capture the experience of those allegedly abducted by aliens. Failing to find psychological explanations (e.g., dream, curable mental disorder, etc.) for their encounters with radical otherness, abductees must struggle to accept the reality of aliens. Mack's account is, needless to say, highly controversial. Abductees commonly identify aliens with angels in their accounts (48, 397, 407). This assimilation of aliens to angel imagery is a commonplace of high- and popular-culture angelology alike, as evidenced, e.g., by Prior's jokey allusion to *Close Encounters of the Third Kind* at the moment of the angel's descent, or by the fact that previous to playing an angel in *Michael,* John Travolta had last been seen onscreen in *Phenomenon,* in the role of a man who experiences an alien encounter.

9. I am grateful to Hank Lazer for calling my attention to Olson's differences with Duncan over esoteric "wisdom," and to Fredman's account in particular.

10. Auden's "posthumous ephemera" appear in "Mirabell" 8.2, 246; 3.6, 161; 3.9, 165; 8.6, 252; 8.7, 254; 9.0, 259; "Scripts" Yes, 345, 353, 365; &, 372; No, 438. Yeats's posthumous poem appears in "Scripts" No, 486. Stokes (229–30) finds the Auden poetry so believable that he is led to wonder what "Auden scholars will make of his posthumous work."

11. Note also the allusions to Wagner, which link this metaphorization of the word processor to fantastic opera and beyond that to the masque; see above, section III.

12. According to Wills (66–99), cyberspace is itself a species of prosthesis; so by extension we could say that Merrill's other world is a prosthetic device in its own right, associated with the prosthetic writing machine, the Ouija board, analogously to the way cyberspace is associated with the computer.

CHAPTER 3

1. Tolson, in Nelson, ed., *"Harlem Gallery" and Other Poems,* "Upsilon" 312; "Xi" 274–75. All subsequent references to *Harlem Gallery* will be to this new 1999 edition and will be inserted parenthetically in the text, giving the title of the section, named by Tolson using the twenty-four letters of the Greek alphabet ("Alpha" through "Omega"), and page number.

2. Dorn, *Gunslinger* II.79. All subsequent references to *Gunslinger* will use this edition and will be inserted parentheticaly in the text, giving number or title of the book (I, II, "The Cycle," III, IIII) and page number.

3. On Reed's postmodernism, see Gates 302, 316; Bérubé 214; McGee 74, 102–03, 127–33. Whenever Jameson lists representative postmodernists, he never fails to include Reed on that list; see, e.g., Jameson, *Postmodernism* 1, 26.

4. The cinematic origins of Dorn's Gunslinger character are readily documented. The Gunslinger makes his first appearance in a separate poem entitled "An Idle Visitation," published in Dorn's book-length sequence *The North Atlantic Turbine* (1967). This poem would later be reused, with minor changes, as the opening passage of *Gunslinger*. In its original context, however, it is preceded by a poem entitled "A Notation on the Evening of November 27, 1966," set in England during Dorn's sojourn there, and recording an outing by the poet and his friends to the local Odeon to see "an old classic flick," *The Magnificent Seven* (Dorn, *Collected* 225). Given this context, it is hard to read of the Gunslinger's "impeccable personal smoothness/and slender leather encased hands" (I.3) without being reminded of the dandified gunslinger character of *The Magnificent Seven*, played by Robert Vaughn.

5. Equally typical, and if anything, less reassuring, is the poem that Larry Neal, an important poet of the Black Arts Movement, dedicated to Melvin Tolson. Entitled "Harlem Gallery: From the Inside," and carefully dated "Spring 1966" (i.e., predating Tolson's death in August of that year), Neal's poem seems to challenge Tolson to acknowledge the desperate reality of the contemporary "inner city" that has displaced the glamorous, nostalgic Harlem of the Renaissance (and presumably of *Harlem Gallery*). If Tolson is actually the intended addressee of the poem, and not just its dedicatee, then Neal's stance is not just reproachful but downright aggressive:

Listen baby, to the mean scar-faced sister,
between you and her and me and you there are no
distances. short reach of the .38, a sudden
migraine hammering where your brain used to be;
then it's over. . . . (24–5)

The poem ends with a catalogue of names—jazz musicians, folk figures, Harlemites—constituting, presumably, Neal's alternative cultural repertoire, replacing the high-culture repertoire proposed by *Harlem Gallery*.

6. There is persuasive evidence for this view in the text of *Harlem Gallery*. For instance, among the African-American symposiasts of the Zulu Club one of the recurrent topics of conversation is a poem entitled "Ode to the South" and ascribed to a certain "Dolph Peeler" ("Xi" 180; "Phi" 328). As most critics have recognized (e.g., Farnsworth, *Plain Talk* 245), this poem is a thinly disguised version of Allen Tate's widely anthologized "Ode to the Confederate Dead." What the critics have overlooked, however, as far as I'm aware, is Tolson's derisive troping here on Tate's name. Detach the suffix "-er" from Peeler and attach it to Tate, and one gets "Tater,"

as in "'tater peel," or "to peel 'tater(s)." Now shift the initial A from Allen to Dolph, and one gets Adolph—as in Hitler, I suppose. Scrutinized closely enough, the allusion here to Tate's anthology piece begins to look less like an homage and more like revenge. If this doesn't qualify as signifying, I don't know what does.

7. There is precedent for affiliating these poems with Menippean satire, at least in the case of *Gunslinger,* whose family resemblance to certain other texts in the Menippean tradition—*Gulliver's Travels, The Dunciad, Don Juan*—has long been a staple of the criticism (see, e.g., Paul 156; Davidson, "To eliminate" 117; Lockwood 177). The connection is made less regularly in the case of *Harlem Gallery,* though even here critics have occasionally associated Tolson's poem with earlier Menippean satires such as the *Satyricon* (e.g., Woodson 37).

8. *Harlem Gallery* is particularly haunted by verbal echoes of the modernists, including Pound, Frost, Yeats, Allen Tate, and especially Eliot; citations of romantic poetry (Keats, Shelley, Coleridge, especially Blake) also abound. Dorn's text is saturated with Shakespearean quotations and allusions, and with echoes of Renaissance poetry generally (e.g., a pastiche of a Petrarchan blason, II.55), but there are also conspicuous quotations from, among many others, Shelley (I.16), Keats (IIII.128), Thoreau (II.97), Blake (II.120, IIII.161), Eliot (IIII.179), and Dorn's friend and contemporary, the British postmodernist poet J. H. Prynne (III.145, 147), to whom book IIII of *Gunslinger* is dedicated.

9. For other examples of literalized figures, see I.27–28, I.23, 29, III.161, all analyzed by Von Hallberg ("Marvellous" 73–74), and IIII.163, analyzed by Davidson ("To eliminate" 144).

10. Confirmation of this hypothesis, if any were needed, arrives a few pages later, when it is explained why there is no mustard on this particular burger: "They must be ready at a moments notice/To Take Off, and mustard, whatever else it may do/Has an exceedingly long Take-Off Roll" ("The Cycle," 94). No doubt Robart's peculiar disguise also arises in part from literalizing the fixed idiom, "the Big Cheese." Incidentally, later in the poem, when Robart and his crew reach the Southwest, there is some discussion about camouflaging his vehicle as a chile relleno, with "a full set of tortillas" for tires (IIII.150, 151).

11. Proper names are peculiarly unstable throughout *Gunslinger.* The Gunslinger is Slinger for short, but also Zlinger, for no particular reason. Howard Hughes is also Robart, which, apart from being Hughes's middle name, puns on Rob Art (Perloff, "Introduction," ix) and possibly alludes to Jules Verne's Robur the Conqueror. Robart's right-hand man (or android, or whatever) is called Al, but code-named Rupert, inviting confusion with Robart.

12. I detect at least two other puns in this brief passage, apart from the quibble on Everything's name: first, the new medium is "revolutionary" in the etymological sense of "turning things around," and secondly, "everybody" is a "tangible change" because it introduces the "body," both touchable and endowed with the sense of touch, where before there had only been a "thing."

13. Alternatively, one might think in terms of *Pop-Up Videos,* a popular feature

on the VH1 cable-television channel, where music video clips are subjected to running commentaries, sometimes informative but often smart-alecky and ironic. Appearing as printed words intruded directly into the image-space, like comic-strip speech balloons, these commentaries wreck the "suspension of disbelief" indispensable to fiction, reducing the virtual world of the video to no more than a flat image-track. In other words, where pop-up books project a flat world into 3-D, *Pop-Up Videos* have the opposite effect of flattening a 3-D world. "Pop" here also overlaps with the use of the terms "pop" and "push" in software design, where one "pops" up from a lower level to a higher one in a stack of levels (read: worlds) and "pushes" back down from the higher to the lower level; see Hofstadter; Ryan; and cf. McHale, *Postmodernist Fiction* 112–24.

14. In an earlier appearance (III.135–39), Flamboyant had arrived in a Turing Machine, i.e., a thought experiment (never an actual machine) by means of which Alan Turing proposed to determine whether a computer had achieved intelligence. So the machine is a literalized metaphor, and Flamboyant himself literalizes the Cartesian metaphor of the "ghost in the machine." Moreover, he arrives a piece at a time—first a toe and an ear, later a hand, and so on—literalizing the figure of synecdoche, *pars pro toto.*

15. See, e.g., "Upsilon" 312–16. Dr. Nkomo asks the Curator why he prefers cream to milk, to which the Curator responds with a figure comparing "the opacity of cream" with "the dusk of human nature"; Nkomo caps the Curator's figure by interpreting the preference for cream as racist; the Curator responds by adducing a relevant piece of proverbial wisdom ("cream rises to the top"); another speaker intervenes, inverting the racist reading and attributing "rich opacity" to cream by contrast with the "poor whiteness of skim milk"; the Curator weighs in with a newly coined aphorism ("*taste* the milk of the skimmed/and *sip* the cream of the skimmers"), and Nkomo tops this by quoting Virgil and referring cryptically to "the homogenized milk of multiculture." Game, set, and match to Nkomo. A similar contest ("Xi" 280–81; "Phi" 328–42) involves successive rounds of interpretation and reinterpretation of a figure extracted from a poem, Dolph Peeler's "Ode to the South" (see note 6). Hideho Heights wins this competition, trumping all other contestants with his parable of the sea turtle and the shark.

16. By a striking coincidence, Covarrubias retired from his New York career as caricaturist to become curator of the Department of Primitive Art of the National Museum of Mexico. One wonders whether the collection he curated would have been a potential target for Ishmael Reed's *Mu'tafikah* art terrorists, or whether it was just the sort of venue to which they would have repatriated the indigenous art they sought to "liberate."

17. *The Cycle* appeared in an oversize format, resembling a children's picture book, with color illustrations on the front and back cover, and several others interspersed throughout the text; the illustrator is unidentified. *Recollections of Gran Apachería* mimics a comic book in its size (9½ inches by 6¾ inches), its glossy,

colored cover, and its pulp pages; the cover drawing is by Michael Myers, as are two line drawings in comic-book style interpolated in the text.

18. Or perhaps Dorn has in mind, instead, the surrealist collages of Dick Tracy comic-strip imagery produced even earlier, from 1958, under the series title "Tricky Cad" (an anagram of "Dick Tracy"), by Jess [Collins], a San Francisco artist on the fringes of pop; see Auping; Varnedoe and Gopnik 192–94. Dorn might have been exposed to Jess's proto-pop sensibility through the poet Robert Duncan, Jess's companion, and like Dorn an alumnus of Black Mountain College.

19. For instance, the Slinger identifies the Velvet Underground as his "second favorite group" (III.130) and plays a tape of their song, "European Son." The Velvet Underground, of course, was the band Warhol induced to play for his Exploding Plastic Inevitable happenings, and for whom he designed a notorious album cover. (But which is the Slinger's favorite band? He never says.)

20. Sherman Paul contends that Dorn uses popular-culture materials "to impugn the means and mentality of popular culture" itself (165–66), but surely this is too simple. Sometimes, indeed, Dorn does seem to "impugn" popular culture, but at other times his attitude varies from mild satire, through a kind of tolerant campiness, to outright endorsement (e.g., in the case of rock music). See also McPheron 5; Dewey 58–64; Michelson; and especially Foster.

21. In the absence of allusions to more recent art anywhere in the poem, it is tempting to try interpreting the art exhibited in the Harlem Gallery as belonging to the Harlem Renaissance period, and maybe even reflecting particular Renaissance-era styles. Unfortunately, Tolson's account of what hangs in the gallery's four wings ("Iota" 248–51; see Farnsworth, *Plain Talk* 240–41) is so nearly opaque as to frustrate any attempt to match up his descriptions with specific historical styles or schools (let alone specific painters or paintings). It is not even clear whether the four wings are distinguished by medium (murals in the east wing? oils in the west? etchings, or tempera, in the north? but what in the south?) or by style and subject matter (modernist primitivism in the west? social realism in the north? portraits in the south? but what in the east?).

CHAPTER 4

1. One valuable shared characteristic that will not, I fear, figure much in the discussion that follows is humor: *Mercian Hymns* and *The Tablets* are both comic poems. The humor of the *Hymns,* while relatively muted, nevertheless makes its presence felt in the absurd, Monty-Pythonesque funerals of hymns IX and XXVII, in the slapstick of hymn XV (see Hart 153), and in the punning crossword-puzzle clues of hymn II, to each of which the answer is "Offa." (What is a "best-selling brand"? Offa.; A "curt graffito"? Offa.; "A specious gift"? Offa.; etc.) The humor of *The Tablets* is more robust, often turning on wild incongruities of tone between the scholar-translator's pedantic manner and the scatological, obscene, or nonsensical materials of his texts. Other comic effects depend on anachronisms (see below) or

on the bathetic spectacle of the scholar-translator inadvertently undermining, as he frequently does, his own (dubious) authority.

2. Schwerner's scholar-translator might almost have been modelled on a figure such as Julian Jaynes, the Princeton psychologist and author of *The Origins of Consciousness in the Breakdown of the Bicameral Mind* (1976). Jaynes speculated that people in the ancient world—the world of *The Iliad,* Hammurabi's Code, and the cities of the god-kings; the world of *The Tablets*—literally lacked consciousness in the modern sense, and instead received directions from the other hemisphere of their own brains, perceived as divine voices. Not until the breakdown of this experience of "bicamerality," which Jaynes dates to the world-historical crises of the second millennium B.C., does consciousness, subjecthood, the experience of inwardness in something like the form with which we are familiar, emerge. While this is not Schwerner's scholar-translator's thesis—apart from anything else, Jaynes's date for the onset of modern consciousness is a thousand years too late—and Schwerner could not literally have had *The Origins of Consciousness* in mind, since the first of *The Tablets* precedes it by some eight years, nevertheless there are intriguing similarities between Jaynes's somewhat manic scholarship and the scholar-translator's.

3. For a markedly different evaluation of Schwerner's ironic structure from my own, consult Lazer, "Sacred Forgery." For Lazer, the distance that Schwerner opens between himself and his text by interposing the scholar-translator and other unreliable mediators constitutes a serious self-limitation, a form of self-imposed austerity and reticence. Moreover, where I see the appended "Journals/Divagations" as heightening the indeterminacy of the text, Lazer finds in its record of Schwerner's creative process compensation for the loss of immediacy that the poem's ironic structure entails.

4. Elsewhere (McHale, "Topology") I have compared Schwerner's *Tablets* to the paintings of the Belgian surrealist Paul Delvaux. In the foregrounds of his paintings, female nudes mingle with fully dressed bourgeois gentlemen, while in the background, a ruined classical city recedes in foreshortened perspective. The closer we scrutinize these ruins, the more they appear to be stage sets, or scale models made to appear full-size by a trick of perspective, or perhaps trompe l'oeil backdrops—sham ruins, in short. It is this trompe l'oeil effect of Delvaux's ruins that led Alain Robbe-Grillet to base his novel *Topologie d'une cité fantôme* (1976) on Delvaux's imagery.

5. Behind my discussion of fragments and hoaxes lies a larger issue, which I can only mention here, involving the relations among fragmentation, forgery, and the construction of national or ethnic identity. The connection is transparent in cases such as Ossian and *The Kalevala,* but it may even be faintly discerned in the Piltdown hoax, which was embraced in part because it seemed to vindicate British paleoarchaeology, and even to stake a claim for the primacy of the English race: journalists and popularizers regularly referred to Piltdown Man as "the first Englishman." It would be pertinent to reflect on the "national" subtexts of the scandals surrounding such recent hoaxes as the Ern Malley hoax, the Alan Sokal/*SocialText*

hoax or the Yasusada case. See McHale, "A Poet May Not Exist"; and on the complex motives of ethnic identity construction (or is it identity evasion?) in *The Tablets*, see Finkelstein 110–20.

6. My discussion implies a typology of hoaxes something along these lines: (1) "genuine" hoaxes, intended never to be exposed; e.g., Macpherson's Ossian poems, the Piltdown skull, the art forgeries of Hans van Meegeren, Clifford Irving's fake biography of Howard Hughes, the forged Hitler Diaries; (2) "entrapments," hoaxes designed to deceive, with the intention that they will be revealed by the hoaxer in order to discomfit the gullible; e.g., the Sokal hoax, the Ern Malley hoax, possibly Tom Keatings's art forgeries, allegedly designed to expose venal practices of the art-world establishment; (3) mock hoaxes, intended never to deceive, but to be recognized as hoaxes (almost) immediately; at most, to deceive momentarily, the deception to be followed by a moment of recognition; e.g., Koch's "Some South American Poets," Schwerner's *Tablets*, possibly William Boyd's biography of the nonexistent painter Nat Tate. The most controversial and disturbing cases are those which we cannot securely place in one category or another: where, exactly, do Thomas Chatterton's writings belong? Do the Yasusada notebooks belong to the category of entrapments or that of mock hoaxes? The outrage of the deceived editors of *American Poetry Review, Conjunctions,* and other journals might even lead one to believe that Yasusada ought to be grouped with genuine hoaxes, but that would probably be unjustified. For further details, see McHale, "A Poet May Not Exist."

7. Reportedly, listeners at Schwerner's readings, convinced that what they are hearing is a genuine translation, sometimes failed to grasp the mock hoax character of *The Tablets*. Schwerner complicates matters by incorporating in one tablet (tablet XII) a genuine translation of a Sumerian text—an authentic text masquerading as a hoax text, a pseudo-pseudo-translation!

8. Alternatively, as my epigraph is meant to suggest, there is also Walter Benjamin; but I have no space here to consider the Benjaminian model of archaeology. For that, see instead Frisby; Buck-Morss.

CHAPTER 5

1. Some would disagree. Lehman (*Last Avant-Garde* 356–57), for instance, argues that, while Ashbery's devices may be postmodernist, the metaphysical uses to which he puts them are not: "The questions Ashbery raises are not the questions of postmodernism."

2. On shifting frames of reference in Ashbery's poetry, see Shetley 113, 125. On the poetics of disjunction generally, see Forrest-Thomson, *Poetic Artifice;* C. Bernstein, *A Poetics;* and Quartermain.

3. "The Skaters," I, in Ashbery, *Mooring* 195. All subsequent references to "The Skaters" will be to this edition, and will be noted parenthetically in the body of the text, citing section (I, II, III, IV) and page number.

4. This is also the substance of McHoul and Wills's (108–30) objection to the critical literature on Pynchon, another fiction writer who, like Barthelme, poses her-

meneutic difficulties comparable to those posed by Ashbery. Critics typically pro-mote to the status of "keys" a mere handful of passages from Pynchon's texts (often the same passages, from one critic to the next), leaving vast stretches of text effec-tively unread. McHoul and Wills wickedly characterize this as a "conspiracy-to-succeed between the letter of the text and the critical argument" (109).

5. See, for instance, Ross's insights ("Doubting" 189–90, 204–05) into the way compositional principles of Ashbery's earlier poetry are thematized by his later po-etry, as though Ashbery were conducting a running commentary on his own corpus, in hopes of heading off his critics; by the time of *Shadow Train* (1981) Ashbery has caught up with himself, so to speak, and the enactment and its commentary occur in the same poem, sometimes in the same line (194). See also Ward on the tendency of New York School poetry generally to render commentary redundant by antici-pating and preempting it—and this includes even (or especially) psychoanalytic and deconstructive commentary. This perspective on Ashbery owes much to Forrest-Thomson (*Poetic Artifice* 152–9), not only one of Ashbery's earliest close readers, but one whose readings have yet to be bettered.

6. The skating scene is briefly reprised later in part I, inside an analogy ("As skaters elaborate their distances,/Taking a separate line to its end"; I.197), and once again, in an ironically backhanded way, at the very end of part I, when a "No Skat-ing" sign is mentioned (I.201).

7. The effect of artificiality is hardly lessened by the discovery in part III of an image strikingly parallel in construction to those in part IV: "The west wind grazes my cheek, the droplets come pattering down" (III.214).

8. Compare Shetley's observation (123) that Ashbery's frequent recourse to col-loquialism seems less like a representation of colloquial voice than like the citation of popular (film, television) representations—"a representation of a representation, doubly removed from the voice of any actual speaker."

9. Two books appeared during the nineties from critics with unprecedented ac-cess to Ashbery and his papers, namely John Shoptaw's *On the Outside Looking Out* (1994) and David Lehman's *The Last Avant-Garde* (1998). Shoptaw, while usually circumspect in his claims about the poems' autobiographical dimension (see below), occasionally uses the autobiographical key to "unlock" a cryptic text, as in his read-ing of the short lyric, "They Dream Only of America" (from *The Tennis Court Oath),* in terms of an episode from Ashbery's private life (65–66). Lehman, on the other hand, insisting that Ashbery is "the least autobiographical of modern poets" (94), takes Shoptaw severely to task for his biographism, particularly in the case of "They Dream Only of America" (155–59).

10. Contrast the earlier reading of "The Skaters" by David Shapiro, who does indeed attempt to construe the poem's childhood memories as authentically Ash-bery's (102). Lehman, as might be expected (see the preceding note), is categorical in his denial of personal reference: "in a crucial sense John Ashbery does not exist in his poems. . . . The speaker in an Ashbery poem has a curiously distant relation

to the living man" (*Last Avant-Garde* 97). On Ashbery's confounding of conventional expectations about "voice" in poetry, see also Ross, "Doubting" 182.

11. With respect to "The Skaters," see Keller's reading (*Re-making It* 29–33), which revisits some of the same quotations already canonized by Bloom. See note 4 above.

12. Ashbery's "fire fountain" also has a canonical precursor in Coleridge's "Kubla Khan," where the fountain, upwelling violently from subterranean depths, functions as a scale model of the creative imagination, much as Ashbery's fire fountain models the "subterranean" sources and spontaneous, improvisatory character of writing: "it is the fire demon/Who has created [the scene], throwing it up on the dubious surface of a phosphorescent fountain /For all the world like a poet" (II.211).

13. The continuation of this passage, in which the poem's form is compared with that of falling snow, is also a candidate for ars-poetic reading; see, e.g., Mohanty and Monroe 43–44.

14. Elsewhere (McHale, *Constructing* 81–114) I have advanced a parallel argument for the instructive or educative value of our failure to "solve" *Gravity's Rainbow.*

15. See also the related images of the "ocean of language" through which such waves sweep (*A Wave* 71), and of the mind as the beach on which rocks are exposed when the tide ebbs (70).

CHAPTER 6

1. The Left poet James Scully corroborates Jameson's approach in his reading of a comparable Perelman text, where he dismisses Language poetry as "just another symptomatic literature" (*Line Break* 121–22; "Line Break" 103–04). On the surprising failure of Marxist criticism generally to value contemporary innovative writing, see Lazer 85–86.

2. As it turns out, "China" is also, despite its stylistic homogeneity, a found object, though of a different kind from "Confidence Trick." Its disjunct "lines" are ad hoc captions that Perelman supplied for images from a Chinese primer he found (176, n.37)—not a book of photographs, as Jameson says (*Postmodernism* 30). The tone of resentment one detects in Jameson's "revelation" of the poem's "found" status is curious, and perhaps goes some way toward explaining his characterization of "China" as schizophrenic.

3. In this respect it is an exemplary "New Sentence" poem; see Silliman; Perelman, 59–78. On sentence-measure versus phrase-measure poetry, see Shoptaw, "Music of Construction."

4. All subsequent references will be to the 1997 complete edition of *Letter to an Imaginary Friend* and will be incorporated parenthetically in the body of the text, specifying part, section, chapter, and page number, thus: (part 1, I.1.3), except for part 4, which lacks sections. All emphases and ellipses are McGrath's, except where otherwise noted.

5. One might also hope that such a poem would be efficacious—that it would change hearts and minds, promote solidarity, move people to action, and so on—but

I do not see how the criterion of efficacy can be built into the definition of political poetry. Efficacy is a matter of how (and whether) poems are taken up and used, and so has less to do with the poems themselves than with the historical circumstances in which they find themselves. The most that a poem can do is make itself available for use; whether it is actually used or not is literally beyond its, or the poet's, control.

6. McGrath was intimate in Los Angeles with Edwin Rolfe (1909–1954) during the latter's last years. Rolfe is mentioned at least twice in part 1 of the *Letter* (I.5.7., XII.4.128). On Rolfe, see Nelson, "Lyric Politics."

7. Particularly heterodox is McGrath's attempt, especially in parts 3 and 4, to marry materialism with an eclectic spirituality derived from Hopi mythology and from the Roman Catholicism of his own upbringing. His motives, especially in the case of his use of Catholicism, are hard to determine and seem profoundly mixed: is he seeking to "redeem" Catholicism for a materialist, revolutionary politics, on the analogy, perhaps, of Third-World liberation theology? or vice versa, using Catholic myths and metaphors to "redeem" secular politics? I leave out of my account here attitudes McGrath displays that appear "politically incorrect" by current standards, since it would be deeply anachronistic to expect a white man born in 1916 to adhere to turn-of-the-millennium standards of correctness with respect to, e.g., Native Americans or women. On the other hand, it is striking that in later parts of his poem McGrath seems deliberately to revisit and revise less-than-enlightened attitudes displayed earlier in the poem; compare, for instance, the respectful elegy in an Indian graveyard in part 2, V.1–2 with the Indian-fighter fantasy of part 1, III.2.17, or the sexual initiation of part 2, IV.2, involving a recognizably real woman, with the fantasy women of part 1, IV.

8. McGrath's potential to develop in a postmodernist direction can perhaps be traced to his schooling in orthodox New Criticism by Cleanth Brooks at LSU in the late thirties (see Stern, *Revolutionary Poet* 159), an experience that forms the basis of *Letter,* part 1, IX.4. This positioned him in the first generation of poets to encounter modernism as a canonized poetics, rather than a transgressive one—as a period style, from which one could distance oneself, rather than the style of present innovation. Unlike others of his literary generation with similar training (but a middle-class background)—Lowell, Berryman, Jarrell—McGrath did, in fact, go on to distance himself from canonical modernism. Compare McGrath's position with respect to New-Critical modernism to Melvin Tolson's belatedness with respect to the African-American modernism of the Harlem Renaissance; see chapter 3.

9. McGrath's antics here place his poem firmly in the tradition of "learnéd wit" that passes from Erasmus, Rabelais, and Cervantes through Sterne and Diderot down to the Joyce of "Cyclops," "Circe," and *Finnegans Wake* and finally to postmodernist fiction and postmodernist long poems such as Dorn's *Gunslinger* and Schwerner's *Tablets* (see chapters 3 and 4).

10. Another Yeats text that echoes throughout the *Letter* is the refrain of "Easter 1916": "All changed" (1, XII.1.124); "All to be changed" (2, VI.2.266). The presence of Yeats is perhaps unsurprising for an Irish-American poet trained by New Critics (see

note 8); nevertheless it does appear paradoxical in view of the incompatibility of McGrath's and Yeats's respective politics.

11. Interestingly, in one place McGrath actually directs his invective *against* Baraka (here still called LeRoi Jones): "El Roy Bones/Is preparing his nation's house: i.e. to yell *Motherfucker*/In the Mies van der Rohe jakes of the Anglo-Saxon death" (2, II.6.169). What is at stake here, apparently, is Baraka's/Jones's Black Nationalism, which McGrath sees as compromising working-class solidarity: "At the congress of the colorblind/I put up the communist banner my father signed and sang:/LABOR IN A BLACK SKIN CAN'T BE FREE WHILE WHITE SKIN LABOR IS IN CHAINS!" (169–70).

12. This latter seems almost certain to be an allusion, not to real TV quiz shows, but to the radio-comedy troupe The Firesign Theater and its parody of a quiz show, "Beat the Reaper!" in their routine entitled, "Waiting for the Electrician or Someone Like Him" (1968).

13. A comparable volatility characterizes the behavior of the second-person addressee; see, for instance, the shifting and elusive addressees in the passage cited above: "Dog eats dinner on *your* bed [. . .] Get tension wire brakes in her brain pan, if I were *you* [. . . .] I want the same ouput *you* want" (emphases and ellipses mine).

14. On the day that I began revising this passage, November 28, 1999, National Public Radio news reported that an anti-World Trade Organization activist had greeted fellow activists, gathering in Seattle to protest WTO policies, with the words, "Welcome to the revolution! And it appears that it *will* be televised." The use of his phrase in this context would presumably be somewhat more palatable to Gil Scott-Heron than its use in the Turner Broadcasting context—but probably not much more.

15. Barnard is referring here to Kenneth Fearing's precocious awareness of the power of mass-media discourse. Fearing, she writes, unlike Muriel Rukeyser, "seems concerned with the possibility that the revolution itself may be 'televised' (if I may anachronistically apply the phrase from the sixties)" (94).

16. Interestingly, the texts in Andrews's *Get Em Enough Rope*, including "Confidence Trick," date from precisely the same years, the late seventies and early eighties, when hip-hop music was just emerging from the South Bronx, only a few miles from where Andrews taught at Fordham.

17. I am indebted to Matthew Remski for making this point to me in a discussion after my presentation of this material at the "Assembling Alternatives" conference at the University of New Hampshire in August and September of 1996.

CHAPTER 7

1. On the history and impact of *HOW(ever)* see Kinnahan 183–236, Fraser 25–38, Vickery 88–100. On women's poetry communities generally see Vickery, especially 77–87 on Howe's poetry program for Pacifica Radio in the late seventies. Howe has also been associated, if somewhat problematically, with the L=A=N=G=U=A=G=E poets; see McGann "Composition" 104; Back 13–15.

2. On the "unity" of Howe's volume *Singularities* (1990), which like *The Eu-*

rope of Trusts juxtaposes three separate long poems (or sequences), "Articulation of Sound Forms in Time," "Thorow," and "Scattering as Behavior Toward Risk," see Back 50.

3. The same problems of organization and integration that characterize the whole of *The Europe of Trusts* recur at the level of its third part, "The Liberties." Ambiguities abound with respect to how we ought to understand the divisions and subdivisions of this part. There are three numbered sections, one of which also has a title ("*God's Spies*"), another of which may or may not have a title ("TRAVELS"), as well as two titled sections ("THEIR/*Book of Stella*," "WHITE FOOLSCAP/*Book of Cordelia*") that might constitute subdivisions of part I, but then again might occupy the same level of organization as the numbered sections. See Keller's excellent but inevitably inconclusive account of these difficulties (*Forms* 207, 212). On the difference in layout between the original Loon Books edition of *The Liberties* and the later Sun & Moon Press edition, see Back 196, n.2.

4. Recent scholarship has begun to document in greater detail Howe's use of her source material; see, e.g., Green and Back 21–32 on the sources of *Secret History of the Dividing Line,* and Vanderborg 65–69 on "Scattering as Behavior Toward Risk."

5. All references to *The Europe of Trusts* will be noted parenthetically in the text, using the following abbreviations: *T* for the preface, "There Are Not Leaves Enough to Crown to Cover to Crown to Cover"; *PS* for "Pythagorean Silence"; *DP* for "Defenstration of Prague"; *L* for "The Liberties."

6. I am simplifying here. In fact, immediately after the passage I quoted above from "Pythagorean Silence" (23), Howe cuts away from *Hamlet* to a different text, indeed a different author altogether, introducing verbal material sampled from Bunyan's *Pilgrim's Progress:* "wicket-gate," through which Bunyan's pilgrim passes at the outset of his progress; "TALKATIVE," a character encountered on the road.

7. Perhaps, too, Shakespeare's figure "As mad as the vexed sea" contributes to the maritime imagery of Howe's passage.

8. The notion of a rhyme on the level of topic, as distinct from the level of sound, originates in Kenner's account (92–93 and passim) of the organization of Pound's *Cantos.* Keller (*Forms* 198–99) makes the connection with Howe's practice in "The Liberties." By contrast, Perloff ("Collision" 305) denies that Howe employs the Poundian technique of subject rhyme.

9. Moreover, "darkling" itself is an interesting poeticism, a word that, over time, has lost its currency *except as* a word used in poems. In effect, it contains and recapitulates in miniature a whole genealogy of "poeticalness." Beginning its career as an adverb in current use, meaning "in the dark," "darkling" becomes a marker of the "poetic" register thanks to its use by Shakespeare (in *King Lear* and elsewhere) and Milton (e.g., *Paradise Lost,* III, l. 39). It survives as an archaism, as in Keats's "Ode to a Nightingale" (l. 50), ultimately undergoing a shift of grammatical function from adverb to adjective, as in Hardy's "The Darkling Thrush" and many other Romantic and post-Romantic poems. (Compare Susan Stewart's account ["Lyric Possession" 40] of the poeticism "guerdon.") By isolating this particular charged

word from *Lear,* Howe implicates the entire sequence of (male) "major poets" in the cultural identity of "Shakespeare."

10. The story of Florimell in fact figured conspicuously in one of the canonical narratives of poetic descent: writing in the mid-eighteenth century, the poet William Collins, in his "Ode on the Poetic Character," made Spenser's episode of the competition for possession of Florimell's girdle (originally Venus's) into a myth of the continuity of poetry. Spenser's version is narrated in *Faerie Queene* IV.v.

11. Dworkin (400) observes that, in associating printed words with woods, Howe foregrounds the physical basis of books (*i.e.,* wood pulp), which has left its etymological traces in many of the everyday words we use in connection with books, including "book" itself, as well as "folio," "biblio-," "codex," "leaf," even "paper"—all derived from words for the various fibrous plants from which books and book materials were once made. Cf. McGann, "Composition" 104.

12. See also *PS* 78, *PS* 82, *PS* 84, and the "Formation of a Separatist" sequence, *L* 204–08, reprised on *L* 216. Such word grids abound in Howe's other poetry as well, for instance in *Secret History of the Dividing Line, Articulation of Sound Forms in Time,* "Thorow," and elsewhere.

13. Howe's practice of the visual page flows from, or converges with, the spatial poetics of some of her immediate precursors and contemporaries, especially Charles Olson and others associated with the Black Mountain group, but also mavericks like Paul Metcalf and Armand Schwerner (see chapter 4), and even poets farther afield, such as Francis Ponge and Edmond Jabès. Particularly relevant to Howe's practice is the precedent of Robert Duncan in poems like "The Fire/Passages 13" (from *Bending the Bow,* 1968), where words are disposed on the page in grids similar to Howe's (Butterick 318; Fraser 185). On Howe's spatial poetics, see Golding, "Drawing"; on women poets' practice of visual poetics, see Fraser 174–200; on Duncan as forerunner of women's avant-garde practice generally, see Keller, *Forms* 241–52.

14. In the Garden of Adonis canto, "form"—differently spelled—appears in two combinations: "forme and feature" (vi.37) and "forme and outward fashion" (vi.38). In the Oxford *Poetical Works* of Spenser, edited by DeSelincourt, the first of these combinations is printed with so little spacing between the words that one wonders whether it might have inspired Howe's telescoped "formandform(s)."

15. Note how, in at least two cases—"twyne," "paramoure"—Howe selects words that reflect archaic orthography, one of her fascinations throughout her writing (see my discussion of her borrowings from Spenser's *View,* below). Spenser's orthography is not only archaic, of course, but actively *archaizing,* i.e., pseudo-medieval.

16. Other strings of orthographic variants from the *View* variorum appear on *DP* 87: "egeiptes aegistes aegiptes egeps Egipp/ egypt"; "slayius slamius stanius."

17. It is also, of course, Beckett's city, as allusions to Beckett throughout "The Liberties" attest. See Back's (91–94) impressive documentation of Howe's "dialogue" with *Waiting for Godot* in *God's Spies,* the second part of "The Liberties"; and see below for other Beckett allusions. The Becketts belonged to the same Protestant social circles in Dublin as Howe's mother's family, the Mannings, and Mary Manning

Howe, a childhood friend of Beckett's, evidently had a brief affair with him ("all but an affair" says one of his biographers, circumspectly; Cronin 23) in the summer of 1936.

18. Deviant "found" orthography, mysteriously "damaged" words, and verbal errors of all kinds abound in Howe's poetry, conspicuously in *Cabbage Gardens* (1979), *Secret History of the Dividing Line* (1979), *Articulation of Sound Forms in Time* (1987), *A Bibliography of the King's Book* (1989), and "Melville's Marginalia" (in *The Nonconformist's Memorial,* 1993). Intriguingly, her book *Frame Structures* (1996) comes with an erratum slip: a self-reflexive gesture? or something more like the ironic "revenge" of language on its abuser? "Howe makes of error a new text," writes Michael Davidson (*Demarcations* 90), and in this respect her poetics has much in common with that of other poets of the *HOW(ever)* group. For what amounts to a manifesto of the poetics of accident, see Kathleen Fraser's "Faulty Copying" (Fraser 77–88). For examples of this poetics in practice, see Fraser's own "boundayr" (in *Notes preceding trust,* 1987) or "Giotto: ARENA" (from *when new time folds up,* 1993), or almost any of the installments of DuPlessis's ongoing long poem *Drafts.* See also Joan Retallack's *Errata 5uite* (1993).

19. Reinfeld (127, n.10) has traced this strangely damaged sentence back to a source in Beckett's *Murphy:* "Do not come down the ladder, they have taken it away." I also hear in it an echo of the penultimate proposition of Wittgenstein's *Tractatus,* where the *Tractatus* itself is figured as a ladder to be kicked away once we have climbed past the end of it.

20. Marjorie Perloff asserts that "there is not . . . so much as a trace in Howe's work of the 'I-centered' mode so ubiquitous in the poetry of the early seventies" ("Collision" 299). This is overstated, I think; there are, precisely, "traces" of this mode in her poetry, though it is hard to distinguish its traces from those of other modes that also employ the first-person pronoun.

21. Dworkin (402, n. 84), for instance, reads the "I" in the last example above ("Often I hear Romans" etc.) as referring to the poet herself, and the entire couplet as referring to her preoccupation with etymology, which is as plausible as any other reading—but not *more* plausible than any other reading.

22. Middleton (1991) relates Howe's motif of "ice," no doubt correctly, to the topos of glaciation in the poetry of Charles Olson and those who came under his intellectual influence, such as J. H. Prynne. But equally relevant to Howe (as the passage from *PS* 35 makes clear) is the way that "ice" encrypts the first-person pronoun.

23. Here, obviously, Howe puns on the "I" in "Ireland" to foreground and reflect on her own personal identification with her mother's homeland. See also the last page of "The Liberties" (which is to say the last page of *The Europe of Trusts* as a whole), where a fragment of an old map is reproduced, showing an island labelled "Irelands Eye"—another resonant pun on the first-person pronoun (see Keller, *Forms* 237).

24. A preoccupation with proper names is a hallmark of Howe's entire oeuvre. See, e.g., her punning on "mark" (the name of both her father and her son) through-

out *Secret History of the Dividing Line* (see Green 86–87; Back 21–23), as well as her encryption of her own presence in the lower-case initials "sh" (*Frame Structures* 116, 122; see DuPlessis, *Pink Guitar* 123–24; Green 100); her fascination with the recurrence of the same Christian names from generation to generation of her family in the prefatory "Frame Structures" essay; the anagrams for the names of Thomas Shepard, Anne Bradstreet, and Anne Hutchinson that she records in *The Birth-mark* (45, 64, 67, 110, 115); and so on.

25. Those who prefer to solve the rebus for themselves should ignore this note; but the solutions are: 1 and 3, "S"; 2, "ewe" or "yew," i.e., "U"; 4, the first letter of the alphabet, "A" ; 5 and 7 together spell "no"; 6, 7, and 8 together spell "how" ("a question or salutation"); 6, 7, 8, and 9 together spell "howe" ("a depression"). See Keller (*Forms* 235) and Back 100 for partial solutions.

26. Interestingly, Dworkin reads Howe's poetics of the visual page (her "visual prosody," in his terms) as figuring "noise" instead of silence. Contrast Keller (*Forms* 231) and Back (107, 112, 119–20), who assume, as I do, that Howe's near-empty pages and sparse, spaced-out typography figure silence.

27. Howe very likely derived her title from John Dryden's "A Song for St. Cecilia's Day, 1687" (subsequently set to musc by Handel), which famously ends, "*The dead shall live, the living die,/ And Music shall untune the sky.*" John Hollander's book (1961) on the doctrine of the music of the spheres, which includes a close reading of Dryden's ode, itself bears the title, *The Untuning of the Sky,* another possible source for Howe's title.

28. In the Pythagorean view, the cosmos is structured according to ten oppositions, or rather, according to ten variations on a single opposition, which can be expressed as the opposition of limit versus the unlimited, or odd versus even, or one versus plurality, or right versus left, or rest versus motion, or straight versus crooked, or light versus darkness, or square versus oblong, or good versus evil, or (finally) male versus female. All the first terms of these oppositions, viz. limit, odd, one, right, rest, straight, light, square, good, male, are equivalent to one another, just as all the second terms are all equivalent to one another and opposed to the respective first terms; see Guthrie 245–46. Howe must have seen in such a binary-structured universe an opportunity for ironic reversal, for her poetics conforms to the aesthetics implicit in Pythagorean doctrine, albeit ironically, in the sense that her practice consistently values the second terms of the oppositions over the first—the unlimited over limit, plurality over the one, motion over rest, the crooked over the straight, the "dark side of history" over the well-lighted—and of course the silent woman over the silencing, misogynous male.

CODA

1. In the "S+7" procedure, one begins with an already existing text and, for each of its nouns (*substantives,* hence the "S" of "S+7") one substitutes the seventh noun to appear after it in the entries of some dictionary; see Mathews and Brotchie 198–200. A famous, not to say notorious, example of an "S+7" poem is Larry Fagin

and Clark Coolidge's "On the Pumice of Morons" (1994), which rewrites Maya Angelou's "On the Pulse of Morning," delivered at the 1993 Clinton inauguration (pulse+7=pumice; morning+7=moron; and so on).

2. Consult the list of "Experiments" (procedures, for the most part) drawn up by Bernadette Mayer and members of the St. Mark's Poetry Project workshop in the early seventies, and reprinted in various places, including the little magazine *L=A=N=G=U=A=G=E, The L=A=N=G=U=A=G=E Book* (1984), and Ron Silliman's anthology *In the American Tree* (1986); Charles Bernstein augments and updates Mayer's list in the special Bernstein issue of *boundary 2* 23:3 (Fall 1996). See also the 1997 issue of the poetry annual *Chain*, devoted to procedures, in which most of the poems are followed by an account of the methods used in their composition.

References

Aarseth, Espen. *Cybertext: Perspectives in Ergodic Literature.* Baltimore: Johns Hopkins UP, 1997.

Abrioux, Yves. *Ian Hamilton Finlay: A Visual Primer.* Cambridge, MA: MIT P, 1992.

Alderman, Nigel. Introduction. *Pocket Epics: British Poetry after Modernism.* Ed. Nigel Alderman and C. D. Blanton. *The Yale Journal of Criticism* 13.1 (Spring 2000): 1–2.

Altieri, Charles. "Without Consequences Is No Politics: A Response to Jerome McGann." *Politics and Poetic Value.* Ed. Robert von Hallberg. Chicago: U of Chicago P, 1987. 301–07.

Amossy, Ruth, and Elisheva Rosen. *Les discours du cliché.* Paris: CDU et SEDES réunis, 1982.

Anderson, Brooke Davis. *Darger.* New York: American Folk Art Museum, Abrams, 2001.

Andrews, Bruce. *Ex Why Zee: Performance Texts, Collaborations with Sally Silvers, Word Maps, Bricolage, & Improvisations.* New York: Roof, 1995.

——. *Getting Ready to Have Been Frightened.* New York: Roof, 1988.

——. *Give Em Enough Rope.* Los Angeles: Sun & Moon, 1987.

——. *Paradise & Method: Poetics & Practice.* Evanston, IL: Northwestern UP, 1996.

——. "Work." *Aerial* 9 (1999): 284–88.

Antin, David. "Modernism and Postmodernism: Approaching the Present in American Poetry." *boundary 2* 1.1 (Fall 1972): 98–133.

Ashbery, John. *The Mooring of Starting Out: The First Five Books of Poetry.* Hopewell, NJ: Ecco, 1997.

——. *A Wave.* New York: Viking Penguin, 1984.

Auping, Michael. "Jess: A Grand Collage." *Jess: A Grand Collage 1951–1993.* Buffalo, NY: Albright-Knox Art Gallery, 1993. 31–65.

Back, Rachel Tzvia. *Led by Language: The Poetry and Poetics of Susan Howe.* Tuscaloosa: U of Alabama P, 2002.

Baker, Houston. *Modernism and the Harlem Renaissance.* Chicago: U of Chicago P, 1987.

Bakhtin, Mikhail. *Problems in Dostoevsky's Poetics.* 1963. Ed. and trans. Caryl Emerson. Minneapolis: U of Minnesota P, 1984.

———. *Rabelais and His World.* Trans. Hélène Iswolsky. Cambridge, MA: MIT P, 1968.

Barnard, Rita. *The Great Depression and the Culture of Abundance: Kenneth Fearing, Nathanael West, and Mass Culture in the 1930s.* Cambridge: Cambridge UP, 1995.

Barthes, Roland. "That Old Thing, Art . . . ". *Pop Art: A Critical History.* Ed. Steven Henry Madoff. Berkeley: U of California P, 1980. 370–74.

Beach, Christopher. *ABC of Influence: Ezra Pound and the Remaking of American Poetic Tradition.* Berkeley: U of California P, 1992.

Benjamin, Walter. *The Origin of German Tragic Drama [Ursprung des deutschen Trauerspiels].* 1928. Trans. John Osborne. London: New Left, 1977.

Ben-Porat, Ziva. "The Poetics of Literary Allusion." *PTL* 1 (1976): 105–28.

Berger, Charles. "Merrill and Pynchon: Our Apocalyptic Scribes." Lehman and Berger 282–97.

———. "Vision in the Form of a Task: *The Double Dream of Spring.*" Lehman, *Beyond Amazement* 163–208.

Berger, Peter L. and Thomas Luckmann. *The Social Construction of Reality: A Treatise in the Sociology of Knowledge.* Garden City, NY: Doubleday, 1966.

Bernstein, Charles. *My Way: Speeches and Poems.* Chicago: U of Chicago P, 1999.

———. *A Poetics.* Cambridge, MA: Harvard UP, 1992.

———, ed. *The Politics of Poetic Form: Poetry and Public Policy.* New York: Roof, 1990.

Bernstein, Michael André. *The Tale of the Tribe: Ezra Pound and the Modern Verse Epic.* Princeton, NJ: Princeton UP, 1980.

Berryman, John. "Homage to Mistress Bradstreet." 1953. *Collected Poems 1937–1971.* Ed. Charles Thornbury. New York: Farrar, 1989. 131–48.

———. *77 Dream Songs.* New York: Farrar, 1964.

Bertens, Hans. *The Idea of the Postmodern: A History.* London: Routledge, 1995.

Bérubé, Michael. *Marginal Forces/Cultural Centers: Tolson, Pynchon, and the Politics of the Canon.* Ithaca, NY: Cornell UP, 1992.

Bezner, Kevin. "Edward Dorn: An Interview." *American Poetry Review* 21.5 (1992): 43–46.

Blasing, Mutlu Konuk. *Politics and Form in Postmodern Poetry: O'Hara, Bishop, Ashbery, and Merrill.* Cambridge: Cambridge UP, 1995.

Bloom, Harold. "The Charity of the Hard Moments." 1976. Bloom, *John Ashbery* 49–79.

———. Introduction. Bloom, *John Ashbery* 1–16.

———. "Introduction: The Survival of Strong Poetry." Hill, *Somewhere* xiii–xxv.

———, ed. *John Ashbery: Modern Critical Views.* New York: Chelsea, 1985.

Brossard, Nicole. "Poetic Politics." Bernstein, *Politics of Poetic Form* 73–86.

Buck-Morss, Susan. *The Dialectics of Seeing: Walter Benjamin and the Arcades Project*. Cambridge, MA: MIT P, 1989.

Bunting, Basil. *Collected Poems*. New York: Oxford UP, 1988.

Butterick, George. "The Mysterious Vision of Susan Howe." *North Dakota Quarterly* 55.4 (Fall 1987): 312–21.

Butwin, Joseph. " 'The Winter Count': Politics in the Poetry of Thomas McGrath." *North Dakota Quarterly* 50.4 (Fall 1982): 59–68.

Calinescu, Matei. *Five Faces of Modernity: Modernism, Avant-Garde, Decadence, Kitsch, Postmodernism*. Durham, NC: Duke UP, 1987.

Campbell, Mary Schmidt, et al. *Harlem Renaissance: Art of Black America*. New York: Studio Museum in Harlem, Abrams, 1987.

Carroll, Paul. "If Only He Had Left from the Finland Station." *The Poem in Its Skin*. Chicago: Follett, 1968. 6–26.

Castle, Terry. *Masquerade and Civilization: The Carnivalesque in Eighteenth-Century English Culture and Fiction*. Stanford, CA: Stanford UP, 1986.

Cavanagh, Sheila T. " 'The fatal destiny of that land': Elizabethan Views of Ireland." *Representing Ireland: Literature and the Origins of Conflict, 1534–1660*. Ed. Brendan Bradshaw, Andrew Hadfield, and Willy Maley. Cambridge: Cambridge UP, 1993. 116–31.

Clark, Katernia and Michael Holquist. *Mikhail Bakhtin*. Cambridge, MA: Harvard UP, 1984.

Conrad, Peter. *Romantic Opera and Literary Form*. Berkeley: U of California P, 1977.

Conte, Joseph M. *Unending Design: The Forms of Postmodern Poetry*. Ithaca NY: Cornell UP, 1991.

Cope, Jackson I. *Joyce's Cities: Archaeologies of the Soul*. Baltimore: Johns Hopkins UP, 1981.

Costello, Bonnie. "John Ashbery's Landscapes." Schultz 60–80.

Coughlan, Patricia, ed. *Spenser and Ireland: An Interdisciplinary Perspective*. Cork: Cork UP, 1989.

Cronin, Anthony. *Samuel Beckett: The Last Modernist*. New York: HarperCollins, 1997.

Culler, Jonathan. "Apostrophe." Culler, *Pursuit* 135–54.

———. "Beyond Interpretation." Culler, *Pursuit* 3–17.

———. *The Pursuit of Signs: Semiotics, Literature, Deconstruction*. London: Routledge Kegan Paul, 1981.

Damon, Maria. *The Dark End of the Street: Margins in American Vanguard Poetry*. Minneapolis: U of Minnesota P, 1993.

Davenport, Guy. "Olson." *The Geography of the Imagination: Forty Essays*. San Francisco: North Point, 1981. 80–99.

Davidson, Michael. "Archaeologist of Morning: Charles Olson, Edward Dorn, and Historical Method." *ELH* 47.1 (1980): 158–79.

———. "Discourse in Poetry: Bakhtin and Extensions of the Dialogical." *Code of Signals: Recent Writings in Poetics*. Ed. Michael Palmer. Berkeley, CA: North Atlantic, 1983. 143–50.

———. *Ghostlier Demarcations: Modern Poetry and the Material Word*. Berkeley: U of California P, 1997.

———. *The San Francisco Renaissance: Poetics and Community at Mid-Century*. Cambridge: Cambridge UP, 1989.

———. " 'To eliminate the draw': Narrative and Language in *Slinger*." Wesling 113–49.

De Jongh, James. *Vicious Modernism: Black Harlem and the Literary Imagination*. Cambridge: Cambridge UP, 1990.

Derrida, Jacques. *Of Grammatology*. 1967. Trans. Gayatri Spivak. Baltimore: Johns Hopkins UP, 1976.

Derrida, Jacques and Peter Eisenman. *Chora L Works*. Ed. Jeffrey Kipnes and Thomas Leeser. New York: Monacelli, 1997.

Des Pres, Terence. *Praises and Dispraises: Poetry and Politics, the Twentieth Century*. New York: Viking, 1988.

Dewey, Anne. "The Relation between Open Form and Collective Voice: The Social Origin of Processual Form in John Ashbery's *Three Poems* and Ed Dorn's *Gunslinger*." *Sagetrieb* 11.1–2 (1992): 47–66.

Dick, Bruce and Amritjit Singh, eds. *Conversations with Ishmael Reed*. Jackson: UP of Mississippi, 1995.

Dickie, Margaret. *On the Modernist Long Poem*. Iowa City: U of Iowa P, 1986.

Disposable Heroes of Hiphoprisy, The. *Hypocrisy Is the Greatest Luxury*. 4th & B'way/Island Records, 1992.

Dodsworth, Martin. "*Mercian Hymns:* Offa, Charlemagne, and Geoffrey Hill." Robinson, *Geoffrey Hill* 49–61.

Dorn, Edward. *The Collected Poems, 1956–1974*. Enlarged edn. San Francisco: Four Seasons Foundation, 1983.

———. *The Cycle*. West Newbury, MA: Frontier P, 1971.

———. *Gunslinger*. Durham, NC: Duke UP, 1989.

———. *Interviews*. Ed. Donald Allen. Bolinas, CA: Four Seasons Foundation, 1980.

———. *Recollections of Gran Apachería*. San Francisco: Turtle Island Foundation, 1974.

Douglas, Ann. *Terrible Honesty: Mongrel Manhattan in the 1920s*. New York: Farrar, 1995.

Dove, Rita. "Telling It Like It I-S *IS:* Narrative Techniques in Melvin Tolson's *Harlem Gallery*." *New England Review and Bread Loaf Quarterly* 8.1 (1985): 109–17.

DuPlessis, Rachel Blau. "Manifests." *Diacritics* 26.3–4 (Fall–Winter 1996): 31–53.

———. "On Drafts: A Memorandum of Understanding," *TO: A Journal of Poetry, Prose, and the Visual Arts* 1.1 (Summer 1992): 72–77.

———. *The Pink Guitar: Writing as Feminist Practice*. New York: Routledge, 1990.

———. "Surface Tensions: Thinking about Andrews." *Aerial* 9 (1999): 49–61.

Dworkin, Craig. "'Waging political babble': Susan Howe's Visual Prosody and the Politics of Noise." *Word & Image* 12.4 (October 1996): 389–405.

Edwards, Michael. "Hill's Imitations." Robinson, *Geoffrey Hill* 159–71.

Eisenman, Peter. *House of Cards*. New York: Oxford UP, 1987.

———. *House X*. New York: Rizzoli, 1982.

———. "Misreading." Eisenman, *House of Cards* 167–86.

Eliot, T. S. "What Is Minor Poetry?" 1944. *On Poetry and Poets*. New York: Farrar, 1957. 34–51.

Eskin, Michael. "Bakhtin on Poetry." *Poetics Today* 21.2 (Summer 2000): 379–91.

Even-Zohar, Itamar. "The 'Literary System'." *Poetics Today* 11.1(Spring 1990): 27–44.

Ewbank, Inga-Stina. "'These pretty devices': A Study of Masques in Plays." *A Book of Masques: In Honour of Allardyce Nicoll*. Cambridge: Cambridge UP, 1967. 407–48.

Farnsworth, Robert M. Afterword. Tolson, *Gallery of Harlem Portraits* 255–71.

———. *Melvin B. Tolson, 1898–1966: Plain Talk and Poetic Prophecy*. Columbia: U of Missouri P, 1984.

Finkelstein, Norman. *Not One of Them in Place: Modern Poetry and Jewish American Identity*. Albany: SUNY Press, 2001.

Fischer, Lucy. "*A Question of Silence:* Ritual in Transfigured Time." *Shot/Countershot: Film Tradition and Women's Cinema*. Princeton, NJ: Princeton UP, 1989. 282–300.

Flasch, Joy. *Melvin B. Tolson*. New York: Twayne, 1972.

Fogarty, Anne, ed. *Spenser in Ireland:* The Faerie Queene *1596–1996*. Spec. issue of *Irish University Review* 26.2 (Autumn/Winter 1996).

Folkenflik, Robert. "Macpherson, Chatterton, Blake, and the Great Age of Literary Forgery." *Centennial Review* 18.4 (1974): 378–91.

Forrest-Thomson, Veronica. *Collected Poems and Translations*. London: Allardyce, 1990.

———. *Poetic Artifice: A Theory of Twentieth-Century Poetry*. Manchester: Manchester UP, 1978.

Foster, Thomas. "'Kick[ing] the Perpendiculars Outa Right Anglos': Edward Dorn's Multiculturalism." *Contemporary Literature* 38.1(1997): 78–105.

Foucault, Michel. *The Archaeology of Knowledge and the Discourse on Language*. Trans. A. M. Sheridan Smith. New York: Pantheon, 1972.

Fox, Robert Elliot. "Ishmael Reed: Gathering the Limbs of Osiris." *Conscientious Sorcerers: The Black Postmodernist Fiction of Leroi Jones/Amiri Baraka, Ishmael Reed, and Samuel R. Delany*. New York: Greenwood P, 1989. 39–92.

Frank, Robert and Henry Sayre, eds. *The Line in Postmodern Poetry*. Urbana: U of Illinois P, 1988.

Frank, Suzanne. *Peter Eisenman's House VI: The Client's Response*. New York: Whitney Library of Design, Watson-Guptill, 1994.

Fraser, Kathleen. *Translating the Unspeakable: Poetry and the Innovative Necessity*. Tuscaloosa: U of Alabama P, 2000.

Fredman, Stephen. *The Grounding of American Poetry: Charles Olson and the Emersonian Tradition.* Cambridge: Cambridge UP, 1993.

Fredman, Stephen and Grant Jenkins. "First Annotations to Edward Dorn's *Gunslinger.*" *Sagetrieb* 15.3 (1996): 57–176.

Friedman, Susan Stanford. "When a 'Long' Poem Is a 'Big' Poem: Self-Authorizing Strategies in Women's Twentieth-Century 'Long Poems'." *LIT* 2 (1990): 9–25.

Frisby, David. "Walter Benjamin: Prehistory of Modernity." *Fragments of Modernity: Theories of Modernity in the Work of Simmel, Kracauer, and Benjamin.* Cambridge, MA: MIT P, 1986. 187–272.

Frye, Northrop. *Anatomy of Criticism: Four Essays.* Princeton, NJ: Princeton UP, 1957.

Gamwell, Lynn and Richard Wells, eds., *Sigmund Freud and Art: His Personal Collection of Antiquities.* New York: Abrams, 1989.

Gandelsonas, Marcel. "From Structure to Subject: The Formation of an Architectural Language." 1978. Eisenman, *House X* 7–31.

Gates, Henry Louis, Jr. "The blackness of blackness: a critique of the sign and the Signifying Monkey." *Black Literature and Literary Theory.* Ed. Henry Louis Gates, Jr. New York: Methuen, 1984. 285–321.

Gery, John. "Ashbery's Menagerie and the Anxiety of Affluence." Schultz 126–45.

Gibbons, Reginald and Terrence Des Pres, eds. *Thomas McGrath: Life and the Poem.* Urbana: U of Illinois P, 1992.

Gibson, William. *Neuromancer.* New York: Ace, 1984.

Gifford, Henry. "Hill and the Dictionary." Robinson, *Geoffrey Hill* 149–58.

Gingerich, Willard. "Armand Schwerner: An Interview." *American Poetry Review* 24.5 (1995): 27–32.

———. "An Interview with Armand Schwerner." *Hambone* 11(1994): 28–51.

Gintz, Claude. "Neoclassical Rearmament." *Art in America* 76.2(1987): 110–17.

Glob, P. V. *The Bog People: Iron-Age Man Preserved.* Ithaca, NY: Cornell UP, 1969.

Golding, Alan. "Bruce Andrews's Poetics and the Limits of Genre." *Aerial* 9 (1999): 196–207.

———. "'Drawing with Words': Susan Howe's Visual Poetics." *We Who Love to Be Astonished: Experimental Women's Writing and Performance Poetics.* Ed. Laura Hinton and Cynthia Hogue. Tuscaloosa: U of Alabama P, 2002. 152–64.

———. "History, Mutation, and the Mutation of History in Edward Dorn's *Gunslinger.*" *World, Self, Poem: Essays on Contemporary Poetry from the "Jubilation of Poets".* Ed. Leonard M. Trawick. Kent, OH: Kent State UP, 1990. 44–58. Reprinted from *Sagetrieb* 6.1(1987): 7–20.

Green, Fiona. "'Plainly on the Other Side': Susan Howe's Recovery." *Contemporary Literature* 42.1 (2001): 78–101.

Greenberg, Harvey. Rev. of *The Piano. Film Quarterly* 47.3 (Spring 1994): 46–50.

Greenblatt, Stephen. "To Fashion a Gentleman: Spenser and the Destruction of the Bower of Bliss." *Renaissance Self-Fashioning.* Chicago: U of Chicago P, 1980. 157–92.

Greene, Thomas. *The Descent from Heaven: A Study in Epic Continuity.* New Haven: Yale UP, 1963.

Grooms, Red. *Ruckus Rodeo.* New York: Abrams, 1988.

Guthrie, W. K. C. *The Earlier Presocratics and the Pythagoreans.* Cambridge: Cambridge UP, 1962.

Hadfield, Andrew. *Edmund Spenser's Irish Experience: Wilde Fruit and Salvage Soyl.* Oxford: Oxford UP, 1997.

Hafif, Marcia. "Silence in painting: Let me count the ways." *Silence: Interdisciplinary Perspectives.* Ed. Adam Jaworski. Berlin: Mouton de Gruyter, 1997. 339–49.

Hall, Donald. "McGrath's Invective." *North Dakota Quarterly* 50.4 (Fall 1982): 90–91.

Halliday, M. A. K. and Ruqaiya Hasan. *Cohesion in English.* London: Longman, 1976.

Harbison, Robert. *The Built, the Unbuilt, and the Unbuildable.* Cambridge, MA: MIT P, 1991.

Harrison, Robert Pogue. *Forests: The Shadow of Civilization.* Chicago: U of Chicago P, 1992.

Hart, Henry. *The Poetry of Geoffrey Hill.* Carbondale: Southern Illinois UP, 1986.

Hartley, George. *Textual Politics and the Language Poets.* Bloomington: Indiana UP, 1989.

Hartman, Charles O. *Virtual Muse: Experiments in Computer Poetry.* Hanover, NH: UP of New England, Wesleyan UP, 1996.

Harvey, David. *The Condition of Postmodernity: An Enquiry into the Origins of Cultural Change.* Oxford: Blackwell, 1989.

Hassan, Ihab. *The Dismemberment of Orpheus: Toward a Postmodern Literature.* 1971. 2nd ed. Madison: U of Wisconsin P, 1982.

———. *The Literature of Silence: Henry Miller and Samuel Beckett.* New York: Knopf, 1967.

Haywood, Ian. *Faking It: Art and the Politics of Forgery.* New York: St. Martin's P, 1987.

———. *The Making of History: A Study of the Literary Forgeries of James Macpherson and Thomas Chatterton in Relation to Eighteenth-Century Ideas of History and Fiction.* Rutherford, NJ: Fairleigh Dickinson UP; London: Associated Univ. Presses, 1986.

Heaney, Seamus. *North.* New York: Oxford UP, 1976.

Heidegger, Martin. "Letter on Humanism." 1947. Trans. Frank A. Capuzzi and J. Glenn Gray. *Basic Writings from* Being and Time *(1927) to* The Task of Thinking *(1964).* Ed. David Farrell Krell. New York: Harper, 1977. 193–242.

Henderson, Stephen. "Introduction: The Forms of Things Unknown." *Understanding the New Black Poetry: Black Speech and Black Music as Poetic References.* New York: Morrow, 1973. 3–69.

Henley, Pauline. *Spenser in Ireland.* 1928. New York: Russell, 1969.

Higgins, Dick. *A Dialectic of Centuries: Notes toward a Theory of the New Arts.* New York: Printed Editions, 1978.

Hill, Geoffrey. *Collected Poems.* New York: Oxford UP, 1986.

———. *Somewhere Is Such a Kingdom: Poems 1952–1971.* Boston: Houghton, 1975.

Hirshkop, Ken. "Dialogism as a Challenge to Literary Criticism." *Discontinuous Dis-*

courses in Modern Russian Literature. Ed. Catriona Kelly, Michael Makin, and David Shepherd. New York: St. Martin's P, 1989. 19–35.

Hofstadter, Douglas. *Godel, Escher, Bach: An Eternal Golden Braid.* Harmondsworth: Penguin, 1980.

Holden, Jonathan. *The Rhetoric of the Contemporary Lyric.* Bloomington: Indiana UP, 1980.

Hollander, John. *The Untuning of the Sky: Ideas of Music in English Poetry, 1500–1700.* Princeton, NJ: Princeton UP, 1961.

Holly, Grant I. "The Ruins of Allegory and the Allegory of Ruins." *Postmodernism across the Ages: Essays for a Postmodernity That Wasn't Born Yesterday.* Ed. Bill Readings and Bennet Schaber. Syracuse, NY: Syracuse UP, 1993. 188–215.

Hoover, Paul, ed. *Postmodern American Poetry: A Norton Anthology.* New York: Norton, 1994.

Howe, Susan. *The Birth-Mark: Unsettling the Wilderness in American Literary History.* Hanover, NH: UP of New England, Wesleyan UP, 1993.

———. *The Europe of Trusts.* Los Angeles: Sun & Moon P, 1990.

———. *Frame Structures: Early Poems, 1974–1979.* New York: New Directions, 1996.

———. *My Emily Dickinson.* Berkeley CA: North Atlantic, 1985.

Hrushovski [Harshav], Benjamin. "Poetic Metaphor and Frames of Reference." *Poetics Today* 5.1 (1984): 5–43.

———. "The Structure of Semiotic Objects: A Three-Dimensional Model." *Poetics Today* 1.1–2 (1979): 363–76.

Humphries, Jefferson. "The Voice within the Mirror: The Haunted Poetry of James Merrill." *boundary 2* 15.3 (spring/fall 1988): 173–94.

Hutcheon, Linda. *A Poetics of Postmodernism: History, Theory, Fiction.* New York: Routledge, 1988.

Huyssen, Andreas. *After the Great Divide: Modernism, Mass Culture, Postmodernism.* Bloomington: Indiana UP, 1986.

Inman, P. "Early/Later (2 Scenarios for/on Bruce Andrews)." *Aerial* 9 (1999): 88–90.

Jacoff, Rachel. "Merrill and Dante." Lehman and Berger, 145–58.

Jameson, Fredric. "Architecture and the Critique of Ideology." 1982, 1985. Jameson, *Syntax* 35–60.

———. *The Ideologies of Theory: Essays 1971–1986.* Vol. 2. *The Syntax of History.* Minneapolis: U of Minnesota P, 1988.

———. "Periodizing the Sixties." 1984. Jameson, *Syntax* 178–208.

———. "Postmodernism, or, The Cultural Logic of Late Capitalism." *New Left Review* 146 (July–August 1984): 53–94.

———. *Postmodernism, or, The Cultural Logic of Late Capitalism.* Durham, NC: Duke UP, 1991.

Janowitz, Anne. *England's Ruins: Poetic Purpose and the National Landscape.* Cambridge, MA: Blackwell, 1990.

Jaynes, Julian. *The Origins of Consciousness in the Breakdown of the Bicameral Mind.* Boston: Houghton, 1976.

Jencks, Charles. *The Language of Post-Modern Architecture.* 4th ed. London: Academy Editions, 1984.

———. "Postmodern Architecture and Time Fusion." *International Postmodernism: Theory and Literary Practice.* Ed. Hans Bertens and Douwe Fokkema. Amsterdam: Benjamins, 1997. 123–28.

———. *What Is Post-Modernism?* London: Academy Editions; New York: St. Martin's P, 1986.

Jenkins, Grant. "*Gunslinger*'s Ethics of Excess: Subjectivity, Community, and the Politics of the Could Be." *Sagetrieb* 15.3 (1996): 207–42.

Johnson, Philip and Mark Wigley. *Deconstructivist Architecture.* New York: Museum of Modern Art; Boston: Little, Brown, 1988.

Jonson, Ben. *Epicoene, or The Silent Woman.* 1609. *The Complete Plays of Ben Jonson.* Ed. G. A. Wilkes. Vol. 3. New York: Oxford UP, 1982. 121–222.

Joyce, James. *Ulysses.* Harmondsworth: Penguin, 1973.

Kalaidjian, Walter. *American Culture between the Wars: Revisionary Modernism and Postmodern Critique.* New York: Columbia UP, 1993.

Kaminsky, Stuart M. "Variations on a Major Genre: The Big Caper Film." *American Film Genres: Approaches to a Critical Theory of Popular Film.* Dayton, OH: Pflaum, 1974. 74–99.

Kane, Paul. "An Australian Hoax." *Raritan* 11.2 (1991): 82–98.

Karatani, Kojin. *Architecture as Metaphor: Language, Number, Money.* Trans. Sabu Kohso. Ed. Michael Speaks. Cambridge, MA: MIT P, 1995.

Keller, Lynn. *Forms of Expansion: Recent Long Poems by Women.* Chicago: U of Chicago P, 1997.

———. *Re-making It New: Contemporary American Poetry and the Modernist Tradition.* Cambridge: Cambridge UP, 1987.

Kenner, Hugh. *The Pound Era.* Berkeley: U of California P, 1971.

Kinnahan, Linda. *Poetics of the Feminine: Authority and Literary Tradition in William Carlos Williams, Mina Loy, Denise Levertov, and Kathleen Fraser.* Cambridge: Cambridge UP, 1994.

Kirk, G. S., J. F. Raven, and M. Schofield. *The Presocratic Philosophers: A Critical History with a Selection of Texts.* 2nd ed. Cambridge: Cambridge UP, 1983.

Knapp, Steven. *Personification and the Sublime: Milton to Coleridge.* Cambridge MA: Harvard UP, 1985.

Knottenbelt, E. M. *Passionate Intelligence: The Poetry of Geoffrey Hill.* Amsterdam: Rodopi, 1990.

Koch, Kenneth. *The Pleasures of Peace and Other Poems.* New York: Grove, 1969.

Krauss, Rosalind. "Death of a Hermeneutic Phantom: Materialization of the Sign in the Work of Peter Eisenman." 1977. Eisenman, *House of Cards* 166–84.

Kuberski, Philip. "'The Metaphysics of Postmodern Death': Mailer's *Ancient Evenings* and Merrill's *The Changing Light at Sandover*." *ELH* 56.1 (Spring 1989): 229–54.

Kushner, Tony. *Angels in America, Part Two: Perestroika.* New York: Theatre Communications Group, 1994.

Kuspit, Donald. "A Mighty Metaphor: The Analogy of Archaeology and Psycho-analysis." Gamwell and Wells 133–51.

Lakoff, Robin. "Cries and Whispers: The Shattering of the Silence." *Gender Articulated: Language and the Socially Constructed Self.* Ed. Kira Hall and Mary Bucholtz. New York: Routledge, 1995. 25–50.

Landau, Misia. *Narratives of Human Evolution.* New Haven: Yale UP, 1991.

Lazer, Hank. "Sacred Forgery and the Grounds of Poetic Archaeology: Armand Schwerner's *The Tablets.*" *Chicago Review* 46.1(2000): 142–54.

———. " 'To make equality less drab': The Writings of Bruce Andrews." *Readings.* Vol. 2 of *Opposing Poetries.* Evanston IL: Northwestern UP, 1996. 77–94.

Lehman, David, ed. *Beyond Amazement: New Essays on John Ashbery.* Ithaca, NY: Cornell UP, 1980.

———. "Elemental Bravery: The Unity of James Merrill's Poetry." Lehman and Berger 23–60.

———. "The Ern Malley Hoax: Australia's 'National Poet,'" *Shenandoah* 34.4 (1983): 47–73.

———. *The Last Avant-Garde: The Making of the New York School of Poets.* New York: Doubleday, 1998.

Lehman, David and Charles Berger, eds. *James Merrill: Essays in Criticism.* Ithaca, NY: Cornell UP, 1983.

Levinson, Marjorie. *The Romantic Fragment Poem: A Critique of a Form.* Chapel Hill: U of North Carolina P, 1986.

Levy, Andrew. "Fluoroscopy of the Text: Reflections on Bruce Andrews's *Give Em Enough Rope* and *I Don't Have Any Paper So Shut Up.*" *Aerial* 9 (1999): 82–87.

Lewin, Roger. *Bones of Contention: Controversies in the Search for Human Origins.* New York: Simon, 1988.

Lindroth, James. R. "From Krazy Kat to Hoodoo: Aesthetic Discourse in the Fiction of Ishmael Reed." *Review of Contemporary Fiction* 4.2 (1984): 227–33.

Lockwood, William J. "Art Rising to Clarity: Edward Dorn's Compleat *Slinger.*" Wesling 150–207.

Lyons, John. *Semantics.* Vol. I. Cambridge: Cambridge UP, 1977.

Lyotard, Jean-François. "Appendix: Answering the Question: What Is Postmodernism?" *The Postmodern Condition: A Report on Knowledge.* Minneapolis: U of Minnesota P, 1984. 71–82.

Mack, John E. *Abduction: Human Encounters with Aliens.* New York: Scribner's, 1994.

Mackey, Nathaniel. *Discrepant Engagement: Dissonance, Cross-Culturality, and Experimental Writing.* Cambridge: Cambridge UP, 1993.

Macrae-Gibson, Gavin. *The Secret Life of Buildings: An American Mythology for Modern Architecture.* Cambridge, MA: MIT P, 1985.

Maley, Willy. " 'Who knowes not Arlo-hill?': Changing Places in *The Faerie Queene.*" *Salvaging Spenser: Colonialism, Culture, and Identity.* New York: St. Martin's P, 1997. 78–98.

Manfred, Frederick. "Tom." Stern, *Revolutionary Poet.* 55–58.

Martin, Stephen-Paul. "Susan Howe: The Book of Cordelia." *Open Form and the Feminine Imagination: The Politics of Reading in Twentieth-Century Innovative Writing.* Washington, DC: Maisonneuve, 1988. 159–71.

Mathews, Harry and Alastair Brotchie, eds. *Oulipo Compendium.* London: Atlas P, 1998.

Mazzocco, Robert. "The Right Stuff." 1983. Polito 208–21.

McCaffery, Larry. "Avant-Pop: Still Life after Yesterday's Crash." *After Yesterday's Crash: The Avant-Pop Anthology.* Ed. Larry McCaffery. New York: Penguin, 1995. xi–xxxi.

McElroy, Joseph. *Women and Men.* New York: Knopf, 1987.

McFarland, Thomas. *Romanticism and the Forms of Ruin: Wordsworth, Coleridge, and Modalities of Fragmentation.* Princeton, NJ: Princeton UP, 1981.

McGann, Jerome. "'The Apparatus of Loss': Bruce Andrews Writing." *Aerial* 9 (1999): 183–95.

———. "Composition as Explanation (of Modern and Postmodern Poetries)." *Black Riders: The Visible Language of Modernism.* Princeton, NJ: Princeton UP, 1993. 76–117.

McGee, Patrick. *Ishmael Reed and the Ends of Race.* New York: St. Martin's P, 1997.

McGrath, Thomas. "From *Letter to an Imaginary Friend.*" *Passages toward the Dark.* Port Townsend, WA: Copper Canyon P, 1982. 97–131.

———. *Letter to an Imaginary Friend.* Port Townsend, WA: Copper Canyon P, 1997.

McHale, Brian. "Against Interpretation: Iconic Grammar, Anxiety of Influence, and Poetic Artifice." *Poetics Today* 3.1 (1982): 141–58.

———. "Brit-Pop, or Bringing It All Back Home: On Andrew Greig's *Western Swing.*" *The Yale Journal of Criticism* 13.1 (Spring 2000): 195–205.

———. *Constructing Postmodernism.* London: Routledge, 1992.

———. "Gravity's Angels in America, or, Pynchon's Angelology Revisited." *Pynchon Notes* 42–43 (Spring–Fall 1998): 303–16.

———. "Making (Non)sense of Postmodernist Poetry." *Language, Text, and Context: Essays in Stylistics.* Ed. Michael Toolan. London: Routledge, 1992. 6–35.

———. "Modernist Reading, Postmodernist Text: The Case of *Gravity's Rainbow.*" *Poetics Today* 1.1–2 (Autumn 1979): 85–110.

———. "'A Poet May Not Exist': Mock-Hoaxes and the Construction of National Identity." *Faces of Anonymity.* Ed. Robert Griffin. New York: Palgrave, 2003. 233–52.

———. "Poetry as Prosthesis." *Poetics Today* 21.1 (Spring 2000): 1–32.

———. *Postmodernist Fiction.* New York: Methuen, 1987.

———. "Postmodernist Lyric and the Ontology of Poetry." *Poetics Today* 8.1 (1987): 19–44.

———. "Telling Stories Again: On the Replenishment of Narrative in the Postmodernist Long Poem." Ed. Nicola Bradbury. *Yearbook of English Studies* 30 (2000): 250–62.

———. "Topology of a Phantom City: *The Tablets* as Hoax." *Talisman* 19 (Winter 1998/99): 86–89.

———. "Weak Narrativity: The Case of Avant-Garde Narrative Poetry." *Narrative* 9.2 (May 2001): 161–67.

McHale, Brian and Moshe Ron. "On Not-Knowing How to Read Barthelme's 'The Indian Uprising'." *Review of Contemporary Fiction* 11.2 (Summer 1991): 50–68.

McHoul, Alec and David Wills. *Writing Pynchon: Strategies in Fictional Analysis.* Urbana: U of Illinois P, 1990.

McPheron, William. *Edward Dorn.* Boise, ID: Boise State UP, 1988.

Megill, Allan. *Prophets of Extremity: Nietzsche, Heidegger, Foucault, Derrida.* Berkeley: U of California P, 1985.

Merrill, James. *The Changing Light at Sandover.* New York: Atheneum, 1982.

———. *A Different Person: A Memoir.* New York: Knopf, 1993.

———. *Recitative: Prose.* Ed. J. D. McClatchy. San Francisco: North Point, 1986.

———. *A Scattering of Salts.* New York: Knopf, 1985.

Michelson, Peter. "Edward Dorn, Inside the Outskirts." *Sagetrieb* 15.3 (1996): 177–206.

Middleton, Peter. "On Ice: Julia Kristeva, Susan Howe, and Avant-Garde Poetics." Ed. Antony Easthope and John O. Thompson. *Contemporary Poetry Meets Modern Theory.* Toronto: U of Toronto P, 1991. 81–95.

Miller, R. Baxter, ed. *Black American Poets between Worlds, 1940–1960.* Tennessee Studies in Literature, Vol. 30. Knoxville: U of Tennessee P, 1986.

Moffett, Judith. *James Merrill: An Introduction to the Poetry.* New York: Columbia UP, 1984.

Mohanty, S. P. and Jonathan Monroe. "John Ashbery and the Articulation of the Social." *Diacritics* 17.2 (Spring-Summer 1987): 37–63.

Molesworth, Charles. "Scripts for the Pageant." 1980. Polito 173–77.

Møller, Lis. *The Freudian Reading: Analytical and Fictional Constructions.* Philadelphia: U of Pennsylvania P, 1991.

Moore, Steven. "Alexander Theroux's *Darconville's Cat* and the Tradition of Learnéd Wit." *Contemporary Literature* 27.2 (1986): 233–45.

Morrison, Blake. *Seamus Heaney.* London: Methuen, 1982.

Morson, Gary Saul and Caryl Emerson. *Mikhail Bakhtin: Creation of a Prosaics.* Stanford, CA: Stanford UP, 1990.

Mosher, Harold F. "Toward a Poetics of 'Descriptized' Narration." *Poetics Today* 12.3 (Fall 1991): 425–45.

Murphy, Andrew. *But the Irish Sea Betwixt Us: Ireland, Colonialism, and Renaissance Literature.* Lexington: UP of Kentucky, 1999.

Murphy, Patrick. "De/Reconstructing the 'I': PostFANTASTICmodernist Poetry." *Journal of the Fantastic in the Arts* 1.4 (1988): 39–47.

Neal, Larry. *Hoodoo Hollerin' Bebop Ghosts.* Washington, DC: Howard UP, 1974.

Nelson, Cary. "Lyric Politics: The Poetry of Edwin Rolfe." *Collected Poems of Edwin Rolfe.* Ed. Cary Nelson and Jefferson Hendricks. Urbana: U of Illinois P, 1993. 1–55.

———. *Our Last First Poets: Vision and History in Contemporary American Poetry.* Urbana: U of Illinois P, 1981.

———. *Repression and Recovery: Modern American Poetry and the Politics of Cultural Memory, 1910–1945*. Madison: U of Wisconsin P, 1989.

Nemoianu, Virgil. "Societal Models as Substitute Reality in Literature." *Poetics Today* 5.2 (1984): 275–97.

Nielsen, Aldon L. *Black Chant: Languages of African-American Postmodernism*. Cambridge: Cambridge UP, 1997.

———. *Writing between the Lines: Race and Intertextuality*. Athens: U of Georgia P, 1994.

Novak, Estelle Gershgoren. "The Dynamo School of Poets." *Contemporary Literature* 11.4 (Autumn 1970): 526–39.

Nussbaum, Emily. "Turning Japanese: The Hiroshima Poetry Hoax." *Lingua Franca* 6.7 (1996): 82–84.

Olsen, Tillie. *Silences*. New York: Seymour Lawrence-Delacorte, 1978.

Olson, Charles. "The Present Is Prologue." 1952. *Collected Prose of Charles Olson*, Ed. Donald Allen and Benjamin Friedlander. Berkeley: U of California P, 1997. 205–07.

Ondaatje, Michael, ed. *The Long Poem Anthology*. Toronto: Coach House P, 1979.

Orgel, Stephen. *The Jonsonian Masque*. Cambridge, MA: Harvard UP, 1965.

Paul, Sherman. "Edward Dorn." *The Lost America of Love: Rereading Robert Creeley, Edward Dorn, and Robert Duncan*. Baton Rouge: Louisiana State UP, 1981. 77–169.

Paxson, James J. *The Poetics of Personification*. Cambridge: Cambridge UP, 1994.

Peebles, Curtis. *Watch the Skies! A Chronicle of the Flying Saucer Myth*. Washington: Smithsonian Institution P, 1994.

Pentikäinen, Juha Y. *Kalevala Mythology*. Trans. and ed. Ritva Poom. Bloomington: Indiana UP, 1989.

Perelman, Bob. *The Marginalization of Poetry: Language Writing and Literary History*. Princeton, NJ: Princeton UP, 1996.

Perloff, Marjorie. " 'Collision or Collusion with History': Susan Howe's *Articulations of Sound Forms in Time*." *Poetic License: Essays on Modernist and Postmodernist Lyric*. Evanston, IL: Northwestern UP, 1990. 297–344.

———. "From Image to Action: The Return of Story in Postmodern Poetry." *The Dance of the Intellect: Studies in the Poetry of the Pound Tradition*. Cambridge: Cambridge UP, 1985. 155–71.

———. "In Search of the Authentic Other: The Poetry of Araki Yasusada." *Doubled Flowering: From the Notebooks of Araki Yasusada*. Trans. and ed. Tosa Motokiyu, Ojiu Norinaga, and Okura Kyojin. New York: Roof, 1997. 148–68.

———. Introduction. Dorn, *Gunslinger* v–xviii.

———. *The Poetics of Indeterminacy: Rimbaud to Cage*. Princeton, NJ: Princeton UP, 1981.

———. *Radical Artifice: Writing Poetry in the Age of Media*. Chicago: U of Chicago P, 1991.

———. "A Syntax of Contrariety." *Aerial* 9 (1999): 156–60.

———. *21st-Century Modernism: The "New" Poetics*. Malden, MA: Blackwell, 2002.

Polito, Robert. "Afterword: Tradition and an Individual Talent." Polito, *James Merrill's* 231–63.

———. "Introduction: Sibylline Listening." Polito, *James Merrill's* 1–15.

———, ed. *A Reader's Guide to James Merrill's* The Changing Light at Sandover. Ann Arbor: U of Michigan P, 1994.

Potter, Russell. *Spectacular Vernaculars: Hip-Hop and the Politics of Postmodernism.* Albany: SUNY P, 1995.

Powell, Richard J., et al. *Rhapsodies in Black: Art of the Harlem Renaissance.* Hayward Gallery, Inst. of Intl. Visual Arts, U of California P, 1997.

Pynchon, Thomas. *The Crying of Lot 49.* New York: Bantam, 1967.

———. *Gravity's Rainbow.* New York: Viking, 1973.

Quartermain, Peter. *Disjunctive Poetics: From Gertrude Stein and Louis Zukofsky to Susan Howe.* Cambridge: Cambridge UP, 1992.

Quilligan, Maureen. *The Language of Allegory: Defining the Genre.* Ithaca, NY: Cornell UP, 1979.

Rajan, Balachandra. *The Form of the Unfinished: English Poetics from Spenser to Pound.* Princeton, NJ: Princeton UP, 1985.

Ramanathan, Geetha. "Murder as Speech: Narrative Subjectivity in Marleen Gorris's *A Question of Silence.*" *Genders* 15 (Winter 1992): 58–71.

Rasula, Jed. "Andrews Extremities Bruce." *Aerial* 9 (1999): 23–27.

Reed, Ishmael. "Cab Calloway Stands In for the Moon." *19 Necromancers from Now.* Ed. Ishmael Reed. Garden City, NY: Doubleday, 1970. 293–309.

———. *Mumbo Jumbo.* New York: Bantam, 1973.

———. *Yellow Back Radio Broke-Down.* New York: Bard-Avon, 1977.

Reinfeld, Laura. "Susan Howe: Prisms." *Language Poetry: Writing as Rescue.* Baton Rouge: Louisiana State UP, 1992. 120–47.

Relihan, Joel C. *Ancient Menippean Satire.* Baltimore: Johns Hopkins UP, 1993.

Reynolds, Gary A. and Beryl J. Wright, eds. *Against the Odds: African-American Artists and the Harmon Foundation.* Newark NJ: Newark Museum, 1989.

Rich, Adrienne. *On Lies, Secrets, and Silence: Selected Press 1966–1978.* New York: Norton, 1979.

Richter, David H. "Dialogism in Poetry." *Studies in the Literary Imagination* 23.1 (1990): 9–27.

Riddel, Joseph. "A Somewhat Polemical Introduction: The Elliptical Poem." *Genre* 11 (1978): 459–77.

Riffaterre, Michael. *Semiotics of Poetry.* Bloomington: Indiana UP, 1978.

Robinson, Peter, ed. *Geoffrey Hill: Essays on his Work.* Milton Keynes: Open UP, 1985.

———. "Reading Geoffrey Hill." Robinson 196–218.

Rose, Tricia. *Black Noise: Rap Music and Black Culture in Contemporary America.* Hanover, NH: Wesleyan UP, UP of New England, 1994.

Rosenthal, M. L. and Sally Gall. *The Modern Poetic Sequence: The Genius of Modern Poetry.* New York: Oxford UP, 1983.

Ross, Andrews. "Doubting John Thomas." *The Future of Modernism: Symptoms of American Poetry.* New York: Columbia UP, 1986. 159–208.

Rotella, Guy, ed. *Critical Essays on James Merrill.* New York: Hall, 1996.

Ryan, Marie-Laure. *Possible Worlds, Artificial Intelligence, and Narrative Theory.* Bloomington: Indiana UP, 1991.

Sabatini, Arthur. "Armand Schwerner." *American Poets Since World War II, Fourth Series.* Ed. Joseph Conte. Vol. 165 of *Dictionary of Literary Biography.* Detroit: Gale, 1996. 242–53.

Sacks, Peter. "The Divine Translation: Elegaic Aspects of *The Changing Light at Sandover.*" Lehman and Berger 159–85.

Saez, Richard. "'At the Salon Level': Merrill's Apocalyptic Epic." Lehman and Berger 211–45.

Saunders, George R. "Silence and Noise as Emotion Management Styles: An Italian Case." Tannen and Saville-Troike 165–83.

Saville-Troike, Muriel. "The Place of Silence in an Integrated Theory of Communication." Tannen and Saville-Troike 3–18.

Schama, Simon. *Landscape and Memory.* New York: Knopf, 1995.

Schroeder, Patricia. "Point and Counterpoint in *Harlem Gallery.*" *CLA Journal* 27.2 (1983): 152–68.

Schultz, Susan M., ed. *The Tribe of John: Ashbery and Contemporary Poetry.* Tuscaloosa: U of Alabama P, 1995.

Schwerner, Armand. *The Tablets.* Orono, ME: Natl. Poetry Foundation, 1999.

Scott-Heron, Gil. *Pieces of a Man.* LP. Flying Dutchman Records/RCA, 1971.

Scully, James. "Line Break." Frank and Sayre 97–131.

———. *Line Break: Poetry as Social Practice.* Seattle: Bay Press, 1988.

Serres, Michel. *Angels: A Modern Myth.* Trans. Francis Cowper. Paris: Flammarion, 1995.

Shapiro, David. *House (Blown Apart).* Woodstock, NY: Overlook P, 1988.

———. *John Ashbery: An Introduction to the Poetry.* New York: Columbia UP, 1979.

Shapiro, Karl. Introduction. *Harlem Gallery: Book I, The Curator.* By Melvin Tolson. New York: Twayne, 1965. 11–15.

Sherry, Vincent. *The Uncommon Tongue: The Poetry and Criticism of Geoffrey Hill.* Ann Arbor: U of Michigan P, 1987.

Shetley, Vernon. *After the Death of Poetry: Poet and Audience in Contemporary America.* Durham, NC: Duke UP, 1993.

Shklovsky, Viktor. *Theory of Prose.* Trans. Benjamin Sher. Normal, IL: Dalkey Archive P, 1990.

Shoptaw, John. "James Merrill and John Ashbery." *The Columbia History of American Poetry.* Ed. Jay Parini and Brett C. Miller. New York: Columbia UP, 1993. 750–76.

———. "Lyric Cryptography." *Poetics Today* 21.1 (Spring 2000): 221–62.

———. "The Music of Construction: Measure and Polyphony in Ashbery and Bernstein." Schultz 211–57.

———. *On the Outside Looking Out: John Ashbery's Poetry.* Cambridge, MA: Harvard UP, 1994.

Shumway, David. *Michel Foucault.* Charlottesville: UP of Virginia, 1992.

Shusterman, Richard. "Art in Action, Art Infraction: Goodman, Rap, Pragmatism (New Reality Mix)." *Practicing Philosophy: Pragmatism and the Philosophical Life.* New York: Routledge, 1997. 131–53.

———. "The Fine Art of Rap." *New Literary History* 22 (1991): 613–32.

Silliman, Ron. "From *The New Sentence.*" 1980. *In the American Tree: Language, Realism, Poetry.* ed. Ron Silliman. Orono, ME: Natl. Poetry Foundation, 1986. 561–75.

Silliman, Ron, et al. "Aesthetic Tendency and the Politics of Poetry: A Manifesto." *Social Text* 7.1–2 (1988): 261–75.

Smitherman, Geneva. *Talkin and Testifyin: The Language of Black America.* 2nd ed. Detroit: Wayne State UP, 1986.

Sontag, Susan. "The Aesthetics of Silence." 1967. Sontag, *Sontag Reader* 181–204.

———. "Notes on 'Camp'." 1966. Sontag, *Sontag Reader* 105–19.

———. *A Susan Sontag Reader.* New York: Farrar, 1982.

Spence, Donald P. *The Freudian Metaphor: Toward Paradigm Change in Psychoanalysis.* New York: Norton, 1987.

Spencer, Frank. *Piltdown: A Scientific Forgery.* London: British Museum (Natural History), Oxford UP, 1990.

Spenser, Edmund. *Poetical Works.* Ed. J. C. Smith and E. De Selincourt. London: Oxford UP, 1970.

———. "A View of the Present State of Ireland." *The Works of Edmund Spenser: A Variorum Edition. The Prose Works.* Ed. Rudolf Gottfried. Baltimore: Johns Hopkins UP, 1949. 39–231.

Spiegelman, Willard. "Breaking the Mirror: Interruption in Merrill's Trilogy." Lehman and Berger 186–210.

Stallworthy, Jon. "The Poet as Archaeologist: W. B. Yeats and Seamus Heaney." *Review of English Studies* NS 33.130 (1982): 158–74.

Stallybrass, Peter and Allon White. *The Politics and Poetics of Transgression.* Ithaca, NY: Cornell UP, 1986.

Steiner, George. *Language and Silence: Essays on Language, Literature, and the Inhuman.* New York: Atheneum, 1967.

Stepto, Robert. "Afro-American Literature." *Columbia Literary History of the United States.* Ed. Emory Elliot. New York: Columbia UP, 1988. 785–99.

Stern, Frederick C. "'The Delegate for Poetry': McGrath as Communist Poet." *North Dakota Quarterly* 50.4 (Fall 1982): 107–15.

———, ed. *The Revolutionary Poet in the United States: The Poetry of Thomas McGrath.* Columbia: U of Missouri P, 1988.

———. "The Revolutionary Poet in the U.S.: The Poetry of Thomas McGrath." Stern, *Revolutionary Poet* 1–46.

Stewart, Susan. "The Birth of Authenticity in the Progress of Anxiety: Fragments of an Eighteenth-Century Daydream." *Crimes of Writing: Problems in the Containment of Representation.* New York: Oxford UP, 1991. 102–31.

———. "Lyric Possession." *Critical Inquiry* 22 (Autumn 1995): 34–63.

Stokes, Geoffrey. "The Red Eye of God: James Merrill's Reasons to Believe." 1983. Polito, *James Merrill's* 222–30.

Sukenick, Ronald. *Doggy Bag.* Boulder, CO: Black Ice, Fiction Collective Two, 1994.

——. "Thirteen Digressions." 1973. *In Form: Digressions on the Act of Fiction.* Carbondale: Southern Illinois UP, 1985. 16–33.

Suleiman, Susan Rubin. *Subversive Intent: Gender, Politics, and the Avant-Garde.* Cambridge, MA: Harvard UP, 1990.

Swift, Jonathan. *Journal to Stella.* Ed. Harold Williams. 2 vols. 1948. New York: Barnes, 1975.

——. *Poems.* Ed. Harold Williams. Vol. 2. Oxford: Oxford UP, 1937.

——. *The Prose Works. Miscellaneous and Autobiographical Pieces, Fragments, and Marginalia.* Ed. by Herbert Davis. Vol. 5. Oxford: Oxford UP, Blackwell, 1962.

Sword, Helen. "James Merrill, Sylvia Plath, and the Poetics of Ouija." *American Literature* 66.3(Sept. 1994): 553–72.

Tafuri, Manfredo. "Peter Eisenman: The Meditations of Icarus." 1980. Eisenman, *House of Cards* 167–87.

Taggart, John. "Play and the Poetry of Susan Howe." *Songs of Degrees: Essays on Contemporary Poetry and Poetics.* Tuscaloosa: U of Alabama P, 1994. 114–122.

Tannen, Deborah and Muriel Saville-Troike, eds. *Perspectives on Silence.* Norwood, NJ: Ablex, 1985.

Thesen, Sharon, ed. *The New Long Poem Anthology.* Toronto: Coach House P, 1991.

Thompson, E. P. "Homage to Thomas McGrath." Stern, *Revolutionary Poet* 104–49. Repr. in Gibbons and Des Pres 106–57.

Thompson, Gorden E. "Ambiguity in Tolson's *Harlem Gallery.*" *Callaloo* 9.1(1986): 159–70.

Tolson, Melvin B. *A Gallery of Harlem Portraits.* Ed. Robert M. Farnsworth. Columbia: U of Missouri P, 1979.

——. *Harlem Gallery, Book I: The Curator.* 1965. *"Harlem Gallery" and Other Poems of Melvin B. Tolson.* Ed. Raymond Nelson. Charlottesville: UP of Virginia, 1999. 207–469.

Torgovnik, Marianne. "Entering Freud's Study." *Gone Primitive: Savage Intellects, Modern Lives.* Chicago: U of Chicago P, 1990. 194–209.

Trevor-Roper, Hugh. "The Invention of Tradition: The Highland Tradition of Scotland." *The Invention of Tradition.* Ed. Eric Hobsbawm and Terence Ranger. Cambridge: Cambridge UP, 1985. 15–41.

Tschumi, Bernard. *Architecture and Disjunction.* Cambridge, MA: MIT P, 1994.

Tynyanov, Yury. "The Literary Fact." Trans. Ann Shukman. *Modern Genre Theory.* Ed. David Duff. Harlow, Eng.: Longman, 2000. 29–49.

Vanderborg, Susan. *Paratextual Communities: American Avant-Garde Poetry since 1950.* Carbondale: Southern Illinois UP, 2001.

Varnedoe, Kirk and Adam Gopnik. *High & Low: Modern Art & Popular Culture.* New York: Museum of Modern Art, 1990.

Vendler, Helen. "Mirabell: Books of Number." 1979. Polito, *James Merrill's* 162–72.

Venturi, Robert. *Complexity and Contradiction in Architecture.* 2nd edn. New York: Museum of Modern Art, 1977.

Venturi, Robert, Denise Scott Brown, and Steven Izenour. 1972. *Learning from Las*

Vegas: The Forgotten Symbolism of Architectural Form. rev. ed. Cambridge, MA: MIT P, 1977.

Vickery, Ann. *Leaving Lines of Gender: A Feminist Genealogy of Language Writing.* Hanover, NH: Wesleyan UP, UP of New England, 2000.

Vine, Richard. "Thank Heaven for Little Girls." *Art in America* 86.1 (January 1998): 72–79.

von Hallberg, Robert. *American Poetry and Culture 1945–1980.* Cambridge, MA: Harvard UP, 1985.

———. "This Marvellous Accidentalism." Wesling 45–86.

Wald, Alan. *The Revolutionary Imagination: The Poetry and Politics of John Wheelwright and Sherry Mangan.* Chapel Hill: U of North Carolina P, 1983.

Ward, Geoff. *Statutes of Liberty: The New York School of Poetry.* New York: St. Martin's P, 1993.

Watten, Barrett. *Bad History.* Berkeley, CA: Atelos, Hip's Road, 1998.

———. "Social Formalism: Zukofsky, Andrews, and Habitus in Contemporary Poetry." *North Dakota Quarterly* 55.4 (Fall 1987): 365–82.

Werner, Craig Hansen. *Playing the Changes: From Afro-Modernism to the Jazz Impulse.* Urbana: U of Illinois P, 1994.

Wesling, Donald, ed. *Internal Resistances: The Poetry of Edward Dorn.* Berkeley: U of California P, 1985.

Westover, Jeff. "Writing on the (Sur)face of the Past: Convivial Visions and Revisions in the Poetry of James Merrill." Rotella 215–30.

Whitman, Walt. *Leaves of Grass: A Textual Variorum of the Printed Poems.* Vol. I. *Poems, 1855–1856.* Ed. Sculley Bradley, et al. New York: New York UP, 1980.

Wigley, Mark. *The Architecture of Deconstruction: Derrida's Haunt.* Cambridge, MA: MIT P, 1993.

Williams, Adriana. *Covarrubias.* Ed. Doris Ober. Austin: U of Texas P, 1994.

Williams, Linda. "A Jury of Their Peers: Marleen Gorris's *A Question of Silence.*" *Postmodernism and Its Discontents: Theories, Practices.* Ed. E. Ann Kaplan. London: Verso, 1988. 107–15.

Wills, David. *Prosthesis.* Stanford, CA: Stanford UP, 1995.

Wines, James. *De-Architecture.* New York: Rizzoli, 1987.

Woodson, Jon. "Melvin Tolson and the Art of Being Difficult." Miller 19–42.

Yacobi, Tamar. "Ashbery's 'Description of a Masque': Radical Interart Transfer across History." *Poetics Today* 20.4 (Winter 1999): 673–707.

Yenser, Stephen. *The Consuming Myth: The Work of James Merrill.* Cambridge: Harvard UP, 1987.

Zimmerman, Leo. "Against Apocalypse: Politics and James Merrill's *The Changing Light at Sandover.*" Rotella 175–89.

Zorn, John. Liner notes. *Spillane.* LP. *Elektra/Nonesuch,* 1987.

Zucker, Paul. "Ruins—An Aesthetic Hybrid." *Journal of Aesthetics and Art Criticism* 20.2 (1961): 119–30.

Index

Library of Congress Cataloging-in-Publication Data

McHale, Brian.
  The obligation toward the difficult whole : postmodernist long poems / Brian McHale.
      p. cm. — (Modern and contemporary poetics)
  Includes bibliographical references and index.
    ISBN 0-8173-1305-2 (cloth : alk. paper) —
    ISBN 0-8173-5037-3 (pbk. : alk. paper) 1. American poetry—20th century—History and
  criticism. 2. Postmodernism (Literature)—United States. 3.Literary form. I. Title. II. Series.
  PS310.P63 M34 2004 810.9′113—dc22

                                                                                    2003010221

British Library Cataloguing-in-Publication Data available